Song, Landscape, and Identity in Medieval Northern France

Song, Landscape, and Identity in Medieval Northern France

Toward an Environmental History

JENNIFER SALTZSTEIN

OXFORD
UNIVERSITY PRESS

OXFORD
UNIVERSITY PRESS

Oxford University Press is a department of the University of Oxford. It furthers
the University's objective of excellence in research, scholarship, and education
by publishing worldwide. Oxford is a registered trade mark of Oxford University
Press in the UK and certain other countries.

Published in the United States of America by Oxford University Press
198 Madison Avenue, New York, NY 10016, United States of America.

CIP data is on file at the Library of Congress

ISBN 978-0-19-754778-6 (pbk.)
ISBN 978-0-19-754777-9 (hbk.)

DOI: 10.1093/oso/9780197547779.001.0001

Paperback printed by Marquis Book Printing, Canada
Hardback printed by Bridgeport National Bindery, Inc., United States of America

The publisher gratefully acknowledges support from the Claire and
Barry Brook Fund, Kenneth Levy Fund, and General Fund of the American
Musicological Society, supported in part by the National Endowment for
the Humanities and the Andrew W. Mellon Foundation.

For Brian and Remi

Contents

PART I. LANDS AND IDENTITIES

PART II. SONG AND SPRING IN TOWN AND COUNTRY

Tables

Figures

Examples

Introduction

Landscape, Group Identity, and the Songs
of the Trouvères

This book explores how medieval song expressed relationships between people and their environments. Its primary source base derives from the works of the trouvères, composers who were active primarily in the areas of present-day Northern France and Flanders (especially the medieval counties of Artois, Champagne, and Flanders, as well as Chartres, which included the Parisian basin). The trouvères wrote songs in Old French during the late twelfth century through the early fourteenth centuries. I examine how the songs they wrote may have reflected their lived experiences in their own surroundings or the lands they wished to inhabit. I argue that these songs often reflected how their authors (or their patrons and audiences) saw themselves, how they hoped to be seen by others, or how they wanted to be remembered by their descendants and admirers after death. That is, songs influenced the ways particular groups of medieval people defined who they were, often through ways of belonging to specific landscapes. My focus is thus on identity. Modern readers might define "identity" as one's individual personality or sense of self, but for medieval people, group identities were often equally important, or even more so.[1] Although most of the songs in this book were written in the first-person voice, they were not necessarily always modes of individual expression; they could also serve as expressions of group identity, particularly for members of two elite groups (the nobility and clergy). Set in the outdoors, these songs placed recognizable social types (knights, ladies, clerics, and peasants, among others) onto specific landscapes. Both the authors of and the audiences for these songs (those who consumed, patronized, sang, and preserved them) may have conceived of their own

---

[1] My thinking about medieval identity is especially inspired by Bynum's classic article, "Did the Twelfth Century," which continues to influence more recent accounts of medieval identity (see, for example, Newman, *The Permeable Self*).

Song, Landscape, and Identity in Medieval Northern France. Jennifer Saltzstein, Oxford University Press.
© Oxford University Press 2023. DOI: 10.1093/oso/9780197547779.003.0001

identities through them or in opposition to them. When songs associated social types with specific topographical configurations, they presented models
of identity for others to emulate. By influencing the ways subsequent generations of performers, listeners, patrons, or readers defined themselves
through their connection to certain kinds of landscapes, such songs could
project into the future particular ways of being on the land.[2] The trouvère
songs I explore were thus cultural products that both reflected and shaped
the configuration of the land, demonstrating a cycle of mutual impact between nature and culture.

Trouvère songs are often set in a landscape. As I use the term, "landscape"
signifies a physical place articulated by a particular configuration of geographical features and vegetation, as described by a narrator. "Landscape" is
thus different from "land" because in an overt or implied way it is governed
by a human perspective—a frame of vision and a point of view.[3] A landscape presented in a song can be realistic or fictional (or have elements of
both). Although the trouvère songs that form my primary source base are
the products of human imagination and dwell on human emotions, my
interpretations of them tend to start from the place they describe. I then investigate how (or whether) sung landscapes reflect the natural surroundings
in which their authors (and/or the characters that populate them) lived and
walked, to the extent to which this can be known. The question of whether
these songs were based on observation or first-hand experience (rather than,
for example, literary imitation or modelling) can be clarified through the
insights of medieval environmental historians, who offer a detailed view of
medieval land.[4] Throughout, I engage in a process of comparison between
the way the land is described in trouvère songs (its literary representation as
landscape) and the historical environmental conditions that prevailed on the
land at the time that individual songs were written or recorded. Comparing a
trouvère's lived circumstances (the climate, topography, and local patterns of
land use) to their sung landscapes reveals both how songwriters represented
the land and their attitudes toward it, which could be realistic, idealistic, or
nostalgic.

---

[2] My examples resonate with Boym's view that expressions of nostalgia are often oriented toward a
desired future. See Boym, *The Future of Nostalgia*, 351–54.

[3] See especially Mitchell, *Landscape and Power*, and the recent review of relevant literature
in Merriman et al., "Landscape, Mobility, Practice." Berberich, Campbell, and Hudson discuss
distinctions between land and landscape and identify ways the intertwining of land, landscape,
space, and place often combines the material and the ideological. See "Introduction," 19–20.

[4] Key studies include Hoffman, *An Environmental History*; Campbell, *The Great Transition*; and
Keyser and Dowling, *Conservation's Roots*.

To write an environmentally minded history of medieval French song requires paying attention to plant-life. This is somewhat unusual in the humanities, which, by definition, foreground human activity. As Michael Marder states, "If animals have suffered marginalization throughout the history of Western thought, then non-human, non-animal living beings, such as plants, have populated the margin of that margin"[5] Moreover, I operate from the premise that in medieval Europe, at all social levels, knowledge of plant-life was high. Medieval society was, first and foremost, agrarian. The vast majority of people were directly engaged in farming,[6] and most of those who dwelled in burgeoning, cosmopolitan cities had either recently poured in from the countryside or were not more than a few generations removed from village life.[7] The elites were mindful that their wealth derived from the land even when they were prosperous enough not to work it themselves. Most of the favored leisure activities of elite men and women took them outdoors. Piero de' Crescenzi's treatise on horticulture (*Liber ruralium commodorum*, completed in 1309) emphasized that lingering in the garden renewed the spirits of kings and queens, that viewing his orderly fields from the castle should give the lord pleasure, and that the lord should create an abundance and variety of trees on his estate by moving specimens and grafting them.[8] Agricultural knowledge was essential, ubiquitous, and self-evident.[9] Medieval plant-life was importantly shaped by human activity, especially farming and animal husbandry. My purpose in investigating animal activity will most often lie in determining its impact on the land and its vegetation.

For medieval people, the natural world was divinely created. The clergy understood the supernatural world through the imagery of sacred trees and

---

[5] Marder, *Plant-thinking*, 2. For accounts of medieval song that highlight animals (notably birds), see especially Kay, *Parrots and Nightingales*; Leach, *Sung Birds*; and Zingesser, *Stolen Song*. For a recent musicological study that focuses on plants, see Watkins, *Musical Vitalities*.

[6] Nine out of every ten medieval people were engaged in farming. See Freedman, *Medieval Peasant*, 2–3.

[7] Kowaleski, "Medieval People," 600.

[8] Piero de' Crescenzi, *Liber ruralium commodorum*, 102, 105, and 107. In his song "Tout autresi con l'ente," the highest-ranking of all the trouvères, Thibaut IV, count of Blois and Champagne and (from 1234) king of Navarre, writes: "Just as falling water/makes the grafted scion grow,/so does remembrance give birth to true love/and make it grow and flower through habit and use," suggesting his own understanding of grafting. Thibaut de Champagne, *Lyrics of Thibaut*, 96–101. The symbolism of grafting in the context of the Old French song genre known as the *motet enté* has received considerable attention. See especially Butterfield, "Enté," "Peraino," "Monophonic Motets." The relationship between musical quotation and horticultural metaphors focused on grafting receives extensive and thoughtful treatment in Plumley, *Grafted Song*.

[9] See comments in Winiwarter, "Making the Earth Fruitful," 95.

gardens.[10] The biblical tree of knowledge, which God planted in Paradise but whose fruit he forbade Adam and Eve to eat, became a common heuristic for the process of attaining knowledge.[11] In the medieval experience of time, seasonal time was tied to sacred liturgical time, where the arrival of spring was understood as an earthly reminder of the resurrection of Christ.[12] The kingdom of heaven was believed to await the deserving after death, but not before a stay in heaven's waiting room—Paradise, or the Garden of Eden, lost to humanity but still flourishing somewhere on earth.[13] Medieval cloister gardens were modeled directly on the description in Genesis of the Garden of Eden, which was irrigated by four rivers and was planted with every herb-bearing seed and every tree.[14]

Judging by their songs, medieval people also experienced joy and wonder over the workings of plant-life. God promised them dominion over the earth, a responsibility that was much desired. Yet medieval people could also see the tenuousness of their dominion, which they believed had been tainted by the Fall. It was humanity's imperfect dominion that explained, for medieval theologians, the creation's barren wastes, wild beasts, as well as poisonous snakes and plants. Alexander Neckham argued that the irritations of insects were intended as a living reminder to man of his deceit and his better state before the Fall—examples of incomplete dominion.[15] In the decades around 1300, this fragile dominion became evident to medieval people in a destabilizing series of natural disasters that they viewed as punishment from God. Unbeknownst to them, they were experiencing the negative impacts of climate change—the gradual onset of the Little Ice Age, a phenomenon they lacked the scientific understanding to comprehend.[16] The authors featured in this book span this era of climatic disruption and offer an opportunity to explore relationships between nature, culture, and change through the lens of medieval song.

[10] The scriptural symbolism of good and bad trees is explained in Robertson, "Doctrine of Charity."
[11] See Armstrong and Kay, *Knowing Poetry*, 107–16.
[12] See especially Rothenberg, *Flower of Paradise*, chap. 3; "Springtime Renewal over the *In Seculum* Tenor"; and Caldwell, *Devotional Refrains*, 33–38.
[13] Delumeau, *History of Paradise*, 23–25.
[14] Genesis 1:29. See Morgan, "Early Modern Edens," 145.
[15] Glacken, *Rhodian Shore*, 205–6.
[16] A coherent discourse for concepts such as "ecology" or "environment" is not evident in medieval European thinking. See Hoffman, *An Environmental History*, 86. The onset of the Little Ice Age is described in Campbell, *The Great Transition*, 335–49; and Hoffman, *An Environmental History*, 323–29.

Medieval People and Their Environments

The ways in which most medieval people viewed their relationship toward their natural surroundings—their "environment"—were fundamentally shaped by the Scriptures, which conceptualized the earth as an ideal habitat for humans, planned and designed for them by God. Some modern ecocritical scholars eschew the word "environment" because of the way it suggests an artificial separation between human beings and the other forms of life on earth.[17] Although medieval people do not use the term "environment" (a word for which Old French lacks a direct equivalent), the separation it implies is exactly how they understood their position with regard to their terrestrial home. Consequently, I use the term "environment" to signify the way individuals perceived their relationship to topography and climate. Although the creation story in Genesis situated the earth as a home divinely designed for humans, the creation also required their constant care and concern.[18] Even before the Fall, Adam was placed in the Garden of Eden "to till and keep it."[19] Postlapsarian earth was no longer this ideal home;[20] after the Fall and the expulsion of Adam and Eve from the Garden of Eden, God cursed the ground in response, henceforth demanding that humans engage in agricultural toil for their survival. Human beings were held responsible, as a result of their original sin, for improving nature—medieval Christians thus believed their charge was to co-create their environment with God, an undertaking they viewed not only positively but also redemptively.[21] During the twelfth and thirteenth centuries, people in Northern France made dramatic changes to the land on which they lived, clearing forests, draining marshes, and diverting rivers. In notable contrast to post-Romantic environmental attitudes, which often prize wilderness as land existing in a state uncontaminated by human civilization,[22] medieval thinkers held little admiration for wilderness. Although Bernard of Clairvaux famously remarked, "Believe me, I have discovered that you will find far more in the forests than in books; trees and stones will teach you what no teacher permits you to hear,"[23] at his

---

[17] See the discussion in Allen and Dawe, "Ecomusicologies," 1–15, esp. 9–10.

[18] See Glacken, *Rhodian Shore*, 151–53 and Hoffman, *An Environmental History*, 94–112.

[19] Genesis 2:15.

[20] Epstein, *Medieval Discovery of Nature*, 13.

[21] Aberth, *An Environmental History*, 6–7.

[22] Such attitudes remain common in the modern environmental movement, as Cronon influentially argued in "The Trouble with Wilderness."

[23] From Bernard's letter to Heinrich Murdach, quoted in Leclercq, *Love of Learning*, 135–36.

own cloister, the monks and lay brothers enthusiastically domesticated the wilderness by clearing land and diverting rivers, re-creating, through their labor, a small-scale version of Eden.[24]

Modern environmental historians emphasize the interaction between nature and culture, underscoring that the two are in constant cycles of mutual influence, and that human colonization of the natural sphere is almost always driven by the demands of culture.[25] For medieval people, this mutual influence was everywhere in evidence and the human manipulation of nature was viewed as valuable. Many medieval people ascribed to what some would today call environmental determinism—the belief that environmental factors (such as the topography within which one lived or the moisture of the air) impacted the bodily humors, directly altering the disposition and character of human beings.[26] They saw clearly their ability to influence the natural world through their actions and believed they had been commanded by God to improve upon nature.[27] Although they lacked understanding of genetics or sexual reproduction in plants, they understood the principle of inheritability in plants and animals, having observed that "like produces like."[28] Medieval horticultural treatises such as that of Albertus Magnus espouse a theory of environmental influence, advising the domestication of plant-life through cultivation, clearing, and grafting.[29] The widespread shaping of nature through cultural forces is particularly evident in the temporal and geographical context explored in this book, a period during which the Northern French landscape of the long thirteenth century was being (or had already been) actively shaped by cultural forces, particularly by dietary preferences, which were a key driver of the clearance of woodland in favor of cereal crops.[30]

It is perhaps not surprising that the cultural artifacts of a society so invested (spiritually and materially) in shaping nature would highlight relationships between humans and the natural world. "Natura" was a common character in allegorical fiction of this era,[31] and garden and forest settings were pervasive

---

[24] Glacken, *Rhodian Shore*, 213–14. The role of the Cistercian order in forest clearance has been overstated; Cistercians often created new cloisters on previously settled land. See discussion in Aberth, *An Environmental History*, 94.

[25] See Hoffman, *An Environmental History*, 5–10.

[26] Glacken, *Rhodian Shore*, 82–94 and 256–57, and Weeda, "Geographical Determinism."

[27] Epstein, *Medieval Discovery of Nature*, 148.

[28] Epstein, *Medieval Discovery of Nature*, 4 and 26–27.

[29] Epstein, *Medieval Discovery of Nature*, 25–29.

[30] Hoffman, *An Environmental History*, 119. These changes are discussed in detail in Chapter 1.

[31] The allegorical representation of Nature lies outside the scope of this study but receives careful attention in Robertson, *Nature Speaks*.

in medieval French romances and narrative *lais*.[32] In trouvère song, outdoor settings dominated. Most of the major genres of Old French song from the long thirteenth century are set in the open air and are saturated with images of the natural world: countless love songs begin with the "nature opening" in which the first-person speaker is inspired to love or sing by the beauty of a springtime landscape; *pastourelle* songs feature encounters between men and women in agricultural hinterlands; *rondets* often describe dances that occur in meadows and under trees. Although such outdoor settings are widespread, this book is the first to examine this Old French song corpus systematically from the perspective of landscape and environmental history.[33] I explore how the song traditions of medieval Northern France depicted relationships between medieval people and the land, and also how song helped to influence that relationship by forging identities grounded in particular patterns of land use.

Of Songs and Identities: Authorship, Anonymity, and Group Identities

Landscape implies a viewer. It has often been connected to powers of surveillance and of representation.[34] Focusing on landscape thus foregrounds questions of access, since the experience of landscape is always contingent. The ability to view a large expanse of land is often a coveted symbol of wealth and status.[35] The experience of viewing land is unlikely to be shared equally, but rather, is exploited in hierarchical systems of domination that are dependent on age, gender, kin, and lineage, as Tilley explains: "Knowledge and experience of particular locales and tracts of the landscape may be restricted

---

[32] See the survey in Gallé and Quéruel, "La forêt" and especially Whalen and Pickens, "Gardens and Anti-gardens."

[33] Medieval nature imagery has often been dismissed as merely symbolic or rhetorical, mechanically copied from classical or biblical sources. See Curtius, *European Literature*, 183–92, echoed in Pearsall and Salter, *Landscapes and Seasons*. Studies of trouvère song and motets that address nature imagery include Clark, "When Words Converge"; Leach, *Sung Birds*; Rothenberg, *Flower of Paradise*; Zingesser, *Stolen Song*; and my "Songs of Nature." Troubadour nature imagery has received considerably more attention. See Scheludko, "Zur Geschidite des Natrueinganges"; Wilhelm, *The Cruelest Month*; and the excellent recent study, Thiolier-Méjean, *Voici l'arbre d'amour*. Literature discussing the contacts between the troubadours and trouvères is summarized in Zingesser, *Stolen Song*, 8–11. Although a comparative study of relationships between song, landscape, and identity in song traditions in other regions (such as that of the troubadours of medieval Occitania) would surely prove illuminating, it lies outside the scope of this book.

[34] See Mitchell, *Landscape and Power*.

[35] Mitchell calls landscape "the 'dreamwork' of imperialism." See his "Imperial Landscape," 9.

and hidden from particular individuals and groups."[36] Most of the songs I explore in this book feature a first-person narrative perspective—that is, they are told from the point of view of an "I" who observes, comments, feels, speaks, and sings. It is through the filter of this "I" that trouvère songs reveal their landscapes (as opposed to the land that inspires them) to listeners and readers. I examine the degree of alignment between the landscapes described by the song's "I" and the rank, status, and lived circumstances of the song's author, to the degree to which these are known. I ask: do the landscapes described in these songs resemble the land as it was configured in the regions and periods when their authors wrote them?

To ask this question immediately raises interpretive issues to which scholars have adopted strikingly different responses over the centuries. During the twentieth century, the interpretive pendulum shifted dramatically from the assumption that trouvère songs were mostly or always autobiographical[37] to the assumption that they rarely were—that trouvère love song was a bravura rhetorical exercise in which the song referred only to itself.[38] The former approach could be criticized as an example of the "authorial assumption" (or worse, the "intentional fallacy"), that is, either the assumption that there is a direct relationship between an author's biography and the works s/he produced or that the author is referring to him or herself when using the first-person voice. Yet the latter approach arguably negates the author in favor of an autonomous work of art and the structures of language. More recent studies have charted a middle ground that considers details of biography without assuming that all songs were autobiographical.[39] I will not interpret every work written in the first-person as autobiographical or assume that its author's intentions conditioned a song's reception. Nor will I assume that this was never the case, particularly since many medieval songs are preserved in ways that implore readers to associate their author with the textual first-person voice.

[36] Tilley, *A Phenomenology of Landscape*, 26–27.

[37] Haines discusses the biographical approach preferred during the nineteenth century, an era when songs were connected to legends of their authors' lives. See *Eight Centuries*, 52–56 and 160–61. The songbooks are not always specific about the identities of the authors, even when author rubrics were included. Philologists undertook significant archival work to establish many of the identities that lay behind author rubrics that indicated only titles or identified persons who were not otherwise known. See especially Guesnon, "Nouvelles recherches," and "Recherches biographiques"; and Dyggve, "Chansons françaises," *Onomastique des trouvères*, and "Personnages historiques."

[38] See especially Dragonetti, *Technique poétique*; Guiette, *D'une poésie formelle*; and Zumthor "De la circularité."

[39] See Kay, *Subjectivity*, 112, and the review of relevant literature in Peraino, *Giving Voice to Love*, 17–22.

Even in those cases in which it is not clear that a given song represents the individual, subjective expression of its author, it may nonetheless be expressive of a *group identity* with which its author associated.[40] The identities that are placed front and center in this song corpus are those of the knight, the lady, the cleric, and the peasant, a configuration that quickly conjures up the "three orders" of medieval society: the warriors, worshipers, and workers. This vision of a tripartite medieval society was seemingly first articulated by bishop Adálberon de Laon in the early eleventh century. Its ideological purpose was to express harmony, interdependence, and solidarity within and between the orders, a harmony guaranteed by the presence of a strong ruler.[41] This ideal of the three orders was, by the thirteenth and fourteenth centuries, so well known that it become the object of frequent ridicule in the popular "estates satire."[42] Rather than merely echoing the literature of the medieval estates, the image-making at work in trouvère song represents a celebration of group identities. The compilation of manuscripts preserving these songs preserved these identities as models for future generations to emulate. This song tradition is thus an apt expression of the medieval valuation of models and types—ideals of behavior to which people ascribed and attempted to mold themselves, and through which people identified with their peers and differentiated themselves from those who belonged to other social groups. That this is so should also come as no surprise: song was (and is) a particularly potent vehicle for transmitting such behavioral models, helping to foster the group identities through which individuals configured and understood relationships between themselves and their communities.[43]

Most of the manuscripts that transmit my song corpus were luxury items produced at great expense, likely funded by elite members of medieval society who possessed the utmost status and wealth. Many of these books give pride of place to the highest-ranking songwriters and are organized and illustrated in ways that idealize knightly identity. They transmit more than the songs of the knightly classes; they also include songs by clerics and professional entertainers, artistic products that may have reflected the patronage

---

[40] My focus on group identity differs from Peraino's exploration of subjectivity trouvère song (grounded in the ideas of Althusser), in which she compellingly argues that authorial subjectivity is visible in strong departures from stylistic and generic convention. See *Giving Voice to Love*, 10–17.

[41] See Le Goff, "Société tripartite," 80–90 and Freedman, *Medieval Peasant*, 6.

[42] See Mann, *Estates Satire*.

[43] On medieval group identities, see Bynum, "Did the Twelfth-Century." On constructions of identity through songbook compilation through strategies such as naming and the adjacency of materials, see Galvez, *Songbook*, chap. 2, "Lyric Presence and Names," and *Subject of Crusade*, 162–71.

or taste of the elite. The group identity of the clerics is pronounced in some songbooks, their differently high status based not on wealth, but on their learnedness and the abilities needed to notate cultural artifacts like songs into manuscripts.

Anonymous songs also form a significant portion of my corpus; in these cases, the sex and rank of the song's author were unspecified in the surviving manuscripts. Theoretically, the authors of these anonymous songs (although not necessarily their patrons or transmitters) could be men or women of any rank.[44] Some scholars argued that these songs bore hallmarks of involvement by the lower classes, people who undoubtedly participated in music-making but lacked the wherewithal to preserve their songs in manuscripts. Songs scholars viewed as "popular" in their rhetoric and style were seen as products of oral transmission reflecting the voice of the people.[45] However, these arguments have now been thoroughly questioned.[46] In response to this compelling body of criticism, I operate on the premise that most of the songs discussed in this book (whether they are attributed or not) likely reflect an aristocratic or clerical milieu. Songs attributed to bourgeois authors seem to offer us a glimpse into the mentalities of a middle stratum—however, these may also speak to the influence and taste of patrons, most of whom were aristocrats or wealthy merchants who aspired to the trappings of aristocratic status. Although it is certainly possible that the grammatically feminine lyrics that appear in anonymously preserved songs could represent the voices of female authors, it is also possible that these songs convey the voices of fictive

[44] Although the trouvère songbooks focus overwhelmingly on male authors, scholars have long argued in favor of the robust role women played in vernacular song traditions, uncovering a variety of evidence in support. See especially the compelling treatment of this subject in Boynton, "Women's Performance"; Coldwell, "*Jougleresses* and *Trobairitz*"; and Haines, *Medieval Song*, 51–82. Recent studies of contrafacta further illuminate the participation in and representation of historical medieval women through vernacular song. See especially Quinlan's exploration of a contrafactum commenting on the regency of Blanche of Castille (Quinlan, "Courtly Song Invades"), as well as Dolce's exploration of the songs of the Brabantine mystic Hadewijch, some of which share metrical structures with trouvère songs (Dolce, "'Soit hom'"). The small number of named female authors associated with trouvère lyric is discussed in Doss-Quinby et al., *Women Trouvères*, 26–33. The most comprehensive review of relevant literature on medieval female-voiced lyric is Golden and Kong, "Introduction," 12–16.

[45] See especially Jeanroy, *Origines*. More recent studies of trouvère song identified hierarchies of genre, style, or register, and attached these to aristocratic or popular categories. See, for example, Bec, *Lyrique française*; Page, *Voices and Instruments*.

[46] In the context of trouvère song, especially the landmark study, Aubrey, "Reconsidering 'High Style.'" For a critique of purported connections between oral song traditions and the medieval refrain, see Saltzstein, *Refrain and the Rise*, 8–16. Although she continues to rely on notions of "courtly" or "popular" poetic register as being potentially tied to social categories (see, for example, *Poetry and Music*, chap. 8, "Urban Culture: Arras and the *puys*"), Butterfield critiques arguments that extant medieval sources directly transmit oral literature or song. See *Poetry and Music*, 42–63.

female bodies (characters and protagonists). I recognize that the identities of women and peasants we find in medieval songs could be introduced by authors who did not share their sex, their rank, or both.[47] In the context of the songbooks that are central witnesses to the song tradition I explore, acknowledging the importance of elite patronage and the dominance of male authorship does not preclude exploring how songs might represent the experiences of women or peasants. The challenge lies in balancing the constellation of roles a song or songbook may connect (authors, patrons, textual characters, and, implicitly, performers and audiences) and examining how these roles converge in song to express identities tied to specific landscapes.

The Design of This Book

This book is organized around medieval identities (knights and clerics, peasant women and aristocratic women) and their association with specific configurations of land usage (meadows and woodlands, cityscapes, farmland, and gardens). Part I, "Lands and Identities," sketches the physical topography of Northern France as well as the historical rank and status of the book's named author figures, providing an overview of the historical conditions of the land and the biographies and identities of the trouvères who sang about it. Chapter 1, "The Lay of the Land," surveys dominant patterns of land use as described by archaeologists and environmental historians, offering an image of the terrain and prevailing environmental conditions of the region during the long thirteenth century. Chapter 2, "Trouvère Identities: Rank, Status, and Geography," addresses the biographies of individual trouvères who will figure prominently in later chapters (especially Chapter 3 and Chapter 4), most of whom were either knights or clerics. These two social groups each promoted a strong sense of collective identity, identities that I show that some songbooks highlighted through their organization and illustration. The framework of these two chapters provides a necessary foundation for Parts II and III, which address how land and biography come to be represented in songs and songbooks—that is, how they are expressed culturally as landscape and identity. Comparing the historical conditions to their

---

[47] The most thorough consideration of female authorship in the trouvère song corpus remains Doss-Quinby et al., *Women Trouvères*. My approach to questions of gender and voice in anonymous Old French songs is indebted to the classic study, Burns et al., "Feminism and the Discipline," 238–43.

sung representation allows me to assess whether the relationships individual songs project between landscape and identity were authentic to a specific trouvère's biography or a character's status or, in contrast, whether the relationship may have been aspirational, satirical, or nostalgic.

Part II, "Song and Spring in Town and Country," focuses on songs written in the first-person voice by members of the knightly classes and by clerics. I explore how these two groups of authors promoted, through song, group identities that reflected differing ties to specific kinds of landscapes. Chapter 3, "In the Meadows: Feeling the Landscape through the Songs of the Knightly Trouvères," explores songs by prominent knightly trouvères that use what has been called the "nature opening" (or *Natureingang*) in which the trouvère begins with a description of a beautiful landscape and then explains that this landscape prompts them to feel love and sometimes to sing the very song their audience is hearing. As a social group, knights strove for an ideal balance of traits (a concept conveyed through the Old French term *mesure*) that combined licit violence, military prowess, and horsemanship with the expression of intense emotion and a new language of love.[48] In their songs (particularly those by Gace Brulé, the Châtelain de Couci, the Vidame de Chartres, and Raoul de Soissons), knightly trouvères highlighted the emotion of love and its expression through singing. They described this emotional and artistic impulse as being generated by a solitary experience on a landscape that bears the hallmarks of the aristocratic estate. In keeping with recent studies that highlight the way in which music can encode experience and feeling,[49] I show how these songwriters harnessed musical structure (namely, *pedes cum cauda* form) to help listeners experience the emotional pull of landscape, feeling the shift from sensation to singing alongside them. Chapter 4, "In the City: Landscape, Season, and Plant-Life in the Works of Cleric-Trouvères," continues to focus on the nature opening, this time exploring its use (or lack thereof) in the works of songwriters who were also clerics. Overall, songwriters from this group such as Adam de la Halle, Richard de Founival, and Moniot d'Arras either eschew the nature opening entirely in their love songs or treat it with parody or inversion. In the genre of the motet, I explore commentary on the nature opening in works by Petrus

---

[48] For my understanding of the culture of the chivalry, I am informed by the rich picture that emerges from studies such as Baldwin, *Knights, Lords, and Ladies*; Kaeuper, *Chivalry and Violence*, *Medieval Knighthood*, and *Chivalry and Violence*; and Taylor, *Ideals of Knighthood*.

[49] On the role of emotion, I am influenced by Rosenwein, *Generations of Feeling*. My exploration of relationships between embodied experience and medieval vernacular song resonates with studies such as Dillon, *Sense of Sound* and Golden, *Mapping Medieval Identities*.

de Cruce as well as an interrelated group of pieces connected to the prominent theologian Philip the Chancellor, several of which suggest more appropriate spiritual endpoints for the plant imagery found in vernacular song.

Part III, "In the Pasture and the Garden," focuses on how trouvère songs represent the experiences of women and peasants on the landscape. The songs in this section, many of which are anonymous, were most likely written about, rather than by, women and peasants. Nevertheless, I explore how these songs articulated the rank and status of elite women and peasants through the placement of characters representing these social types on specific landscapes. Chapter 5, "Rural Landscapes and the *Pastourelle*: Boundaries, Spatial and Social," focuses on songs from the genre of the *pastourelle*, which often feature an encounter between a knight and a shepherdess in a geographical hinterland—a location between castle and city that was marked by roads and mixed agricultural land usages. In *pastourelle* songs, this encounter had a range of narrative outcomes including dialogue, seduction, refusal, as well as violence and rape. I establish the terrain these songs describe and the narrative outcomes with which that terrain was associated. I then provide a systematic account of the landscape found in those songs in which rape or attempted rape is depicted, exploring the relationship between landscape and sexual violence. In addition to a large corpus of anonymous *pastourelles*, I highlight works by the bourgeois professional trouvère Jehan Erart and the cleric-trouvères Jehan Bodel and Adam de la Halle (namely, Adam's dramatized *pastourelle*, the *Jeu de Robin et Marion*), all three of whom were active in the urban context of Arras. Although the songs medieval peasants undoubtedly sang left us no known examples, I explore how the reception of the *pastourelle* is suggestive of the ways that the knightly classes, wealthy urbanites, and ordinary urban dwellers who had recently migrated from the surrounding countryside may have defined their own identities against the figure of the medieval peasant. Chapter 6, "The Song-Space of the Garden: Performance and Privacy in the Medieval *Rondet*," focuses on a refrain song genre called the *rondet* that often features scenes of women dancing in cultivated outdoor spaces. These songs have traditionally been understood as representing peasant women engaged in social dances, and their written traces were long thought to represent vestiges of lost popular song cultures. I show that the landscapes they describe most closely resemble the aristocratic estate, their garden settings expressive of the strong associations between aristocratic women and garden landscapes. These songs illustrate how feminine aristocratic identities were tied to gardens, their dynamics of place and space indicative of associations between gardens and pleasure and display, as well as privacy.

The trouvère corpus is vast and rich, encompassing well over two thousand individual songs.[50] The corpus divides nearly evenly between authored and anonymous songs.[51] Although this book is the result of my study of hundreds of trouvère songs, it would be impossible, in a single account, to address the full trouvère corpus meaningfully. The authored repertoire on which I focus is centered around trouvères whose creative output was noteworthy as evidenced by factors musicologists traditionally favor such as compositional productivity, innovation, imitation by others, and wide manuscript transmission. My readings of individual songs are placed within the context of broader stylistic features of authorial corpora or generic conventions. I have tended to place this contextualization in tables and notes where musicologists can easily locate it but where it may prove less distracting to readers in other fields. In my transcriptions, slurred notes are used to indicate ligatures in the manuscripts. Modern scholars rely on the foundational work of nineteenth-century philologists who carefully catalogued songs, motets, and refrains found in medieval manuscripts; I use their numbering systems throughout.[52] Medieval songbooks do not always agree on the attribution of the songs they transmit. For this reason, the song totals that appear in this book should be regarded as approximations that reflect those songs that are always or largely attributed to an author. They are not intended to establish canons for these songwriters, but rather, to illustrate the relative sizes of corpora with which individual trouvères can reasonably be associated.[53] I have attempted, wherever possible, to use published translations of song

[50] The standard catalog, Spanke, G. Raynaud's Bibliographie, includes 2,130 entries. Haines estimates that around 2,800 melodies survive in about 4,600 different readings. See Haines, Eight Centuries, 23.

[51] This is evident in Linker, A Bibliography.

[52] The numbering of songs follows Spanke, G. Raynaud's Bibliographie, motet numbering follows Gennrich, Bibliographie der ältesten, rondet/rondeau and refrain numbering follows Boogaard, Rondeaux et refrains, and the numbering of poetic rhyme schemes refers to Mölk and Wolfzettel, Répertoire métrique.

[53] In cases of conflicting attribution, I have favored those identifications made in the songbooks K, N, P, and X or M, T, A, and a. I tended to omit from author corpora the odd song in which those manuscript groupings disagree. I have generally given less weight to attributions found exclusively in songbooks such as C, which (although interesting in their own right) were added in a later hand and often conflict with those of other sources. See the discussion in Gatti, "Author Ascriptions," 76–79. On the filiation of trouvère manuscript sources, see Schwan, Die altfranzösischen Liederhandschriften. Parker argued that Schwan's schema, which was based on primarily on literary features, was also largely correct for the melodies. See Parker "Tradition manuscrite des trouvères," 182–85. Problems of attribution in trouvère songbooks are discussed in Rosenberg, "Colin Muset" and, most recently, Gatti, Repertorio delle attribuzioni.

lyrics. Where translations were not available, I have noted those translations that are my own. The spelling of Old French is not consistent across different manuscripts and I have not regularized it.

Overall, the songs explored in this book often included realistic representations of the land, yet in many cases, the images they presented were out of date, reflecting the land usage patterns of earlier generations. This book thus illustrates that the ways that some trouvères expressed relationships between song, landscape, and identity were remarkably durable in the face of both changes in land management and shifts in the climate, which intensified in the decades around 1300. Indeed, this altered relationship between medieval people and the land was rarely reflected in the landscapes of their vernacular songs. Rather, these songs continued to project idealized, harmonious relationships between humans and the natural world. In other words, the relationships between identity and landscape demonstrated in the book's chapters remained constant even as both medieval society and medieval environments changed. In my final chapter, "Conclusions: Nature, Culture, and Change in the Middle Ages and Beyond," I explore legacies of the nature imagery found in trouvère song in the middle ages and modern era. I explore Guillaume de Machaut's treatment of the nature opening in his *Remede de Fortune*, a narrative into which he inserted his own songs. I argue that Machaut's treatment of the nature opening, which he extrapolates into his narrative, is importantly continuous with that of many thirteenth-century trouvères and the ways they configured relationships between song, landscape, and identity. The persistence of these relationships is a testament to the cultural durability of identities, even amid change. I close with an example of medievalism in modern environmental writing—a passage in Aldo Leopold's *Sand County Almanac* that holds unexpected thematic parallels with trouvère nature openings—to consider how the medieval song traditions explored in this book speak to modern relationships between nature, culture, and change.

PART I

LANDS AND IDENTITIES

1

The Lay of the Land

What were the contours of the land in medieval Northern France? How was this region shaped by climate, demography, and ways of life? Later chapters will focus on the way the trouvères represented the land in their songs (their sung landscapes). In order to evaluate what those cultural representations might say about the attitudes toward the natural world held by the people who produced and consumed them, it is necessary to first gain an understanding of the outdoor surroundings of the trouvères at the time they wrote their songs. I aim to illustrate the plant-life, topography, climate, and patterns of land use that likely surrounded these songwriters in their daily lives. This chapter harnesses literature from the fields of environmental history and archaeology to sketch the contours of the medieval Northern French terrain, focusing on the urban and rural spaces in which most of the known trouvères lived and worked and that are represented across the trouvère song corpus, authored and anonymous. The Introduction underscored that medieval people held instrumentalist views of nature. They did not place value on ostensibly untrammeled wilderness or "virgin forest" since such spaces were reminders of the Fall. Even the Cistercians believed men were meant to improve upon nature with their labor, transforming chaotic wilderness into a recreation of paradise.[1] The Northern French terrain (whether urban or rural) reflected those values—land was actively and relatively thoroughly managed. Few European localities at this time were devoid of settlement or economic activity.[2] Medieval people deliberately reshaped the physical terrain in response to cultural preferences such as diet, fashion, and architecture. Exploring landscape in this particular context is thus a reminder that the word "culture" derives from "cultivation." As Aaron S. Allen and Kevin Dawe explain, it was only much later that the tending and management of natural growth (cultivation) took on the more abstract, expressive concepts with which the word "culture" is now associated.[3] We will see that in this

---

[1] Glacken, *Rhodian Shore*, 213–14.
[2] Campbell, *The Great Transition*, 62.
[3] Allen and Dawe, "Ecomusicologies," 9.

Song, Landscape, and Identity in Medieval Northern France. Jennifer Saltzstein, Oxford University Press.
© Oxford University Press 2023. DOI: 10.1093/oso/9780197547779.003.0002

particular historical and geographical context, there was often little to divide nature from culture. For many medieval people, self-image and identity were importantly tied to built environments (meaning human-made surroundings), whether these were composed of wood, stone, earthworks, or managed plant-life. Nature, culture, and identity were tightly intertwined and in constant interaction.[4]

This chapter explores what Northern France likely looked like during the long thirteenth century. My survey of the physical terrain is framed by the ways people lived in, mediated, and altered the land—what some have called the "dwelling perspective."[5] At a time in which humans intentionally and actively sought to shape their environment, imagining the lay of the land will require attending to cultural values such as diet and acknowledging the profound influence that animals had on medieval plant-life configurations. I start by sketching salient characteristics of the medieval climate; I then examine urban and rural topographies.

Medieval Environments: Climate and Human Flourishing

Between 1000 and 1300, scholars have estimated that the population of Europe doubled, and that of France and the low countries may have more than tripled.[6] This dramatic increase in the sheer number of human beings had many causes, including political and economic conditions. The period saw, for example, the stability and centralization of the Latin Church,[7] as well as international commercialization spurred by increased property rights and the rise of guilds, communes, and fairs.[8] Recent research by, in particular, historians Bruce M. S. Campbell and Richard C. Hoffmann has shown that a significant contributor to this period of demographic increase and overall flourishing was the climate.[9] As scholars have brought traditional historical sources into dialogue with data collected through archaeology, dendrochronology, and the study of ice cores, a sophisticated picture of medieval climatological conditions has emerged. Based on a synthesis of such

---

[4] On the interaction model of nature and culture and its relevance to environmental history, see Hoffman, *An Environmental History*, 8–10.

[5] See the discussion in Tilley, *Phenomenology of Landscape*, 13–23.

[6] Campbell, *The Great Transition*, 58–60 and Hoffman, *An Environmental History*, 159.

[7] Campbell, *The Great Transition*, 66–76.

[8] Campbell, *The Great Transition*, 79–83.

[9] Campbell, *The Great Transition* and Hoffman, *An Environmental History*.

sources, Campbell has called thirteenth-century Europe a "climatically favored age,"[10] characterized by high solar irradiance, slightly above-average
temperatures, and settled atmospheric circulation patterns. This "medieval
climate anomaly" (MCA) was stable and resilient. Favorable atmosphere-
ocean interactions led to increased rainfall and fewer bouts of cold, dry polar
air.[11] Across Europe, people enjoyed mild, rainy winters and warm summers,
conditions that caused plants and the life forms they sustained to thrive.
Coupled with agricultural innovations, the MCA contributed to historic
increases in farm productivity. In Northern France, grain yields were typically three-to-one but could be as high as ten-to-one.[12] The Alpine tree line
ascended and grapes were grown in England as well as southern Scotland
and Norway.[13] The advantageous conditions of the MCA were enjoyed across
western Europe and eastern Asia.[14]

The MCA lasted until the 1270s, when the medieval climate began to
change. The "Little Ice Age," which set in around 1450, was characterized by
very long winters, lasting two to three months longer than before. The slow
onset of the Little Ice Age caused shifting ecological boundaries, pushing the
vines and trees back from the northern locations where they had flourished
during the MCA.[15] Between the late MCA and the onset of the Little Ice
Age, a period of climatic instability that Campbell calls the "great transition"
brought an increase in unpredictable and often disastrous weather events.[16]
Many factors contributed to the great transition. Ice cores from Greenland
show signs of space debris indicating the presence of meteors (which
were also described by several medieval chroniclers), suggesting an extra-
terrestrial bombardment.[17] A dramatic succession of volcanic eruptions in
1269, 1276, and 1286 increased volcanic aerosols in the Earth's atmosphere.
A period of absent sunspot activity called the Wolf Solar Minimum began
in the 1290s. These factors (and others) contributed to downward trends
in temperature, changes that substantially impacted oceanic circulation
patterns. As oceans alternately cooled and rewarmed and the global climate system reorganized, the climate became unstable and unpredictable.[18]

[10] Campbell, *The Great Transition*, 65.
[11] Campbell, *The Great Transition*, 45–50.
[12] Jordan, *Great Famine*, 25.
[13] Hoffman, *An Environmental History*, 322–23.
[14] Campbell, *The Great Transition*, 5.
[15] Hoffman, *An Environmental History*, 328–29.
[16] Campbell, *The Great Transition*, 10 and Hoffman, *An Environmental History*, 323.
[17] Campbell, *The Great Transition*, 202.
[18] Campbell, *The Great Transition*, 198–99.

Dramatic fluctuations in European tree ring widths from the early decades of the fourteenth century show years of both abnormally rainy and abnormally dry weather.[19] An instance of ocean warming seems to have produced the prolonged summer rains[20] that led to catastrophic crop failures between 1315 and 1317, and precipitated the Great European Famine of 1315 to 1322.[21] The great transition coincided with a prolonged commercial recession in Europe as well as increased warfare.[22] Much of my song corpus was written by trouvères who lived during the efflorescence of the MCA, as well as songwriters who would have experienced the instability and shocks that coincided with the great transition. The quality of life they enjoyed may have been quite different depending on the portion of the century during which they lived.

Northern French Cities and their Rural Surroundings

I have just noted the natural forces that shaped Northern French land and plant-life of the long thirteenth century. Yet any investigation of medieval land use must confront the ways in which the physical terrain is shaped by cultural values—nature and culture exist in cycles of mutual interaction. In the medieval context, it is often impossible to separate identity from the lay of the land since identity was a key driver of land management.

The population increases of the thirteenth century transformed the landscapes of urban and rural areas alike. In the countryside, new towns (*neuvilles*) proliferated creating a densely settled landscape.[23] Although the precise character of each medieval city must be explored individually, there were features that were common across urban areas from the late twelfth century through the first half of the fourteenth. Most medieval cities experienced dramatic population increases during this time period. By 1300, a dozen European cities had populations of over fifty thousand.[24] Largest of all was Paris. By 1190, the Parisian population had grown so much that Philip Augustus built new fortifications around the left and right banks,

---

[19] See Campbell, *The Great Transition*, 201 and Jordan, *The Great Famine*, 17.
[20] Campbell, *The Great Transition*, 205 and Hoffman, *An Environmental History*, 323–24.
[21] See Campbell, *The Great Transition*, 189–97 and Jordan, *Great Famine*.
[22] Campbell, *The Great Transition*, 10.
[23] Jordan, *Great Famine*, 47.
[24] Campbell, *The Great Transition*, 126.

significantly expanding the area of the city.[25] Paris was a true international metropolis with a population somewhere between one hundred fifty thousand and two hundred thousand.[26] Flanders had an urbanization rate of as much as thirty-five percent,[27] and Arras had thirty-five thousand inhabitants at its height.[28] Most medieval cities were also densely populated. By the early fourteenth century, Artois and Picardy had population densities sometimes exceeding one hundred per square kilometer.[29] Around 1300, Paris had a population density about twenty percent higher than present-day London, but with few buildings higher than three stories.[30]

Medieval urban areas were surrounded, often for many miles, by the farmland and villages that supplied their inhabitants with food. Urban ecosystems are populated by people engaged in non-agricultural activities; they can only be maintained by cultural inputs. In 1287, Engelbert of Admont, an Austrian monk, estimated that four agricultural laborers were needed to support each urban dweller.[31] Cities brought agricultural change to distant landscapes.[32] The grain-provisioning hinterlands might extend ten to twenty miles beyond even a small city.[33] Around 1300, supplying London with grain required an arable zone of over ten thousand square kilometers.[34] London's demand stretched to Dover, and Sicily produced the grain that fed half of the central-northern Italian cities.[35] Grain fields would thus have been a common sight in the lands surrounding most medieval cities.

It would also be difficult to overstate the importance of wood to Northern European civilization at this time. Wood cultivation was common near medieval cities; it was the primary fuel for everything from cooking, to smelting, to salt making. In cities, it was the building material of choice for dwellings and fencing, applications for which the need was virtually insatiable. A typical medieval house often contained a few hundred small oak trees.[36] In the thirteenth century, France moved toward a market-oriented, extractive

---

[25] Baldwin, *Paris, 1200*, 25–28.
[26] Wickham, *Medieval Europe*, 130.
[27] Campbell, *The Great Transition*, 91n201.
[28] Symes, *Common Stage*, 181.
[29] Campbell, *The Great Transition*, 64.
[30] Hoffman, *An Environmental History*, 229.
[31] Hoffman, *An Environmental History*, 231.
[32] See Hoffman, *An Environmental History*, 236; Wickham, *Medieval Europe*, 135; and Jordan, *Great Famine*, 127.
[33] Campbell, *The Great Transition*, 118–19.
[34] Campbell, *The Great Transition*, 118.
[35] Wickham, *Medieval Europe*, 135.
[36] Rackham, "Medieval Countryside," 17.

Figure 1.1 Harvesting Poles of Small Wood. Courtesy of the Walters Art Museum, Baltimore, MD, Manuscript W90, fol.7v

system of woodland management that favored intensive, small wood production.[37] Since large trees were difficult and labor-intensive to work with using medieval tools,[38] the preferred method of wood cultivation was coppicing, a remarkably productive and sustainable process in which a tree is cut down and the stump is left undisturbed for a period ranging from four to ten years. During this time, the stump would regenerate through (depending on the tree species) sprouting or suckering around the base. Those sprouts or suckers would be allowed to grow and widen into poles of "small wood" that were in heavy demand for fencing, firewood, furniture, tools, and many other uses.[39] Figure 1.1 provides an illustration from the calendar of an early fourteenth-century Book of Hours produced in Northern France, which shows a laborer hauling a bundle of poles of small wood harvested from a severely pruned tree (perhaps a coppice).[40]

[37] Keyser, "Woodland Management."
[38] Hoffman, *An Environmental History*, 183.
[39] Rackham, "Medieval Countryside," 16–17.
[40] The Walters Art Museum, Baltimore, manuscript W90, fol. 7v.

In a woodlot full of coppices is a thoroughly colonized landscape in which trees are small and brushy.[41] Coppices required sunlight; thus the height of the tree canopy was restricted to no more than 25 feet in some woodland regulations, ensuring that tall trees would not overshadow new growth.[42] Animals were kept away from coppices because they grazed on the sprouts.[43] A woodlot was essentially a field where wood was grown for economic use and would have borne little resemblance to a wild woodland or forest.[44] Intensive wood cutting was especially common near cities;[45] the trees in view around Paris and Arras, for example, would most likely have been woodlots composed primarily of coppices.

By 1230 in Paris and 1250 in Picardy most suitable land was cultivated. This change was driven by both increases in grain farming and the rise of intensive wood production.[46] Europe was in the midst of what has been called the "great clearance"—an era in which forested land shrank significantly, reduced to twenty to thirty percent from a height of around fifty percent.[47] The reductions of woodland intensified in the decades around 1200[48] and may have been the most dramatic in England. Domesday Book (the land use survey undertaken by agents of William the Conqueror) records just fifteen percent woodland in England, and by the time of the Black Death that figure had fallen to six percent.[49] Earlier in the middle ages, Paris had been surrounded by a ring of woods a short walk from the city center; this had ceased to be the case by the twelfth century.[50] Managed timber preserves one hundred kilometers up and down the Seine were used to supply the city with

---

[41] Hoffman, *An Environmental History*, 186.

[42] Keyser, "Woodland Management," 380.

[43] Hoffman, *An Environmental History*, 186.

[44] As Rackham explained, by the middle ages, wilderness or ("wildwood") "lay in the very distant past. Medieval Europeans had no more direct experience of it than modern Europeans, indeed less than modern Americans." Rackham, "Medieval Countryside," 14.

[45] Keyser, "Woodland Management," 382.

[46] Duby, *Rural Economy*, 86.

[47] See Hoffman, *An Environmental History*, 119–22 and Beck and Guizard, "La forêt resources," 107–21.

[48] Bernard et al., "Ressources forestières," 243–58.

[49] Rackham, "Medieval Countryside," 15. Some argue that Domesday Book may understate the woodlands. These figures would also exclude game parks, which will be discussed further below. See Dyer, "Woodland and Wood-Pasture," 106. For a revised dating of Domesday Book, see Symes, "Domesday Book."

[50] The story of Abbot Suger's attempt to procure twelve roof beams for his monastery's church demonstrates that even in the woodlands in the forest of Yvelines, 50 km west of Paris, few tall trees remained. See Keyser, "Woodland Management," 353–54. The same was true of the great forest of Marchiennes near Douai; what was not taken over for game parks was used extensively for timber and firewood. See Duceppe-Lamarre, *Chasse et pâturage*, 81.

wood.[51] Planted fields and managed woodlots would thus have surrounded most medieval cities and could stretch well beyond a day's walk from the city walls.

Many modern readers are accustomed to cities that are interspersed with parks. Green spaces were rarer in medieval urban areas, many of which were "a terrain of beaten earth, of buildings, of increasingly paved squares, streets, and courtyards."[52] I show in Chapter 2 that most of the trouvères who were associated with cities were connected to either Amiens, Arras, or Paris, each of which had its own unique character. The impression of Paris, in particular, is of an urbanized landscape where "rural patches remained here and there in the city, but they were in retreat as building campaigns multiplied."[53] The city did boast the grassy the *Pré aux Clercs* and *Saint-Germain-des-Prés*,[54] and professors at the University of Paris reportedly grew basil in small gardens attached to their rooms.[55] But by the end of the thirteenth century, Paris was filled with buildings up to its walls.[56] During the thirteenth century, Amiens would have been a compact city surrounded by the wall built by Philip Augustus. By the time the walls were extended after Philip VI's defeat at the battle of Crécy in 1346, the area enclosed by the new wall was already heavily populated.[57] Vineyards would have been a common sight on the land surrounding Amiens, whose merchants, along with those of Arras and Saint Quentin, held a royal monopoly on the sale of wine in Picardy. The river valleys of the Somme just north of Amiens were a source of woad (*isatis tinctoria*), a weedy biennial plant that produces a profusion of yellow flowers in May and June. The leaves of the woad plant (once dried, fermented, and milled in urban facilities) were used to make a blue dye that was sought after for cloth production and over which the commune held a royal monopoly. It was cultivated extensively in the river valleys upstream of the city.[58] In Arras, the area known as "The Town" (La Ville) grew significantly during the twelfth century. Accounts illustrate a steady influx of new arrivals and a scarcity of lodging; the parish of Sainte-Croix leased their garden to accommodate new

---

[51] Hoffman, *An Environmental History*, 232. The roof beams of the Gothic churches of Paris were sourced from coppice stools that were used to produce tall, straight, uniform poles of wood. See Épaud, "Les forêts," 142–53.

[52] Hoffman, *An Environmental History*, 229.

[53] Jordan, *Great Famine*, 132.

[54] Harvey, *Medieval Gardens*, 51.

[55] Harvey, *Medieval Gardens*, 107.

[56] Baldwin, *Paris, 1200*, 25–28.

[57] Johnson, "Music at the Cathedral of Amiens," 46.

[58] Johnson, "Music at the Cathedral of Amiens," 23–24.

arrivals.[59] The intricate web of roads suggest that most areas were densely populated, very few areas retaining the character of the countryside.[60] The "Grand Market" covered more than a hectare and hosted markets as well as tournaments.[61] To the west of The Town, the terrain in the Episcopal City would have had a comparatively bucolic character. This area (where the cathedral of Notre Dame d'Arras and the episcopal house were located) was sparsely populated and had few public roads.[62] The bishop maintained an urban park of several hectares enclosed by a wall that, at the end of the fourteenth century, was home to deer and rabbits.[63] The houses inhabited by cathedral canons were located within this urban park.[64] The landscape of Arras was thus unevenly dense, and its character could be dramatically different depending on one's location and status.

The cultural choices of medieval urban dwellers—their architecture, non-agrarian occupations, and their diets—ensured that their view would most often have been framed by the buildings of dense cityscapes or by the coppices, vineyards, and fields that supplied the population with building materials, food, and drink.

Rural Topographies: Forests, Fields, Meadows, Parks, and Gardens

For medieval aristocrats, rural lands were intimately connected to their values, lifestyles, and identities. The countryside was shaped by their architectural tastes and their dietary preferences. The rural topography was dotted with castles owned by everyone from emperors, kings, dukes, viscounts, and bishops, to petty lords.[65] The creation of elevated castle towers "forcefully stamped the seigneurial mark on the locality."[66] Castles were an imposing visual reminder of military power and wealth, qualities that were also symbolically communicated through manipulation of the lands surrounding them. Many castles were built on large, constructed mounds of earth called "mottes"

[59] Berger, *Littérature et société*, 39.
[60] Berger notes the lack of roads in pockets in the west. See Berger, *Littérature et société*, 43.
[61] Berger, *Littérature et société*, 51.
[62] Berger, *Littérature et société*, 31.
[63] Duceppe-Lamarre, *Chasse et pâturage*, 134–37. This park was closed in 1395 and its deer transferred to the famous Park of Hesdin. See ibid., 134.
[64] Berger, *Littérature et société*, 29.
[65] Creighton, *Early European Castles*, 48.
[66] Creighton, *Early European Castles*, 61.

that were designed to elevate their structures, making them appear larger and more imposing.[67] These mottes are an emblem of the way aristocratic identities and lifestyles drove a unique ecology marked by the desire to shape and control the natural world.[68] The landscape of the medieval estate was, above all, a built environment designed to support the meat-based aristocratic diet and the leisure pursuit of hunting. Rural lands were transformed by such values.

On elite estates, animals played an outsized role in the configuration of the land. Because elites demonstrated their high social status in part through meat consumption and the leisure pursuit of hunting, animals shaped, to a large extent, the topography and plant-life of the areas on which they were housed. Few activities were more closely tied to medieval elite identity than hunting,[69] and the ideal context for this activity was a forest. Castles were often planned and built next to forests for hunting purposes.[70] Most aristocrats held exclusive rights in their woodlands.[71] Peasants were technically forbidden from hunting, from hunting grounds, and from game itself; however, they did hunt some venison and small game. Noble treatises on hunting show disdain for peasant hunting methods, particularly their use of traps and nets.[72] Medieval sources recognize a hierarchy of arboreal landscapes, from the bushy areas that cropped up after woodland clearances, to glades and copses, to the hedges used as barriers, to woodlands, parks, and at the very top, forests.[73] The *forête* (a term denoting a landscape covered with trees mostly not planted by men) could be very large, covering hundreds or even tens of thousands of hectares.[74] The counts of Hainaut owned more than thirty forests; the counts of Artois occupied about the same number, but their forests were of less significance.[75] Descriptions of Northern French woodlands most often name oak, ash, and beech trees. In wet meadowland, willows, alder, and linden were common. The forest floor would also have had a shrub layer, which was important for hunting strategy.[76] The pasturage

---

[67] Creighton, *Early European Castles*, 90.

[68] Creighton, *Early European Castles*, 124.

[69] Hunting rights are discussed in records dating back to the Merovingian era. See Duceppe-Lamarre, *Chasse et pâturage*, 140–41. Aristocratic women participated in avian hunting. See Duceppe-Lamarre, *Chasse et pâturage*, 152. There is evidence to suggest that some elite women hunted on horseback. See Richardson, "Riding Like Alexander."

[70] Colvin, "Royal Gardens in Medieval England," 11.

[71] Keyser, "Woodland Management," 377.

[72] Duceppe-Lamarre, *Chasse et pâturage*, 148–49.

[73] On these terms see Duceppe-Lamarre, *Chasse et pâturage*, 142–48.

[74] Duceppe-Lamarre, *Chasse et pâturage*, 69.

[75] Duceppe-Lamarre, *Chasse et pâturage*, 39.

[76] Duceppe-Lamarre, *Chasse et pâturage*, 66.

of animals, which suppresses new tree growth through grazing as well as soil compaction, likely resulted in a structure in which the forest was composed primarily of tall trees and laced with clearings.[77]

For modern readers, the term "forest" may conjure up a wild space, untrammeled by human intervention. But wilderness is a cultural construct—only after the Romantics did Europeans view human intervention in the natural world as somehow contaminating.[78] In medieval forests, the economic demand for timber and livestock, as well as the cultural obsession with hunting game, resulted in a managed ecosystem created through intentional and often elaborate human interventions.[79] The explicit purpose of a forest was to be a refuge for game. In England, forest-dwellers were forbidden bows and arrows and forbidden to construct any impediment to the free-movement of game. Their dogs' claws were cut close to the pads of the feet so that they could not chase game and the tree-cover was protected as shelter for the deer. Penalties for transgressing such laws were harsh.[80] Aristocrats went to great lengths to suppress the natural predators that endangered those species they preferred to hunt.[81] The woodlands of Northern France (particularly in Flanders and Artois) also functioned as an important pasture where pigs, cows, and bees were raised.[82] Successful pasturing of these domesticated species required that they be separated from game and rabbits.[83] Sheep and goats were thus kept out of the forests and woods because of the damage they did to the plants and trees; they were pastured exclusively on wet meadowland.[84] In many areas, neighboring peasants had common rights to graze their animals in aristocratic woodlands, an additional complexity that was also a frequent source of conflict.[85]

Although elite men fostered strong ties to the forest and the hunt, grain fields, pastures, and meadows would have covered significant portions of most Northern French estate landscapes during the thirteenth century.[86]

---

[77] Duceppe-Lamarre, *Chasse et pâturage*, 70.

[78] Cronon, "The Trouble with Wilderness," 80.

[79] Duceppe-Lamarre, *Chasse et pâturage*, 82.

[80] Short, "Forests and Wood-Pasture," 133–34.

[81] Duceppe-Lamarre, *Chasse et pâturage*, 130.

[82] On the pasturing of animals in medieval woodlands, see Duceppe-Lamarre, *Chasse et pâturage*, 50–63.

[83] Duceppe-Lamarre, *Chasse et pâturage*, 53.

[84] Duceppe-Lamarre, *Chasse et pâturage*, 60–62 and 71.

[85] Common rights varied according to region and time period. A helpful discussion appears in Martina De Moor, et al., "Comparing the Historical Commons," 15–31. See also Duceppe-Lamarre, *Chasse et pâturage*, 51–53, 84, and 130.

[86] See Duby, *Rural Economy*, 67–86 and Hoffman, *An Environmental History*, 114–19.

Eating meat was a daily reminder of the lord's position at the top of the food chain.[87] Yet the cultural goals of facilitating both recreational hunting and extensive meat consumption were surprisingly at odds. Although venison was particularly favored, in practice, game hunting supplied a very small portion of the meat that made its way to aristocratic tables. Archaeozoology shows that the aristocratic diet was largely composed of grain-fed pork and beef; game represented only around ten percent of the meat consumed.[88] Since the grounds of the domain (the portion of a lord's lands that he cultivated directly) were relied upon to produce meat for the castle's inhabitants (who could number in the thousands),[89] the demand for meat ironically drove the conversion of much of the wooded lands on estates that had once been deer habitats into grain fields that supplied livestock feed. Cattle ate the most grain, but pigs also fed on grain much of the time, since they grazed on mast (acorns and nuts from trees) only in the autumn and only every second or third year.[90]

The mere presence of animals on the land alters ecosystems. Grazing animals create and maintain areas of grassland; without such animals compacting the ground and eating tree and bush seedlings, grassland quickly reverts to woodland.[91] Horses, which were important for both elite hunting and warfare, grazed on meadowland. Meadowlands were not sown crops, they occurred naturally in the flood-plains of rivers, and aristocrats preserved them carefully for use by their horses as well as to provide a valued source of the hay needed to overwinter livestock.[92] Because their status-consciousness inspired European aristocrats to imitate the cultural practices of others in their social group, these land management systems were found in a relatively uniform state across the continent.[93] The very presence of medieval aristocrats on the land tended to result in a specific ecosystem.[94] Creighton argues that this living "animalscape" was part of the material culture of the aristocracy, signaling "a fundamentally different sort of relationship between elite society and nature, with the desire to change and shape

---

[87] See Pluskowski, "Predators in Robes."
[88] Creighton, *Early European Castles*, 114–17.
[89] Johnson, *Behind the Castle Gate*, 42.
[90] Hoffman, *An Environmental History*, 180.
[91] Rackham, *Medieval Countryside*, 26.
[92] Rackham, *Medieval Countryside*, 28 and Hoffman, *An Environmental History*, 175. Farmer argues that count Robert II d'Artois acquired marshland specifically for grazing his treasured horses. Farmer, "Aristocratic Power," 674.
[93] Hoffman, *An Environmental History*, 115.
[94] Creighton, *Early European Castles*, 118.

the flora and fauna of the countryside becoming part of the European aris-tocratic mindset."[95] It is a powerful reminder of the role of culture in shaping nature. The relationship between the elite knightly classes and animals had a profound impact on the plant-life that surrounded them, whether this took the form of grain fields, pasture lands, or heavily managed woodlands.

In addition to grazing lands and woodlands, elite estates also housed arti-ficial, intensively managed habitats on their land for introduced and some-times exotic animal species. Rabbits benefited enormously from the clearance of woodlands, which formerly sustained the weasels, martins, and foxes that had been their main predators.[96] From the twelfth century on, aristocrats bred rabbits in large numbers, constructing artificial habitats called warrens where the rabbits were fed, enclosed, and protected.[97] Mounded, elevated rabbit warrens were a common sight on aristocratic estates, as were dovecotes holding thousands of birds[98] and fish ponds stocked with imported carp.[99] Estate gardens and orchards, in turn, required extensive protection from the imported species. These manmade animal habitats and their inhabitants were thus costly status symbols prized for their ornamental value as well as their ability to contribute luxurious meats for the table.[100]

The largest and most significant artificial animal habitat was the deer park. Although true forests were a luxury affordable only to princes, counts, and barons, wooded hunting grounds were desired across the knightly classes. Those who could not afford to keep forests constructed deer parks,[101] which were the visual backdrops for palaces, manor houses, monasteries, and castles. They were found even on lower-ranking estates.[102] Parks were, in some ways, pastures that served the utilitarian function of raising deer that were then hunted for meat.[103] At first, the parks housed native red deer; later, fallow deer were imported from Southwest Asia specifically for their ability to thrive on smaller areas of land.[104] Deer parks enclosed their cervine inhabitants within a substantial wall or pale flanked by an interior ditch to

[95] Creighton, *Early European Castles*, 119.

[96] van Dam, "New Habitats," 57–58.

[97] van Dam, "New Habitats, 59; Farmer, "Aristocratic Power," 656–57; Duceppe-Lamarre, *Chasse et pâturage*, 165–71.

[98] Dovecotes often had cells for 4,500 pigeons. See Jordan, *Great Famine*, 56.

[99] Farmer, "Aristocratic Power," 658–60.

[100] Creighton, *Designs Upon the Land*, 114–15 and Dowling, "Landscape of Luxuries."

[101] Rackham, *Medieval Countryside*, 22.

[102] For a description of deer parks, see especially Rackham, "Pre-Existing Trees."

[103] Fallow deer were imported from China, likely through Persia. See Hoffman, *An Environmental History*, 192.

[104] Rackham, *Medieval Countryside*, 22 and Farmer, "Aristocratic Power," 648–73.

keep the animals inside.[105] Their owners would likely have shaped the park's tree cover and its density through clearing and/or planting, creating a miniature image of an ideal forest.[106] Some parks were created whole cloth by planting trees in non-wooded areas,[107] while others contained a mix of newly planted trees and existing trees that were kept for the air of antiquity they lent to the built environment.[108] Deer parks were created as a more affordable substitute for hunting forests, but their grounds did not directly replicate the landscape of the forest—the parks were quickly transformed by the deer themselves. As they ate not only grass, brambles, and acorns, but also tree leaves, suckers, and saplings, their hungry mouths enforced a "browsing line" that prevented the trees' natural modes of regeneration. New trees had to be planted and protected from the deer, who created a new landscape composed of tall trees separated by areas of grass.[109] Human intervention and imported animals thus shaped the park's vegetation.

Deer parks were very numerous by the thirteenth century. Magnates often held dozens of them.[110] Although hunting was prohibited by canon law because of the violence involved,[111] deer parks were even a presence at bishops' residences.[112] They ably served the utilitarian purpose of supplying venison, yet parks were more than medieval feed lots. They were a palpable expression of aristocratic power, status, and wealth: "The right to empark was a jealously guarded privilege and badge of lordly authority, while another type of social statement was implicit in the very act of enclosing, quite tangibly and visibly, a large tract of landscape, and sometimes taking it out of agricultural production."[113] If a forest was the status symbol of kings and princes, a park

---

[105] Rackham, "Pre-existing trees," 9 and Creighton, *Designs Upon the Land*, 129.

[106] Cummings, "Hunting and the 'Natural' Landscape," 47.

[107] Zadora-Rio, "Parcs a gibier," 133.

[108] Rackham, "Pre-existing trees," 5. Records attest to the existence of a nursery industry that supplied aristocrats with saplings, nuts, and acorns meant to be sown into forest groves. See Harvey, *Medieval Gardens*, 15–17.

[109] Rackham, "Pre-existing trees," 2–3 and Short, "Forests and Wood-Pasture," 136.

[110] They were especially common in England. Nearly two hundred are recorded in Staffordshire in Wiltshire alone. See Dyer, "Woodlands and Wood-Pasture," 110. In England as a whole, there were as many as 1,900 parks in existence, most between one hundred and two hundred acres, and even larger royal parks. See Short, "Forests and Wood Pasture," 136–37.

[111] Sometimes gifts of forested land from lay nobles to religious institutions go so far as to reserve their right of hunting on the land while explicitly excluding clerics from hunting. Other documents recognize the right of religious regulars to hunt. See Duceppe-Lamarre, *Chasse et pâturage*, 153.

[112] Creighton, *Designs Upon the Land*, 127 and Duceppe-Lamarre, *Chasse et pâturage*, 172. Although there were many prohibitions against clerical hunting, it was critics who alleged that abbots and archbishops engaged in the practice. According to Creighton, "direct evidence for the involvement of ecclesiastics in hunting is on the whole sparse." Creighton, *Designs Upon the Land*, 128.

[113] Creighton, *Designs Upon the Land*, 124. See similar comments in Farmer, "Aristocratic Power," 647.

was a marker of status that reached down to minor aristocrats.[114] The access that non-aristocrats had to the parks was carefully controlled. Grazing and service-work permitted by custom to villagers was timed carefully so as not to disrupt the seasonal rhythms of the deer.[115] Woodlands were strongly tied to male aristocratic identity.

Gardens, the most intentionally cultivated of all outdoor spaces, were tied to female aristocratic identity. By the thirteenth and fourteenth centuries, increasing portions of medieval aristocratic estates began to be cultivated specifically to furnish pleasurable sensory experiences in the outdoors. Aristocratic gardens could house theatrical spaces meant for social display as well as contemplative spaces designed to provide privacy.[116] Gardens had long been mainstays of the monastic cloister.[117] However the creation and maintenance of large-scale ornamental gardens were the province of the elite,[118] who spent lavish sums on the design, building, and maintenance of their gardens.[119] Payment records show that improvements to the gardens sometimes took decades to complete and that their owners were constantly tinkering with them at steady expense, sometimes even importing master gardeners from other regions.[120] Garden spaces were strongly associated with the aristocratic women who were often charged with their initial de-sign and management. Queen Eleanor of Castile (queen of Edward I) per-sonally oversaw her own royal gardens, employing Aragonese gardeners and an Italian vintner and importing apple cuttings from France.[121] Similarly, countess Mahaut of Artois carefully managed the 2,200-hectare garden park at Hesdin not only for the pleasure of her guests but also to produce luxury products for her household.[122]

Estates were characterized by mixed agricultural uses and were shaped by the animals on which elite diet and leisure pursuits depended. The presence of gardens, meadowlands, and the wooded deer park (and, more rarely, the forest) set estate topography apart and served as markers of high social status.

---

[114] Rackham, *Medieval Countryside*, 22 and Creighton, *Designs Upon the Land*, 153.

[115] Creighton, *Designs upon the Land*, 153.

[116] Creighton estimates that in fourteenth-century England, ornamental landscapes could account for as much as five percent of the *demesne*. See *Designs Upon the Land*, 13.

[117] Indeed, Isodore of Seville specifies the need for a garden in the cloister. See Harvey, *Medieval Gardens*, 26.

[118] Harvey, *Medieval Gardens*, 51.

[119] For example, when Sir Paulin Pever, steward to Henry III, d.1251, bought a large, landed estate, he employed at least 50 men to improve and maintain the gardens. Harvey, *Medieval Gardens*, 12.

[120] Harvey, *Medieval Gardens*, 78–79.

[121] Harvey, *Medieval Gardens*, 175.

[122] See Dowling, "Landscape of Luxuries."

In medieval Northern France, outdoor spaces (even forests) were rarely wild; rather, they were intensively managed in ways that were driven by cultural values. The terrain was shaped by intensive intervention, and this human mediation of nature was viewed positively. Both land management schemes and the access individuals had to particular types of topography were often correlated with wealth, status, and/or identity. For the trouvères of the thirteenth century, their status and geography would thus have influenced the terrain that surrounded them as well as the topography and plant-life they saw on a regular basis. There were often significant differences in land usage between urban and rural areas, even when these areas were in relative proximity. The quotidian field of view of a songwriter living in an urban center such as Paris or Arras would likely have been dominated by the built environment of the city, a densely populated space with significantly less plant-life than many modern cities. An urbanite who had occasion to walk beyond the city walls may been surrounded by vineyards, grain fields, coppices, and other intensively managed agricultural spaces. Woodlands composed of tall trees, wet meadowlands, and large-scale gardens would rarely have been in view. Knightly trouvères, whether on their own domain or while visiting others of higher rank, would have spent considerable time outdoors in rural lands characterized by mixed uses. They may have walked in expansive meadows, grasslands, woodlands, and parks with tall trees. Such men may have hunted in deer parks or, if they were particularly high ranking, tall-growth forests where they would have been surrounded by a carefully curated population of favored plants, animals, and birds. When anonymous songs placed female characters in gardens or under tall trees, they signaled, through the topography, the high status of these women and their location within an elite context.

Having sketched historical conditions that can help us to imagine the contours of the land of medieval Northern France, I now turn to the trouvères themselves, situating individual authors according to their social rank and geographical context. This topographical and biographical foundation will serve as a necessary groundwork for Parts II and III, which explore how trouvère song could reflect attitudes toward the land and forge models of identity that were tied to specific topographies.

2

Trouvère Identities

Rank, Status, and Geography

Armed with an understanding of the lay of the land in medieval Northern France, it is now time to learn more about the songwriters who inhabited it. In this chapter, I address what is known about the historical biographies of the trouvères, the medieval Northern French songwriters who wrote most of the songs featured in this book. Interest in the biographies of medieval vernacular songwriters has enjoyed a nearly unbroken tradition. The thirteenth-century scribes and compilers who first preserved the songs of the troubadours and trouvères in manuscript form took, as I will show, a scholarly approach to the repertoire and its authors.[1] Tales of the lives of the knightly trouvères were published well into the nineteenth century.[2] The biographical sketches that opened many of the first modern editions of trouvère songs were based primarily on the song lyrics, reflecting the editor's assumption that the songs were authentic, reliable representations of the lives, experiences, and emotions of their authors. Before I explore potential relationships between trouvère songs and the lives of their authors, I seek first to review the available documentary evidence of the lives of key trouvères, focusing on their historical rank and status, and their association with specific geographical regions. In certain ways, my focus on biography harkens back to the (questionable) Romantic ideal that an artist's life and works should be intimately connected; it was this ideal that drove many editors to deduce elements of biography directly from trouvère song lyrics. Yet as Leach rightly explains, the desire to examine culture through the lens of biography is also thoroughly medieval: "there is ample evidence that it replicates medieval understandings of the correct relation between a first-person narrator and his or her text."[3] This chapter examines the trouvères and the known details

[1] See Haines, "The First Readers," chap. 1 in *Eight Centuries*.
[2] See Haines, *Eight Centuries*, 52–56 and 160–61.
[3] Leach, *Guillaume de Machaut*, 27.

Song, Landscape, and Identity in Medieval Northern France. Jennifer Saltzstein, Oxford University Press.
© Oxford University Press 2023. DOI: 10.1093/oso/9780197547779.003.0003

of their biographies, focusing especially on figures whose songs are featured in Chapters 3 through 6. I then provide an overview of the group identities with which many of those authors were affiliated (most were knights or clerks). Finally, I examine how a specific group of songbooks drew on both individual and group identities to represent the authors of song corpora, tying songs to the figure of the trouvère in ways that were both biographical and symbolic of social status. These songbooks, in turn, helped to articulate the elite identities of their patrons at the time of compilation and beyond, by projecting ideal types into the future.

By "identity," I mean an image a person or group of persons adheres to, or projects, of themselves. Identities can be projected outward, relating a self to externalities, but can also later be internalized and reabsorbed into an interior self.[4] A specific identity could be cultivated as a matter of self-presentation or imposed upon a person by others.[5] An identity also may or may not align closely with reality; it could be accurate or aspirational, broadly consistent or fluid.[6] In an influential study, Bynum discussed the novel attention paid to identity during the twelfth century, a development that earlier accounts had connected to the rise of the individual. Contrary to these accounts, Bynum emphasized that self-discovery and psychological self-examination (which had been interpreted as an emergent individuality) coincided with "self-conscious interest in the process of belonging to groups and filling roles." The discovery of the inner dimensions of the self thus went hand-in-hand with discovery of the group.[7]

The two groups to which many of the most celebrated trouvère author figures belonged were the knightly classes and the clergy. Both cultivated strong group identities. Because women are so seldom represented among the identified authors of trouvère song, this chapter pays the greatest attention to

---

[4] Kelly, "Medieval *Moi Multiple*," 15.

[5] Numerous studies shed light on medieval modes of identity formulation and presentation. Crane explores self-presentation and the performances of the self among medieval courtiers. See Crane, *Performance of the Self*. For an argument that medieval identity fragmented the self and spread it across other objects, bodies, and events, see Cohen, "Chevalerie," chap. 2 in *Medieval Identity Machines*. Newman argues that medieval selves were often constituted through various kinds of "indwelling" in which selves could merge or overlap. See Newman, *The Permeable Self*. My exploration of relationships between biography and identity is distinct from Peraino's approach to trouvère song, which focuses on subjectivity. See Peraino, "The Turn of the Voice," chap. 1 in *Giving Voice to Love*. My emphasis in this book on the ways in which individual medieval identities emerge from within larger group identities differs from that of Golden, who situates trouvère crusade song as an articulation of individual identity and "selfhood." See *Mapping Medieval Song*, 233–34.

[6] Newman argues that medieval selves tended to be permeable rather than discrete. See *The Permeable Self*.

[7] Bynum, "Did the Twelfth Century," 3.

elite men and masculine identities.[8] Chapters 5 and 6 however will deal extensively with the literary representation of the identities of other members of medieval society, including peasants, noble women, and urbanites. An important group of songbooks produced in the second half of the thirteenth century carefully configured and highlighted trouvère authorial identities through schemes of organization, classification, and illustration. These songbooks distinguished between the trouvères based on these (and other) identities. Placing available biographical data in dialogue with the cultural image-making practices of the songbooks shows how the trouvères were connected to both individual and group identities, identities forged through status and geography, both urban and rural. Later chapters will rely on this framework to determine how individual songs could foster identities tied to specific landscapes.

Knightly Trouvère Biographies: Lives and Careers

The lives of the trouvères have received sustained attention from scholars since the accounts of sixteenth-century antiquarians, as Hanes has shown.[9] The earliest accounts paid most attention to the noble songwriters, many of whom were credited with large numbers of songs that were widely transmitted. The surviving biographical data varies; certain lives are amply documented, whereas others are a matter of conjecture. Some of these

[8] Manuscript rubrics credit two elite women as trouvère song authors: Blanche of Castille and the Duchess of Lorraine. The fragmentary songbook *j* credits "Amours, u trop tart" (RS 1604a) to Blanche of Castille, wife of Louis VIII of France and mother of Louis IX (Saint Louis), who was regent queen during her son's minority. Blanche is also listed as co-author of the *jeu-parti* "Dame, merci, une riens vous demant" (RS 335) with Thibaut de Champagne in the manuscript *b* (fol. 169v) through the rubric "Le roi de Navarre a la roine blanche" (the other ten manuscripts in which this *jeu-parti* is found extant do not name her). These attributions, and the views of scholars who have accepted or rejected their veracity, are discussed in Doss-Quinby et al, *Songs of the Women Trouvères*, 30–31. The songbook *C* credits the Duchess of Lorraine with "Par maintes fois" (RS 1640) and "Un petit devant le jour" (RS 1995). Although *C* does not indicate which holder of the title "Duchess de Lorraine" was the author, Lévêque-Fougre argues that it was likely Marguerite de Champagne, daughter of Count Thibaut IV of Champagne, and wife of Duke Ferri III of Lorraine. See "Lorraine Repertory," 30. In addition to these attributed examples, there are also women who are named as participants and judges in some *jeux-partis* (see Doss-Quinby, et al., *Songs of the Women Trouvères*, 26–28 and 32–33). Although authorial attribution of specific songs to women is uncommon, there is ample evidence to indicate women's participation as performers and musical professionals in thirteenth-century Northern France (see, for example, Boynton, "Women's Performance"; Coldwell, "*Jougleresses* and *Trobairitz*"; Doss-Quinby et. al., *Songs of the Women Trouvères*, 14–26; Dolce, "'Soit hom'"; and Haines, *Medieval Song*, 51–82). I discuss questions of gender and anonymity in the Introduction.

[9] Fauchet's *Recueil des poetes François* (1581) examined 127 trouvères active before 1300, based on his consultation of medieval sources. See Haines, *Eight Centuries*, 51–52.

biographies were the stuff of legend: an alleged love affair between Thibaut IV and regent queen Blanche of Castille;[10] Conon de Béthune's supposed rescue of King Richard the Lionhearted from prison during the third crusade; and the tale of the lady tricked by her husband to eat the heart of her dead lover, the Châtelain de Coucy. These tales were often constructed from literary accounts and embellished freely by nineteenth-century editors.[11] This creative approach to biography, in which literary sources (and sometimes even the editor's imagination) were used to fill in the gaps left by the archival record, prevailed beyond the turn of the twentieth century, long after the emerging science of philology had introduced a rigorous, systematic approach to editing the lyrics of the trouvères.[12]

Among the named authors in the trouvère song corpus, those who were knights represent some of the most prolific and best-preserved. Two of the most significant trouvères were knights with strong ties to the county of Champagne: Thibaut IV (who was count of Blois and Champagne and, from 1234, king of Navarre) and Gace Brulé. Countess Marie de Champagne had established Champagne as a vernacular literary center during the twelfth century through her patronage of the romance author Chrétien de Troyes and several trouvères.[13] Some trouvère songbooks open with an author section devoted to the songs of Thibaut IV. Thibaut's grandmother was Eleanor of Aquitaine, who as the granddaughter of Guillaume IX, Duke of Aquitaine (widely viewed as the earliest troubadour). Thibaut IV was among the most productive of the trouvères, having written around sixty songs in a wide variety of genres. Little is known about the life and career of the prolific trouvère Gace Brulé. However, several documents tie him to the Paris region. Gace is known to have owned land in Dreux (north of Paris). He enjoyed an annual cash payment (*fief-rente*) from the *prévôté* of Mantes (Paris region) that is noted in the registers of Philip Augustus.[14] He may have been related to Henry Brullé and Hugh Brullé, knights who held fiefs in the county of Champagne in the 1170s, although Gace does not himself appear in the fief rolls or comital acts. References in his song corpus suggest he, like Thibaut

---

[10] On the sourcing of this rumor in medieval chronicles, see Jordan, "Representation of the Crusades," 28. Songs that attempt to slander the reputation of Blanche de Castille are discussed in Quinlan, "Courtly Song," 106–8.

[11] Haines, *Eight Centuries*, 34–37, 104–106, and 160.

[12] Haines, *Eight Centuries*, 160.

[13] Benton, "Court of Champagne," Evergates, *Marie of France*, 58–62; Peraino, *Giving Voice to Love*, 140.

[14] See Baldwin, *Aristocratic Life*, 15–16; Baldwin, *Knights, Lords, and Ladies*, 15–16.

IV, may have been from Champagne.[15] His claim to have written one of his songs at the command of Countess Marie de Champagne lends further support to his connection to this region.[16]

Several knightly trouvères likely knew one another and fought in the same expeditions in the Holy Land. Thibaut IV fought in the Albigensian Crusade alongside the trouvère Thibaut de Blaison, who was present at the siege of Toulouse.[17] Song references hint further at the acquaintance of the two knightly songwriters: Thibaut IV dedicated his song "De ma dame" (RS 1467) to Thibaut de Blaison and modeled his Marian song "De chanter" (RS 1475) on Thibaut de Blaison's "Amours, que porra devenir" (RS 1402).[18] Thibaut IV commanded the Baron's Crusade of 1239–1240,[19] and he was joined on this expedition by the trouvère Raoul de Soissons.[20] Raoul spent years in the Holy Land, participating in three separate expeditions. After the Barons' Crusade, he stayed behind to marry Alice of Champagne, making him a contender for the throne of Jerusalem and leading to a long struggle with emperor Frederick II.[21] Among the earliest generation of knightly trouvères, the Châtelain de Couci (likely Guy IV, Castellan of Coucy, who fought in the third and fourth crusades and died at sea during the latter),[22] Conon de Béthune,[23] and Gautier de Dargies all fought in the Third Crusade. The Châtelain and Conon would also join the Fourth Crusade along with the Vidame de Chartres[24] and Hughues de Berzé.[25] Other trouvères such as count Charles II of Anjou (later king of Jerusalem and Sicily), Raoul de Soissons, and the Vidame of Chartres (Guillaume de Ferrières) fought together in the seventh crusade in Egypt. The songs of the trouvère-crusaders, particularly those who fought in the fourth and seventh crusades, are showcased in the songbook *M*.[26]

---

[15] See Evergates, *Marie de France*, 138n130.

[16] See "Bien cuidai toute ma vie" (RS 1232). This reference is suggestive but is not proof that Gace ever attended court of Champagne. See Benton, "Court of Champagne," 566-67.

[17] Thibaut's participation in the Albigensian Crusade is discussed in Evergates, *Feudal Society*, 2–4. Documents pertaining to the life of Thibaut de Blaison are summarized in Newcomb, "Introduction," in Thibaut de Blaison, *Les poésies* 15–20.

[18] See Karp, "Thibaut de Blaison," *Oxford Music Online*, https://www-oxfordmusiconline-com.

[19] See the account in Lower, *The Barons' Crusade*.

[20] See Griffiths, "Royal Counselors and Trouvères," 133.

[21] See Griffiths, "Royal Counselors and Trouvères," 134.

[22] On the identification of the Châtelain de Couci, see Lerond's introduction to Châtelain de Couci, *Chansons attribués*, 16–18. Guy's death is described in Villehardouin, "Conquest of Constantinople," 33.

[23] On Conon's involvement in the crusades see Wallensköld, *Conon de Béthune*, iv–vii.

[24] The Vidame was likely Guillaume de Ferrières. See Dyggve, "Personnages historiques," 161–85.

[25] Villehardouin, *Chronicles of the Crusades*, 14.

[26] See the discussion in Haines, "Songbook for William," 72–83.

Clerkly Trouvère Biographies: Lives and Careers

Although the knightly trouvères had traditionally attracted the greatest attention from the earliest observers, many non-noble trouvères were also
credited with songs in medieval manuscripts. Careful archival work by the
philologist Adolphe Guesnon established that there were trouvères who were
members of the clergy and who were associated with urban environments.[27]
The cleric-trouvères were a diverse assemblage of scribes, masters, canons,
deacons, priests, deans, and even a cantor and a chancellor. Some clerical
songwriters (such as Guibert Kaukesel and Gaidifer d'Avion) produced just
a handful of songs whereas others are among the most prolific, well-studied
author-figures of the period: Jehan Bodel, Adam de la Halle, Guillaume
de Machaut, Gautier de Coinci, and Richard de Fournival.[28] Other cleric-
trouvères produced significant song corpora but have received less critical
attention, figures such as Guillaume le Vinier, Simon d'Authie, and Moniot
d'Arras. The cleric-trouvères dominate the vernacular songwriters who
wrote, or may have written, polyphonic motets.[29] As I discuss in greater detail
in Chapter 4, we should probably view some portion of the hundreds of other
unattributed vernacular motets that survive from the thirteenth and early
fourteenth centuries as the likely work of cleric-trouvères. For the moment,
it is notable that there were at least twenty cleric-trouvères active during the
twelfth and thirteenth centuries who were named in surviving songbooks.
They represent a significant portion of the vernacular songwriters active
in their day. Collectively they produced around three hundred fifty songs,

---

[27] Guesnon, "Recherches biographiques"; Guesnon, "Nouvelles recherches." See also Berger,
Littérature et société, 435–42. The existence of urban, clerical trouvères is mentioned in Dragonetti,
Technique poètique, 366; Räkel *Die Musikalische Erscheinungsform*, 135–37, 259–61, and 337–41;
and Ungureanu, *La bourgeoisie naissante*, 118–21. Page discusses references in the Occitan *vidas* and
in canon law that suggest the relatively robust presence of "jongleur-clerics." See Page, *Owl and the
Nightingale*, 73–74. Haines and Peraino argue that the songbooks *M* and *T* implicitly stage the emergence of the urban and/or clerical trouvère in the later thirteenth century. See Haines, "Songbook for
William," 73–75; Peraino, *Giving Voice to Love*, 127–54.

[28] On the significance of Jehan Bodel's life and works, see Symes, *A Common Stage*, 37–43. For a re-
cent synthesis of the vast literature on Adam de la Halle, see the essays in Saltzstein, *Musical Culture*.
The most comprehensive recent treatment of Machaut's works is Leach, *Guillaume de Machaut*,
which updates Earp's still essential *Guillaume de Machaut*. The most recent syntheses of research on
Machaut can be found in the chapters in McGrady and Bain, *Companion to Guillaume de Machaut*.
On Gautier de Coinci, see especially Krause and Stones, *Gautier de Coinci*. On Richard de Fournival,
see, most recently, Leach and Morton, "Intertextual and Intersonic Resonances"; Zingesser, "From
Beak to Quill," chap. 4 in *Stolen Song*. The anonymous author of *Les règles de la seconde rhétorique*
claimed that in addition to motets, the clerical composer Philippe de Vitry also wrote *balades*, *lais*,
and *rondeaux* (Plumley, *Art of Grafted Song*, 279); had these vernacular songs survived, we might also
count Philippe among the ranks of the cleric-trouvères.

[29] See Saint-Cricq, "Genre, Attribution, and Authorship," 187 and 195.

which represent a significant portion of the surviving trouvère song corpus of roughly two thousand one hundred songs.

The lives of the cleric-trouvères speak to the breadth of career paths which medieval clerics pursued. Some were ordained members of the major clergy, and several individuals also led distinguished and well-documented ecclesiastical careers. Richard de Fournival was a canon of Rouen and Amiens and was promoted to the dignity of chancellor of the Amiens chapter of Notre Dame, a position he occupied for nearly two decades from 1241 until his death in 1260. Although canonicates, which provided their recipient with an income, did not always require residency in the city to which they were attached, Richard held capitular land and was strictly bound to residence in Amiens for at least six months per year.[30] As chancellor, Richard significantly expanded the cathedral school at Amiens, which began to attract students from Tournai, Arras, Béthune, and Soissons.[31] Richard also authored a corpus of around twenty-five songs and polyphonic motets, as well as a variety of Latin treatises and vernacular poems, including his widely transmitted *Bestiaire d'amour*. Richard was not the first prominent cleric of Amiens to combine his ecclesiastical duties with vernacular song composition. His predecessor Simon d'Authie (credited with nine songs and three *jeux-partis*) was a canon at Amiens cathedral, a university graduate (*magister* or *maistre*), and a talented jurist. Simon's involvement in court proceedings in Paris and Arras are well documented during the 1220s and 1230s, including his involvement in a dispute in 1229 between the students of the University of Paris and the French crown.[32] Simon was also elected dean of the cathedral chapter by the canons of Amiens in 1226, a dignity that required enormous competence and was normally reserved for priests.[33] The trouvère Adam de Givenchi, like Simon, held the dignity of dean[34] and worked as clerk to the bishop of Arras.[35] He was also a noted jurist who (with the help of cleric-trouvère Gilles le Vinier)[36] argued against Simon in a legal dispute in

---

[30] See Johnson, "Music at the Cathedral of Amiens," 62 and 288.

[31] See Johnson, "Music at the Cathedral of Amiens," 84–86.

[32] Johnson, "Music at the Cathedral of Amiens," 258.

[33] Deans were responsible for the service, fundraising, giving counsel to the bishop, and other duties. See Barrow, *Clergy in the Medieval World*, 303.

[34] Adam was dean at Lens cathedral. See Guesnon, "Recherches biographiques," 425–27.

[35] Adam is cited in two charters from 1230 as clerk to the bishop. In 1243 he is listed with the title "dominus" and finally, in 1245, he is listed as the dean of Lens. See Guesnon, "Recherches biographiques," 425–27.

[36] Gilles le Vinier is twice named clerk to the bishop in documents from 1232. See Guesnon, "Recherches biographiques," 430.

1232.[37] Outside of court, Simon and Gilles collaboratively composed a debate song (*jeu-parti*) that includes references to clerical culture.[38] Other trouvères who led ecclesiastical careers include: Guibert Kaukesel of Arras, a canon who held the positions of scholasticus and cantor at the cathedral and served as chaplain to Pope Urban IV;[39] Gaidifer d'Avion, who was likely a canon and provost;[40] the canon Guillaumes Veaus;[41] as well as the master, canon, and deacon Pierre de Corbie.[42] Monks are credited with vernacular songs, most notably Gautier de Coinci of Soissons, who transformed trouvère songs to serve the purposes of Marian devotion in his widely transmitted cycle of vernacular miracles. Two trouvères about whom we otherwise lack biographical information wear their status as monks in their names: Moniot (Little Monk) d'Arras and Moniot de Paris.[43]

Other cleric-trouvères belonged to the minor clergy. Jehan de Grieviler of Arras, for example, was a married cleric who, along with a number of other married clerics, Jehan petitioned for tax exemption in 1254. He was also a prolific trouvère credited with over forty songs.[44] Guillaume le Vinier, to whom a varied musical corpus of around thirty-five songs is attributed, was a married cleric and university graduate.[45] In some cases, we lack historical evidence demonstrating a trouvère's clerical status, but literary or circumstantial sources strongly suggest it. Jehan Bodel (d. ca. 1210), for example, tells us in his *Congé* that he worked as a clerk to the elected officials (*échevins*) who governed the Town of Arras. Although no records of his employment survive, Carol Symes argues that there is no reason to doubt Bodel's own claims,

---

[37] Guesnon summarizes the legal dispute in "Recherches biographiques," 429–30. Later accounts include Gennrich, "Simon d'Authie," 52, Berger, *Littéraire et société arrageoises*, 436 and Johnson, "Music at the Cathedral of Amiens," 259–60.

[38] See my reading of their *jeu-parti* "Maistre Simon," (RS 572) in "Cleric-Trouvères," 155–58.

[39] See Berger, *Littérature et société*, 441.

[40] Guesnon argued that Gaidifer was the "Gautier d'Avions" who was canon of Cambrai and, in 1250, provost of Saint-Géry. See Guesnon, "Nouvelles recherches," 148–49.

[41] Guillaume was canon of Notre-Dame d'Arras and occupied a house in the cloister. See Guesnon, "Nouvelles recherches," 141–42.

[42] Guesnon discusses the three charters that name "Petrus de Corbeia" (likely Pierre de Corbie) as a canon and deacon. See "Recherches Biographiques," 422–24. Berger questions whether Petrus and Pierre were the same person because Pierre is referred to as "mesire." *Littérature et société*, 437. Guesnon indicates, however, that it was not only nobles but also priests who were referred to as "mesire." See Guesnon, "Recherches biographiques," 422.

[43] Dyggve, "Moniot d'Arras et Moniot de Paris."

[44] Berger, *Littérature et société*, 438. Clerical marriage was common through the twelfth century before crackdowns in the thirteenth. See Barrow, *Clergy in the Medieval World*, 139.

[45] A charter of 1245 identifies the trouvère Guillaume le Vinier as *magister*. This document is discussed with the passage quoted in full in Ménard, *Poésies de Guillaume le Vinier*, 2–3.

particularly since the constant references to charters, seals, and accounts in his works as well as the quasi legal language of parts of his *Congé* amply attest to his familiarity with legal procedure and scribal culture.[46] Adam de la Halle of Arras (d. ca.1285–88), who composed in most of the song genres of his day and produced two of the earliest vernacular plays, may have also self-consciously styled his own career after that of Bodel's.[47] Historical documentation related to Adam's life and career is scarce,[48] but through his works, Adam constructed an authorial persona for himself as a cleric and reluctant trouvère who hoped to return to the University of Paris to complete his studies.[49] Adam's father and nephew were both clerics.[50] Their relationships match a common pattern for children to be primed for clerical careers by their clerical fathers or uncles.[51] The literary identity Adam constructed for himself is also reinforced by his peers and immediate successors. In a *jeu-parti* composed with Adam, "Adan, amis, je vous dis" (RS 1833), Jehan Bretel calls Adam "bien letrés" (well lettered) and complains that Adam speaks "en clergeois" (in clerical parlance). Adam is depicted tonsured[52] and described as a master (*maistre*) in songbooks.[53] Although no biographical data about the trouvère Richart de Semilli has emerged, he was also identified as a master in songbooks[54] and set several of his songs in Paris, suggesting that he may have been a cleric.[55] Finally, the trouvère Jacques d'Amiens may also have been a cleric. An author by the same name translated Ovid's *Ars amatoria*

[46] See Symes, *A Common Stage*, 41–42.

[47] Adam wrote in many of the same genres as Jehan and directly imitated Jehan's *Congé; W* links the works of the two poets. See discussion in Symes, "'School of Arras," 22–28.

[48] For the most recent accounts of the available information, see my "Introduction," 1–13 and Symes, "'School of Arras," 28–32.

[49] He introduces this persona in the first verses of his *Jeu de la feuillée*, and aspects of it are reiterated in his other works. See my *Refrain and the Rise*, 114–23.

[50] Adam's father Henri is listed in the register of the Carité de Notre Dame des Ardents of Arras as "Maistre Henri Bochu." See Berger, ed., *Nécrologe*, 1:62a. Jehan Mados, a married cleric from Arras, identifies himself in a manuscript colophon as Adam's nephew (and indicates that Adam is dead). See Guesnon, "Nouvelles recherches," 144.

[51] See Barrow, "Clergy as Family Men," chap. 4 in *Clergy in the Medieval World*.

[52] *A* 142v. See discussion in Huot, *Song to Book*, 59–60.

[53] *W*, 1r. According to Guesnon, rubrics applied the Old French term *maistre* (master) to canons, clerics, doctors, and architects. See "Recherches biographiques," 422–423n4. When used in songbooks, it may not have corresponded directly to the Latin title *magister* (master), which certified a university education and the possession of the *licentia docendi* (teaching license) granted by the chancellor. On the Latin term *magister*, see Baldwin, *Masters, Princes, and Merchants*, 74; Barrow, *Clergy in the Medieval World*, 175–76 and 208–11.

[54] These "maistre" author rubrics appear consistently with Richart's songs across the *K, N, P, X* group of songbooks.

[55] Johnson, *Lyrics of Richard de Semilli*, 3.

from Latin into Old French (this work was a common school text used to teach clerics Latin grammar).[56]

Several clerical-trouvères are known to have worked in aristocratic households, including Adam de la Halle and Oede de la Couroierie, as well as the most well-known among them, Guillaume de Machaut. Oede de la Couroierie served Count Robert II d'Artois between 1270 and 1295, a period during which he would have accompanied the count on his international travels and, during the 1280s, worked alongside Adam de la Halle.[57] Guillaume de Machaut, the most prominent of the vernacular composers featured in this book, was an ordained cleric—a subdeacon who worked in both courtly and ecclesiastical roles.[58] He spent decades as an administrator in the court of king John of Bohemia as an almoner, notary, and from 1333 onward, secretary, likely remaining in John's service until the king's death in 1346.[59] As one of the king's secretaries, Machaut would have been intimately involved in scribal culture; his responsibilities included signing the king's private correspondence and authorizing official documents.[60] After John's death in 1336, circumstantial evidence suggests that Machaut was connected to other prominent aristocrats who may have been his patrons.[61] In addition to his music and literature, Machaut composed chivalric biographies such as La prise d'Alexandrie (c. 1369–1371), which celebrated the life of King Peter I of Cypress. His Confort d'ami was a work of consolation, in a genre of texts designed to soothe leaders beset by difficult political and military circumstances (in this case, Charles II of Navarre). Machaut understood chivalric mentalities and values; he emphasized peer assessments of honor by incorporating the views of other knights into the Prise.[62] As a high-ranking domestic servant in a royal household, Machaut would have partaken, to some extent, of the luxurious lifestyle of the court. The composer was also granted three different canonicates and eventually (probably by 1360) became a resident canon at the cathedral of Notre Dame of Rheims. Machaut's

[56] No historical documentation of Jacques survives. See discussion in Johnson, "Music at the Cathedral of Amiens," 386–91. On the vernacular translation of Ovid by Jaques d'Amiens, see Hexter, Ovid and Medieval Schooling, 21. His devotional contrafacta (found in songbook C) are discussed in Callahan, "Strategies of Appropriation."

[57] On Oede, see Guesnon, "Nouvelles recherches," 53; on Adam's service to Robert II, see Symes, "School of Arras," 29 and 31.

[58] On the life and career of Guillaume de Machaut, see esp. Leach, Guillaume de Machaut, 7–18.

[59] See Leach, Guillaume de Machaut, 12–13 and 31.

[60] Leach, Guillaume de Machaut, 14–15.

[61] Leach, Guillaume de Machaut, 25–26, 29–30, and 33.

[62] Taylor, Ideals of Knighthood, 63.

life and career thus harnessed clerical skills in royal and aristocratic contexts (which would have been both urban and rural) and concluded his career in an urban, ecclesiastical post. Within this context, we are encouraged to view the two best known composers of medieval France, Adam de la Halle and Guillaume de Machaut, as luminaries within a relatively broad cohort of composers in possession of some form of Latinate training who applied their skills to songwriting.

Group Identities, Knightly and Clerical

The surviving repertoire of trouvère songs divides roughly in half between authored and anonymous songs. Chapters 3 and 4 focus on songs attributed respectively to knights and clerics. In Chapter 1, my discussion of land was quickly entangled with questions of identity, since identity shaped the way people interacted with the land. A similar dynamic will hold in my consideration of trouvère biographies, which were importantly overlaid with (and difficult to disentangle from) group identities. The knightly and clerical classes each cultivated strong group identities through which they distinguished themselves from others. Although the ranks of the clergy and nobility could overlap in important ways (indeed, the clergy were often brothers, sisters, and cousins of the ruling classes), to be a knight or a cleric in Northern France entailed deliberate modes of self-presentation that were clearly enough understood to be the subject of ready parody,[63] as the popular stereotypes of the medieval estates satire demonstrate.[64] Yet they were also identities that many medieval people valued deeply and actively fostered. Because the vast majority of the trouvères to whom songs were attributed were men, my treatment of the authored corpus will focus on masculine identities.

Male elite identity was intrinsically bound up in knighthood, which emphasized status, prowess, and adherence to an accepted set of ideals. Knighthood was not a military rank; it was an ethos that referred to "the entire social body of knights considered as a group stretching across space and time."[65] During the twelfth and thirteenth centuries, elite warrior status

---

[63] In the anonymous *fabliau*, "Des chevaliers, des clers, et des villains," the poet describes a beautiful glade and discusses the various ways in which aristocrats, clerics, and peasants respond to it: the aristocrats admire it as a site for a courtly picnic, the clerics eye it as the stage for a romantic rendezvous, and the peasants aim to use it as a latrine. See Dubin, *Fabliaux*, 14–17.

[64] On the estates satire, see Mann, *Medieval Estates Satire*.

[65] Kaeuper, *Chivalry and Violence*, 4.

trumped, in certain ways, social status. The identity of the knightly warrior was adopted by kings as well as the fighters of little wealth who served them.[66] Kings considered themselves members of the knighthood and personally led knights into battle.[67] Warrior identity was thus shared among the knightly class regardless of rank, from kings, counts, barons, and castellans (those in possession of a castle), to common knights (*vavassores*) like the iconic Guillaume le Maréchal, who, according to his biographer, held not a strip of land to his name, only his chivalry.[68] Guillaume's acts of prowess during tournaments won him ransoms and horses, lucrative prizes that furnished his rise from a landless knight dependent on patronage to a man of enormous wealth.[69] The ideals of knighthood emerged as a core cluster of common values involving lay piety, loyalty, generosity (largesse), intense male friendship, a new framework for heterosexual love and gender relationships, and above all, prowess, with its attendant emphasis on social dominance and licit violence.[70] Heraldry demonstrates the direct intertwining of combat and identity among the knightly classes, since its emergence in the late twelfth and thirteenth centuries directly coincides with the adoption of cylindrical helmets that completely obscured the knight's face, necessitating new modes of identification on the battlefield and during tournaments.[71] Based on texts written by knights themselves and those who were close to them, Kaeuper argues that the chivalrous believed they were set apart from others by their prowess and the largesse it supplied: "they possessed castles, or at least fortified dwellings of some sort; they pictured themselves fighting from the backs of noble warhorses; they enthusiastically participated in the defining sport of tournament; they displayed appropriately refined manners in court and courtship; they provided patronage and audience for literature of a specific, and ideally exclusive sort."[72] This knightly identity was formed early and held lifelong. From early childhood, male aristocratic children were trained to master horses and weaponry. They were fed a cultural diet of epic and chivalric romance that steeped them in knightly values and imagery.[73]

---

[66] Kaeuper, *Medieval Chivalry*, 94 and Baldwin, *Knights, Lords and Ladies*, 101.

[67] Kaeuper *Medieval Chivalry*, 235 and 243.

[68] Kaeuper, *Medieval Chivalry*, 57, citing *History of William Marshal*, ll.2071–2096. This is not to say that nobility was not recognized among the knightly classes. Nobles were distinct from knights and few knights would ever be castellans or exercise more than limited lordship. See Evergates, "Nobles and Knights," 15–17.

[69] See Baldwin, *Knights, Lords and Ladies*, and 219–20.

[70] Kaeuper, *Medieval Chivalry*, 22.

[71] Baldwin, *Knights, Lords and Ladies*, 71.

[72] Kaeuper, *Chivalry and Violence*, 302.

[73] Taylor, *Ideals of Knighthood*, 100–1.

Knightly bravery was viewed as an inherent quality that was genetically passed down to male children.[74] After death, prominent aristocrats projected their identities as warriors for the ages on their tombs, where their effigies often represent them in armor with swords and heraldry.[75]

Knightly identity was also importantly tied to the land, which was itself an expression of noble values and lifestyles. Off the battlefield, the favored pastime of the knightly classes was hunting, an activity that they had cultivated for centuries.[76] Recall that Chapter 1 showed that forests composed of tall trees, which formed the best hunting grounds, were rare status symbols owned by only the wealthiest, most elite families. These associations between knightly identity, hunting, and the forest are evident in the fact that castles were often planned and built next to forests specifically for hunting purposes,[77] and that the planted, walled environment of the deer park was a substitute for the forest sought by even relatively low-ranking landowners. The few board games that have been unearthed by archaeologists incorporate iconography of game animals, demonstrating how ingrained hunting was in the self-image of the knightly classes.[78] The violence involved in hunting was also a preparation for warfare; hunting aided in the development of the equestrian skills on which medieval military strategy relied.[79] Eating meat was symbolic of the lordly position at the top of the food chain, both literally and sociologically.[80] The value placed on the hunt thus made woodlands a potent symbol of male knightly identity.

Land was arguably the endpoint of knightly prowess. It was the prize to be won through military valor and advantageous marriages and was the single most important source of wealth in the middle ages. The fief, which most knights held from another lord as his vassal, was a primary means of support. By the thirteenth-century in Champagne, a region where the nobility had once been restricted to a small cadre of castle lords, noble status was extended to any person who held a fief, rendering land and status commensurate.[81]

---

[74] Kaeuper, *Medieval Chivalry*, 43.

[75] On aristocratic tombs, see Kaeuper, *Medieval Chivalry*, 102; Taylor, *Ideals of Knighthood*, 61, and Baldwin, *Knights, Lords, and Ladies*, 164–77.

[76] Hunting rights are discussed in records dating back to the Merovingian era. See Duceppe-Lamarre, *Chasse et pâturage*, 140–41. On the participation by elite women in hunting, see Duceppe-Lamarre, *Chasse et pâturage*, 152; Richardson, "Riding like Alexander."

[77] Colvin, "Royal Gardens in Medieval England," 11.

[78] Creighton, *Early European Castles*, 124.

[79] See Kaeuper, *Chivalry and Violence*, 175.

[80] See Pluskowski, "Predators in Robes."

[81] See Evergates, *Aristocracy in the County of Champagne*, 58–61.

Particularly in the late twelfth through the mid-thirteenth centuries, the revenues generated from agricultural lands dwarfed other sources of income.[82] Wheat was the primary crop lords cultivated; the bread it produced for the table was a status symbol, and the revenues gained through its sale represented the largest share of the lord's income.[83] Records of donations from the aristocracy to the church suggest that aristocrats were loath to part with their land, preferring to donate cash and in-kind payments. Purchases of aristocratic land by the church (which were relatively rare) also show that land commanded very high prices.[84] Finally, in one of the more overt examples of the connection between land and knightly identity, aristocrats increasingly advertised their relationship to the land in their names by adopting toponymic surnames (such as Thibaut *de Champagne*), which associated them with specific places or geographical features.[85] Their names thus signaled that knights and lords alike considered themselves lord of a place.[86] Interestingly, toponyms did not necessarily refer to lands from which an individual originated or which their family controlled; they could express one's seat of power or even one's territorial ambitions.[87]

Like the knightly classes, clerics also possessed a strong, shared identity. Theirs was defined by a common set of skills and common educational background. The term "cleric" could refer broadly to any person who was a member of the clergy, from bishops and priests to monks and nuns to university students or choirboys learning chant. Clerics were numerous and their ranks grew steadily throughout the middle ages,[88] growth that was driven by increasingly elaborate liturgies and new demand for private masses.[89] They shared an identity that was deeply rooted and that set them apart from other members of society. Those destined for a clerical life usually joined in childhood or adolescence and some were positioned for it by their relatives even earlier, sometimes even before birth.[90] Clerical identity was visible on the

---

[82] Baldwin, *Knights, Lords, and Ladies*, 124.

[83] Baldwin, *Knights, Lords, and Ladies*, 128.

[84] Baldwin, *Knights, Lords, and Ladies*, 122–27.

[85] See Evergates, *Aristocracy in the County of Champagne*, 133–39.

[86] Baldwin, *Knights, Lords, and Ladies*, 70.

[87] Evergates, *Aristocracy in the County of Champagne*, 133. This is evident in name changes, wherein men might adopt a toponym referring to land acquired by marriage or to aspirational territorial claims. See ibid., 135–36.

[88] On the numbers of medieval clergy see Guillemain, "Chiffres et statistiques."

[89] See Barrow, *Clergy in the Medieval World*, 12.

[90] See Barrow, *Clergy in the Medieval World*, 40–41. Young men whose parents had chosen a clerical life for them were often named after their clerical fathers or uncles, creating dynastic successions that were determined before birth. See Barrow, *Clergy in the Medieval World*, 124.

body through the tonsure (the shaving of the top of the head)[91] and through the ankle-length clothing clerics wore.[92] Although clerics were not the only literate members of medieval society, the term "cleric" came to be synonymous with learning and knowledge of letters.[93] Their early education in Latin (which focused on grammar, rhetoric, and dialectic),[94] whether obtained from a monastic or cathedral school, relied on a fairly uniform set of Latin texts including the Psalter and the Scriptures, as well as classical works such as Ovid's *Metamorphoses* and *Ars amatoria*, texts with which they would have shared an intimate familiarity.[95] The pedagogical methods were broadly similar across institutions of learning.[96] Although education in Latin grammar could be attained in rural monastic schools, higher education, whether with a prominent master at a prestigious cathedral school or at a university, was an urban endeavor. Students were enticed to leave their home dioceses by the opportunity to study specialized subject matter from star teachers attached to urban cathedral schools starting in the eleventh century.[97] The political stability and lodging that cities could provide were necessary preconditions for international centers of learning to develop.[98] A cleric whose education had advanced beyond basic Latin grammar would thus have spent some period of time in an urban cathedral school or a university, and many of these men would remain in the city long afterward, opting to copy charters rather than enter the priesthood.[99] Clerics were particularly numerous in urban areas. In Arras, for example, it has been estimated that one adult man in four was educated and that over the course of a century, the monastic and cathedral schools could have welcomed as many as 8,000–10,000 students.[100] Indeed,

---

[91] The tonsure was established as a marker of the clergy from the sixth century and clerics were required to maintain it for life, even if they had been tonsured as children. See Barrow, *Clergy in the Medieval World*, 31–33. Frequent calls for clerics to uphold their tonsures do suggest that some were lax its maintenance (see, for example, Symes, *A Common Stage*, 157).

[92] See Barrow, *Clergy in the Medieval World*, 31–33.

[93] See "Clergie," in Godefroy, *Dictionnaire de l'ancienne langue française*, II, 151–52.

[94] These language arts were known as the *trivium*, and they were complemented by the *quadrivium* (arithmetic, astronomy, geometry, and music), which received comparatively little emphasis in medieval education. The study of the "seven liberal arts" laid a foundation for higher learning in theology, law, or medicine. See Grant, *God and Reason*, 101.

[95] On widely used texts in medieval curricula, see Barrow, *Clergy in the Medieval World*, 217–27.

[96] The standard treatment of these hermeneutic techniques is Smalley, *Study of the Bible*.

[97] See discussion in Barrow, *Clergy in the Medieval World*, 190–94; Ridder-Symoens, "Mobility," 280–304. The eagerness with which medieval students imitated their teachers, modeling themselves after not only their ideas, but also their gait and facial expressions, is discussed in Newman, "Teacher and Student: Shaping Boys," chap. 1 in *The Permeable Self*.

[98] Barrow, *Clergy in the Medieval World*, 200–201.

[99] Barrow, *Clergy in the Medieval World*, 47.

[100] See Berger, *Littérature et Société*, 110.

there were steady complaints that too few clerics became priests, leaving vacant the rural altars their teachers hoped they would staff.[101]

While they were a distinctive group, clerics were not a uniform social class. Divisions among the medieval clergy could be profound and even violent.[102] There was frequent discord between monastics and the secular (or "worldly") clergy who performed the public sacrament of the Mass.[103] In the twelfth century, bitter disputes arose between monastic theologians and clerics who taught in prominent schools.[104] Within the secular clergy, an important division existed between a higher grade of celibate clerics (subdeacons, deacons, and priests), who performed or assisted in the mass, and the minor clergy (including students and choirboys), who were not yet ordained and many of whom would not ultimately seek the priesthood.[105] The minor clergy often enjoyed privileges such as tax exemption and immunity from civil justice but were not celibate; some adopted worldly lifestyles.[106] Although their upbringing often differed from that of their siblings who underwent military training,[107] many clerics also came from aristocratic families to which they maintained strong ties throughout their lives and careers.[108] Bishops were regularly chosen from lordly families,[109] and they would frequently favor aristocratic brothers and nephews with ecclesiastical positions.[110] The lifestyles bishops led on episcopal estates were as luxurious as those of the wealthiest members of the aristocracy. Other clerics put their literacy and scribal skills to work in aristocratic and episcopal households, which employed significant numbers of clerical administrators (men like the composer Guillaume de Machaut) to serve them as notaries, lawyers, and in other roles that required

[101] Barrow, *Clergy in the Medieval World*, 43. See also Ferruolo, *Origins of the University*, 242–58; Schwinges, "Student Education, Student Life," 199–200.

[102] Ferruolo addresses the conflicts between the monasteries and the urban schools of the twelfth century. See Ferruolo, *Origins of the University*, 47–92. Tensions between Parisian university students and the monks of Saint-Germain-des-Prés escalated into a murderous brawl in 1278. See Skoda, *Medieval Violence*, 156–157.

[103] On monastic campaigns intended to discipline the secular clergy see Barrow, "Rules for Life," chap. 3 in *Clergy in the Medieval World*. On monastic disdain for married clergy see ibid., 93–94.

[104] See Wei, *Intellectual Culture*, 72–78.

[105] The seven grades of ordination are explained in Barrow, "Grades of Ordination," chap. 2 in *Clergy in the Medieval World*.

[106] See Verger, *Men of Learning*, 187n3.

[107] Aristocratic children on a clerical path would often be entrusted to cathedral canons for their education. See Barrow, *Clergy in the Medieval World*, 169.

[108] See Barrow, "Clergy as Family Men," chap. 4 in *Clergy in the Medieval World*; Evergates, *Aristocracy in the County of Champagne*, 161.

[109] Barrow, *Clergy in the Medieval World*, 228.

[110] See Barrow, *Clergy in the Medieval World*, 128–29.

scribal skills.[111] These court clerics emerged in force when Philip Augustus replaced his father's baronial counselors (who perished during the third crusade) with a new, younger, entourage of familiars, including a score of clerks upon whom he relied heavily.[112] As many of a third of those in regular attendance at the twelfth-century court of Marie de Champagne and Henry the Liberal were clerics.[113] By the fourteenth century, the trend had accelerated to the point that clerics outnumbered knights at some courts.[114] Such men would have thought of themselves as members of the court and would have occupied many of the same spaces as the courtiers they served.[115] It was also possible for clerics to move back and forth between ecclesiastical and aristocratic employment over the course of their careers, living and working in both environments. Although clerical lives were conducted in a variety of medieval social and geographical contexts, the clergy was nonetheless a distinct group, sharing attributes that were rare or nonexistent in the rest of the medieval population. This is evident whether we look to their knowledge of Latin and liturgical chant, their scribal skills, or their physical appearance. Like knights, clerics actively cultivated a group identity that marked their difference from other members of medieval society.

Representing Individual and Group Identities in Medieval Songbooks: Knights, Clerics, and Performers

How were the identities of the trouvères represented once their songs were preserved in writing? It was during the thirteenth century that the earliest troubadour and trouvère anthologies transformed a performative repertory into a written tradition.[116] As they worked to record trouvère song in writing from the second quarter of the thirteenth century through the first quarter of the fourteenth, medieval scribes and compilers were the first interpreters of

---

[111] See Baldwin, *Masters, Princes, and Merchants*, I, 179–85; Baldwin, *Government of Philip Augustus*, 119–22. Episcopal households increasingly hired university graduates (*magistri*) to serve in their courts. See Barrow, *Clergy in the Medieval World*, 258.

[112] See Baldwin, *Government of Philip Augustus*, 115–22.

[113] See Benton, "Court of Champagne," 590.

[114] See Vale, *Princely Court*, 103.

[115] On this point, see Vale, *Princely Court*, 31.

[116] The compilation of troubadour *chansonniers* is addressed in Burgwinkle, "*Chansonniers* as Books"; Aubrey, *The Troubadours*, 34–49; Galvez, *Songbook*, 1–16. Trouvère *chansonnier* compilation is addressed in Haines, *Eight Centuries*, 13–25; O'Neill, *Courtly Love Songs*, 13–52. On the ways in which the act of writing it down transformed medieval song, see especially Dillon, "Unwriting Medieval Song."

an already well-established tradition that had long been circulating orally and possibly also through more ephemeral written modes.[117] They transmitted then-current repertories of songs by living trouvères alongside a valued historical tradition of songs by deceased composers.[118] In many cases, scribes were notating melodies that were decades to a century old.[119] The design of some songbooks, some of which included tables of contents (a relatively new feature of thirteenth-century manuscripts that was more common in didactic and historical books)[120] or alphabetic organizational schemes[121] that helped readers access specific songs, were notably scholarly. The surviving songbooks are not monolithic; they represent individual exercises in vernacular song preservation carried out by diverse actors over a long temporal expanse.

In her influential monograph, *From Song to Book*, Huot notes the emphasis that some songbooks place on author identity, which distinguishes them from narrative anthologies of the same period. She attributes this difference to the self-reflexive quality of trouvère lyrics, which center on a poet-protagonist who sings about their own experiences, and to the fact that so many trouvères had aristocratic standing.[122] Huot shows that through organization, rubrication, and iconography, certain songbooks sort the trouvères into categories.[123] In particular, the miniature author portraits found in many songbooks tend to dress their subjects in clothing that reflects their rank. Some of the coats of arms attached to the knightly trouvères are historically verifiable and accurate, grounding the lyric "I" in an external reality.[124] Subsequent accounts have built on Huot's observations, noting that some trouvère *chansonniers* feature author corpora that tend to organize the trouvères in descending order of social rank.[125] Songbooks produced in the mid- to late thirteenth century often

[117] Although it was produced much later, the famous Lambeth Palace scroll (London, Lambeth Palace Library 1681) is suggestive of the kinds of written media of song transmission that may have circulated during the thirteenth century. See discussion in Haines, "Songbook for William," 61–62. The scroll is pictured on ibid., 62.

[118] See, for example, *U*, which includes both living and dead trouvères as well as a corpus of troubadour songs. Lug, "Politique et littérature."

[119] See Haines, "The First Readers," chap. 1 in *Eight Centuries*.

[120] See Hasenohr, "Systèmes de repérage," 277. Medieval tables of contents appear in *I, K, M, R, W, U, a*, and Paris, BNF fr. 22543. See Peraino, *Giving Voice to Love*, 136 and Haines, *Eight Centuries*, 14–15.

[121] See *Eight Centuries*, 14–15. Two songbooks, *C* and *O*, were ordered alphabetically by song title. See discussion in Parker, "Notes on the Chansonnier," 264.

[122] Huot, *Song to Book*, 48.

[123] Huot, *Song to Book*, 47–64.

[124] See *Song to Book*, 57. This is particularly evident in the songbook *M*. See Prinet, "L'illustration héraldique."

[125] Haines, *Eight Centuries*, 18; O'Neill, *Courtly Love Songs*, 18.

Figure 2.1 Author Portrait of Thibaut IV, *T* 1r. Courtesy of Bibliothèque nationale de France, fr.12615

open with the songs of Thibaut IV.[126] The songbooks *K*, *N*, and *V* depict a performer singing to a royal couple, showing Thibaut wearing his crown, seated with his queen.[127] In the songbook *V*, the seated royal figures wear capes displaying the carbuncle cross of the Navarrese flag, highlighting Thibaut's ascent to the throne.[128] In the songbooks *A*, *a*, *M*, and *T*, portraits depict elite trouvères as warriors in full armor, heraldic shields displayed, mounted on a war horse (perhaps the *sine qua non* of male chivalric identity).[129] In some, the horse is in motion, the trouvère warrior's weapon drawn over the head as though he is charging, as seen in Figure 2.1, which shows the author portrait of count Thibaut IV that opens the songbook *T*.

---

[126] Barbieri argues that it is the songbooks produced in the mid- to late thirteenth century that give Thibaut IV pride of place, elevating his status within the trouvère corpus. See Barbieri, "Thibaut le chansonner."

[127] A slightly different version of the scene appears in *P*, which features an aristocratic couple, a man holding a scroll pointing toward a lady whose hand is on her heart, representing the couple as the subject and audience of the songs. *X* presents a similar image, but the man is crowned and not holding a scroll. See the discussion in Huot, *From Song to Book*, 53–64.

[128] See *V* 1r.

[129] On the warhorse as an assemblage that combined into one form man, animal, and objects, see Cohen, *Medieval Identity Machines*, 45–54 and 76. Kaeuper notes that chivalric literature continued to portray knightly warfare as mounted even when knightly combat on foot was increasingly common, demonstrating enduring connections between the warhorse and knightly identity. See Kaeuper, *Chivalry and Violence*, 175.

Along with her discussion of knightly trouvères, Huot also draws attention to the way certain songbooks highlighted the participation of clerics, scribes, and performers such that they became poetic protagonists rather than merely cultural transmitters.[130] Subsequent studies have deepened our understanding of how individual songbooks construct identities for their authors. John Haines' extensive analysis of *M* shows that the manuscript's first half focuses on the knightly traditions of courtly song, featuring crusaders, while the second half highlights urban songwriters from Arras,[131] opening with the songs of Guillaume le Vinier, followed by Moniot d'Arras and Gilles le Vinier (all three were clerics). Although Haines argues that the first half of *M* celebrates the courtly world of the manuscript's likely patron (Charles II d'Anjou) and its probable recipient (the prince of Morea, Guillaume II de Villehardouin), the shift to modern songwriters from Arras in the book's second half reflects the prestige of the new urban song culture where the manuscript was likely produced.[132] Similarly, Peraino has shown that the songbook *T* was organized and illustrated in a way that encoded both geographical and social meanings, representing the trouvère song corpus as moving from an aristocratic tradition to an urban, clerkly one. Bookended by discrete collections (*libelli*) of the songs of Thibaut IV of Navarre and Adam de la Halle, she argues that *T* charts the move away from love songs produced by noble trouvères and "advertises the new voice of the professional cleric" as well as the cultural rise of Arras, displacing Champagne's erstwhile dominance as a literary center.[133]

Two less-examined songbooks (*A* and *a*) similarly project status and identity, in both cases, delineating different social types among their authors. These two songbooks are closely related, and both highlight the group identities of knight and cleric. In their organizational schemes, *A* and *a* also suggest a cultural dynamic similar to that described by Haines and Peraino in the context of *M* and *T*, which bear witness to the rising importance of the figure of the urban and/or clerical trouvère. The love song section of the songbook *A* presents exclusively knightly and clerkly trouvères, as Table 2.1 shows.[134]

---

[130] Huot, *Song to Book*, 59 and 64.

[131] See especially Haines, "Songbook for William," 73.

[132] Haines, "Songbook for William," 91 and 96.

[133] See Peraino, *Giving Voice to Love*, 135–44, quotation at 144. On the cultural importance of the twelfth-century court of Champagne, see Benton, "Court of Champagne."

[134] Table 2.1 is based on my examination of the high-resolution digital facsimile of *A* https://bvmm. irht.cnrs.fr/mirador/index.php?manifest=https://bvmm.irht.cnrs.fr/iiif/24762/manifest. Based on the strong similarity between *A* and *a*, Ferrari and Tyssens have convincingly calculated the number of missing pages in the first and second quaternions of *A*. See Ferrari and Tyssens, *Chansonniers Français 1*, 118–19. Brackets indicate missing folios; a question mark appears when the first page of an author corpus has been removed, indicating the possible presence of an author portrait.

Table 2.1 Trouvère Author Corpora in *A*

Folio #	Opening Rubric	Portrait	# of Songs	Notes
	[Le Roi de Navarre?]	[?]	3 extant [1 partial]	3 pages are missing. Folio 129r starts with the end of "Ausi com l'unicorne sui" by Thibaut de Champagne
130r	None	Equestrian warrior	8	Rubrics "Li Kastelains" or "Li Kastelains de Couci" start on song 5.
133r	"Ce sont les kançons monseigneur Gautier de Dargies"	Equestrian warrior	5	Rubric placed below portrait on 133r. All subsequent songs have rubric "Monsiegneur/Mesires Gautiers de Dargies."
135r	"Ce sont les kançons mon seigneur Ugon de Bregi"	Equestrian warrior	3	All subsequent songs have rubric "Mesire Ugon/Uges de Bregi."
	[Le Vidame de Chartres?]	[?]	2 extant [1 partial]	2 pages missing. Folio 136r starts with the end of "Combien que j'aie demouré" by the Vidame de Chartres. The second and third songs each have the rubric "Li Vidame."
136v	"Mesires Pieres de Molaines"		2	Both songs have rubrics. No space provided for a portrait.
137v	"Le Duc de Brebant"		1	No space provided for a portrait.
	[Guillaume le Vinier?]	[?]	5 [1 partial]	Page missing. Folio 138r starts with the end of "En tous tans." Rubrics "Maistre Wuillaumes li Viniers" start on song two.
140r	"Maistres Richars de Fournival fist ches kanchons a se vie"	Clerk wearing a pileus and long robes seated at a lectern with open book, speaking or singing (lecturing?)	6	Rubric "Maistres Richars" or "Maistres Richars de Founival" precedes all subsequent songs except "Ains ne vi" (RS 685), which is unrubricated.

(*continued*)

Table 2.1 Continued

Folio #	Opening Rubric	Portrait	# of Songs	Notes
142v	"Adans li bocus fist ces kancons"	Tonsured clerk seated at a lectern using a pen and knife on a piece of parchment	5 [1 partial]	Rubric "Adan/s" or "Adans li bochus (d'Arras)" precedes all subsequent songs. The copy of "De cuer pensieu" (song 6) is partial, ending on st.5, l.1.
				Page missing.
145r	None	Two tonsured clerics facing each other both with fingers raised	32 *jeux-partis*	Opening song is "Maistre Symon" by clerics Simon d'Authie and Gilles le Vinier

In *A*, Thibaut de Champagne heads a corpus of knightly trouvère songs. The songbook may have included as many as five equestrian author portraits (attached to knightly trouvères), three of which remain. The knightly songs are followed by a song corpus devoted to the most prolific cleric-trouvères: "master" Guillaume le Viniers, "master" Richard de Fournival, and Adam de la Halle (called "li boçus"). The surviving author portraits for Richard and Adam (which represent Richard as a clerk dressed in a long robe and pileus lecturing from a book and Adam as a tonsured, robed cleric copying text onto parchment) situate the two trouvères as clerics. Huot views these portraits of Adam and Richard as evidence of a new clerkly, "bookish" authorial persona, arguing that the portraits stress the role of the two trouvères in "making" their songs.[135] Following Adam's song corpus, *A* presents a collection of *jeux-partis* headed by the song "Maistre Symon," a debate between Simon d'Authie and Gilles le Vinier, two trouvères active in the second quarter of the thirteenth century who were both high-ranking secular clerics. The portrait that accompanies their *jeu-parti* represents the two trouvères as tonsured clerics performing their debate, their posture bearing a strong resemblance to the academic tradition

---

[135] Huot argues that *A* contrasts the aristocratic articulation of sentiment with its novel appropriation by the two clerical trouvères. See *Song to Book*, 59.

of the disputation.[136] This image thus presents two early cleric-trouvères engaged in a learned, clerical performance tradition. Moreover, the order of the *jeux-partis* in this section also focuses on clerical songwriters. Of the first seven *jeux-partis* included in *A*, five are examples in which two clerics debate each other.[137] The songbook *A* focuses almost entirely on knightly and clerkly trouvères.[138] For our purposes here, it is particularly valuable for its varied representation of the identities of the latter, showcasing generations of clerical trouvères active from the second and third quarters of the century, and depicting them engaged in clerkly activities ranging from notating, to teaching, to disputing.[139]

The songbook *a* (which is extremely close in its contents and order to *A*)[140] also carefully separates the figures of knightly and clerkly trouvères, and these songwriters are also joined by a significant corpus of songs mainly by professionals. Together, these three identities (knight, clerk, and professional songwriter) form the primary organizational scheme for the opening of the manuscript, after which, genre becomes the organizational principle.[141] Further, *a* seems to elevate the figures of the clerical and professional trouvère over the figure of the knightly trouvère. This songbook has

---

[136] See the comments in Saltzstein, "Cleric-trouvères." On the scholastic disputation and its ties to musical traditions, see Novikoff, *Medieval Culture of Disputation*, 147–55.

[137] After no.1, "Maistre Simon" (RS 572, 145r) follows: no.2, "Sires frere" (RS 691, 145v) by Gilles and Guillaume le Vinier, brother clerics from Arras; no.5, "Sire ki fait mieus" (RS 1293, 146v), also by Gilles and Guillaume le Vinier; no.6, "Amis Guillaume" (RS 1085, 147r) by the jurist Adam de Givenchi and Guillaume le Vinier; and "Moines ne vous anuit" (RS 378, 147v) by Guillaume le Vinier and Moniot d'Arras. The same emphasis on clerical participants holds for the closely related songbook *a*, the *jeu-parti* section of which shares the first twenty-five *jeux-partis* found in *a*, both included in the same sequence. On the concordances between these two manuscripts see Ferrari and Tyssens, *Chansonniers Français 1*, 118.

[138] Noted in Huot, *Song to Book*, 59.

[139] Huot influentially argued that the "clerkly trouvère" figure represented by Adam de la Halle and Richard de Fournival (particularly as found in *A*) was a new type of author figure that combined the roles of romance narrator, scribe/compiler, and amorous protagonist. These trouvères, she argued, prefigured the clerkly authorial representation of fourteenth-century figures such as Machaut and Jean Froissart and were evidence of the beginning of a movement "from song to book" referenced in her title. See Huot, *From Song to Book*, 61–64. Huot did not address the portrait of Gilles le Vinier and Simon d'Authie in *A* (which foregrounds an oral, performative mode of clerkliness), nor did she discuss the dominance of cleric-trouvères in the *jeu-parti* section, which foregrounds prominent, productive cleric-trouvères who were active in the first half of the thirteenth century, decades before the careers of both Adam de la Halle and Richard de Fournival. The material presented in this chapter resituates Adam and Richard as the most visible of a much larger group of clerics composing vernacular song in both bookish and performative modes. Cf. Huot, *From Song to Book*, 59 and 64.

[140] There are no songs in *A* that are not also found in *a*. See the careful account of the shared material in Ferrari and Tyssens, *Chansonniers Français 1*, 117–21.

[141] The remainder of the songbook (starting on fol.109r) is organized by genre and includes *pastourelles*, polyphonic motets, *rondeaux*, *jeux-partis*, *vers d'amours* by both Adam de la Halle and Nevelot d'Aimon, and a version of the opening scene of Adam de la Halle's *Jeu de la feuillée*. See O'Sullivan, "The Northern Jeu-Parti," 164–66, for an overview.

a medieval table of contents copied in the same hand as the majority of the songbook.[142] The table of contents makes no omissions; however, twenty-three folios were removed at some point in the manuscript's history; they probably contained attractive illuminations.[143] The songbook begins with a selection of songs by Thibaut IV followed by author sections for each of ten additional knightly trouvères, as shown in Table 2.2a.[144]

Following Thibaut IV, some knightly trouvères are listed by their title (Le Castelains de Couci, Le Vidame de Chartres, Le Duc de Brabant). Those trouvères who are identified by their proper name are also listed as "mon seigneur" or "mes sires" so that there can be no mistaking their status as lords. As Table 2.2b shows, the next section of the songbook is devoted almost exclusively to cleric-trouvères, the majority of whom are referred to as either master (*maistre*) or cleric (*clers*) in the table of contents and the author rubrics in the songbook itself.[145]

The final section of the songbook to preserve author corpora mainly highlights professional performers and tradesmen from Flanders and Artois.[146]

The compilers of the songbook *a* thus present cleric-trouvères and professional trouvères as distinct author groups, carefully separating them into two sections. The surviving portraits of the knights and professionals

---

[142] For a detailed paleographical study of this manuscript, see Ferrari and Tyssens, *Chansonniers Français 1*, 17–31.

[143] See ibid., 18. The stubs of these folios are still visible in most cases. My analysis in this section (and the material in Tables 2.1a–2.1c) is based on my examination of the high-resolution digitized copy of the original manuscript: https://digi.vatlib.it/view/MSS_Reg.lat.1490.

[144] Folio numbers follow the medieval red foliation (the black modern foliation used by many scholars ignores the missing pages). The brackets in Tables 2.1a–2.1c indicate missing folios. In column 4, a question mark appears when the first page of an author corpus has been removed, indicating the likely presence of an author portrait. Column 5 lists the total number of songs indicated in the table of contents, followed by the number of songs present in the manuscript in its current state. I have not included the songs and motets not listed in the table of contents that were added to the ends of many gatherings; for a detailed description of these, see Ferrari and Tyssens, *Chansonniers Français 1*, 15–22.

[145] The two exceptions are Adam de la Halle (listed as "Adan li Bocu") and Moniot d'Arras (listed as "Monios"). It is possible that Adam was not identified as *maistre* or *clerc* because he was so widely known as a cleric. Moniot's status as a monk was evident in his name ("little monk"), perhaps rendering further identification redundant. The only song in this section that does not seem to be by a cleric is "Con plus ain et mains ai joie" (66r), a song unique to *a* attributed to the Flemish trouvère Maihieu de Gant.

[146] Most of the trouvères in this section hailed from the north (various locations in Artois, Picardy, and Flanders). The section opens with an author portrait Colart le Boutellier of Arras holding a bird of prey, a stance Huot argued was a bourgeois pretention to nobility. Huot, *Song to Book*, 61. There are two clerics represented: Jehan de Grievilers and Richard de Fournival. Although his clerical status is not indicated in the table of contents, Jehan (whose songs start on 93r) was a married cleric from Arras. A song by Richard de Fournival was added to 113v with the rubric "Maistre Richars."

Table 2.2a Knightly Trouvères in MS *a*, Gatherings 2–5, fols. [1]–32v

Starting Folio	Rubric in ToC	Rubrics in MS not included in ToC	Portrait	Songs in ToC	Songs in MS
[1r]	Ce sont les chancons le Roi de Navarre		[?]	15	13 [2 missing]
[9r]	Ce sont les chancons le Castelain de Couci		[?]	9	7 [2 missing]
[14r]	Ce sont les chancons mon seigneur Gautier de Dargies		[?]	6	4 [2 missing]
17r	Ce sont les chancons mon seigneur Gasson brule		Equestrian warrior	6	6
20r	Ce sont les chancons le Vidame de Chartres		Equestrian warrior	4	4
21v	Ce sont les chancons mesires Pierres de Molaines	No space provided for a portrait		2	2
22v	mesires quenes de bietune	No space provided for a portrait		2	2
23v	Ce sont les chancons le Duc de Braibant			2	2
[25r]	Ce sont les chancons mon seigneur Ugon de Bregi		[?]	5	2 [2 missing]
27r		Mesires Meurisses de Craon		0	1
[28r]	Ce sont les chancons mon seigneur Jakemon de Cison		[?]	4	2 [2 missing]
30r	Messires Raous de Soisons fist cestes chancons	No space provided for a portrait		5	5
TOTALS	11	1	2 [5 missing]	60	50 [10 missing]

Table 2.2b Cleric-Trouvères in MS *a*, Gatherings 6–11, fols. [33r]–76v

Starting Folio	Rubric in ToC	Medieval Rubrics in MS not included in ToC	Portrait	Songs in ToC	Extant Songs in MS
[33r]	Ce sont les chancons maistre Willaume le Vinier		[?]	16	14 [2 missing]
[41r]	Ce sont les chancons maistre Richart de Fournival		[?]	14	12 [2 missing]
[47r]	Ce sont les chancons Monniot		[?]	9	7 [2 missing]
[51r]	Ce sont les chancons Adan le bocu		[?]	21	19 [2 missing]
[61r]	Ce sont les chancons Gaidifer clerc		[?]	7	5 [2 missing]
[65r]	Cest les chancons maistre Jakemon le Vinier		[?]	6	3 [3 missing]
[68r]	Ce sont les chancons Robert de Castel, clerc		[?]	5	3 [2 missing]
70v	Cest le chancon Jehan le petit clerc			1	1
71r	none	Maistre Will' Veaus		3	3
72v	none	Maistres Baudes au Grenon		1	1
73r	none	Henris Aimons li clers		1	1
74r	none	Maihieu de Gant		1	1
74v	none	Maistre Adan de Givenci		1	1
75r	none	Maistres Simons d'Autie		3	3
TOTALS	8	6	[7?]	90	74

differentiate the status of these groups through their iconography; although the portraits of the clerics do not survive, they may well have mirrored those in the very closely related songbook *A*, which depicted cleric-trouvères engaged in clerkly activities such as lecturing, notating, and debating.[147]

---

[147] On the close ties between these manuscripts, see n140.

Table 2.2c Professional Trouvères in MS *a*, Gatherings 12–18, fols. 77r–123r

Starting Folio	Rubric in ToC	Medieval Rubrics in MS ToC	Portrait	Songs in ToC	Extant Songs in MS
77r	Ce sont les chançons Colart le Boutellier		Standing man with hawk perched on his hand	14	14
[83r]	Ce sont les chançons Jehan Bretel d'Arras		[?]	8	6 [2 missing]
[87r]	Robert de le Piere fist ces chancons		[?]	8	6 [2 missing]
[91r]	Ce sont les chancons Jehan Fremaut de Lisle		[?]	3	1 [2 missing]
93r	Ce sont les chançons Jehan de Grieviler d'Arras		Standing man singing	8	7 [song 8 attributed to Jehan de le Fontaine in MS rubric]
97r	Ce sont les canchons Willamme d'Amiens le paigneur		Illuminator, standing and painting a shield	3	3
[99r]	Ce sont les chançons Blondel de Niele		[?]	7	5 [2 missing]
[103r]	Ce sont les cançons Gilebert de Bernevile		[?]	9	7 [2 missing]
107r	Ce sont les cançons Perrin d'Aucicourt		Man standing holding portative organ	7	7
111r	Ce sont les cançons Cuvelier d'Arras		[?]	6	4 [2 missing]
114r	Ce sont les cançons Martin le begin de Cambrai		Man standing playing bagpipes	4	4
[117r]	Ce sont les cançons Jehan Erart d'Arras		[?]	5	3 [2 missing]
119v	Ce sont les cançons Carasaus			2	2

(continued)

Table 2.2c Continued

Starting Folio	Rubric in ToC	Medieval Rubrics in MS ToC	Portrait	Songs in ToC	Extant Songs in MS
120v		Thumas Heriers		0	2
121r		Wastable		0	3
123r		Crestiens de Troies			1
TOTALS	13	4	12	84	74

Comparing Tables 2.2a, 2.2b, and 2.2c shows that the design of *a* works to elevate clerical and professional songwriters. This book includes larger numbers of individual songs for these groups than it does for the knightly trouvères. The cleric-trouvères' section originally included ninety songs and the section devoted to northern professionals included eighty-four songs. Each of these sections thus transmits significantly more songs than that of the opening section devoted to the knightly trouvères, where sixty songs were originally found.[148] These figures misleadingly suggest that clerical trouvères and professional songwriters were as prolific as their knightly forerunners. For example, the author section devoted to Guillaume le Vinier, which opens the cleric-trouvères section, transmits sixteen songs, one song more than the author section devoted to Thibaut IV. The roughly equivalent poetic stature that these similarly sized author corpora suggest to the reader is striking since Thibaut's total surviving song corpus is, at over sixty songs, nearly double that of Guillaume's, to whom around thirty-five songs are attributed. Adam de la Halle's author section, which includes twenty-one of his monophonic love songs, is the largest in the entire manuscript. Recall that songbook *a* is missing twenty-three folios, many of which occur at the start of author corpora. These may have contained author portraits that collectors removed. It is possible that as many as seven such portraits originally accompanied the author corpora of cleric-trouvères and as many as twelve may have accompanied the professional trouvères, whereas no more than seven were originally included for the knightly trouvères. Although

---

[148] These figures include songs on missing pages that are listed in the table of contents. In some cases, it is possible to see the final verses of these songs at the beginning of the surviving folios, confirming the existence of the missing items.

the songbook begins with the songs of knightly trouvères, the compilers of *a* included many more songs and more author portraits for cleric-trouvères and professionals than for the knightly songwriters. The compilers of *a* thus recognized the importance of the knightly song culture while also conveying the emergence of a new class of urban and clerical songwriters from the north. My analysis of the compilation of *A* and *a* resonates with the observations of Haines and Peraino regarding the songbooks *M* and *T* and underscores the importance of knightly and clerical identity in the compilation and illustration of this group of songbooks.

These books highlight the long participation of clerics in the trouvère song tradition and place the status and importance of the cleric-trouvères on par with or even eclipsing that of the knightly trouvères. The degree to which songbooks and their contents could bear witness to rising urban song traditions, as well as to changes in the knightly culture within which trouvère song had emerged in the late twelfth century, is a theme to which I return in later chapters.

Songbooks and Songbook Patronage as Projections of Noble Identity

Songbooks could express the identities not only of the trouvères whose songs they preserved but also of the patrons who sponsored their compilation.[149] Although it is rarely known for certain which individuals commissioned individual songbooks, nobles were clearly responsible for them. The requisite materials were sourced globally at staggering expense.[150] That the nobility had the funds to acquire the parchment, inks, and skilled labor required is reason enough to assume their involvement. Scholars have suggested probable patrons for some of the surviving songbooks. For example, Symes argues that the songbook *W*, which includes a section devoted to the nearly complete works of Adam de la Halle, may have been commissioned by a grieving

---

[149] Not all surviving sources of medieval vernacular song are presentation manuscripts. The earliest known trouvère songbook, *U*, for example, differs from luxury songbooks in its frequent erasures and crossed-out passages. See Parker, "Notes on the Chansonnier," 274. Songs are also transmitted in miscellanies and scrolls, among other sources. See n117. The range of sources in which medieval song survives is best captured in the essays in Deeming and Leach, *Manuscripts and Medieval Song*. The oldest surviving written sources of trouvère lyric and the evidence for early, informal transmission of trouvère song are discussed most recently in Jacob, "Chevalier mult estes."

[150] Haines, "Songbook for William," 62–63.

Robert II d'Artois after Adam died in the count's service in the Kingdom of Naples. The volume could thus have served as a lavish parchment memorial to honor Adam's death, an event for which Robert may have felt personally responsible.[151] The songbook *P* contains, within its large corpus of over three hundred songs, a small author collection (a "little book" or *libellus*) devoted to the Duke of Brittany. Joseph W. Mason convincingly argues that this *libellus* within *P* and the *jeu-parti* with which it opens (in which the Duke and Bernart de la Ferté debate the merits of the central chivalric virtues of prowess and largesse), position the Duke of Brittany (probably John I) as an ideal chivalric author figure at a time when his family's reputation had been tarnished.[152] Two other songbooks seem to have been commissioned specifically as reminders of francophone identity for audiences in regions at significant geopolitical remove. The songbook *I* was produced in Metz and added, during the fourteenth century, to a larger *messine* literary manuscript featuring the *Tournoi de Chauvency*, a versified account of a tournament held there in 1285. This book reflected aristocratic tastes for both song and combat, and represented an attempt by a wealthy urban family in Metz, which had by then become a francophone city of thirty thousand inhabitants within the German empire, to appropriate an ancient aristocratic culture.[153] The songbook *M*, which, as I mentioned in the previous section, Haines convincingly argues was commissioned by Charles II for Guillaume II de Villehardouin, was produced for the diasporic court of a *champenoise* family ruling the Latin Greek province of Morea.[154] Songbooks could thus function as memorials of valued friends, assertions of chivalric status, or precious reminders of one's membership in communities that were distant geographically.

The knightly elite would have viewed sponsoring a beautifully illustrated repository of songs as an act that increased chivalric honor. For the knightly classes, honor was not understood as an ethical value, but rather, as an expression of status and confirmation of one's place within the social hierarchy.[155] Women were a particularly important audience for performances of chivalric honor. In chivalric romance, women inspire prowess and romantic love is often a catalyst for further acts of prowess. Female characters often

---

[151] Symes, "School of Arras," 31.
[152] Mason, "Debatable Chivalry."
[153] Baldwin, "*Le Tournoi*," 7–24, at 21.
[154] Haines, "Songbook for William."
[155] Kaeuper, *Medieval Chivalry*, 39–43.

witness acts of prowess within the narratives, underscoring their role as a key audience for displays of prowess.[156] It is thus notable that scholars suggest the songbooks *I, M, O,* and *U* may each have been commissioned as aristocratic wedding gifts.[157] Among the aristocracy, largesse (gift giving) was connected with honor: between men of equal status, gifts were a mark of friendship and love that fostered trust, and between men of unequal status, gift-giving marked the recipient as worthy of friendship with a social superior.[158]

Chivalric honor was performative, as Taylor underscores. Since some of the most valued prizes that could be won through prowess were honor, fame, and glory, "Chivalric culture constantly emphasized the importance of impressing other people, from their peers to future generations who would read about them in chronicles and other records."[159] Chivalric texts were meant to confer honor, helping to ensure that a knight's fame and glory would outlive him. Children and tombs could also further this aim; writing however, was viewed as the very best method.[160] Commissioning songs that celebrated chivalric values and recording them in lavish manuscripts for consumption by future generations would surely have been viewed as an act that extended chivalric honor beyond death.

Songbook Portraits and Authorial Persons: Author Portraits as Seals

I have now provided an overview of individual trouvère biographies as well as the identities with which many trouvères affiliated themselves and through

---

[156] Taylor, *Chivalry and the Ideals of Knighthood,* 100–102. See Kaeuper, *Chivalry and Violence,* 220–21.

[157] Leach argues that *I* may have been commissioned for a Chiny/Lorraine wedding in 1313. See Leach, "Provenance, Date, and Patron." For an argument that *U* was a gift from Perrin Noise to his bride Héloise in Metz in 1231 see Lug, "Katharer und Waldenser," 249–74; "Politique et littérature à Metz," 475–76. On the likely status of *M* as a wedding gift for William of Villehardouin and his bride Anna Doukaina of Epiros from Charles d'Anjou, see Haines, "Songbook for William," 57–60. Stones argued in "Aristocratic Context," that *O* may have been created as a wedding gift for Blanche of Burgundy's wedding to Edouard de Savoie in 1307 (256–57). It should be noted, however, that she has since sided instead with Ruffo's argument that *O* was commissioned by Aymon of Savoie in 1297. See Stones, *Gothic Manuscripts,* I, 114.

[158] Taylor, *Ideals of Knighthood,* 75. This aspect of chivalric culture resonates with Symes' argument that the songbook *W* may have been commissioned by a bereft Count Robert II d'Artois upon the death of Adam de la Halle in the Angevin Kingdom of Sicily as a kind of monument. See Symes, *A Common Stage,* 249.

[159] Taylor, *Ideals of Knighthood,* 54.

[160] This, according to Eustache Deschamps. See Taylor, *Ideals of Knighthood,* 61–62.

which they were understood by subsequent generations of manuscript pa-trons, compilers, and readers. I have shown that songbooks reinforced identities not only for the songwriters whose works they preserved but also for their patrons. I close by considering how biography and identity could be intermingled through a specific type of iconographical representation at work in the equestrian author portraits found in the songbooks *A*, *a*, *M*, and *T*. Although many scholars have discussed the representation of certain aristo-cratic trouvères as mounted, armored knights in these books, only the most sporadic mention has been made of the striking resemblance between these author portraits and medieval seals.[161] From the late twelfth century onward, the knightly classes began using wax seals rather than witnesses to authenti-cate documents. Seals became ubiquitous during the twelfth and thirteenth centuries, when, for the first time, lay elites allowed other persons to rep-resent them in important transactions.[162] Seals were an important mode of aristocratic self-representation; their images form a barely differentiated rep-ertoire, depicting kings as seated rulers and magnates as armored equestrian warriors, expressing group identity and conformity to a social type.[163] The seals were particularized and connected to an individual owner by the Latin legend around the seal's perimeter, which almost always specified the place name of the sealer, connecting identity, social type, and geography.[164]

The strong resemblance between the knightly author portraits and seals has interesting implications. For readers of songbooks who were familiar with elite sealing practices (a group that included both knights and clerics), this iconography would have had rather specific associations. Figure 2.2 provides the third grand seal of Thibaut IV.[165]

---

[161] Paulin Paris occasionally noted this resemblance. See Paris, *Histoire littéraire*, 569, 763, and 827. Prinet noted occasional errors in Paris' remarks on the heraldry of the portraits but said little about their relationship to seals. See "L'illustration héraldique," 522 and passim. Page states, without elaborating, that the author portraits resemble seals. See Page, "Listening to the Trouvères," 655n5. Ruffo mentions the resemblance between trouvère author portraits and seals in the context of *M*, arguing that compilers used the imagery to guarantee the noble trouvère's monopoly on courtly lyric at a time of clerkly ascendence in vernacular song. See Ruffo, "Courting Convention," 166–67. Ruffo also explores connections between author portraits and seals in her unpublished dissertation, "Illustration of Notated Compendia," at 95–97 and 103. The only musicological account I am aware of that explores a possible connection between music (in this case, *conductus*) and seals is Maschke, "Porta salutis ave," 170–77.

[162] Bedos-Rezak, *When Ego was Imago*, 110–11.

[163] See Bedos-Rezak, *When Ego Was Imago*, 155.

[164] See Baldwin, *Knights, Lords, and Ladies*, 60.

[165] Archives départementales de l'Aube, © Département de l'Aube, Noël Mazières. I am grateful to Aubin Baudin for his kindness in sharing ultra-high resolution digital images of this and many other seals with me. The seals used by Thibaut IV as count of Champagne and Blois and later as King of Navarre receive extensive treatment in Baudin, *Emblématique et pouvoir*, esp. 70–88; Baudin, "Enquête sur le premier sceau."

Figure 2.2 Third Grand Seal of Thibaut IV, no.155 15089. Archives départementales de l'Aube, © Département de l'Aube, Noël Mazières. Photo courtesy of Aubin Baudin reproduced here with kind permission.

Comparing the author portrait of Thibaut IV from *T* in Figure 2.1 with his seal in Figure 2.2 reveals that the posture of the equestrian, armored knightly figure used in the two images is nearly identical.

Because medieval seals were originally created to extend royal authority beyond the person of the ruler, Bedos-Rezak describes them as "quasi personal beings."[166] Seals were a medieval mechanism for materializing presence.[167] When affixed to a charter gifting land to an ecclesiastical institution, the seal of a medieval aristocrat substituted for their person when they were not present, certifying that a particular action would continue in the sealer's absence and even after their death. The scriptoria that initiated the production of sealed charters were located in abbeys or cathedrals in which debates about eucharistic theology were taking place.[168] The chancery-scholars involved were pre-scholastic theologians, men who would likely have understood the images on seals as a kind of incarnation.[169] Aristocrats themselves demonstrated their understanding of the status of their seal as an embodiment of their person when they embedded what we would today call

---

[166] See Bedos-Rezak, *When Ego was Imago*, 79.
[167] Bedos-Rezak, *When Ego Was Imago*, 151.
[168] Bedos-Rezak, *When Ego Was Imago*, 140–41.
[169] Bedos-Rezak, *When Ego Was Imago*, 127.

biometrics (fingerprints, bite marks, or hair) in the wax before imprinting their seal upon it.[170]

The equestrian author portraits in songbooks are not merely representations of trouvères as knights. I maintain that the strong resemblance between the portraits and seals suggests that some songbook compilers intended to forge for their viewers a much more direct relationship between the person of the knightly trouvère, his social group, his geography, and his song corpus than previous accounts have recognized. The imagery of the seal would likely have meant that for medieval readers of these books, the songs would not only be tied to the group identity of the knightly classes but would also have conjured up a specific person in a quasi-corporeal way. The seal-like portrait would already have had the effect of bringing forth an absent person. The manuscript rubrics that attribute song corpora to individual trouvères function much like seal legends, connecting the generic image of the knight with a specific person. That person was often associated with a regional geography through his toponym. In addition to loudly proclaiming the status, lineage, and geography with which a knightly trouvère was associated, by visually aligning knightly author portraits with the iconography of charter seals, the compilers of *A, M, T,* and *a* (which use these seal-like author portraits) also authenticate the songs that follow as emanating from the body and voice of a specific person, creating further impetus for autobiographical readings of their songs.

In such circumstances, did the songbook conjure up the trouvère's absent voice after death? Let us consider the portrait of Thibaut IV in the songbook *T* (Figure 2.1). Bedos-Rezak argues that seals were adopted in part to rectify the mixed authorial voice of the Latin charters to which they were attached, documents that were composed in the first-person voice of the person responsible for their creation but which written down by someone else (a literate cleric).[171] Just as a seal would, the equestrian portrait in this songbook connects Thibaut IV to a particular social group (the knightly classes). Like a seal legend, the manuscript rubric "Li Roi de Navarre fist ces chancons" particularizes the generic image of the knightly warrior through his title (the King) and associates him with a specific geography (Navarre). It certifies for the reader that the songs to follow were made (*fist*) by him. These gestures of textual authentication precede a song written in the first person that describes

---

personal, emotional experiences. The song would not have been notated by Thibaut himself. Yet the seal-like author portrait identifies the songs following the portrait as emanating from Thibaut's person, materializing his absent body and voice long after his death, and helping readers and listeners connect the emotions that the song's poetic subject describes to the author to whom they are assigned, thereby authenticating the first-person voice of the song's lyrics as the trouvére-king's own voice, the emotions it describes as his own feelings.[172] I imagine that Thibaut IV and other knightly songwriters would have been delighted by the prospect of a posthumous echo of their performing body and voice being conjured up for audiences to behold long after their deaths, thereby increasing their chivalric honor.

Other examples of seal-like knightly author portraits are less faithful to the seal iconography of the associated trouvère and, accordingly, communicate a more generalized focus on identity. The representation of the Vidame de Chartres, for example, presents a more muddled expression of personhood, emphasizing knightly identity instead. Dyggve convincingly identified the "Vidame of Chartres" (a title held by many individuals during the thirteenth century)[173] as Guillaume de Ferrières, a strenuous knight who took the cross in 1202 and probably died en route to Constantinople in 1204 or 1205, making him a member of the earliest generation of trouvères.[174] The two surviving portraits of the Vidame in *M* and *a* have significant discrepancies. The portrait in *a* inappropriately dresses the Vidame's horse in the carbuncle cross of the Navarrese flag (imagery the artist may have copied from an author portrait of Thibaut IV, the King of Navarre),[175] and the heraldry used in the two songbook portraits differs, a factor that led, in the early twentieth century, to conflicting opinions about the Vidame's historical self.[176] The

---

[172] Zink's argument that trouvère song lacked personal identifiers relied in part on the absence of biographical information in the songbooks (specifically, the lack of the *vidas* and *razos* found in some troubadour songbooks). He did not consider the role of portraits, author rubrics, and the other identifiers I have discussed here that have a similar function. See Zink, *Invention of Literary Subjectivity*, 39. On the elevation of the identity of Thibaut IV as a songwriter after his death, see especially Barbieri, "Thibaut le chansonnier."

[173] See Livingstone, *Love of My Kin*, 24–26; Livingstone, "Nobility of Blois-Chartres," 381–94.

[174] Dyggve, "Personnages historiques," 161–85.

[175] The portrait of the Vidame is found on *a* 21r. The compilers of *a* seem to have included a portrait of king Thibaut IV of Navarre, but the first folio has since been removed. The stub preceding *a* 2r is still visible. See https://digi.vatlib.it/view/MSS_Reg.lat.1490.

[176] Based on the heraldry depicted on the warrior's shield in *M* (which features ten blackbirds arranged between two horizontal bars, three on top, four in the middle, and three below), Max Prinet argued that the identity of the Vidame de Chartres was Geoffroy de Meslay, a member of the family who occupied the position of Vidame of Chartres in the second half of the thirteenth century. See Prinet, "L'illustration héraldique," 521–37. Countering Prinet's identification, Dyggve convincingly

portraits of the Vidame in the songbooks *a* and *M* invoke the mounted warrior posture of aristocratic seals and its associations with personhood. Yet, through their inconsistencies, the two songbooks also convert the seal iconography into a representation of status alone, where what is conjured up is not (for those who knew him or were familiar with his heraldry), the historical person, body, or voice of Guillaume de Ferrières. Rather, readers encounter the title of vidame of Chartres, which Guillaume possessed as part of a lineage within his own family and those who followed in that office. In the case of the Vidame, the suggestion of a person recedes in favor of a social type and a lineage tied to a specific geography—status and group identity take center stage.

Group identities (especially the knight and the cleric) were at the forefront of the way several important songbooks represented the trouvère corpus and its most prominent author figures. Whether through schemes of organization or illustration, the songbooks *A*, *a*, *M*, and *T* aligned many individual trouvères with the social rank to which they belonged. Through the striking iconographic similarity between knightly author portraits and seals, songbook compilers drew together the person of the knightly trouvère and the representation of his group identity, comingling biography with social type and aligning the knightly trouvère's body with the first-person poetic voice of his songs. These songbooks projected the elite status of their patrons while also demarcating individual trouvères as members of groups and types. In so doing, they presented images of identity after which later generations could model themselves.

Subsequent chapters will explore specific trouvère songs as expressions of individual and group identities. Particularly in Chapters 3 and 4, I will focus on authorial identity, revealing how a song connects an author figure to particular social and environmental context, projecting a sense of personal identity that is tied importantly to place. I will not, however, assume that authorial identity determined the point of view of every song a given trouvère wrote. The trouvère corpus includes songs by male authors written from the perspective of women, amorous songs written by celibate ecclesiastics, hired performers writing from the perspective of knights in *pastourelle* songs, and many other layered articulations of authorial identity and poetic voice. It

argued, based on the poetic circle suggested by song dedications to and from the Vidame, that the trouvère was Guillaume de Ferrières. Dyggve claimed the painter of the songbook *M*, who was working decades after Guillaume's death, simply painted the wrong arms. Dyggve, "Personnages historiques," 161–85.

will also be evident that medieval songwriters delighted in imagining, and writing from, the perspective of persons whose identities and status differed from their own. In the case of the many anonymous songs that appear in medieval songbooks, compilers and scribes did not reveal to us whether the authors behind these songs were clerical, aristocratic, or professional, or whether they were male or female. Subsequent chapters will show that such songs can still reveal much about the way medieval people projected and received images of identity through song, and how those identities were tied to space and place.

PART II
SONG AND SPRING IN TOWN AND COUNTRY

3

In the Meadows

Feeling the Landscape through the
Songs of Knightly Trouvères

What was the experience of spring on a medieval aristocratic estate? As I showed in Chapter 1, the Medieval Climate Anomaly created weather conditions that were ideal for plant-life. Just as crops flourished, propelling population increases, the short, rainy winters and generally mild weather would surely have caused meadowlands, woodlands, and gardens to thrive, leafing out and blooming earlier and longer than during other, less climatically favored, ages. The oaks, ash, beech, and alder trees that dominated medieval woodlands were deciduous.[1] The emergence of fresh green leaves on the bare branches of the arboreal canopy must have been a welcome sight at the end of winter. The color green, according to humoral medicine, refreshed and nourished the eye, protecting against sight loss and dry eyes in old age; the greening of the landscape was thus therapeutic.[2] Orchards would have been suddenly covered with blossoms and filled their sweet scent. Herb gardens dominated by herbaceous plants (which die back to the ground in winter) would have reemerged with new, green foliage. The roses that songs and romances so often mention were not the modern hybrid varieties that produce waves of blossoms from spring through fall. Medieval rose bushes covered themselves with a mass of blooms just once per year, filling the air with a sudden profusion of color and sweet scent.[3] The fleeting, delicate flowers of lilies would have dotted the landscape with vibrant color. And in contrast to the winter chill of largely unheated castles, milder air must

---

[1] See Duceppe-Lamarre, *Chasse et pâturage*, 69.
[2] Rawcliffe, "Delectable Sightes," 11.
[3] Only one known variety of European rose bloomed for more than a single, brief period per year. It was not until the sixteenth century that continuous-flowering roses were imported to Europe from the East, and these were not in widespread use until the late eighteenth century. Taylor, *Oxford Companion to the Garden*, 415.

Song, Landscape, and Identity in Medieval Northern France. Jennifer Saltzstein, Oxford University Press.
© Oxford University Press 2023. DOI: 10.1093/oso/9780197547779.003.0004

have been eagerly anticipated. For medieval people, this reemergence of greenery, color, flowers, scent, and warmth would not only have offered sensory pleasure, but it would also have been a reminder of the resurrection, a liturgical event to which it was calendrically tied.[4] Fragrant flowers, too, were reminders of Eden and the garden of paradise, which medieval writers imagined was replete with the scent of flowers, trees, and spices.[5]

The love songs of the trouvères often begin with the sensory pleasures of spring. The first-person speaker describes a beautiful landscape then tells listeners that it moves him to sing, to think of his beloved, to feel the joy or bitterness of love, or all of these simultaneously. This "nature opening" (*Natureingang*) appears with such regularity in trouvère songs that it has historically viewed as an abstract rhetorical convention imitated from other texts (biblical, classical, or the songs of the troubadours) rather than being grounded in the poet's observations or genuine sentiments. The nature opening has been compared to the classical *locus amoenus*, a description of a "pleasant place" that normally included a tree (or several trees), a meadow, a spring or brook, birdsong and flowers, and sometimes a breeze.[6] The *locus amoenus* originated in the works of Theocritus and was developed by Virgil and Ovid.[7] Its valorization of shade and water likely reflected Theocritus' own experiences in the parched climates of Sicily and Egypt, but these elements were retained in the topos for centuries, even by poets writing in the wetter, shadier north.[8] The details of the landscape the trouvères describe, however, need not have been drawn from literary sources; they could plausibly be observed in Northern France during our period. The trouvères invoke only a few of the standard elements of the *locus amoenus* with any regularity: meadows, birdsong, and flowers. As evidence that medieval nature descriptions were modelled on biblical and classical texts rather than the

---

[4] See Rothenberg, *Flower of Paradise* and Caldwell, *Devotional Refrains*.

[5] Woolgar, *The Senses*, 120. In his description of the Nile River valley, Jean de Joinville claims that the river flows into Egypt from Eden, and that the cinnamon, ginger, rhubarb, and aloe wood that fishermen find in their nets descends from heaven: "from the earthly paradise, the wind brings them down from the trees in paradise just as in this country [Champagne] the wind brings down the dry wood in the forests." Joinville, "Life of Saint Louis," 192.

[6] The classical *locus amoenus* was influentially described in Curtius, *European Literature*, 192–95. For its use in troubadour songs, see Scheludko, "Zur Geschidite des Natureinganges" and in the songs of the trouvères, see Dragonetti, *Technique poétique*, 166–67.

[7] Curtius, *European Literature*, 183–92. Curtius' view that medieval nature imagery was not based on observation is echoed uncritically in Pearsall and Salter, *Landscapes and Seasons*, 50; Hoffmann, *An Environmental History*, 98–101.

[8] See Gifford, "Pastoral, Anti-pastoral, Post-pastoral," 18; Pearsall and Salter, *Landscapes and Seasons*, 9.

poet's direct observation, Curtius noted the appearance of nonindigenous creatures such as lions in French epics, which could be seen only in royal menageries.[9] The nature openings of the trouvères exclude such exotic flora and fauna—the grassy meadows, rose bushes, woods, and bird species they describe were all found in Northern French landscapes. They also lack the classical, mythological, and allegorical references that permeate the nature openings found in the *Carmina Burana* lyrics.[10] Indeed, there is no clear poetic reason to assume that that the nature imagery found in trouvère song was divorced from direct experience and observation.

The nature opening gracefully combines landscape, sensation, emotion, and sung expression. Focusing on a selection of especially widely transmitted songs by trouvères who were members of the medieval warrior elite, this chapter explores the nature opening as a privileged expression of identity among the knightly classes. Through their use of the nature opening, these knightly trouvères construct a world in which land, love, and song are pleasurably intertwined within the first-person subject. This sung formulation of knightly identity is found in songs composed and copied over the course of a century, often in spite of differences in the status of knights who composed it. Its endurance also conceals changes in elite relationships to the land during the late thirteenth and early fourteenth centuries.

Landscape and Knightly Identity in the Songs of Gace Brulé

Land was central to knightly identity, as I showed in Chapter 1. Aristocrats were, first and foremost, landowners, and land was the most important source of wealth in the middle ages. Particularly in the late twelfth through mid-thirteenth centuries, landowners would have cultivated it directly as their "domain" (the aristocratic *demesne*) while also using other portions to

---

[9] Curtius, *European Literature*, 184.

[10] As in, for example, "Aestivali sub fervore," a *Carmina Burana* lyric featuring a multi-stanza *locus amoenus* in which the poet describes the landscape and remarks "Plato's pen could not have depicted/a more agreeable scene" (Stilo non pinxisset Plato/loca gratiora, l.11–12). The song features river nymphs and Venus, and the poet calls his lady more beautiful than Flora. See the edition in Traill, *Carmina Burana*, I, 328–31. Wilhelm argues that in the *Carmina Burana* lyrics, the spring motif wavers between the physical and metaphysical worlds, intermingling realism and myth. See Wilhelm, *The Cruelest Month*, 125 and 141–42. Wilhelm also notes that the nature opening of medieval vernacular lyric differs from its Latin counterparts by lasting only a few lines and being followed by a monologue focused on the inner world of the speaker. See Wilhelm, *The Cruelest Month*, 3.

generate income through rents.[11] The toponyms through which aristocrats and knights alike named themselves in association with geographical regions or features strongly suggest that they viewed themselves as lords over a place.[12] For most knights, a fief (a parcel of land bestowed upon them by a lord) would be their primary means of support. Holding a fief entailed a personal relationship; vassals submitted to the authority of a lord. Vassals were the lord's "tenant" because they held (*tenere*) his land; they were called a knight's "tenure."[13] Kings and counts had hundreds of these vassals during the twelfth century: Henry the Liberal, count of Troyes in Champagne, had 1,900 and Henry II, duke of Normandy, had 1,500.[14]

For medieval knights, landowning was directly tied to prowess. In his history of the fourth crusade, the knightly chronicler Geoffrey de Villehardouin offers detailed descriptions of the distribution of conquered lands after successful battles.[15] Kings kept extensive records of their fiefs, by which vassals they were held, whether those vassals had vassals of their own, and directly tied this information to descriptions of the vassal's military service.[16] In literature, the relationship between knightly violence and landowning found expression in medieval *chansons de geste*, where violent plots were sometimes generated by the unfair distribution of land, and in chivalric romances, where combat won knights the love of women and the estates that came with them.[17] Patronage, marriage, and the securing of property were among the most desired endpoints of knightly vigor.[18]

The medieval circulation of land was conducted with motives that were primarily non-economic. Land transfer was a social instrument in which gifts of land were used to establish lasting bonds between the two parties involved.[19] As Van Bavel states, "Land was not primarily a commodity to be freely bought and sold, but was embedded in social networks and relationships, and landed property formed the main instrument constituting such social relationships and could be used in several ways as a source of power."[20] This was true whether land provided for the needs of individual

---

[11] See Van Bavel, *Manors and Markets*, 170.
[12] Baldwin, *Knights, Lords, and Ladies*, 70.
[13] Baldwin, *Knights, Lords, and Ladies*, 104.
[14] Baldwin, *Knights, Lords, and Ladies*, 101.
[15] See, for example, Villehardouin, "The Conquest of Constantinople," 72–73.
[16] Baldwin *Knights, Lords, and Ladies*, 102.
[17] Kaeuper, *Medieval Chivalry*, 109.
[18] Kaeuper, *Medieval Chivalry*, 109–10.
[19] Van Bavel, *Manors and Markets*, 162–64.
[20] See Van Bavel, *Manors and Markets*, 52; Bedos-Rezak, *When Ego Was Imago*, 25–26.

consumption, the opportunity to levy a tax or extract a surplus, or to consolidate power relationships through a gift or temporary grant of use. Among the elite, land was the basis for power relationships and the means of their maintenance. It was a symbol of the power it fostered and a visible marker of the status and identity of those who controlled it.

The nature opening found in the love songs written by knightly trouvères is an apt expression of this intertwining of land and identity. It describes and valorizes a direct, sensory experience of an expansive outdoor environment; this experience leads to thoughts of love, song production, and often both at once. The songs emphasize the solitary enjoyment of an outdoor space full of burgeoning plant-life and often birdsong. The song "Au renouveau" by the prolific, widely imitated trouvère Gace Brulé is representative:

> Au renouvel de la douçour d'esté
> Que resclarcist la doiz en la fontainne
> Et que sont vert bois et vergier et pré
> Et li rosiers en mai florist en grainne,
5 > Lors chanterai, que trop m'avra duré
> Ire et esmaiz qui m'est au cuer prochainne;
> Car fins amis, a tort achoisonez,
> Est mout souvent de legier esfraez.

[Upon the return of summer warmth,/when the fountain stream flows clear/ and the woods and the orchards and the fields are green/and the rosebush flowers red in May,/then I will sing, for the pain and distress which grip my heart will have lasted too long;/for a true lover, wrongly blamed,/very often is easily disquieted.][21]

The speaker of this song seems to be embedded in an expansive and productive medieval estate. The speaker's field of vision sweeps across woods, orchards, and greening fields, as well as a flowing stream. The reference to flowering roses and the mixed usages of the land in relatively close proximity suggest an aristocratic landscape that includes ornamental as well as agricultural areas. The land is not merely a setting for this song, in the sense of being a neutral backdrop. Rather, the song articulates a causal connection between the return of warm weather, the awakening of plant-life, and the speaker's decision to sing in expression of the emotions that have gripped his heart. His

---

[21] RS 437. Gace Brulé, *Lyrics and Melodies of Gace*, 100–101.

vantage point and position are in keeping with that those of a landowner. In this song and many others like it, the landscape is his alone to behold—it is noticeably devoid of laborers and livestock. The nature opening seemingly presents the unfiltered feelings and sensations of the subject as being unique to landowners—the position of being lord of a place and enjoying it in ways that are unavailable to others. Although the plant-life described is realistic, the speaker's claim to being alone on the land is not. Since landowners of the knightly classes did not work the land themselves, the tenants or hired laborers who extracted its value for them would have been a constant presence. Moreover, even the most powerful landowners did not hold exclusive property rights in the middle ages. Their neighbors and tenants were allowed to graze animals and collect firewood on lands held by the aristocracy at certain times of year.[22] The absence of animals is thus particularly conspicuous. Songs like this one project the solitary enjoyment of the land as an expression of identity; they articulate an intimate, sensory, and emotional relationship between the knightly classes and the land that was their desired source of wealth and power.

The nature opening was a mainstay of the songs attributed to Gace Brulé; twenty-four of his seventy-eight love songs begin with it.[23] When considering these songs as a group, the topography they describe is notably wide-ranging, embracing features such as gardens, woodlands (including brushland and coppices), and meadows, as well as fountains and rivers. The garden (*li vergiers*) receives frequent mention, and meadows, woods, and brushland also appear often. His landscapes rarely include spaces marked by direct agricultural cultivation such as planted orchards (*l'arbroie*),[24] focusing instead on descriptions of woodlands, flowers, birdsong, open meadows, and unplanted fields covered in greening grasses. These songs draw special attention to the absence of human (and animal) activity in these spaces through references to grass that is wet with dew, suggesting a speaker who is the first to tread on the morning landscape. In "Biaus m'est estéz," the speaker sings of his love of the summer, when the birds sing, "and the green grass is wet with dew/which makes it shimmer along the river bank."[25] In "Lanque voi l'erbe," the speaker is inspired to sing after seeing the shimmering (presumably dewy) fields of

---

[22] I discuss these common rights at greater length in Chapter 5.

[23] These figures are based on the corpus of songs in the edition of Rosenberg and Danon, Gace Brulé, *Lyrics and Melodies*.

[24] See "Quant voi renverdir" (RS 1690).

[25] "Et l'erbe vert de rosee se muille,/Qui resplandir la fait lez le rivage" (RS 1006). St. 1, ll. 3–4. See Gace Brulé, *Lyrics and Melodies*, 80–81.

grass: "When I see the grass shimmer/in the fields and grow green,/then I wish to turn to song."[26] The landscape described is often notably expansive. We have already seen the panorama of "Au renovel" (quoted above). In "A la douçor" the speaker gazes across greening meadows, orchards, and thickets,[27] and in "Biaus m'est estéz," the shimmering green grass wet with dew (noted above) is found along a riverbank.[28] At the time this song was written, grassy meadows were not sown crops; they thrived in wetlands and small river floodplains.[29] These descriptions linking the meadow to the riverbank were thus true to the topography and emphasize non-cultivated areas. References to water features such as fountains and brooks are otherwise rare in trouvère nature openings, and Gace seems to have been the only trouvère whose songs include a river.[30]

The sweeping landscapes and the mixture of fields, woodlands, and gardens that we encounter in these songs suggest a speaker in possession of a vantage point that offers a far-reaching geographical perspective. As I noted in the Introduction, the concept of surveillance has long linked landscape to power.[31] Tilly reminds us: "What space is depends on who is experiencing it and how. Spatial experience is not innocent and neutral, but invested with power relating to age, gender, societal position and relationships with others."[32] Surveillance was also an important function of all medieval castles, which, as I noted in Chapter 1, were often built on mottes, elevated from the ground. The sweeping landscapes we find in the songs of Gace Brulé suggest just such an expansive aristocratic vantage point defined, implicitly, by lordship over a large tract of land.

Autobiography, Variability, and Authorial Persons: Approaching Trouvère Song in Manuscripts

Gace Brulé was a landowner. A charter surviving from 1212 indicates that he owned an estate at Groslières, west of Paris in Dreux.[33] The identity he

[26] "Lanque voi l'erbe resplandre/Par les prez et renverdir/Lors vuil a chanter entendre" (RS 633). St.1, ll.1–3. See Gace Brulé, Lyrics and Melodies, 52–53.

[27] RS 1893. See Gace Brulé, Lyrics and Melodies, 130–31.

[28] RS 1006. Gace Brulé, Lyrics and Melodies, 80–81.

[29] Hoffmann, An Environmental History of Medieval Europe, 175.

[30] Dragonetti, La technique poétique, 172. Gace's "Quant voi la flor betoner" (RS 772) also mentions shimmering riverbanks.

[31] See, Creighton, Early European Castles, 120. Mitchell, "Imperial Landscape."

[32] Tilley, Phenomenology of Landscape, 11.

[33] See Dyggve, Gace Brulé, 91. Gace also enjoyed a fief-rente of 24 livres per year from King Philip Augustus. See Page, "Listening to the Trouvères," 643.

projects through the nature opening is thus in alignment with his historical status. During the reign of Philip Augustus, in the decades around 1200
when Gace was presumably writing, aristocrats lived deep in the countryside
even when they held property in cities like Paris.[34] It would be reasonable to
suppose that Gace wrote these songs based on observation of his own land
and that they communicated his own feelings and sensations. One might
make the same assumption about the songs of other landowning trouvères
such as Thibaut IV, the Châtelain de Coucy, and many others. Interpreting
the songs in this way (as straightforwardly autobiographical) would resonate with nineteenth- and early twentieth-century accounts of trouvère song,
which, as I discussed in Chapter 2, took for granted that the song lyrics were
transparent records of the ideas and sentiments of their authors and often
constructed biographies based in part on references in the song lyrics.[35] This
autobiographical approach largely fell out of favor during the second half of
the twentieth century, when critical attention shifted away from authors and
biography; rather than looking to songs for information about the history of
their authors, scholars looked to songs for information about the history of
artistic forms.[36]

Interpreting the nature imagery found in trouvère songs as a manifestation
of the feelings and sensations that the authors who wrote them experienced
in their lived environment introduces methodological problems, particularly related to the manuscript transmission of this repertory. The clerical

---

[34] Baldwin, *Knights, Lords, and Ladies*, 94.

[35] See, for example, Paris' belief in the sincerity of the songs of Gace Brulé: "The amorous pursuits of Gace were not a simple poetic fiction. After having read his songs, one remains convinced of the reality of the sentiments he expresses in them" (Les amours de Gasse ne furent pas une simple fic- tion poétique. Après avoir lu ses chansons, on demeure convaincu de la réalité des sentiments qu'il y exprime). Paris, *Histoire littéraire*, 565. In spite of the problematization (and even outright rejec- tion) of the approach in many studies of trouvère love lyric, the practice of reading trouvère songs autobiographically has continued in the literature on crusade songs, where modern scholars often interpret the verb tenses used in the songs as evidence of whether or not a trouvère has already left for the holy land at the time of writing. This approach is evident in the biographical essays in Paterson, *Troubadours, Trouvères, and the Crusades*: https://warwick.ac.uk/fac/arts/modernlanguages/resea rch/french/crusades/. Compare this approach to the treatment of biography and identity in Galvez, *Subject of the Crusade*.

[36] The idea that troubadour and trouvère song referred only to itself and excluded external, bio- graphical referents was influenced by, in particular, Dragonetti, *Technique poétique*, Guiette, "D'une poésie formelle"; Zumthor, *Toward a Medieval Poetics*. Zink advocated for a limited literary subjec- tivity in certain medieval genres that he argued manifested themselves as "the product of a particular consciousness." *Invention of Literary Subjectivity*, 4. However, he argues that the exclusion of personal anecdotes and the presence of melody in trouvère song are features designed to render these songs assimilable by the performer and listener. This assimilation was made possible, he argued, by the in- tentional effacement of authorial expression. See ibid., 38–39 and 45. These views are productively challenged in Peraino, *Giving Voice to Love*, 10–17.

composer Guillaume de Machaut was intimately involved in the preservation of his songs in manuscript form, overseeing their historical compilation and extensively thematizing his role as an artistic creator across his narrative works.[37] We lack this kind of clear evidence (and the increased confidence it might give regarding authorial intention) in the case of the twelfth- and thirteenth-century trouvères.[38] Although the cleric-trouvères, whom I explore at length in Chapter 4, could theoretically have been involved in the written preservation of their songs, most trouvères were not trained scribes, and many were long dead by the time the extant versions of their songs were recorded on parchment. In Chapter 2, I showed that the compilers of medieval songbooks often went to great lengths to identify the authors of their songs as singular individuals, through strategies such as illustration, naming, and organization by author. Some songbooks associated trouvères with specific social groups (such as aristocrats, clerics, and professionals) and others used seal-like author portraits that were functionally tied to the person they represented.

It is, however, important to keep in mind the long temporal gap that separates most of the surviving songbooks (produced during the mid to late thirteenth century) and the heyday of trouvères like Gace Brulé in the decades around 1200. The earliest surviving songbook, *U*, may have been compiled during the 1220s and completed in 1231,[39] during Gace's period of activity, but this manuscript does not provide authorial attributions for its songs. Further, songs attributed to Gace and other early trouvères continued to be copied at the turn of the fourteenth century and beyond. This long transmission history seems to explain the variation that often exists between versions of songs recorded across multiple manuscripts: the number or order of stanzas recorded in individual manuscripts is sometimes different and the melodies found in different copies of the same song normally include some degree of variation, at times diverging significantly. Zumthor famously argued that the instability of medieval poetry was such that there was no one version of any text.[40] When textual transmission diverges, which (if any)

---

[37] See especially Leach, "Creation," chap. 3 in *Guillaume de Machaut*.

[38] An ambiguous remark in the *Grandes Chroniques de France* describes the copying of songs by Gace Brulé and Thibaut IV, Roi de Navarre, in Thibaut's palaces at Provins and Troyes at the King's behest. See the discussion in Haines, *Eight Centuries*, 34–35.

[39] Lug argues the oldest portion of *U* was compiled in the 1220s and completed in 1231. See Lug, "Politique et Littérature," 475.

[40] See Zumthor, "Poet and Text," chap. 2 in *Toward a Medieval Poetics* and Cerquiglini, *Éloge de la variant*.

surviving version reflects the song as the trouvère-author conceived it? Was the song itself always viewed as fluid, allowing room for such variation? Did the song change during this long process of transmission, performers, and/ or scribes introducing their own variations found across the manuscript tradition? It might be tempting to view the lyrics and melodies found in an early manuscript (such as U, which is often closest temporally to the phenomena it records) as more likely to reflect trouvère songs as their composers intended them. The differences found in copies made decades later could be viewed as the result of error or reinterpretation by later historical actors. While it is clear that songbooks were copied from written exempla that were circulating during the first half of the thirteenth century,[41] such ephemeral traces of the material transmission of trouvère song are mostly lost to us.[42] Assuming they did exist, we might wonder just what those exemplars were a copy *of*. Were they based on the scribe's memory of a performance? Were they dictated by the composer to a scribe?[43] It is important to recognize the multiplicity of actors lying behind a song's first-person voice as encountered in a medieval manuscript, a factor that complicates any attempt to view a specific song as the expression of an individual trouvère's sensory experiences in the natural world and their emotional reactions to it.

Yet it is also important to recognize that the very concepts of an "original" and a "copy" may have made little sense to medieval composers and scribes. As Bedos-Rezak elucidates, *all* medieval documents were originals in the sense that they were unique and handmade. Originals were abundant—it was the exact replica that was hard to produce. In a documentary environment in which memory and reenactment continued to play important roles, Bedos-Rezak argues that authenticity was more important than temporal primacy; a document might be viewed as more authentic if it bore a seal, even if an earlier version of the same text existed. Documents gained authority in part through their recopying and reenactment; repetition worked

[41] Evidence in the form of references to now lost author *libelli* (including one for Gace Brulé) and songbooks in inventories as well as similarities between the author corpora preserved in different manuscripts indicate that written exemplars were circulating in the first half of the thirteenth century, and that the songbooks were copied from such exempla. See the discussion in Haines, "Songbook for William," 60–75 and Poe, *Compilatio*, 15.

[42] Lambeth Palace scroll (London, Lambeth Palace Library 1681), which preserves songs by *arrageois* songwriters, suggests the possibility that more ephemeral written modes of song transmission may have existed. See discussion in Haines, "Songbook for William," 61–62. The scroll is pictured on ibid., 62. The survival of this scroll may stem from the fourteenth-century Latin and French memoranda written on its reverse side, as noted in Philips, "Songs without Borders," 60.

[43] Historical approaches to the editing of medieval musical texts are addressed in Haines, *Eight Centuries*, 178–87; O'Sullivan, "Editing Melodic Variance."

to validate them. Viewed in this light, a song transmitted in *A*, *a*, *M*, or *T* may have been understood as being more authentic than a much older version of the same song in *U* if, in the later version, the song was accompanied, for example, by an authorial rubric identifying its composer, placed within an author section, accompanied by an author portrait, or attributed to an author within an index. The recopying and sung performance of many versions of a particular song, even versions that differed considerably from one another, might be understood to further authenticate a song.[44] In Chapter 2, I showed that the strong resemblance between aristocratic seals (which functioned as substitutes for the persons they represented) and the author portraits found in the songbooks *A*, *a*, *M*, and *T* suggests that the compilers and patrons of those books may have expressly desired for readers to align the first-person speaker found in trouvère songs with their author. The portraits represent knightly trouvères as warriors, while their rubrics and the heraldry often found on their shields connect the men to kin networks and to the land itself.[45]

What is more, the degree of variation across surviving versions is often not great enough to cast doubt on a song's status as the intentional artistic expression of a singular author figure. Even in songs attributed to the earliest generation of trouvères—those for whom the temporal gap between the song's creation and its written transmission is often the greatest—trouvère melodies can be stable across a wide array of manuscripts copied at far temporal remove from one another. To demonstrate, it is worth considering Gace Brulé's song "Au renouveau,"[46] which survives with music notation in ten different manuscripts, the copying of which probably spanned nearly a century (see Table 3.1).

"Au renouveau" appears in the oldest part of *U* (possibly compiled in the 1220s), the closely related songbooks *K*, *N*, *P*, and *X*, as well as the songbooks *L*, *M*, *O*, *R*, and *V*.[47] The attribution of "Au renouveau" to Gace across these songbooks is strong; Table 3.1 shows that six include an author rubric identifying the author as "me sire" or "monseigneur" (my lord) Gace. Six

[44] See Bedos-Rezak, *When Ego Was Imago*, 37–40.

[45] Bedos-Rezak, *When Ego was Imago*, 154. The heraldry depicted in *M* is discussed in Prinet, "L'illustration héraldique."

[46] RS 437.

[47] Its lyrics (without the melody) are also preserved in *C* as well within the *Roman de la Châtelain de Couci*, where the author Jakemes assigns them (wrongly) to his hero the Châtelain de Couci. See Jakames, *Roman du Châtelain*, v.5952–5991. Misattribution, which is common across the trouvère corpus, could represent mistaken identity or possibly an attempt to confer greater authority on an author by associating their name with a song elsewhere attributed to a trouvère of greater renown.

Table 3.1 Transmission of "Au renouveau" by Gace Brulé

Manuscript	Medieval Rubric	In Author Section	Decorative Initial	Music
M 32r	Me sire Gasse	Yes	Yes	X
K 54	Ci faillent les chancons le Roi de Navarre et conmencent les chancons mon seigneur Gace brullez	Yes (first song in section)	Yes	X
N 15v	Same as above	Yes (first song in section)	Yes	X
X 43v	Same as above	Yes (first song in section)	Yes	X
P 17r	Me sire Gaces	Yes	No	X
V 27r	None	Yes	No	X
O 3r	None	No	No	X
R 114r	None	No	No	X
L 48r	None	Yes (first song in section)	Yes	X
U 23r	None	No	No	X
C 7v	Yes (marginal)	No	Yes	Empty Staves

songbooks highlight the presence of the song with a large decorative letter "A." At the start of Gace's author section in *K*, "Au renouveau" begins with a large, ornately decorated initial.[48] All but four of the songbooks include this song within a section of songs by Gace.[49] Gace's works are among the oldest trouvère songs in the repertoire, and the majority of the surviving manuscripts (with the possible exception of *U*) were being written out long after any performer or scribe could have heard the trouvère sing his songs with his own voice. Yet as Appendix I shows, the surviving melodies of "Au renouveau" preserve a strong sense of musical resemblance.

Appendix I presents six of the ten melodies arranged in descending order of resemblance. All but one of the melodies attached to "Au renouveau" are in *pedes cum cauda* form, the most common arrangement of melodic and textual repetition in trouvère songs. In *pedes cum cauda* form, an initial melodic phrase (usually associated with lines 1 and 2 of the poetry) is repeated with

---

[48] *K* 54r. See https://gallica.bnf.fr/ark:/12148/btv1b550063912/f80.item.
[49] There would be no expectation of this in *O*, which is organized alphabetically rather than by author and *U*, which is organized generically, without author rubrics.

different lyrics (usually in lines 3 and 4). These repeated melodies are the *pedes* (or feet); and they are followed by a new melody called the *cauda* (or tail).[50] Musicologists express this form by referring to each *pes* as "A" and the *cauda* as "B," resulting in the form AAB (marked in Appendix I). The versions of the song in the *KNPX* group of songbooks as well as *L* are so similar that Appendix I provides the melody of *K* as representative of all five melodies. Moreover, the versions of "Au renouveau" in the songbooks *M* and *O* are broadly similar to the melody of *K* (and, by proxy, *L*, *N*, *P*, and *X*). All seven of these manuscripts transmit the melody at the same pitch level with minor variations such as the presence or absence of neighboring pitches (pitches a step above or below a common pitch); the differences we find between them rarely extend beyond a single syllable of text. The other three melodies are not as similar to these seven versions however, their divergence is largely saved for the *cauda*. *U*, the oldest surviving version, is notated at a pitch level a fifth higher than the other melodies; to facilitate comparison, it has been transposed in Appendix I. The *pedes* of the song as written in *U* are very similar to those of *K* (and related manuscripts), *M*, and *O*.[51] The same could be said for the melody in *V*.[52] The melody of *R* is the only surviving copy of "Au renouveau" that is not in *pedes cum cauda* form; it is through-composed, meaning a different melody is used for each line of poetry within the first stanza. Yet even *R* begins with a melody in lines 1 and 2 that is recognizably the same basic *pes* melody found in all of the other versions before diverging from the other versions starting in line 3. All ten of the manuscripts thus notate the song's first two lines to melodies that are either nearly identical or recognizably similar to each other. The melodies in the group represented by *K* continue to resemble the melody of *M* and *O* throughout the *cauda*, while the *cauda* melodies of *R*, *U*, and *V* differ from the other melodies. One certainly encounters variation when comparing these surviving melodies. Yet particularly for hand-written replicas, they confirm a strong sense of the song's melody and form as relatively stable entities: seven melodies

---

[50] On the musical structure *pedes cum cauda* form, see especially Peraino, *Giving Voice to Love*, 47–49 and 164–76; Saint-Cricq, "A New Link."

[51] The motif that accompanies the lyric "par la fonteine" in line 2 is written a step below that of the others (see Appendix I). This is probably a copying error since the parallel passage in the repetition of the *pes* in line 4 of *U* ("en mai et graine") is very close to the versions of the melody in the other songbooks.

[52] Although the melody in *V* on the phrase "et vergiers" (line 3) diverges more significantly from the others, ending on a different cadential pitch, the melody used in line 4 is more closely related to the other versions. Because lines 3–4 are a close but not strict repetition of the melody of lines 1–2, the form is AA[1]B.

are broadly similar throughout; one more version is similar to those seven throughout the *pedes* and into the first phrase of the *cauda* (U); all versions but one (R) present the song in *pedes cum cauda* form; and all versions agree on the song's first two lines. The lessons this comparison provides will apply to other songs in this book, although each must be evaluated individually.[53] For our purposes here, it is noteworthy that even when a particular melody differs significantly from most of the other recorded versions of the song, it often shares the form of the others and often diverges significantly only in the *cauda*.[54] By preserving opening portions of the melody, such otherwise differing renderings would probably still be recognized initially as a version of the same song.

This song by Gace Brulé demonstrates that trouvère songs could maintain a stable melodic identity even when all versions were not identical. Further, as we saw in Chapter 2, when scribes and compilers tied them to features such as author portraits, rubrics, or tables of contents, they work hard to authenticate songs like "Au renouveau" as the work of Gace Brulé. This kind of authentication could be seen to overcome the existence of different renderings of portions of a melody, whether these variations originated with the author, other performers of their corpus, or the scribes who notated them.[55] Much like chivalric literature, the songbooks likely represented knightly trouvères like Gace as they saw themselves and as they and their patrons wanted others to see them. Not every song explored in this book will feature such careful alignment between the poetic speaker of the song and its author figure that I will demonstrate in the analyses that follow. Later on, I will explore that are not well authenticated and songs in which the author seems to be playing a part, intentionally exploring an identity different from his or her own. But

---

[53] In spite of centuries of scholarship on trouvère song, there is still not a systematic account of melodic stability across the surviving corpus. This continues to be the case despite the existence of two comparative editions, one partial (van der Werf, *Trouvères-Melodien*) and one complete (Tischler, *Trouvère Lyrics with Melodies*), which provide most or all of the manuscript versions of individual melodies for comparison. Few of the editors of individual trouvère corpora provide melodies and even fewer extend their analyses to the melodies. The value of a comprehensive approach is demonstrated in the recent edition of the lyrics of Thibaut IV edited by Callahan et al. See Thibaut IV, *Les chansons*. Since over two thousand songs survive (often in many individual versions) attributed to 264 individual trouvères, the scope of such a project would be too large for this study. An account of melodic stability in the songs of Audefroi le Bastard and Gautier de Dargies is conducted with clarity in O'Neill, *Courtly Love Songs*, 64–79 and 98–101.

[54] The tendency for significant variation to occur in the *cauda* was noted by van der Werf. See his *Troubadours and Trouvères*, 83–89.

[55] It is important to remember however, that scribes were often careful to faithfully reproduce their written exemplars, making frequent erasures and corrections. See especially Haines, "Erasures in Thirteenth-Century Music."

in the case of the knightly trouvères who are the focus of this chapter, the confluence of medieval authentication as well as the alignment between the author's rank and the status of first-person speaker provide ample reason to believe that these trouvères, compilers, and scribes hoped readers and listeners would interpret the songs as autobiographical, or, at minimum, as promoting an authorial identity that was meant to be understood as emanating from a specific person.

Feeling the Landscape in the Songs of Gace Brulé

In the nature opening, the sensory perception of nature often leads to emotional expression; feeling the landscape and its sensations prompts the expression of feelings of love. The lack of personalizing details and the presence of rhetoric shared broadly across the trouvère corpus has often been viewed as evidence of the absence of sincere feeling or self-expression—claims that the nature opening was merely rhetorical.[56] Yet emotional expression is always, to some degree, rhetorical, as Rosenwein has convincingly argued. Rather than representing a generic template whose repetition would signal a lack of individual feeling, the commonly held rhetoric linking nature imagery to emotional expression in trouvère song would, in her formulation, constitute an "emotional inheritance" available to contemporaries and subsequent generations. People who share a common vocabulary for describing their emotions constitute an "emotional community."[57] The medieval knightly classes were unquestionably an emotional community of this sort, as evidenced in the intensity of male friendship that they valued, the oaths of loyalty required for land transfer, or the shared rhetoric of *fin'amour* (or "courtly love").[58] Indeed, knights were sure that only they experienced love,[59] their elevated language of love (so intensely felt it was most often described as

---

[56] See n36 above.

[57] Rosenwein, *Generations of Feeling*, 9 and 125–27.

[58] Kaeuper, *Medieval Chivalry*, 315–16.

[59] See, for example, Gace Brulé, "A la douçor" (RS 1893), st.1, ll.5–7: "then I rejoice, for everyone else abandons love,/so that no more do I see any loyal lover but myself./I alone wish to love and I alone wish to have that honor" (Lors sui joianz quant tuit lessent amor,/Qu'ami loial n'i voi mes se moi non./Seus vueil amer et seus vueil cest honor), Gace Brulé, *Lyrics and Melodies*, 130–31, and "Biaus m'est estez" (RS 1006), st.1, ll.5–6 "I wish my heart to be afflicted by good love,/for no one but me has a heart true to love" (De bone amour vuil que mes cuers se duille,/Que nuns fors moi n'a vers li son corage), Gace Brulé, *Lyrics and Melodies*, 80–81.

painful) distinguishing them from peasants and town-dwellers.[60] The songs of the knightly trouvères suggest relationships between convention and expression, the affective qualities of artistic forms, and the power of form to encode and generate experiences for an audience. When combined with melody, the nature opening could be a potent mechanism for expressing emotion and connection to the land. The trouvères also used form strategically to generate perceptual reactions in their audience, prompting them to sense emotional change and feel it alongside the poem's speaking subject.[61]

As a poetic device, the nature opening can convey a remarkable sense of immediacy. It is set in the present tense and the first person. Those songs in which the experience in the landscape directly prompts the subject to sing within the diegetic space of the song's narrative seem to offer a model of spontaneous, oral song composition that unfolds in real time while the singer reacts to an outdoor scene in which they are embedded.[62] They ask listeners to imagine that they record a live compositional scenario developing in a specific place, as seen in Gace Brulé's "Quant noif":[63]

> Quant noif et giel et froidure
> Remaint o le tens felon,
> Que flors et glais et verdure
> Vient o la bele saison,
> 5   Lors chant sanz renvoiseüre,
> Dont je ai droite achoison,
> Que j'ai d'amours qui trop dure
> Sanz gré et sanz guerredon.

[When snow and frost and cold/come to an end with the harsh season,/when flower and lily and greenness/return with the beautiful season,/then I sing

---

[60] Kaeuper, *Medieval Chivalry*, 318 and 325.

[61] Many studies highlight the centrality of melodic form in trouvère song. This reflects the influence of Gennrich, who showed that the structure of the melody usually played the most important role in determining the form of a trouvère song. See Gennrich, *Grundriss einer formenlehre*. Productive approaches to relationships between form and expression or poetic meaning in medieval vernacular monophony include Aubrey, "Form," chap. 5 in *Music of the Troubadours*; Aubrey, "Genre as a Determinant"; Haines, "Vers une distinction"; Leach, "Trouvère Melodies"; Mason, "Structure and Process"; and Switten, *Cansos of Raimon de Miraval*.

[62] My interest in orality with regard to these songs is discursive. The question of whether trouvère songs were composed and transmitted orally or through writing (a topic too vast to receive consideration here) is explored extensively in Van der Werf, *Chansons of the Troubadours*; O'Neill, *Courtly Love Songs*.

[63] RS 2099. Lyric modified slightly from that of Rosenberg and Danon in Gace Brulé, *Lyrics and Melodies*, 42.

without mirth,/and for good cause,/for I love with a love that has lasted too long/without favor and without reward.]

Songs like this one ask listeners to believe that their composition is unfolding before our eyes and ears; since they are monophonic, the notion that their composition could occur anywhere (including outdoors) is also plausible. The lyrics suggest that the singer wrote the song while watching the last remnants of winter melt away, and that the impulse to generate its rhyme and melody came upon him while viewing the greening landscape. The opening word "Quant," which begins many of these songs, places it temporally. After the description of winter's waning and spring's emergence, the poetic "I" is ushered in conspicuously by the adverbial phrase "lors chant," introducing the speaker in a specific moment of seasonal change and in the act of singing.[64] This "when/then" formulation implies a causal relationship between the physical setting and the subject's decision to begin singing; it presents a compositional model as well as a record of a sensory experience. Many nature openings place the observer within the landscape from the start by opening with some version of the phrase "When I see" (*quant je voi*), marking the verses that follow as the speaker's direct, sensory observations.[65]

The firsthand, present-tense description of the trouvère's sensory experience is immediate and immersive. The nature opening asks listeners to imagine two performances: a first that was sung by the singing subject (whom we presume to be aligned with the trouvère) for an audience that consisted of himself alone and a second that occurs as we listen.[66] As heard or read, the song presents itself as a recreation of that original, spontaneous act of singing and the embeddedness in the landscape that it records. The artifact that survives, whether sung or written, seems to emanate from the singer's memory of its first oral performance.[67] Listeners are free to engage in a vicarious experience of being in nature and feeling

---

[64] Zink notes the orientation of the springtime opening at a moment of change: Zink, "Place of the Senses," 96.

[65] See Gace Brulé: "Lanque voi l'erbe" (RS 633), "Quant je voi la noif" (RS 1638), "Quant je voi le dous tens" (RS 1486), "Quant voi la flor betoner" (RS 772), "Quant voi le tans" (RS 838), "Quant voi paroir" (RS 550), and "Quant voi renverdir" (RS 1690). Across the trouvère song corpus, Raynaud records no fewer than seventy-four songs that begin "Quant je voi" or "Quant voi" and seven others that begin "Quant j'oi."

[66] For a brilliant discussion of the temporality of "songs about singing" in the troubadour corpus, see Dillon, "Unwriting Medieval Song," 599–606.

[67] Compare this to the split temporality art historians discuss with regard to the viewing of landscape paintings, as in, for example, Koerner, *Caspar David Friedrich*, 17–19. Also relevant is Dillon's discussion of temporality in songs that end with a *tornada*, wherein the song first characterizes itself as a performance occuring in the present, then, in the *tornada*, as a repeatable, dispatchable thing. See Dillon, "Unwriting Medieval Song," 606.

its sensations, channeled through the voice of the singer. The present tense encourages listeners to place themselves in the first-person perspective, feeling the encounter with nature as it unfolds. The springtime opening thus represents the song and the embeddedness in nature it describes as being unmediated. It communicates a harmonious, fruitful relationship between the singing subject and the land that surrounds them. Indeed, in songs such as "Quant noif" the environment itself seems to help generate the song, prompting the singer directly to produce the sounds we hear, as though it possesses a kind of agency. The outdoor locale is not merely a setting or background for the song that it introduces but, rather, a precondition for its production.

As a device for generating feeling and simulating experience, the nature opening often relies further on melody. The adverbial phrase "Then I sing" (*lors chant* and its variations), which signals the landscape's power to prompt the speaker to sing, feel, or think of the beloved, is often placed strategically at a moment of musical change within the form of these songs. Many trouvères structure the relationship between words and melody such that the phrase "then I sing" actually sounds different from the portion of the song that came before, aurally marking the shift to song for listeners. Through musical novelty, a composer can generate a perceived sensory shift that coincides with the speaker's description of their own shift from perception to emotion (love) or action (song). The vehicle for this device is *pedes cum cauda* form, which is found across hundreds of trouvère songs representing a wide variety of genres, but which takes on a special significance when combined in this particular way with the nature opening. When the nature opening is aligned with *pedes cum cauda* form, the immediacy of its rhetoric is amplified, particularly when the phrase "lors chant" or its variations occurs at the start of the *cauda* section (normally line 5 within the stanza). In songs like this one, the rhetorical shift from perception to feeling and/or action is accompanied by a new melody previously unheard. Listeners feel a shift in their perception of the musical pattern at the same moment that the speaker describes being prompted by the landscape to sing.

The adverb "lors" marks the shift from the nature opening to the moment of singing, feeling, or thoughts of the beloved in eight of the twenty-four songs attributed to Gace that use the nature opening. In six of these, Gace musically positions the shift to emotion, song or both, at the *cauda*, as Table 3.2 shows.

Table 3.2 Structural position of the adverb *Lors* in the songs of Gace Brulé

Song #	Title	Position of *lors* in stanza	Position of *lors* in musical form
RS 1893	"A la douçor"	v.5	B
RS 437	"Au renovel"	v.5	B
RS 1977	"Quant define fueille"	v.3	A
RS 633	"Quant je voi l'erbe"	v.3	A
RS 1638	"Quant je voi la noif"	v.5	B
RS 1486	"Quant je voi la douz tens"	v.5	B
RS 1795	"Quant l'erbe muert"	v.5	B
RS 2099	"Quant noif"	v.5	B

Example 3.1 provides the melodies used in the first stanza of "Quant noif" in the songbooks *K*, *M*, *O*, and *V*.[68] In the *K* melody (which is also representative of the versions of the song found in *L*, *N*, and *X*), "lors" (line 5) is positioned at the start of the *cauda* (marked "B"), the moment of musical change in Example 3.1.

This relationship, moreover, is retained in manuscripts that otherwise transmit versions of this song that vary significantly from that found in the *K* group. The melodies used in the songbooks *M*, *O*, and *V* also appear in Example 3.1. The melody of *O* appears closely related to that of the *K* group during the song's *pedes*, sharing the overall contour, range, and opening and cadential pitches (lines 1–2 and lines 3–4 of *O* are marked A^1 to reflect this similarity). In lines 5–6 of the *cauda*, however, *O* provides a new melody that is seemingly unrelated to that found in the *cauda* of the *K* group (this is marked "C" in Example 3.1). In lines 7–8, the resemblance between the *O* melody and the melody of the *K* group returns. The version of the song in *O* thus differs audibly from that found in the *K* group; however, it preserves the *pedes cum cauda* form and places the *cauda* at line 5, in the same structural position. This ensures that the melody in *O* still aligns the phrase "lors chant" (line 5) with a new melody, creating the same correspondence of melodic and poetic novelty. The songbook *M* provides a melody that is unrelated to that of either the *K* group or *O*, but it, too, provides the lyrics with a melody

---

[68] "Quant noif" (RS 2099) is preserved in eleven songbooks, seven of which provide a melody. The melody in *K* is so similar to that found in *L*, *N*, and *X* that it has been used to represent all four versions. The song also is found in *C*, *P*, *T*, and *U* with staves ruled for music but none entered.

Example 3.1 Gace Brulé, "Quant noif"

in *pedes cum cauda* form, and it, too, places the lyric "lors chant" (line 5) at the beginning of its *cauda* (*pedes* are marked "D" in lines 1–2, "D" in lines 3–4, and "E" at the start of the *cauda* at line 5). Only the songbook *V* provides a version of "Quant noif" that differs from the others both melodically and structurally—its melody is through-composed. Across the seven surviving melodic versions of "Quant noif," there is considerable stability of melodic structure, but more striking, in all but one manuscript (*V*), the structural relationship between melodic change and the shift to the act of singing (the positioning of "lors" at the *cauda*) is retained even in cases when the individual melodies diverge significantly from one another. The stability of this relationship across manuscripts (even those that transmit variant melodies), and the frequency with which this device occurs across the corpus of songs attributed to Gace suggests that it was used intentionally and recognized and retained by the performers or scribes who may have been in a position to alter it. Across this song's complicated and lengthy transmission history, many medieval actors (including, probably, the author) found this particular combination of melodic and rhetorical structuring to be a meaningful mechanism for enacting the transfer from feeling the sensations of nature to feeling love, beginning to sing, or both at once.

Generating Feeling: Landscape and Melodic Form in the Songs of Knightly Trouvères

Active in the decades around 1200, Gace Brulé was the most prolific and one of the earliest knightly songwriters; his songs were copied and recopied into the fourteenth century. His songs were clearly loved by compilers and audiences and they enjoyed wide influence among other songwriters.[69] While we cannot know for certain whether they directly imitated Gace's songs and the way those songs aligned the nature opening with *pedes cum cauda* form, we find this device in the works of many other knightly songwriters.[70] This section focuses on examples that were particularly widely transmitted and thus seemingly well loved by medieval poets, patrons, and

---

[69] This is evident in the large number of his melodies that were set to new lyrics (*contrafacta*), one of which specifically associates Gace's songs with the nature opening. An anonymous trouvère who wrote a pious *contrafactum* of Gace's song "Au renovel" (RS 437) named Gace as the author of his model and associated Gace strongly with the nature opening: "All his songs are about summer flowers/or green woods or spring waters, or some woman to whom God has lent,/in this world, a bit of hollow beauty" (st.2, ll.1–4: Trestuit si chant sont de la fleur d'esté,/Ou de vert bois, ou de ru de fontaine,/Ou d'aucune a qui Dieus a presté/En cest siècle un pou de biauté vaine." RS 425). Translation follows that of Rosenberg and Danon in Gace Brulé, *Lyrics and Melodies*, 300. On the centrality of Gace in the trouvère corpus, see also Barbieri, "Thibaut le *Chansonnier*," 218–19. On Gace's influence on Thibaut IV, see Grossel, "Thibaut de Champagne et Gace Brulé."

[70] In an earlier study I surveyed the usage of the springtime opening among a range of aristocratic trouvères, exploring the ways in which the season served as an impetus for song production. See my "Songs of Nature."

manuscript compilers. The songs, by the Châtelain de Couci, Thibaut de Blaison, the Vidame de Chartres, and Raoul de Soissons, demonstrate the enduring relevance of the nature opening, which continued to provide knights with a model of identity in which sensory immersion in a landscape prompts emotion and its expression through song.

The nature opening figures prominently in the songs of the Châtelain de Couci, a strenuous (meaning violent) knight whose death on the fourth crusade is noted in Geoffrey Villehardouin's chronicle,[71] and whose life was turned into a legend and his songs immortalized by the medieval poet Jakemes in the medieval *Roman du Châtelain de Coucy*.[72] Half of the songs attributed to the Châtelain used the nature opening.[73] The treatment of the opening is varied. For example, it is subjected to inversion in "Lanque rose ne feuille," in which a description of wintertime prompts love to flower within the speaker's heart.[74] We saw how the songs attributed to Gace paired the novel *cauda* melody with the poetic subject's response to the natural setting and his emotional outburst or his inspiration to begin singing. The Châtelain's songs also tend to place the speaker's reaction in the *cauda*, using the new "B" melody to highlight the shift to the expression of feeling. Moreover, these songs often differentiate the *pedes* and *cauda* melodies in a way that increases the effect, moving from melodies in narrow ranges in the *pedes* to more expansive melodies in wider ranges in the *cauda*. This strategic expansion of melodic range aligns with and amplifies the listener's sensation of the poetic shift from observation of nature to feeling, causing the *cauda* to open outward, sonically. See, for example, the much-loved song "La douce voiz":[75]

> La douce voiz du rosignol sauvage
> Qu'oi nuit et jor cointoier et tentir
> Me radoucist mon cuer et rassouage.
> Lors ai talent que chant pour esbaudir.
> 5   Bien doi chanter puis qu'il vient a plesir

---

[71] Villehardouin, "Conquest of Constantinople," 33.

[72] Jakemes, *Roman du Châtelain du Coucy*.

[73] As the corpus of the Châtelain, I adopt those Lerond deems "authentic" as well as "A la douçor" (RS 1754), "Bien cuidai vivre" (RS 1965), "En aventure conmens" (RS 634), "Quant li estez" (RS 1913), "Tant ne me sai dementer" (RS 127), and Conment que longe" (RS 1010). See Lerond, *Chastelain de Couci*.

[74] RS 1009, ll. 1–4.

[75] RS 40. This song is never attributed to anyone other than the Châtelain and nine *contrafacta* survive, attesting to its authenticity and medieval popularity. In addition to the items in Table 3.3, the song is also found in Jakemes, *Roman du Châtelain de Couci*, 29.

Cele que j'ai de cuer fet lige honmage;
Si doi avoir grant joie en mon corage,
S'ele me veut a son oés retenir.[76]

[The sweet voice of the wild nightingale/which I hear night and day ornamenting and resounding/softens me and calms heart./Then I have the desire to sing out of lightheartedness./I must indeed sing, since that pleases/her to whom I have done heartfelt liege homage;/thus I must have great joy in my heart/if she really desires to retain me for her pleasure.]

As Table 3.3 shows, "La douce voiz" was consistently attributed to the Châtelain.

Table 3.3 Transmission of "La douce voiz" by the Châtelain de Couci

#	Manuscript	Medieval Rubric	Melody	Notes on Transmission
1.	*a* 13r	Li castelains de couci	Yes	
2.	*A* 131v	Li kastelains	Yes	
3.	*K* 99	Li chastelains de couci	Yes	
4.	*N*			Recorded in a portion of this manuscript that is now lost
5.	*X* 71v	Li chastelains de couci	Yes	
6.	*P* 33v	Li chastelains de couci	Yes	
7.	*V* 76v	none	Yes	In a section of songs elsewhere attributed to the Châtelain de Couci.
8.	*M* 54v	Li chastelains de couci	Yes	
9.	*T* 157r	Li chastel'	Yes	
10.	*O* 74v	none	Yes	
11.	*C* 135	Li chastelai de couci	No	Staves ruled, no notation entered
12.	*F* 108v	Castellain de Couchy	Yes	

---

[76] The text follows edition of Rosenberg, Switten, and le Vot, *Songs of the Troubadours*, 254, which is based on *K*. The translation is my own.

Example 3.2 "La douce voiz" by the Châtelain de Couci, st.1

Example 3.2 provides the first stanza of "La douce voiz."[77] The *pedes* and *cauda* in this song are linked formally and semantically: "I desire to sing" ("Lors ai talent que chant," in the *pedes*, l.4) becomes "I must sing" ("Bien doi chanter" at the start of the *cauda*, l.5).[78] The nightingale directly inspires the speaker to begin singing, and his shift to song in the *cauda* is distinguished melodically from the *pedes* melodies that preceded it. As Example 3.2 shows, the *pedes* meander through a range of a sixth, hovering noticeably around the pitch "a" in syllables 6 through 10; this portion of lines 1 and 3 is bracketed in Example 3.2. A leap of a fifth draws attention to the fifth syllable of lines 1 and 3 (rosignol/mon cuer: nightingale/heart), marked with an asterisk in Example 3.2.[79] In the *cauda*, a striking melodic contrast accompanies line 5, "I must indeed sing" (Bien doi chanter), which starts a seventh above the cadence of the second *pes* (marked B in Example 3.2).[80] After this large melodic

---

[77] The melody in Example 3.2 follows *K* 99–100.

[78] See the exhaustive linguistic reading of this song in Zumthor, *Toward a Medieval Poetics*, 147–58.

[79] Particularly given that ten versions of this song survive, the melody is remarkably stable in the *pedes*, showing only ornamental differences that rarely extend beyond a single syllable in all versions except *F*, which has its own, unique melody.

[80] The songbooks vary more in their notation of the *cauda*; however, this leap and extension of the song's range occurs in all versions except for those found in *T* and *F*. See the comparative edition in Van der Werf, *Trouvères-Melodien*, I, 186–93.

Example 3.3 "Quant li estez" by the Châtelain de Couci, st.1

leap, the *cauda* continues in an expansive musical idiom, exploring the full ninth of the song's range.[81] The novelty of the *cauda* melody and its soaring character align the listener's perception of change with the shift to the desire to sing that the speaker describes within the text.

A similar technique can be found in "Quant li estez,"[82] which appears in Example 3.3. In this song, the beauty of springtime causes others to sing but makes the speaker sigh and cry. The recitational *pedes* use lengthy passages of repeated pitches (such as the "a" in syllables 4–10 of lines 1 and 3, marked in brackets in Example 3.3); the melodies used in this section span just a sixth in range. The restrained *pedes* contrast sharply with the speaker's emotional outpouring in the *cauda* on the exclamation "Alas!" (*Las*). Just as he did in "La douce voiz," the Châtelain leaps up a seventh to begin the *cauda* melody

---

[81] This stylistic differentiation between the *pedes* and *cauda* occurs in half of the Châtelain's fourteen songs and correlates strongly with the nature opening. In addition to "La douce voiz" (RS 40), the Châtelain sets the *cauda* to a wider melodic range than the *pedes* in "Li nouveau tens" (RS 985), "L'anque rose" (RS 1009), "Quant li estez" (RS 1913), and "Mout m'est bele" (RS 209), all of which use nature openings. Only two of the Châtelain's songs that use the nature opening do not differentiate the *pedes* and *cauda* through range, melodic contour, or both: "A la doucour" (RS 1754) and "Quant voi venir" (RS 1982).

[82] RS 1913. C 205 (ruled for music, none entered), *M* 55v, *R* 34, *T* 158, and Jakemes, *Roman du Châtelain de Couci*, 87 (2591 ff.).

of "Quant li estez," and the restrained *pedes* are replaced by leaping, arc-shaped melodies, as shown in Example 3.3.[83]

Gace Brulé and the Châtelain de Couci, both active in the earliest decades of the trouvère song tradition, established the nature opening as a vehicle for connecting a sensory experience of the land with the expression of emotion, often through singing. Their influence is evident in the songs of the next generation of knightly songwriters, men such as Thibaut de Blaison. Thibaut was a landowner and sénéchal of Poitou between 1227 and 1229, and he continued to use the nature opening, similarly exploiting musical form to highlight the shift from natural description to the expression of feeling in his songs.[84] Of the ten songs attributed to Thibaut, only "Quant je voi esté"[85] uses the nature opening. Like the others we have just seen, this song positions the description of viewing the greening landscape and blossoming rose in the *pedes* and the speaker's personal emotional expression in the *cauda*. The adverb "adonques" (now) ushers in a torrent of emotion: the subject sighs, cries, laments, and desires. The shift to this emotional outpouring is accompanied by a new melody at the *cauda*.[86] His treatment, like that of other knightly trouvères, aligns the solitary, sensory experience of nature with feeling, uniting land and love in song.

The knightly identity projected in the nature openings of Gace, the Châtelain, and Thibaut was, to a great extent, in alignment with their biographical status as landowners. I wish to shift, now, to knightly songwriters whose biographies seem to fit less comfortably within that identity but who also use the nature opening. The Vidame de Chartres, who, as we saw in Chapter 2, was likely Guillaume de Ferrières, begins his well-loved song

[83] Example 3.3 follows *M* 55v. The melody of *R* is unrelated to that of *M*, *T*, and *U*. Although only small differences in the *pedes* occur in *M*, *T*, and *U*, the *cauda* of *T* uses a different melodic contour than that of *M* and *U*. The *cauda* of *T* is arc-shaped rather than recitational, and, like the versions in *M* and *U*, it explores a broader, range (an octave) compared to its *pedes* (which stay within a fifth). Although the melody differs, the effect is thus similar. For comparison, see Van der Werf, *Trouvères-Melodien*, I, 273–76; and see the Châtelain's similar treatment of the *pedes* and *cauda* in "L'an que rose ne fueille" (RS 1009), ibid., I, 251–59.

[84] Thibaut may also have been a crusader who played an important role in Las Navas de Tolosa in Andalusia in 1212 and participated in the siege of Toulouse in 1218 during the Albigensian Crusade. Some scholars argue that two different men by the name Thibaut de Blaison participated in these battles and that they were father and son. See the discussion of attribution in Newcomb, *Thibaut de Blaison*, 15–20.

[85] RS 1488. See *C* 74v–75r (ruled for music but with lyrics only), *K* 124v–125r, *M* 18r–v, *N* 73v–74r, *O* 116v–117r, *P* 63r–v, *T* 107v–108r, *V* 81r, and *X* 87r–87v.

[86] In the eight songbooks that notate "Quant je voi esté," we find three differentiated melodies, yet all three are in *pedes cum cauda* form, and all place the shift to emotion in the *cauda*, enacting the shift to emotional expression for listeners through a new melody. See Tischler, *Trouvère Lyrics*, X: no.841.

Table 3.4 Transmission of "Quant la saisons" (RS 2086) by the Vidame de Chartres

	Manuscript	Rubric	Music	Notes on Transmission
1.	*a* 21r	Ce sont les chancons le vidame de chartres	Yes	Opening song in author section
2.	*M* 7v	Li vidames de chartres	Yes	
3.	*T* 105v	Li vidame de Chartres	Yes	
4.	*B* 6r	None	Yes	
5.	*K* 179	Li vidame de Chartres	Yes	
6.	*N* 85r	Li vidame de chartres	Yes	
7.	*P* 67v	Vidame de chartres	Yes	
8.	*V* 48v	none	Yes	In a section of songs elsewhere attributed to the Vidame de Chartres
9.	*X* 128r	Le vidame de chart	Yes	
10.	*C* 197r	Messires gaises	No	Staves with no musical notation entered.
11.	*O* 6v and 122v	none		Alphabetical organization. This song is entered as "A la saison . . . " on 6v in the "A" section, and "Quant la saison . . . " on 122v in the "Q" section.
12.	*U* 23v	none	No	Staves; no musical notation entered.
13.	*R* 49r	Li chastelains de Coucy	Yes	

"Quant la saisons"[87] with the nature opening. As Table 3.4 shows, this song was a medieval favorite, appearing in thirteen surviving songbooks. This song opens the author section devoted to the Vidame in the songbook *a*. It was also cited in Jean Renart's romance the *Roman de la Rose*[88] and is found in the oldest portion of songbook *U*,[89] which was compiled during the 1220s

[87] A second song using the nature opening is possibly by the Vidame: "Quant foillissent" (RS 14) is attributed to the Vidame in the *K, N, P, X* group but is also credited to Pierre de Molins (*M* and *T*) and Amauri de Craon (*C*), both contemporaries of the Vidame. Like "Quant la saison" and the songs of Gace Brulé explored earlier, "Quant foillissent" features a nature opening in the *pedes* and positions the shift to feeling and singing in the *cauda*. An account of problems of attribution and the style of the Vidame's corpus, particularly centered around issues of tonal coherence, appears in McAlpine, "Trouvère Musical Style."

[88] Rome, Vat. Reg. 1725, 90v (vv.4127–4140). See Renart, *Romance of the Rose*, 74.

[89] Lug argues that the first 92 folios of *U*, where this song appears, were completed by 1231. See Lug, "Politique et littérature," 452–53.

just decades after the Vidame's death. The song continued to be copied into compendia throughout the thirteenth century and into the early fourteenth.

The Vidame plays in multiple ways with relationships between the lyrics and the *pedes cum cauda form* established in the songs of Gace Brulé and the Châtelain de Couci:

> Quant la saisons del douz tanz s'asseüre,
> Que biauz estez se raferme et resclaire,
> Que toute rienz a sa droite nature
> Vient et retrait, se trop n'est de mal aire,
> Lors chanterai, que pluz ne m'en puis taire,
> Pour conforter ma crüel aventure,
> Qui m'est tournee a grant desconfiture.

[When the season of sweet weather gives way/and beautiful summer sparkles and reaffirms itself/and to its own true nature every thing/comes (unless too much is wrong),/then, I will sing, for I can no longer be silent,/to ease my cruel fate,/which has returned me to great discomfort.]

The nature opening is situated at a moment of seasonal change. The Vidame uses the causal when/then formulation that we saw in songs by his prolific peer Gace Brulé. Here, the causal connection between seasonal change and poetic inspiration applies directly to the speaker, who promises that the change of season will cause him to sing, allowing him to express his emotional distress and find comfort in voicing it. Just as we have seen in other songs by knightly trouvères, the Vidame positions the phrase "then, I will sing" (lors chanterai) in line 5 at the song's *cauda*, ensuring that listeners hear the novel "B" melody set to these words, underscoring our perception of the speaker's shift to song. The statement in line 4 that spring is a time when every thing comes to its true nature implies that for the speaker in this song, turning toward his true nature entails intense feeling, which he must express by singing. The Vidame positions this statement in line 3, playing with the relationship between form and lyrics by aligning the textual sense of turning to one's true nature with the melodic repetition of the "A" melody; the melody literally returns. These relationships are maintained across all twelve of the surviving melodic versions of this song, since each surviving melody is in *pedes cum cauda* form.[90] In all but one of

---

[90] In the six songs that constitute the main corpus attributed to the Vidame, *pedes cum cauda* form dominates; the form is normally maintained even when individual melodies differ from one

Example 3.4 "Quant la saisons" by the Vidame de Chartres, st.1

the surviving songbooks, the "A" melody is recognizably the same, having only minor variations (variations across the *caudae* are more significant).

Example 3.4 provides the rendering of "Quant la saisons" from the songbook *M*, which records "A" and "B" melodies that have very different characters. The song's range is wide, spanning the interval of a ninth. The "A" melody used in the *pedes* meanders in mostly stepwise motion around the pitch "A," reaching its peak a seventh higher on E on the seventh syllable ("tanz"/"droite"), marked with an asterisk in Example 3.4. The end of each phrase in the *pedes* comes to its cadence with a gentle stepwise arc hovering around the pitch A and a cadence that falls by step, giving the "A" melody a gentle and static quality. The cauda melody in begins on C, a fifth higher than the pitch on which the song started and sweeps upward dramatically to the song's melodic apex on G at the end of the phrase "Then I sing" ("lors chanterai"), an octave above the final cadence on G. Line 6 uses a dramatic octave leap on syllable 5 ("ma"), marked with an asterisk in Example 3.4, as the speaker mentions his painful state of emotion ("ma cruël aventure"). As listeners to this version, we perceive the speaker's shift to emotional expression and the act of singing at the *cauda* both

another. In two cases, the melodies used in *V* are through-composed while the melodies found in other songbooks are in *pedes cum cauda* form. See the melodies used in *V* in "Chascuns me sermont" (RS 798), Tischler, *Trouvère Melodies*, VI, no.468 and "Tant ai d'amours" (RS 130), Tischler, *Trouvère Melodies*, II, no.74.

through melodic novelty (after the repetition of the *pedes*) and the sweeping character of the "B" melody.[91]

In "Quant la saisons," the Vidame uses intimate connections between melodic form and lyrical content to intensify ties between the speaker's identity, intense emotion, musical production, and the sensory experience of seasonal change. The songbook *a* records this song at the start of the Vidame's author section, accompanied, as shown in Chapter 2, by the equestrian portrait associated with the knightly classes. The songbook *M* also provides him with a similar knightly author portrait. The strong relationships between song, landscape, and knightly identity in this song by the Vidame are interesting given that the position of "vidame" of Chartres was by nature an urban one. The office was created early in the tenth century so that the bishop of Chartres could have a lay administrator to manage his extensive landholdings and provide him with protection.[92] Rather than being gifted a fief from the bishop, the Vidame was given a house in the city, directly beside the cathedral,[93] and would have spent a good deal of his time in this urban residence. And further, while the Vidames of Chartres had been powerful landholders in the eleventh century through the mid twelfth, Livingstone's extensive research into the property transactions of this family indicates that by the mid-twelfth century, the practice of partible inheritance had strained their finances and weakened their landed base.[94] Guillaume de Ferrières seems to have held less land than his forebears, and his grasp of what land he did hold may have been somewhat more tenuous. The image of the Vidame is nonetheless aligned strongly with landed trouvères like Gace Brulé and the Châtelain de Couci, demonstrating his affiliation with the group identity of the knightly trouvère, an identity with which his biography was in a different alignment.

In these very widely transmitted and seemingly well-loved songs, Gace Brulé, the Châtelain de Couci, Thibaut de Blaison, and the Vidame de Chartres

---

[91] The ascent to G in the *cauda* is unique to the version in *M*; however, the versions in *K, N, P, X, T,* and *O* similarly differentiate the *cauda* by exploring a different, broader range. Within the corpus of songs ascribed to the Vidame, see the similar effect in most versions of "Chascuns me sermon de chanter" (RS 798) in Tischler, *Trouvère Songs*, VI, no.468, "D'amours vient joie" (RS 663), ibid., V, no.387, "Tant ai d'amours" (RS 130) in ibid., II, no.74, and "Tant con je fusse" (RS 502), ibid., IV, no.291.

[92] The vidames of Chartres acquired their office through their capabilities rather than their birth. By the mid-eleventh century, in addition to the bishop, they were vassals of the counts of Anjou and lords of Alluyes-Brou. Livingstone, *Love for My Kin*, 24–26.

[93] Dyggve, "Personnages Historiques," 161–85.

[94] Although Guillaume's uncle, Hugh of Chartres, was a direct vassal of Thibaut III, and thus a member of an elite few who held their land directly from the count of Blois-Chartres, the family's increasingly humble donations to the Church show signs of economic decline. See Livingstone, "Nobility of Blois-Chartres," 381–94.

projected an image of knightly identity that connected song and intense emotion to the sensory appreciation of landscape. This was true even when, in the latter case, the identity projected was tied less clearly to the songwriter's biography. I close with a late engagement with the nature opening: "Quant voi la glaï" by Raoul de Soissons, a strenuous knight who spent years in the holy land, participating in three crusades and most likely meeting his fate in Egypt in the early 1270s.[95] Raoul's songs articulate a model of chivalric identity in which the experiences of battle and love converge directly. The songs include events clearly drawn from his life that attest to his prowess, often directly referring to his time in Outremer. In "E! Cuens d'Anjou," the speaker claims that Amors tested him in Syria and Egypt.[96] His songs twice use variations of the figure of the separated heart,[97] a device common in crusade songs. Raoul even compares his imprisonment in Egypt directly with his metaphorical status as a prisoner of Amors, the God of Love.[98] The nature opening finds new inflection in Raoul's hands, perhaps attesting to differences in his personal relationship to the land. Although Raoul's reputation was of the highest order, he was not wealthy and his ambitions for power, status, and territory were never fulfilled. The nature opening in Raoul's song "Quant voi la glaie" (When I see the water iris bloom) is distinct from those of earlier generations of knightly trouvères in its wistful tone. "Quant voi la glaie" was a medieval favorite, as evidenced by its wide transmission history (summarized in Table 3.5). The song's popularity with compilers and presumably audiences stretched into the first half of the fourteenth century, when it was copied, in a fourteenth-century hand, into the last folio of a manuscript devoted to an Anglo-Norman translation of the books of Samuel and Kings.[99]

---

[95] Raoul fought in the Barons' Crusade (led by Thibaut IV) as well as both of Saint Louis' Egyptian expeditions.

[96] St.3, ll.1–2 or 19–20 (RS 1154). See Raoul, *Die lieder*, 46. Raoul took part in Saint Louis' first expedition to Egypt (1248–1250). He returned to Egypt with Saint Louis' second expedition in 1270 and disappears from medieval documents after 1272. See Griffiths, "Royal Counselors and Trouvères," 134. The fact that Raoul refers to Charles of Anjou as count, rather than king, of Sicily suggests that the lyrics may have been written before Charles' coronation in 1266; some have argued this would mean the song was written upon Raoul's return to France after the first crusade in Egypt. See discussion in Paterson, *Troubadours, Trouvères, and the Crusades*: https://warwick.ac.uk/fac/arts/mode rnlanguages/research/french/crusades/texts/of/rs1154/#page2.

[97] See "Rois de Navarre" (RS 2063) and "Quant je voi fueille" (RS 1978). On the motif of the separated heart in crusade song, see especially Galvez, "The Unrepentant Crusader," chap. 1 in *Subject of Crusade*.

[98] "E! Cuens d'Anjou" (RS 1154). In "Quant je voi fueille" (RS 1978) the lady holds his heart hostage.

[99] Item 13 in Table 3.5 is Paris, Mazarine Library 54, fol.194v (an Anglo-Norman translation of the Books of Samuel and Kings: *Li quatre livre des reis*), where, according to de Lincy, the full first stanza of Raoul's song appears, written in a fourteenth-century hand, on the verso of the last folio; at the bottom of the same page (in a different fourteenth-century hand) is the note "Madame suer Blanche,

Table 3.5 Transmission of "Quant voi la glaie" by Raoul de Soissons

	Manuscript	Medieval Rubric	Melody	Notes on Transmission
1.	*a* 29r	"Me sire" Raoul de Soissons	Yes	
2.	*K* 141	"Me sire" Raoul de Soissons	Yes	
3.	*N* 65v	"Me sires" T de Soissons	Yes	
4.	*P* 85r	"Me sire" Raoul de Soissons	Yes	
5.	*X* 97r	Raoul de Soissons	Yes	Author section begins on fol. 95v with rubric "Ci comencent les chancons mesire Raoul de Soissons"
6.	*V* 118r	None	Yes	
7.	*R* 93v	None	Yes	
8.	*S* 231r	None	Lyrics only	
9.	*F* 101r	"Mesir" Raoul	Yes, erased	Song melody and lyrics erased and overwritten with the Latin responsory "Qui sunt isti qui ut nubes"
10.	*U* 128r	None	No	Space left for melody; no staves or notes provided.
11.	*C* 197v	Perrin d'Angicourt	No	Staves; no notes provided.
12.	Metz 535, fol. 162			Lost
13.	Paris, Bibl. Mazarine 54, fol.194v	None	No	First stanza written in a fourteenth-century hand on the verso of the final folio.

If Raoul's predecessors, knights like Gace Brulé and the Châtelain de Couci, used the nature opening in ways that suggested a landowner's perspective (marked by the masterful, solitary, enjoyment of expansive landscapes), Raoul's nature opening in "Quant voi la glaie" differs from these confident expressions of lordship, presenting images of seasonal cyclicity and decay:

fille de roy de France, (signed) Blanche," an inscription by Blanche, the last daughter of Philippe V, who entered the convent at Longchamp in 1318 and may have been one of the manuscript's first owners. See de Lincy, *Les quatre livres des rois*, xlvi–xlviii. On the identity of Thierri de Soissons (noted in item 5 of Table 3.5), see the discussion in Paterson, *Troubadours, Trouvères, and the Crusades*, "Historical Context and Dating: RS 1204." https://warwick.ac.uk/fac/arts/modernlangua ges/research/french/crusades/texts/of/rs1204/#page2

Quant voi la glaie meüre
Et le rosier espanir
Et seur la bele verdure
La rousee resplendir,
5   Lors souspir
Pour cele que tant desir,
He las, j'aim outre mesure.
Autresi conme l'arsure
Fet quanqu'ele ataint brouir,
10   Fet mon vis taindre et palir
Sa simple regardeüre,
Qui me vient au cuer ferir
Pour fair la mort sentir.

[When I see the water iris bloom/and the sweet rose bloom/and the dew shine/on the greenery,/then I sigh/for the one whom I so desire,/whom I love, alas, beyond measure./Just as the ember/burns everything it touches/ my face changes color and turns pale/just by her glance/which struck me in the heart/to make me feel death.][100]

Raoul's first stanza distills a speaker's emotional reaction to a springtime scene. The description is realistic; the blooming times of irises and roses do often overlap. The reference to water irises, which thrive on the soggy edges of ponds and streams, suggests an expansive, possibly aristocratic, landscape. The banks of streams and small rivers produced the meadowlands that provided the best grazing areas for horses.[101] Such features were carefully preserved when naturally occurring on the landscape and were often created whole cloth; large-scale water features such as fishing ponds were manufactured through elaborate earth works.[102] The speaker in this song also mentions that the blooming rose is sweet, presumably referring to its scent. Raoul's images of spring are pointedly marked as temporal, all soon to disappear. The speaker notes that the greenery shines with dew; dew will soon succumb to evaporation. The blossoms of the water iris are delicate and appear only briefly in late spring. Like irises, medieval roses were a fleeting adornment to the landscape, their beauty and sweet scent ending with the decay

---

[100] The translation is modified slightly from that of Rosenberg, Tischler, and Grossel, *Chansons des trouvères*, 634–39.

[101] Thirsk, *Agrarian History*, 33–34.

[102] Ponds were particularly costly and were often used to separate estates from the lands surrounding them. See Creighton, *Designs upon the Land*, 115.

of the first and only flush of blooms. Drawing on a natural image that is not unknown but is relatively rare in trouvère songs, the speaker compares the lady's effect on his complexion to an ember that burns everything it reaches, another image of fleeting natural transformation.[103] The closing reference to death underscores the ephemeral qualities of the stanza's nature imagery.

As in most of the knightly nature openings I have explored thus far, Raoul's song shifts in line 5 from the description of spring to an ambiguous emotive utterance: "then I sigh." The familiar causal connection ("when/then") suggests that the springtime landscape has turned the speaker's thoughts to love, and the object of his desire. And just as in the songs of Gace Brulé, the use of *pedes cum cauda* form in "Quant voi la glaie" ensures that in line 5, the "A" melody that his listeners have now heard twice accompanying the description of the landscape is suddenly withdrawn and replaced by a new melody; the shift to the speaker's expression of emotion is enacted perceptually through melodic transformation. Example 3.5 provides the first stanza of "Quant voi la glaie."[104]

All of the songs attributed to Raoul use *pedes cum cauda* form.[105] Although it is reasonable to segment this song in the same AAB form we have seen earlier (these segments are marked in Example 3.5), it is an unusual variation of the structures we have seen thus far.[106] The rhyme scheme of "Quant voi la glaie" is rare,[107] shared exclusively with five other songs that were very likely based upon it.[108] In each stanza, the seven-syllable lines are interrupted by a

[103] Compare to Raoul's "Chanson m'estuet et faire" (RS 1267) st.5, ll.41–44.

[104] RS 2107. The example is based on *K*, 141–42. The seven other notated versions of the song all preserve a melody that is recognizably like that of *K*, while including the kinds of minor variations that we have seen in earlier examples. The melodies in *R* and *V* disagree most often with the other versions.

[105] I focus here on the six songs most securely attributed to Raoul: "E! Cuens d'Anjou" (RS 1154), "Sire, loez moi a choisir" (RS 1423a), "Chançon m'estuet" (RS 1267), "Quant je voi fueille" (RS 1978), "Rois de Navarre" (RS 2063), and "Quant je voi la glaie" (RS 2107). It is an open question whether the songs attributed to "Tierri de Soissons" (primarily in *N*) are also by Raoul. See the discussion in Paterson, *Troubadours, Trouvères, and the Crusades*: https://warwick.ac.uk/fac/arts/modernlangua ges/research/french/crusades/texts/of/rs1204/#page.

[106] Gennrich interprets the melody of line 5 as a kind of tag attached to the repetition of the A melody, although he views it as distinct enough to provide it with its own, Greek letter (*omega*). His segmentation of the form could be simplified as AA¹ BB. See Gennrich, *Grundriss einer Formenlehrer*, 212–13. I view the melody attached to line 5 as its own distinct phrase (rather than as an extension of A) because of its length and because of the close repetition of the opening A phrases that precede it. Such repetition is typical of *pedes cum cauda* form and would lead to the expectation that line 5 marked the start of the *cauda*.

[107] a7'b7a7'b7b3b7a7'a7'b7b7a7'b7b7 (MW 962).

[108] A medieval annotation in *C* above one of these other songs (Jacques de Cambrai's "Meire, douce creature," RS 2091), explicitly identifies it as a *contrafactum* of Raoul's song: "Jaikes de Cambrai ou chant de lai glaie menre." See *C* 143r. The most recent discussion of the contrafacta attributed to Jacques is Callahan, "Strategies of Appropriation." The other *contrafacta* of "Quant voi la glaïe" are "Deus, je n'os nommer" (RS 1104), "Aussi com l'eschaufeüre" (RS 2096) by Philippe de Remy, "Vierge des cieus" (RS 2112), and "O clementie" from the *Ludus super anticlaudianum* of Adam de la Bassée.

Example 3.5 "Quant voi la glaie" by Raoul de Soissons, st.1

three-syllable line in line 5, just after the song's *pedes* (lines 1–4; the melodic segments are marked *x* in Example 3.5). The short line that initiates the cauda, "Then I sigh" ("lors soupir"; marked *Y* in Example 3.5) disrupts the poetic form.[109] Poetically, this is evident immediately in the metrical disruption; we hear line 6 as the return of the regularity of the poetic meter. Moreover, the *enjambement* creates additional ambiguities. Is line 5 the end of the sentence begun in line 1? This would mean the speaker sighs in reaction to the landscape. It is only clear once we hear line 6 that the sentence continues through line 8, and that the speaker is sighing for the one he desires. Melodically, line 5 (*Y*) is a singular phrase differentiated both from the preceding melody used in the *pedes* and from the remainder of the *cauda*. Immediately following line 5 are two nearly identical melodies set to verses 6 through 9 and 10 through 13 (these are marked *Z* in Example 3.5). Line 5, "Then I sigh," is a phrase out of time; a pause in the form that exists for the speaker to feel, react, and exhale before describing the causes of his emotion. It becomes clear that the "Then I sigh" melody sits stubbornly in stasis between two lengthy passages of melodic repetition (*XX Y ZZ*). The *Y* passage recurs across the stanzas but is never repeated internally within them, as both the *X* and *Z* melodies are. The

[109] Other examples of this short, interruptive line are discussed in Dragonetti, *Téchnique poétique*, 392–93.

temporality of the moment of feeling is poetic (*Then* I sigh) and underscored musically (a melody outside the form).

Raoul's unusual form underscores the tension in his lyrics between images of the cycle of flourishing and decay and an expression of stasis. The temporality of spring blossoms, which decay quickly within the season but repeat year after year, is both fleeting and enduring. It is akin to the burning ember that represents both the spark of attraction and the smoldering of desire. The ember burns quickly and destructively yet can also smolder under the ash, ready to reignite. Reinforcing the dual temporality of these images, the musical stasis that sets the phrase "then I sigh" suggests the enduring suffering of unrequited love, brought on by the fleeting moment of attraction, that lies at the heart of love songs of this era. Raoul explores the experience of love through two different ways of experiencing time: fleeting, momentary time subject to decay and the enduring natural temporality that projects cycles of growth and decay indefinitely into the future. Plant-life itself demonstrated these ways of experiencing time—the word "season" comes from "serere," "to sow," which is also the root of "semen," "dissemination," and "seminal."[110] The plant and its "life cycle" are a commonplace metaphor wherein germination, growth, flourishing, blossoming, coming to fruition, fermentation, and decay are indicators of time's passage. Plant temporality is linear, extending to infinity after the seed is thrown, projecting life perpetually into the future. It is also cyclical, plant growth and decay occurring seasonally.[111]

The imagery used in "Quant voi la glaie" is marked by both kinds of temporality. Through its unusual form, Raoul's song thus contrasts cyclical flourishing and decay with stasis. The former suggests the fleeting moment of attraction that has since passed, the latter, the enduring suffering of unrequited love. The speaker desires death (cyclical)[112] as a release from his suffering (indefinite). Later stanzas continue to play with these temporal concepts. In stanza 5, the speaker is defenseless against his fears of death, suffering while awaiting her command;[113] in a gesture that parallels the first

---

[110] Marder, *Plant-Thinking*, 102.

[111] Marder, *Plant-Thinking*, 112–13.

[112] See the edition of Rosenberg, Tischler, and Grossel, *Chansons des trouvères*, 634–39. St. 2, ll.16–19: "But it would be better to feel the prick/of a scorpion/and die/than languish in my pain" ("Mes mieus vendroit la pointure/D'un scorpion sentir/Et morir/Que de ma dolour languir"); st.4, ll.51–52: "But I would rather be dead/if I have lost your love" ("Mes bien voeil ester peri/S'a vostre aour ai faille"); and st. 6, ll. 71–72: "I live under a greater suffering/than that which death brings" ("Vif plus dolereusement/Que cil que mort fet estendre").

[113] This stanza appears in *C, S, V,* and *U*, and is not present in *F* or *K, N, P, R, X,* and *a*. In *U*, it is positioned as the last stanza.

stanza closely, waiting ("ainz atent") is positioned in line 5, aligning formal and emotional stasis. The song ends in stanza 6 by cycling back to the image of the burning ember from the first stanza:[114] "But her sweet, tender face/ where all beauty shines,/inflames me and causes me to feel so strongly in my heart/that the coal under the ashes/does not burn more secretly/than the one who awaits mercy."[115] Here, the concealed ember smolders like the speaker's enduring suffering, yet the smoldering coal also has the potential to reignite, sparking the emotions he felt upon seeing his lady for the first time. The sixth stanza cycles back to the first, balancing the fleeting natural imagery with prolongation of the sense of stasis. In this full-stanza *envoi*, the emotionally paralyzed speaker sends his completed song to his lady while he continues to live in a state of suffering (lines 5–6).[116] "Quant voi la glaie" builds on what was then a long tradition of allowing musical form to communicate a shift from the sensation of nature to personal feeling while adding a new temporal dimension that inflects the nature opening with a reflective sensibility.

Emphasizing the relationships between feeling and landscape that had, by the mid-thirteenth century, become a mainstay of the songs of the knightly trouvères,[117] "Quant voi la glaie" not only demonstrates careful observation of and great sensitivity to landscape, seasonality, and natural processes, but also connects these empathetically to the emotions of the singing subject. Coming late in what was by then an established tradition of love songs written by knightly warriors, Raoul's poignant approach to the nature opening seems to reflect elements of his life.

As the second son of count Raoul I of Soissons, Raoul was a landowner (viscount of Coeuvres, near Soissons), but not a wealthy one.[118] Four years after his older brother, Jean II ("le bon") became count of Soissons (in

---

[114] Stanza 6 appears in most of the manuscript versions of the song: *F, K, N, P, R, X, a, U,* and *V.* In *U* it is positioned as the penultimate stanza.

[115] "Mes a douce face tendre,/Ou toute biauté resplent,/M'art si mon cuer et esprent/Que li charbons sous la cendre/N'art pas plus couvertement/Que cil qui merci atent." See Rosenberg, Tischler, and Grossel, *Chansons des trouvères*, st.6 ll.73–75.

[116] The potency of these images was not lost on Philippe de Remi, whose *contrafactum* "Aussi com l'eschaufeüre" (RS 2096) replaces Raoul's burning ember with the heat that makes water boil (lines 1–2).

[117] Raoul's other song to use the nature opening, "Quant je voi fueille" (RS 1978), functions similarly.

[118] Whereas it does appear to describe Raoul to some degree, it is important not to indulge in the stereotype that younger aristocratic sons were carefree "knights errant." Scholars focused on medieval French aristocratic families have dispelled the simplistic formulations of primogeniture, patrilineage, and patrimony upon which such formulations depend. See especially, for Champagne, Evergates, "The Aristocratic Family" chap. 4 in *Aristocracy* and for the Chartrain, see Livingstone, *Love for my Kin, passim.*

1235),[119] Raoul sold his vineyards to finance his trip on the Barons' Crusade and appears to have had little else to sell.[120] Debts and four additional land sales (including the sale of some of his woodlands) are recorded between 1245 and Raoul's second departure for Egypt in 1270.[121] The expense of his expeditions diminished his land, and Raoul also failed to increase it through marriage. Although he wed Alix of Jerusalem, daughter of Queen Isabel of Jerusalem (making Alix a contender for the throne), Raoul would soon abandon his wife and return to France after Conrad, son of Holy Roman Emperor Fredrick II, successfully claimed the throne of Jerusalem in 1243.[122]

Was Raoul writing as the speaker of "Quant voi la glaie"? The time of composition within his life cycle is unknown, yet it does not seem like a song composed in the youthful vigor of a knight in possession of an estate, hopeful that success in Outremer would net him glory and more land. Rather, it seems more like a song written wistfully after many trials and disappointments on crusade, possibly even expressing regret over the wife he abandoned.[123] The song projects a facet of knightly identity (the connection to land) to which Raoul himself seems to have had a more tenuous relationship than other elite trouvères. If the nature opening articulated, for earlier knightly trouvères, an alignment between the enjoyment of land, the experience of love, and, often, the expression of both in song, Raoul's song suggests instead nostalgia for landed ambitions that seem, in the end, to have been largely aspirational.

Not all elite trouvères used the nature opening with the frequency of Gace Brulé and the Châtelain de Coucy or the subtlety of Raoul de Soissons. Indeed, some of the highest-ranking knightly songwriters do not use it in their songs.[124] Although he shows great sensitivity to plant-life[125] and was

---

[119] On the life of Jean II, see Griffiths, "Royal Counselors and Trouvères."

[120] Griffiths, "Royal Counselors and Trouvères," 134. The raising of funds and settling of land issues was a task that even the wealthiest aristocratic crusaders performed before leaving. Lower, "Burning at Mont-Aimé," 95–96.

[121] He borrowed a large sum from Count Thibaut IV. Griffiths, "Royal Counselors and Trouvères," 134.

[122] This episode and Raoul's life cycle are discussed in Griffiths, "Royal Counselors and Trouvères," 133. Raoul's second marriage was to a woman named Comtesse de Hangest, who, while not an actual countess, was from a family in the king's entourage, allowing Roul to become a member of the king's *hôtel*. See ibid., 134.

[123] This reading seems more plausible when we recall that Raoul was not able to remarry until Alix died. See Griffiths, "Royal Counselors and Trouvères," 134.

[124] This is true of Charles II, Comte d'Anjou (who was also King of Sicily and Jerusalem and brother of King Louis IX of France), Jehan I, count of Brittany, and the Duke de Brabant.

[125] See, for example, "Tout autresi con l'ente" (RS 1497), in which Thibaut compares the way in which remembrance causes love to flower to the way falling water nurtures a grafted scion.

capable of composing nature openings with extraordinary elegance,[126] Thibaut IV rarely did so. Still, the well-loved songs I have explored here demonstrate that generations of knightly trouvères used the nature opening to express their connection to the land.[127] The most prolific among them, Gace Brulé, crafted imagery that conjured up the contours of the estate landscapes that were either held by the knightly classes or were the kinds of landscapes to which they aspired. Songs by the Châtelain de Couci, Thibaut de Blaison, the Vidame de Chartres, and Raoul de Soissons similarly valorized a position of solitary embeddedness on and appreciation of the land. Overall, this group of knightly trouvères employed nature imagery realistically and with sentiment, celebrating a causal relationship between sensory experiences outdoors and outpourings of emotion (as well as its direct expression through song). This relationship between landscape and expression unfolds within *pedes cum cauda* form in ways seemingly aimed at generating a felt response on the part of listeners, encouraging them to experience the singing subject's emotional reaction to the landscape vicariously. Further, I showed that knightly trouvères like the Vidame de Chartres and Raoul de Soissons drew on the nature opening and its overtones of rural lordship even when their actual lifestyles were, in the former case, less rural, and in the latter, less materially secure than many of their elite peers.

The songs featured in this chapter were among the most widely transmitted and best loved in the repertoire, some copied and recopied for a century. Whether courtiers encountered these songs in live performance or through the pages of songbooks, they would have served as a key audience for knightly self-presentation.[128] The long dissemination of the song tradition would not only have recorded but likely also fostered a knightly identity in which land, love, and song were intertwined.[129]

In a way that was immersive, memorable, and culturally durable, the nature opening helped to promulgate through song a specific knightly identity.

---

[126] "In honor of the season dividing/winter from summer's rain,/when the thrush, songless for so long,/sings graciously again" (Contre le tens qui devise/Yver et pluie d'esté/Et la mauvis se debrise/ Qui de lonc tens n'a chanté. RS 1620, ll.1–4). Translation follows that of Brahney in Thibaut de Champagne, *Lyrics of Thibaut*, 10–11.

[127] This evidence contradicts Zink's assertion that the springtime opening fell out of fashion and was no longer appreciated. See *Invention of Literary Subjectivity*, 41–45.

[128] On the importance of performance and self-presentation among the knightly classes, see especially Taylor, *Ideals of Knighthood*, 54–55.

[129] The songs are thus broadly consistent with the cultural function of chivalric romances in not merely reflecting society but rather shaping future ideals of what the knightly classes hoped to become. See Taylor, *Ideals of Knighthood*, 9 Kaeuper, *Chivalry and Violence*, 22 and 30–33, and Kaeuper, *Medieval Chivalry*, 21 and 84.

Johannes de Grocheio, the only medieval music theorist to address the reception of trouvère song in any detail, wrote that the trouvère love song was "sung in the presence of kings and princes of the land so that it may move their minds to boldness and fortitude, magnanimity and liberality . . ."[130] His comments are a veritable laundry list of ideal traits prized by the chivalry, indicating that trouvère love songs were directly implicated in the promulgation of the values of the knightly classes.[131] The songs suggest that we might add to these virtues the sensible appreciation of nature and the sung expression of intense feeling. As they were performed, copied, and recopied across generations through decades of preservation and cultural diffusion, works like those explored here surely helped to increase cultural associations between land, love, and song among knightly trouvères and their audiences. After the point of their composition and immediate reception through performance (perhaps by their composers), manuscript copies worked to solidify and memorialize these associations. Moreover, the songs did not passively reflect relationships between people and the landscape. Rather, they would have helped to shape expectations about this relationship, increasing associations between aristocratic identity and the appreciation and enjoyment of woodland and meadowland, for example.[132] Archaeologists have shown that some castle gardens were designed to mimic the landscapes of medieval romances, allowing aristocrats to act out scenes from their favorite narratives.[133] By associating solitary, immersive encounters in non-agricultural natural settings with elite identity, the songs explored in this chapter likely helped to increase demand for the expansive but carefully curated woodlands and gardens that increasingly surrounded castles, a trend that reached its apex with the elaborate Park of Hesdin, created by count Robert II of Artois.[134] In these heavily manipulated outdoor environments,

---

[130] Grocheio even mentions the song "Toute sole passerai le vert boscage," set in the woods, in this context. See the translation by Page in Johannes de Grocheio, "Grocheio on Secular Music," 23. And see especially the discussion of the performance of trouvère song in medieval courts in Page, "Listening to the Trouvères."

[131] See discussion if these ideal traits in Crouch, *The Chivalric Turn*, 67–77, Kaeuper, *Chivalry and Violence*, 145; Kaeuper, *Medieval Chivalry*, 45–47 and 53–54.

[132] Spiegel underscores the role of chivalric texts in generating, not merely mirroring, social realities among the aristocracy. See Spiegel, "History, Historicism." Similarly, Jaeger addresses "the power of chivalric representation to compel identification," arguing that courtly enculturation through romance was dramatically successful in shaping behavior well into the renaissance and beyond. See "Courtliness and Social Change," 308.

[133] Creighton, *Designs Upon the Land*, 33 and 142.

[134] See Crieghton, *Designs Upon the Land*. On Hesdin, see especially Dowling, "Landscape of Luxuries"; Farmer, "Aristocratic Power."

it would have been possible for members of aristocratic families and their guests to enjoy the kinds of experiences valorized in the songs of Gace Brulé and others. These elaborate, designed landscapes proliferated at the same time that so many meadowlands and wooded areas had been claimed by the plow.

The endurance of the chivalric ideal celebrated in the songs and manuscripts explored in this chapter is striking given the social and environmental changes it conceals. Peraino has illustrated how the representation of Thibaut de Champagne in songbook *T* celebrated an image of independent nobility in ways that masked the increasing dominance of royal power.[135] Haines has underscored the ways in which the compilation of *M*, a songbook he convincingly argues was produced as a gift to Guillaume de Villehardouin, prince of Frankish Greece, highlights trouvère-crusaders.[136] Yet by the time this and other songbooks were being compiled, the successes of the twelfth and early thirteenth-century crusaders lay far in the past, and the future would be marked by a dramatic string of French military losses. By the early fourteenth century, the figure of the knightly trouvère was being replaced by that of the clerical court composer, a shift that tracks with the general increase of court clerics and professionals in royal households.[137] Chivalry itself became more stylized, literary, and performative: the statutes of the newly established chivalric orders shadowed the language of thirteenth-century romances, and tournaments functioned as reenactment of a glorified past.[138] The relationship between aristocrats and the land itself also changed over the course of the twelfth and thirteenth centuries. Hereditary tenancies and in-kind payments (holdovers from the manorial system) were gradually replaced by short-term leasing, which was adjustable and therefore more responsive to inflation.[139] Leasing, rather than direct cultivation of the domain, became the dominant way for lords to extract wealth from

---

[135] Peraino, *Giving Voice to Love*, 143.

[136] Haines, "Songbook for William."

[137] This shift mirrors patterns across medieval courts, in which, by the fourteenth century clerics often outnumbered knights. See Vale, *Princely Court*, 31. Peraino argues that this shift is thematized in the compilation of the songbook *T*, which charts the rise of the clerical trouvère. See *Giving Voice to Love*, 127–54.

[138] Keen, "Chivalry and the Aristocracy," 210–12 and 215. Crane vividly demonstrates how late medieval chivalric selfhood depended on the ritual performance of identity. See Crane, "Chivalric Display," chap. 4 in *Performance of Self*.

[139] Van Bavel stresses that leasing did not signal increasing distance between aristocrats and the land. It was simply as a more efficient way to extract wealth from their lands. See discussion in Van Bavel, "Short-term leasing," 197–98.

their lands;[140] lords gained greater financial control over their land while, in some ways, diminishing their direct, agricultural tie to it.[141] The connection between elites and the land also became much less exclusive—the wealthiest merchants and moneylenders from burgeoning towns and cities began to acquire significant land and country estates.[142] This lessening exclusivity of landowning may have been experienced as a slight to knightly status, even if knightly lands did not actually diminish significantly. Elite families also experienced financial pressures in this period stemming from both inflation and overindulgence in luxuries, rendering the position of some less secure. These pressures in the decades around 1300 coincided with the period during which the Medieval Climate Anomaly was unwinding (discussed in Chapter 1). The associated unpredictable and extreme weather conditions contributed to a series of crop failures that resulted in the Great European Famine, which lasted from 1315 through 1322.[143] Although landowners were spared from the famine's worst impacts, they were not immune to it, experiencing economic disruption and making modifications as a result.[144]

Status and identity are cultural constructions that are tied to but not defined exclusively by historical factors such as rank or wealth. As a result, they can be impervious to changing conditions. The wide variety of societal and environmental pressures I have just outlined tended to cause medieval elites to cling more fiercely to their status and to project it more lavishly.[145] As scholars such as Peraino, Spiegel, and Taylor have argued, this reaction helps to contextualize late thirteenth- and fourteenth-century historicist literary activities such as producing vernacular knights' biographies, chronicles, prose versions of thirteenth-century verse narratives, as well as songbooks that celebrate the works of knightly trouvères.[146] Songbook production could thus signal a nostalgic return to the age of knighthood that lay in the heyday of Gace Brulé and the Châtelain de Coucy;[147] the continuing taste

---

[140] Van Bavel, "Short-term Leasing," 186.

[141] When renting through hereditary leases, the lord could no longer sell the land, encumber it, or pass it on to heirs; short-term leases allowed him to extract a fee without these drawbacks. See Van Bavel, *Manors and Markets*, 170–74.

[142] Van Bavel, "Short-term Leasing," 197–98; Fossier, "Arras et ses campagnes," 23.

[143] See Campbell, *Great Transition*, 191, 205.

[144] Jordan, "Cost of Living," chap. 4 in *Great Famine*.

[145] By, for example, restricting tournament participation to those of noble rank. See Kaeuper, *Medieval Chivalry*, 211.

[146] See Peraino, *Giving Voice to Love*, chap. 3; Spiegel, *Romancing the Past*; Taylor, *Ideals of Knighthood*, 3.

[147] Attempts to reform the knighthood during this period are discussed in Taylor, *Ideals of Knighthood*.

for songs that featured the nature opening may have represented an idealization of relationships toward the land that prevailed in this earlier era.[148] The cultural longevity of the nature opening, particularly amid social change, suggests that song played an important role in formulating and articulating an enduring emotional attachment to the land in the self-image of the medieval elite.

[148] Longing for more favorable climatic conditions may even have inflected elite nostalgia—Jordan notes a continuing refrain in chronicles of the famine years lamenting that not even the birds of spring heralded hope. Jordan, *The Great Famine*, 8.

4

In the City

Landscape, Season, and Plant-Life in the Works of Cleric-Trouvères

"Fine hearts must rejoice in all weather."
(En tous tans se doit fins cuers esjoïr.)
Guillaume le Vinier

"The month of May does not give me the desire to sing."
(Ne me done pas talent / De chanter li mois de mai.)
Moniot d'Arras

In Chapter 3, I showed that for many knightly trouvères the nature opening provided a means to communicate a strong, emotional tie to a particular type of landscape—one that held features of the estates knights owned or to which they aspired. The songs were a reflection of an ideal relationship to the land and, moreover, through over a century of composition, performance, and preservation, undoubtedly encouraged cultural associations between land, love, and song as part of knightly identity. The songs explored were widely known and seemingly well loved, transmitted broadly, some across over a dozen or more manuscripts compiled over the course of nearly a century. Moreover, their influence on other modes of vernacular expression was almost immediate. By the 1230s (when the oldest portion of our oldest surviving songbook, *U*, had just been compiled), Guillaume de Lorris appropriated the springtime opening in his *Roman de la Rose*, perhaps imitating it from the songs of early trouvères like the Châtelain de Couci and Gace Brulé.[1] The *Rose*

---

[1] Guillaume de Lorris' *Rose* was once thought to have predated all surviving chansonniers; however, more recent assessments of the dating of *U* (now believed to have been completed by 1231) place the two in close temporal proximity. This reassessment challenges notions that songbook production only later stabilized the melodic identity of trouvère songs and that at the time when Guillaume de Lorris wrote the *Rose*, each trouvère song "does not have textual ancestors and, indeed, does not even have a fixed text or melody; phoenixlike, it is re-created anew with each performance." Huot, *From Song to Book*, 85. On the dating of *U*, see Lug, "Katharer und Waldenser."

Song, Landscape, and Identity in Medieval Northern France. Jennifer Saltzstein, Oxford University Press.
© Oxford University Press 2023. DOI: 10.1093/oso/9780197547779.003.0005

was the most widely transmitted and widely imitated vernacular romance of the thirteenth century; the narration begins with the springtime opening[2] and includes four full invocations of it as the narrative progresses.[3] Guillaume's adoption and amplification of this element of trouvère song is a testament to influence on literary mentalities by the second quarter of the thirteenth century. In turn, the *Rose* would serve as a catalyst for the still broader cultural dispersal of the nature opening and the particular way it configured a human relationship with landscape.

Yet as we see in the quotes above by Moniot d'Arras and Guillaume le Vinier,[4] the nature opening was not adopted by all trouvères in ways that mirrored the songs of Gace, the Châtelain, and others. And in this chapter, I aim to show that it resonated quite differently in the songs of a specific group of trouvères—those who, in addition to writing vernacular songs, were also clerics. Clerics were prominent and productive participants in the trouvère song tradition from its beginnings, active as early as the decades around 1200 alongside better-studied knightly trouvères such as Gace Brulé and the Châtelain de Couci.[5] Although literary scholars have focused on the way romance authors fused the first-person "lyric voice" of trouvère song with themes of bookmaking and authorial strategies drawn from clerical discourses,[6] the question of how the nature opening was treated by trouvères who were themselves clerics has not yet been explored.[7] The composers featured in this chapter were ordained priests, university masters and students, as well as educated men who led secular lives. With some important exceptions, most of these cleric-trouvères had strong ties to urban areas where the topography in view would have been quite different from that described in the nature opening of the knightly classes. Not all songwriters used the nature

---

[2] By situating the story in the first-person past of the author-protagonist's own dream (which he promises to gloss in the manner of a scholarly commentary), Guillaume de Lorris deftly intermingled the first-person experiential voice we saw in the songs explored in Chapter 3 with the past-tense narration adopted by clerical romance authors who claimed to translate their stories from classical texts. See Uitti, "From *Clerc* to *Poète*," 209–16 and Huot, "Singing, Reading, Writing," chap. 3 in *From Song to Book*.

[3] Hult, *Self-fulfilling Prophecies*, 210.

[4] Guillaume le Vinier, *Les poésies*, 130 (RS 1405) and Moniot d'Arras, *Moniot d'Arras*, 75 (RS 739).

[5] Those who have explored the participation of clerics in the trouvère corpus tend to associate these authors with the second half of the thirteenth century as part of a shift toward urban, bourgeois, or clerical contexts. See, for example, Räkel, *Die musikalische Erscheinungsform*, 135–37 and 259–61.

[6] Huot influentially argued that the fusion of clerkly and "lyrical" (meaning performative, song-like, or related to song) discourse was thematized in medieval French manuscript compilation and illustration, resulting in a new kind of author figure. See *From Song to Book*, passim.

[7] Peraino argues that the compilation of *T* foregrounds the voice of a clerical lyric subject. See *Giving Voice to Love*, 146 and 153–54.

opening in the same ways,[8] yet we will see that on the whole, the resonances this particular kind of nature imagery held for many of the cleric-trouvères appears to have differed from composers of the knightly classes.[9]

In this chapter, I show that nature opening is simply not a mainstay of the extant song corpora by cleric-trouvères, and when it does appear in clerical vernacular songs, the speaker's response is often marked by irony or distance. After demonstrating that many trouvères who were clerics eschewed the nature opening, I explore the way some clerical songwriters, such as Simon d'Authie and the motet composer Petrus de Cruce, invoke it with irony and distance. This same stance is evident in the musical interpolations that the Parisian chancery cleric Chaillou de Pesstain interpolated into a copy of the *Roman de Fauvel* (fr.146). In other cases, including songs by Gilles le Vinier and a motet by Philip the Chancellor, the clerical songwriter rejects the nature opening while positing modes of engagement with arboreal life that remain intensely personal but are directed toward different aims.

Rejecting the Nature Opening in Clerical Song: Adam de la Halle, Moniot d'Arras, Richard de Fournival

Many of the cleric-trouvères active during the late twelfth and thirteenth centuries never used the nature opening.[10] This includes the best known and most prolific among them, Adam de la Halle—none of Adam's thirty-six love songs use the nature opening.[11] Further, some of Adam's songs self-consciously circumvent the formulation we have seen in which sensory experience in nature prompts feeling or song. In "Je sench em moi," Adam adopts the verb *renouveler* (renews), which is strongly associated with

---

[8] I would be loath to situate the nature opening as a universal trope found across the trouvère corpus writ large with little variation as do, for example, Dragonitti, *Technique poétique*, 183–93 and Dembowski, "Old French Courtly Lyrics."

[9] These findings will run counter to claims that clerical trouvères appropriated aristocratic sentiment from the knightly trouvères. See Huot, *Song to Book*, 60.

[10] This constitutes perhaps the clearest evidence that the trouvères did not imitate the nature opening from classical literature, since the cleric-trouvères, of all vernacular songwriters, would have been the best acquainted with such sources.

[11] The closest Adam comes to invoking it may be in "Li dous maus" (RS 612), which begins "Li dous maus mi renouvelle/Avoec le printans," however, Adam inverts the position of spring and the description of his emotional reaction, and he merely mentions, without describing, spring. See Adam de la Halle, *Oeuvres complètes*, 60. The most recent and most comprehensive account of Adam's love songs appears in Ragnard, "Songs of Adam."

seasonal change.[12] Yet the speaker does not describe the springtime or credit its delights with emotion or the urge to sing. On the contrary, the speaker simply declares that he feels love renew within himself, denying the role of external stimuli and fully internalizing his creative process: "I feel renew in myself the love/that before made me feel the sweet pain/which made me sing of desire;/thus my song is reborn—it comes back." Adam fully circumvents the role of nature in prompting feeling or song; what is renewed and causes him to sing is not the season but rather a love fully internal to the speaker.[13] Adam also playfully alludes to the springtime opening in an *envoi*, a passage occurring at the end of some trouvère songs in which the speaker directly addresses the lady or a patron, or simply dispatches the song into the world. Adam's speaker calls out to the months of April and May, personifying them as messengers: "Ho! Gentle May and April,/the sweet place is closed to me:/make it so that my song will be heard and sung there!"[14] Here, the speaker situates himself as spatially distant from the "sweet place" of spring (the invocation is also poetically distant from its traditional position at the song's beginning). The months serve as synecdoche for the full nature opening, which is absent. Indeed, the speaker is not moved to emotion or song through an experiential, immersive encounter with a landscape in this or any of Adam's other songs. Nor is Adam alone among the cleric-trouvères in this regard. Pierre de Corbie, a canon of the cathedral of Notre Dame d'Arras active during the late twelfth century, avoids the nature opening,[15] as does Adam de Givenchi, an ordained priest and administrative cleric active in the mid-thirteenth century.[16] Clerical trouvères such as Oede de la Corroierie, Jehan de Grieviler, Jacques d'Amiens, and Gaidifer d'Avions also avoid the nature

---

[12] On the verb "renouveler" in the nature opening, see Dembowski, "Old French Courtly Lyrics," 768.

[13] St.I, ll.1–4: "Je sench em moi l'amour renouveler,/Ki autre fois m'a fait le douch mal traire,/Dont je souloie en desirant canter,/Par coi mes cans renouvele et repaire" (RS 888). Adam de la Halle, *Oeuvres completes*, 57. Like most of Adam's songs, the form (here, in all surviving manuscripts) is *pedes cum cauda*; see Ragnard, "Songs of Adam," 210.

[14] St.VI, ll.51–54: "Hé! Tres dous mais et avriex,/Devees m'est li dous liex:/Faites que mes cans oïs/Y soit et dis!" See "Si li maus c'Amours" (RS 1715). Adam de la Halle, *Oeuvres completes*, 108.

[15] See Guesnon, "Recherches Biographiques," 422–24.

[16] Adam de Givenchy worked for the bishop of Arras first as a clerk then as a priest and chaplain, and later served as dean of Lens. See Guesnon, "Recherches Biographiques," 425–27. His corpus of eight songs includes two *descorts* and a *jeu-parti* composed with the cleric-trouvère Guillaume le Vinier and judged by the cleric-trouvère Pierre de Corbie, "Amis Guillaume" (RS 1085). Adam also names himself as the author of "Bone Amour" (RS 112), which the surviving manuscripts mistakenly credit to the song's recipient rather than its author. See Guillaume le Viniers, *Les poésies*, 239–44.

opening entirely. Richart de Semilli and Guibert Kaukesel each use it only once.[17]

Moniot d'Arras, a trouvère who flourished during the second quarter of the thirteenth century and who seems to have been (judging by his name) a lapsed monk, was one of the most prolific of the cleric-trouvères, his songs widely transmitted.[18] Moniot used the nature opening in three of the fifteen songs that were credited to him.[19] Yet his nature openings differ significantly from those by the knightly trouvères that I explored in Chapter 3. As we saw at the start of this chapter, the speaker of Moniot's song, "Ne me done pas," matter-of-factly rejects the premise of the springtime opening, stating simply that May does not give him the urge to sing. In two of his songs, the speaker begins with the nature opening, yet instead of the perception of nature directly inspiring love or song, he assigns direct agency for his emotional state to the God of Love.[20] Moniot's song "Li dous termines" begins with a lengthy, evocative springtime opening in which the subject expresses his love of springtime, when meadows blossom, greening woods leaf out, and birds sing at all hours through the bushy copse.[21] Rather than springtime prompting emotion or song, however it reminds the subject of his distance from his beloved, who resides in a different land:

> Li dous termines m'agree
> Del mois d'avril en pascour,
> Ke voi le bois et la pree
> Cargier de foille et de flour
> 5   Et ester en verdour
> Et j'oi chanter nuit et jour

---

[17] Richart de Semilli is identified as a cleric in some songbook author rubrics; his lyrics, which frequently mention Parisian landmarks, suggest he resided in that city. Guibert Kaukesel was a cantor from Arras.

[18] Although we know nothing of the historical identity of this "little monk from Arras," Guillaume le Vinier refers Moniot's stage in the cloister in their *jeu-parti*. See "Moines, ne vous anuit pas" (RS 378).

[19] I adopt as the corpus of Moniot that established by Dyggve in his edition, *Moniot d'Arras et Moniot de Paris*. I have excluded those songs Dyggve published in his edition but convincingly argued were of "uncertain attribution." These songs are associated with the songbook *H*, a manuscript that attributes to Moniot d'Arras an unusually large corpus of songs that are elsewhere credibly attested to others. See Dyggve's comments in ibid., 126–27.

[20] See "A l'entrant de la saison" (RS 1896, st.I, ll.5–7), Moniot d'Arras, *Moniot d'Arras*, 113; and "Quant voi les pres florir" (RS 1259, st.I, ll.2–3), Moniot d'Arras, *Moniot d'Arras*, 111.

[21] RS 490. This song appears in the oldest portion of *U* (c.1231) as well as *K, M, N, R, T, V*, and its lyrics are found in *H* and *I*. For comparison of all versions, see Tischler, *Trouvère Lyrics*, IV, no.281.

> Oiseaus par broelle ramee.
> *Mais* joie eüsse grignor
> Se je fuisse ens la contree
10   Ou cele maint que j'aor.

[The sweet season pleases me/of the month of April at Eastertide,/since I see the woods and fields/bear leaves and flowers/and be green/and I hear singing night and day/birds through the branching copse./*But* I might have had more joy/if I had been in the country/wherein she whom I adore dwells.][22]

Moniot does not use the when/then (quant/lors) formulation we saw in many of the songs explored in Chapter 3 (*when* the speaker observes natural phenomena, *then* they begin to feel and/or sing). The shift from the speaker's description of nature to its impact on him is occurs after the oppositional "but" instead of the causal "then."[23] Further, what follows is not an emotional reaction but a hypothetical musing in which the subject wonders whether his joy might have been greater if he had been with his lady in a different landscape—that of her "country." Feeling, rather than being a direct reaction to sensory experiences in nature, is hypothetical. The imperfect subjunctive mood of his turn inward is self-consciously counterfactual and thus markedly different from songs in which the nature opening presents an immediate, immersive, present-tense encounter with nature that directly causes feeling or song. In the hands of Moniot d'Arras, the nature opening lacks the generative powers it held for many knightly trouvères; the speaker's emotional reactions are deflected to the God of Love or projected back into a wished-for past, not prompted by experiences in the landscape.

The songs of Guillaume le Vinier, a prolific trouvère and married cleric active in Arras in the second quarter of the thirteenth century, also communicate a distanced relationship between landscape and feeling.[24] He actively writes against the kinds of nature openings found in the extraordinarily popular and widely transmitted songs by Gace Brulé and others that I explored

---

[22] Text edition follows that of Dyggve in Moniot d'Arras, *Moniot d'Arras*, 104. Translation my own.

[23] There are four distinct melodies for this song found across its eight surviving manuscripts; all are in *pedes cum cauda* form. See Tischler, *Trouvère Lyrics*, IV, no.281. The nature opening is not coordinated with the *pedes cum cauda* form, as it was in the examples explored in Chapter 3. "Mais" begins line 8, in the middle of the *cauda* that begins on line 5.

[24] Guillaume was held in high esteem; the songbook *M* features his author portrait at the head of a gathering that credits him with a large corpus of twenty-eight songs. See Haines, "Songbook for William," 94–95. In contrast to other cleric-trouvère portraits explored in Chapter 2, Guillaume is depicted regally, seated on a Dante chair and attended by a squire. See *M*, 105r: https://gallica.bnf.fr/ark:/12148/btv1b84192440/f227.item.

Chapter 3. As seen the beginning of this chapter, Guillaume's song, "En tous tans," begins not with a nature opening, but rather, with a proclamation that true hearts should rejoice in *all* weather, rejecting the generative role played by seasonal change, and springtime in particular, in prompting feeling and expression in many trouvère songs.[25] Further, in Guillaume's song "Li louseignoles avrillouz," the speaker argues: "But fine, desirous lovers, held firmly and tight, do not have joy from the beautiful month, nor from sweet songs, nor foolish joys, nor rose, nor lily."[26] Guillaume uses the nature opening in "La flours d'iver," but here the subject is so pleased to contemplate the snow on a branch during winter that Amors, the God of Love, visits him with a new memory and he is prompted to sing.[27] Although the urge to sing follows the contemplation of the snow-covered branch, the God of Love serves as an additional force encouraging the speaker.[28] In Guillaume's song "Flours ne glais," the speaker denies that true lovers are encouraged by flowers, lilies, or birdsong and underscores the power of Amors, rather than nature, in inspiring him.[29] We find a similarly ironic approach toward the seasonal opening in the songs of Richard de Fournival, who was chancellor of the cathedral of Amiens. Richard was one of the most prolific of the cleric-trouvères and a significant vernacular author in many genres.[30] Rather than inspiring the speaker to feel or compose, in Richard's "Quant je voi," for example, seeing the sweet season of summer and hearing birdsong cause the speaker's madness to return. In a cerebral play on the nature opening, the speaker in Richard's song "Quant chant oisiaus" hears birds singing in the flowering bushes and is prompted to remember a pleasure for which he had always hoped but never experienced except in thought, relegating experience to the realm of imagination.[31] As Friedrich Wolfzettel argued, in contrast to

---

[25] St.I, l.1: "En tous tans se doit fins cuers esjoïr" (RS 1405). See Guillaume le Vinier, *Les poésies*, 130.

[26] St.II, ll.6–10: "Maiz les fins amanz desirroux,/Ferm et estroit pris/N'esjoïst biauz mais ne chans douz,/Gaus foillous/Ne rose ne lis" (RS 2042). Translation follows Pfeffer, *Change of Philomel*, 132–33.

[27] St.I, ll.1–4: "La flours d'iver sour la branche/Mi plaist tant a remirer/Ke nouvele remembrance/Mi doune Amours de chanter." Guillaume le Vinier, *Les poésies*, 72.

[28] These verses all fall within the song's *pedes*; the language of the *cauda* (lines 5–9) is general rather than personal: "Ciaus ki sont sous sa puissance/Voel loer,/Et ciaus haïr et blasmer/Ki sans grievance/S'en sevent plaindre" (RS 255). Guillaume le Vinier, *Les poésies*, 72.

[29] RS 131. Guillaume le Vinier, *Les poésies*, 119. See the discussion in Pfeffer, *Change of Philomel*, 133–34.

[30] The most systematic account of Richard's life and works is found in the unpublished dissertation Johnson, "Music at the Cathedral of Amiens," 282–383. Richard's authorial persona, which blends clerkly and lyric elements, is discussed in Huot, *From Song to Book*, 138–41.

[31] RS 1080. This song is through-composed; it does not align formal change with the shift between the natural imagery and the speaker's personal expression. For a modern edition, see Tischler, *Trouvère lyrics*, VII, no.623.

the classic formulation in which a trouvère sings of his desire in the present tense, Richard's lyrics often resemble "a spiritual exercise in which an 'I' seeks to convince itself and console itself by relying on hope."[32]

Is there a relationship between land and identity in the songs of cleric-trouvères? The careers of these trouvères span the late twelfth through the late thirteenth centuries, and their association with the urban centers of Paris and cities in the north, are conspicuous. Richard de Fournival was very likely educated at the University of Paris, and Adam de la Halle claimed to have been.[33] Richard spent much of his life in the city of Amiens.[34] Adam spent much of his in Arras, as did many of the other cleric-trouvères mentioned earlier, who were also associated with Arras: Pierre de Corbie, Adam de Givenchy, Gilles le Vinier, and Guibert Kaukesel, Jehan de Grieviler and Guillaume le Vinier.[35] Gaidifer d'Avion may have resided in Cambrai.[36] Oede de la Corroierie was a truly cosmopolitan figure. A Parisian who became a very highly compensated clerk to count Robert II of Artois, Oede travelled to Rome as a diplomatic emissary on several occasions.[37] Expansive estate landscapes like those conjured up in the songs of Gace Brulé were not readily at hand in these urban centers, which (as I noted in Chapter 1) were surrounded by the miles of provisioning hinterlands that supplied them with food. Grainfields, vineyards, and coppices would have been a much more common sight than meadows or woodlands. This is not to say that urban clerics had no contact with nature. Paris was a densely populated metropolis dominated by hard-packed earth, paved roads, dense buildings, and few green spaces. In Amiens, however, the economic importance of woad (a plant used in dyes that grew wild in the river valleys upstream of the city) necessitated the conservation of the nearby meadowlands.[38] Arras was divided between

[32] "la parole se fait exercice spirituel d'un moi qui cherche à se convaincre et à se consoler lui-même en s'appuyant sur l'*esperanche*." Wolfzettel, "Au carrefour de discours," 59.

[33] On the extant documentation of Adam's life, see especially Symes, " 'School of Arras,'" 28–32.

[34] A papal bull dated 1239 also lists Richard as a canon of Rouen (although it is not known whether he resided there) and as chaplain of Cardinal Robert of Somercote. By 1241, he is identified as chancellor of the cathedral of Amiens, a position he seems to have held until his death in 1260. See Johnson, "Music at the Cathedral," 288–92.

[35] Pierre de Corbie, Adam de Givenchy, Guilles le Vinier, and Guibert Kaukesel were all secular clerics associated with the Cathedral of Notre Dame d'Arras; Jehan de Grieviler and Guillaume le Vinier were minor clerics who lived in Arras.

[36] Gaidifer d'Avions is designated "cleric" in the table of contents of manuscript *a* (but not the internal author rubrics). See Dyggve, "Chansons françaises," 181–83. Guesnon argued that the trouvère Gaidifer was the "Gautier d'Avions" who was canon of Cambrai and, in 1250, provost of Saint-Géry. See Guesnon, "Recherches biographiques," 148–49.

[37] See Spanke, "Die Gedichte," 163–66.

[38] See Johnson, "Music at the Cathedral," 23.

the episcopal city and the town and was unevenly densely populated.[39] The town, where Adam de la Halle and other married minor clerics like Jehan de Grivieler and Guillaume le Vinier probably lived, was packed with buildings. But the episcopal city, where the cathedral canons and clerks to the bishop such as Adam de Givenchy, Gilles le Vinier, or Pierre de Corbie would have spent much of their time or even resided, was far less urbanized.[40] Further, urban clerics did not necessarily spend all of their time in the city; canons, for example, were often required to be in residence only half the year.[41] Those who served bishops may have enjoyed access to portions of the episcopal urban gardens and perhaps also their luxurious country estates, which often rivalled those of the secular lords. Richard de Fournival owned his own garden in Amiens. He called his *Bibliomania* (an organizational guide to his massive personal library) the "key to his garden," which he conceptualized in separate "plots" for philosophy, medicine, and theology; his stated intention in this work was to "plant a garden in his native city where one could discover and savor the fruits of philosophy."[42] Nonetheless, rejecting the nature opening and its alignment between sensory experience, feeling, and poetic production was a poetic stance Richard shared with a significant number of other urban cleric-trouvères. The continuity of their posture is conspicuous and is hard to justify as mere happenstance.

The Nature Opening and Chaillou de Pesstain's Additions to the *Roman de Fauvel* (fr.146)

There are continuities between the way cleric-trouvères responded to the nature opening and the way it is treated in the songs interpolated into a celebrated copy of the *Roman de Fauvel* (fr.146) that was produced by royal chancery clerks in Paris. *Fauvel* is a satirical animal allegory written by Gèrvais du Bus in 1314, which tells the story of a horse named Fauvel, whom Lady Fortune elevates from the stable to the throne. When Fauvel has

---

[39] On the division of Arras between the Episcopal City and the Town (under the jurisdiction of the Abbey of Saint-Vaast) see Berger, *Littérature et société*, 55–87 and Symes, *Common Stage*, 31.

[40] See the description in Berger, *Littérature et société*, 25–32.

[41] This was true in Amiens; see Johnson, "Music at the Cathedral," 62. Many clerics (particularly those who ascended in the church hierarchy) also came from aristocratic families and thus spent their childhoods on estate landscapes.

[42] Johnson, "Music at the Cathedral," 288. See Ibid., 304.

the audacity to attempt to woo Lady Fortune as his bride, she instead weds him to Vaine Glory and their offspring go on to defile the "garden of France." The character of Fauvel represented Enguerrand de Marginy, a minor noble who enjoyed a meteoric rise to the position of royal chamberlain under King Philip IV and was hanged for bribery in 1315.[43] The message of the allegory was seemingly directed at the Capetian royal family as an admonition against bad counselors. Between 1314 and 1317, the Parisian cleric Chaillou de Pesstain dramatically enlarged and expanded Gèrvais' story with 169 musical elements that are inserted within the narrative.[44] Chaillou seems to have authored some of these musical elements; others he drew from liturgical chant and the works of other composers including perhaps Philipe de Vitry. The treatment of the nature opening in Chaillou's additions to the *Roman de Fauvel* resonates strongly with the posture we just saw in the songs of urban cleric-trouvères and the distanced relationship it articulated between identity and landscape.

In spite of the expansive generic range of Chaillou's musical insertions, trouvère song is a conspicuous absence in the interpolated *Fauvel*.[45] The most appropriate place for it might have been Fauvel's first attempt to court Lady Fortune; instead, he makes his request through a series of anti-courtly *ballades*.[46] Fauvel makes his attempt to woo Fortune through a series of interpolated *lais* that encompass his first request, her negative response, and his dejected lament; a final *lai* condemns Fauvel's attempt to pose as a courtly lover.[47] It is in these *lais* that the nature opening appears, and in each appearance, the references are parodic. A *lai* is a lengthy musical genre using (normally) around a dozen stanzas that each have their own textual

---

[43] See Bent and Wathey, "Introduction," 9–10.

[44] Although he was clearly a highly educated cleric associated with the Royal Chancery, the historical identity of Chaillou de Pesstain remains a matter of informed speculation. The prevailing theory is Lalou, "Chancellerie royale," 307–19.

[45] Page rightly notes that the absence cannot be explained by declining interest in trouvère song since the compilation of fr.146 was coterminous with the copying of several important trouvère songbooks. See Page, "Tradition and Innovation," 357.

[46] "A vous douce debonaire," for example, strips the eloquence of trouvère requests for love to their barest culminating elements and, through dialogue, directly interlaces Fortuna's rejections (Rosenberg and Tischler, *Monophonic Songs*, 56–58). On Chaillou's parodic representation of Fauvel as an anti-courtly lover in this sequence, see Brownlee, "Authorial Self-Presentation," 79. On the song's musical features and models, see Plumley, *Art of Grafted Song*, 68–72.

[47] So argues Lecco, who interprets the images of Fauvel leading accompanying the first three *lais* alternate between depicting Fauvel's human and equine face according to his duplicitousness, working to underscore Fauvel's status as a false courtly lover. She sees the illustration of all four *lais* and their narrative placement as a programmatic condemnation of Fauvel's attempt at courtship. See Lecco, "Per un'interpretazione," esp. 203–5 and 210–12.

and musical form.[48] Only the *lai des hellequines* "En ce dous temps" begins with the nature opening, and this song is performed during a raucous chari-vari (a parade that served as a public protest against second marriages)[49] in a parodic inversion of its role in trouvère song.[50] In the heartbroken *lai* "Talant que j'ai d'obeïr" in which Fauvel laments his rejection by Lady Fortuna, trouvère nature imagery is replaced by innuendo.[51] In the *lai* "Pour recouvrer allegiance," Fauvel situates the discourse of the nature opening as lost to him, declaring "my situation has been turned upside down/just as if summer were turned into winter!" (st.3, ll.27–29).[52] Love is not prompted by an experience in a landscape—rather, summer is simply synonymous with being in love.[53] In the sixth stanza, Fauvel similarly elaborates: "For love of her I used to love/roses and flowers,/woods and verdure/and springtime,/ all pleasure, all joy."[54] The speaker's posture toward the nature opening is most striking in the song's close. In this *lai*, the meter, rhyme scheme, and melody of the first stanza are repeated in the last. In the first stanza, Fauvel had bypassed the nature opening, declaring simply that he would compose a *lai* to relieve his pain. The parallelism between the first stanza and the second half of the final stanza (where Fauvel alludes to the nature opening) is notable, as Table 4.1 shows.[55]

The already pronounced parallelism of these stanzas is amplified by their shared music. Fauvel's lament that he is far from his lady (st.1, ll.3) and his request that Love bring them together (st.13, ll.152) share the same stan-zaic position and thus the same melody. In the final stanza, Fauvel projects

---

[48] In some, but not all, *lais*, the final stanza repeats the form of the first, sometimes transposed to a different pitch level. See the extensive treatment in Fallows, "Lai," *Oxford Music Online*. https://www-oxfordmusiconline-com.

[49] On the *charivari* scene in *Fauvel*, see Regalado, "Masques réels," 116–26; Huglo, "Contexte folklorique"; Dillon, *Medieval Musicmaking*, 20 and 238–40; and Lecco, "Lo *charivari*."

[50] A modern edition appears in Rosenberg and Tischler, *Monophonic Songs*, 131–42.

[51] Fauvel says Fortuna's sweet mouth smells better than a flower in the bush: "Mieus flaire que fleur en brueil" (st.3, ll.45–46). In the edition of this song in Rosenberg and Tischler, *Monophonic Songs*, 58–69, at 65, "brueil" is imprecisely translated as "woodland."

[52] This *lai* has attracted significant attention, largely due to its apparent paleographical status as a later addition to the manuscript. See the most recent review of literature in Lecco, "Per un'interpretazione." Dillon makes a case for the careful paleographical integration of the folio on which the *lai* appears. See her "Art of Interpolation."

[53] The melody in this stanza is expansive, descending downward through melodic sequences a range of a ninth, and punctuated conspicuously by the song's first long melismas (which are rare overall). See the modern edition in Rosenberg and Tischler, *Roman de Fauvel*, 106–15, at 108.

[54] St.6, ll.43–47: "Je souloie amer pour s'amour/roses et flour,/bois et verdour/et temps paschour,/ tout deduit, toute joi." Rosenberg and Tischler, *Roman de Fauvel*, 111.

[55] The text edition and translation follow Rosenberg and Tischler, *Monophonic Songs*, 110–14, here at 114.

Table 4.1 "Pour recouvrer alegiance," From Stanzas 1 and 13

St.1, ll.1-7

Pour recouvrer allegiance	To find relief
Des maus que je trai,	from the woes that I have,
En tant que fais elloingnance	while I am far
De celle en qui j'ai	from the one whom I desire
Mis mon desir de cuer vrai,	with a true heart,
Ferai en sa remembrance	I shall in remembrance of her compose
Piteus lay.	a moving lay.

St.13, ll.150-56

Pour ç'amour sanz decebrance	Therefore I beg Love, honestly
Proi au mieus que sai	and as well as I can,
Que de nous deus l'acordance	to bring the two of us together,
Face, et lors serai	and then I shall be
Jolis plus qu'oisiaus en mai	merrier than a bird in May
Et vous en bonne Esperance	and will serve you
Servirai	in full confidence

emotion into a conditional future and indicates that as long as Amors fulfills his request, he will be capable of imitating the happiness that springtime (invoked through synecdoche as "the month of May") prompts in the birds. His proposed bargain has little in common with the nature openings of the knightly trouvères, and further, Fauvel saves the allusion for the song's close, inverting its expected poetic position. Fauvel alludes to the language of the nature opening throughout this *lai* (and other musical interpolations Chaillou assigns to him), yet he never fully voices it. Fauvel's posture toward the nature opening suggests Chaillou's understanding of the knightly identities with which it was especially associated. That it does not function properly in Fauvel's songs underscores Fauvel's lack of knightly status. It is interesting, too, to note that Chailou's own identity as (presumably) a chancery cleric would also have differed from that of the royal and princely audience toward which his book was directed. In a long authorial speech marked with a rubric stating, "So speaks the author" (ci parle l'aucteur), Chaillou describes hearing birdsong at dawn and provides a veritable buffet of springtime topoi. As Brownlee explains, this section is modelled directly on Guillaume de Lorris' *Rose* (and the trouvère songs on which it was based), and it prepares the reader to expect Chaillou to voice a first-person love song.[56] Instead, the

---

[56] See Brownlee, "Authorial Self-Representation," 85–88.

author states that youths languish in love as a result of the season, casting the emotional reaction that should result from his own first-hand experience of spring in the third person and transferring it to others from whom he is disconnected. Chaillou thus self-consciously adopts the voice of the clerkly narrator in a way that recalls the songs of the urban cleric-trouvères explored earlier.[57]

Could it be merely a coincidence that the nature opening is absent, effaced, or treated with irony by Chaillou and by so many cleric-trouvères? This relatively large group of educated, mainly urban composers whose careers collectively spanned over a century seem to have adopted a similar posture toward the nature opening in their songs. Was the alignment between nature, emotion, and song that many knightly trouvères embraced simply unsuited to the self-image of a cosmopolitan, clerical songwriter? Or was expressing distance from nature part of an authorial posture that such men adopted in their songs as an expression of clerical identity, or to signal their difference from the knightly trouvères? Recall that knightly trouvères used the nature opening to communicate dominion over large tracts of land in ways that articulated their identities as fief holders (or fief aspirants). The projection of such a self-image may not have been relevant to the songwriters considered here.

Landscapes and Plant-Life in the Songs of Simon d'Authie and Gilles le Vinier

Cleric-trouvères were not monolithic in their treatment of nature imagery; Simon d'Authie and Gilles le Vinier took a different approach to those explored above. These two men were active during the second quarter of the thirteenth century, in the generation after trouvères like Gace Brule. They clearly knew each other; both were prominent clerics who led distinguished careers, and both were jurists.[58] Simon was based in Amiens; he was university educated canon and was elected to dignity of dean of the

---

[57] Chaillou's rejection of the *Rose* by Guillaume de Lorris (and its fusion of courtly lyricism with the clerical mode of the romance narrator) as an authorial model is direct. Chaillou inverts several of Guillaume's key rhyme words in this section. See Brownlee, "Authorial Self-Representation," 88.

[58] Simon also held the dignity of dean of the cathedral chapter of Amiens. The earliest archival mention of Simon lists him as a *magister*, indicating his possession of a university degree. See Johnson, "Music at the Cathedral," 255.

cathedral chapter in 1226. His considerable legal skills were in demand; he travelled frequently to Arras and Paris.[59] As I noted in Chapter 2, Simon and Gilles found themselves on opposite sides of a legal dispute over the placement of a street altar in Arras. Gilles' activities in Arras are well attested.[60] As a trouvère, he participated in three *jeux-partis* that were each composed with other cleric-trouvères. In two of these debates, Gilles was partnered with his brother, the prolific and celebrated cleric-trouvère Guillaume le Vinier. These debates between the brother clerics very widely transmitted.[61] The significant collection of *jeux-partis* found in manuscript *b* opens with these two songs accompanied by a fitting image of the brothers debating each other dressed in long, clerical robes.[62] In Gilles' third *jeu-parti*, he debated his fellow jurist Simon d'Authie. Their vernacular song contest was memorialized in a portrait in *A* of the two clerics, tonsured and dressed in long clerical robes as they debate each other. Simon wrote a rich and varied corpus of songs, several of which were transmitted widely, as Table 4.2 shows. The manuscript rubrics rarely omit his title "maistre."

Simon d'Authie used the nature opening in four of his love songs. One of these songs operates in a pattern very similar to songs featured in Chapter 3 in which composers positioned the shift from the description of nature to emotion or expression at the point of musical change within the *pedes cum cauda* form. Although Simon does not use the when/then formulation we saw in other songs, he does situate the shift to emotional expression at the *cauda*, the locus of musical change:[63]

---

[59] The documentation of Simon d'Authie's life is discussed in Johnson, "Music at the Cathedral," 255–63. Of the fourteen songs are attributed to Simon, eleven are likely his. The conflicting attributions found across the manuscript transmission of these songs is discussed in Gennrich, "Simon d'Authie," 55–57.

[60] Gilles was canon of Lille in 1221 and became canon of Arras between 1225 and 1232. He acceded to the priesthood prior to April 12th, 1243. See Guesnon, "Recherches biographiques," 430–32; Gennirch, "Simon d'Authie"; and Berger, *Littérature et société*, 416–17.

[61] "Sire frere" (RS 691) is transmitted in *A, G, M, T, R, Z, a,* and *b*; "Frere, qui fait mieus" (RS 1293) is transmitted in *A, C M, R, T, Y, a,* and *b* (where it is wrongly attributed to the King of Navarre). *I* transmits one stanza only.

[62] Although the two are not tonsured, their dress and posture (one uses the raised pointing finger associated with lecturing) mark them as clerics. See *b* 139v (149v): https://digi.vatlib.it/view/MSS_Reg.lat.1522.

[63] Both *M* and *T* provide a melody in *pedes cum cauda* form; the variations between the melodies are very minor. See Tischler, *Trouvère Lyrics*, V, no.361.

Table 4.2 Song Corpus of Simon d'Authie

RS #	Title	Manuscripts	Attributions	Genre
487	Bone amour qui m'agree	*M* (ToC), *T* 37r, *a* 67v; *U* 106r (lyrics only), *C* 29r (staves only)	"Maistre" Simon d'Authie (*M*, *T*) in Simon author section in *a*; Gautier d'Espinal (*C*)	Love song
665	Fols est qui a ensient	*M* 124r (partial), *T* 168v; *I* 149v; *C* 81v	"Maistre" Simon d'Authie (*M*, *T*)	?
183	Li biaus estés	*M* 33r, *T* 39r	"Maistre" Simon d'Authie (*M*, ToC; *T*); "Me sire" Gace (*M*)	Love song
1802	Li nouviaus tens	*M* 124r, *T* 39r	"Maistre" Simon d'Authie (*M*, *T*)	Love song
1460	On ne peut pas	*M* (ToC), *T* 36v, *a* 67r; *K* 185, *N* 88v, *X* 132r, *P* 73v	"Maistre" Simon d'Authie (*M* in ToC; *T*, *a*); Raoul de Ferrieres (*K*, *N*, *P*; in group by Raoul de Ferrieres in *X*)	Love song
1415	Quant je voi le gaut	*M* 123r (end only), *T* 37r	"Maistre" Simon d'Authie (*M* ToC, *T*)	Love song
623	Quant la sesons comence	*M* 123r, *T* 38r	"Maistre" Simon d'Authie (*M*, *T*)	Love song
1381	Quant li dous estés	*M* 123r, *T* 37v; *U* 62v	"M." Simon d'Authie (*M*), "Maistre" Simon d'Authie (*T*)	*pastourelle*
525	Tant ai amours servie	*K* 223, *N* 107v, *P* 105v, in a lost part of *X*; *M* 123v, *T* 38v; *C* 242r	"Maistre" Simon d'Authie (*M*, *P*, *T*); Simon d'Authie (*K*, *N*); King of Navarre (*C*)	Love song
572	Maistre Simon	*A* 145r, *a* (ToC); *b* 160v	Gilles le Viniers to "Maistre" Simon d'Authie (*b*)	*Jeu-parti*
289	Symon, le quel emploie	*b* 169v	Hue to Symon (*b*)	*Jeu-parti*
1818	Symon, or me faites	*b* 170r	Hues li Maronniers to Simon d'Authie (*b*)	*Jeu-parti*

pes:

Quant la saisons conmence
Del novel tanz en mai,

pes:

Que toute rienz s'agence
Et naist la flour el glai,

cauda:

D'amour, dont je sui en esmai,

Ai encore esperance . . .

[When the season begins/in the new weather in May,/when every thing softens itself/and gives birth to the flowers in the place where the lilies grow,/ about love, from which I am in great sorrow,/I still have hope. . . .][64]

In Simon's song "Li biauz estez," however, he underscores separation between the landscape described in the opening and the emotional state of the speaker. In line four, the speaker states "I *should* be joyful" as though nodding to the common association between springtime and joy in such songs:

pes:

Li biauz estez se resclaire

Que nest l'erbe verdoians,

pes:

Que flours et fueille repaire,

Donc *deüsse estre* joianz;

cauda:

Maiz pour cele sui dolanz

Ou il n'a rienz que reprendre. . . .

[Beautiful summer shines again/which gives birth to the green grass,/ and makes flowers and leaves reappear,/then *I should* be joyful;/but I am mournful for the one/who is irreproachable. . . .][65]

Both of the manuscripts that transmit this song provide it with melodies in *pedes cum cauda* form;[66] Simon positions the description of summer in the *pedes* and the shift to the speaker's emotion in the *cauda*. However, he introduces the speaker's expression of emotion with the oppositional "but" (maiz).[67] The shift to emotion occurs at the start of the *cauda*, as we saw in other songs. Yet Simon

---

[64] RS 623. Text edition follows Tischler, *Trouvère Lyrics*, V, no.361. Translation my own.

[65] RS 183. Text edition follows Tischler, *Trouvère Lyrics*, II, 105. Italics added for emphasis. Translation my own.

[66] RS 183. This song is in *M* and *T*. While both melodies are in *pedes cum cauda* form (preserving the relationship between the lyrics and the musical structure), the cauda differs significantly between the two versions. A modern edition of this song can be found in Tischler, *Trouvère Lyrics*, II, no.105.

[67] Dragonetti notes the distance suggested by the word "maiz" in this song, but he wrongly attributes it to Gace Brulé (presumably because the table of contents of *M* lists it in Gace's section) even though the author rubric attached to the notated song in *M* assigns it to Simon. Dragonetti argues, based on this incorrect attribution, that this song demonstrates Gace's opposition to the "external convention" of the nature opening, a position out of keeping with the songs explored in Chapter 3. See Dragonetti, *Technique poétique*, 188.

does not use *pedes cum cauda* form to highlight a generative relationship between nature, sentiment, and song. Here, the *cauda* disassociates the speaker from such songs, the melodic change coinciding with and perhaps amplifying the perception of the speaker's distance from the scene he has described.[68] His use of the nature opening is thus mixed, adopting approaches we saw in the songs of knights as well as the clerical songs explored earlier.

Gilles le Vinier composed a rich and varied corpus of seven songs, which appear in Table 4.3.[69] Two of these songs use the nature opening, and Gilles' approach to it is, like Simon's, mixed.

Table 4.3 Song Corpus of Gilles le Vinier

RS #	Title	Manuscripts	Attributions	Genre
1928	A ce m'acort	*M* 136r (beginning missing), *T* 83r	Giles li viniers (*M* and *T*)	Descort
257	Amours qui	*M* 136, *T* 102v	Maistre Giles li viniers (*M*)	Love song
1280	Biaus m'est prins tens	*M* 136 (beginning missing), *T* 102v; *C* 34v	Maistre Gilles (*T*)	Love song
2101a	Au partir de la froidure	*M* 136r (beginning missing), *T* 102r	Maistre Gilles li Viniers (*T*)	Love song
572	Maistre Simon	*a* (ToC), *A* 145r; *b* 160v	Gilles le Viniers a Maistre Simon d'Authie (*b*)	*Jeu-parti* with Simon d'Authie
691	Sire frere	*M* 112r, *T* 31v, *a* 134r (beginning missing), *A* 145v; *b* 150r (lyrics only); *R* 25v; *Z* 52v; *G* no.7 (lyrics only)	"Maistre" Guillaume le Vinier (*M*); "Maistre" Guillaume "maistre" Gilles le Vinier (*T*); Guillaume le Vinier to "frere" (*b*); "Frere" to King of Navarre (*R*)	*Jeu-parti* with his brother, Guillaume le Vinier
1293	Frere, qui fait mieus	*A* 146v, *M* 111r, *T* 31r, *a* 135v; *b* 149v; *R* 26r; *C* 79v (Guillaume le Vinier); *I* 188r (one stanza); *Y* no.2	"M." Guillaume le Vinier (*M*); "Maistre" Gilles and "maistre" Guillaume le Vinier (*T*); King of Navarre to "frere" (*R*)	*Jeu-parti* with his brother, Guillaume le Vinier

[68] The other two songs in which Simon uses the nature opening are through-composed. See "Li noviaus tans" (RS 1802), Tischler, *Trouvère lyrics*, XII, no.1036, and "Quant je voi le gaut" (RS 1415), Tischler, *Trouvère lyrics*, IX, no.799.

[69] His corpus of eight songs is significant and modern scholars have drawn attention to his formal inventiveness. Although the crusade song "Aler m'estuet" is attributed to Gilles in the *KNPX* group, internal dedications suggest the more likely author was Hue, the Châtelain d'Arras, as *T* indicates. See "RS 140: Historical Context and Dating," in Paterson, *Troubadours, Trouvères, and the Crusades*. https://warwick.ac.uk/fac/arts/modernlanguages/research/french/crusades/. Gilles' *descort* "A ce m'acort" (RS 1928) is one of only eleven songs in this Old French genre. See Spanke "Sequenz und lai." On the *descort* genre, see especially Peraino, *Giving Voice*, 77–81.

In Gilles' "Au partir de la froidure," seasonal change directly prompts emotional expression (in this case, the speaker laments his misfortune in love).[70] Although we have now seen this relationship many times, this song is otherwise highly unusual—its form has been compared to a rare, virtuosic genre called the *descort*, and it uses a panoply of special rhymes including echo-rhymes:[71]

> Au partir de la froidure
> Dure,
> Que voi apresté
> Esté,
> 5   Lors plains ma mesadvanture.
> Cure
> N'ai éu d'amer;
> Car amer
> Ai sovent son gieu trouvé.
> 10   Prove
> Ai soventes fois:
> Male fois
> Fait par tout trop a blasmer.

[At the end of the cold/harsh,/since I see coming/summertime,/then I bewail my misfortune./Remedy/I never had from love/for I have often found its game bitter./Tested/it I have many times./Bad faith/is to be blamed everywhere.][72]

The playful convergence between phonic similarity and semantic difference in Gilles' rhymes is an outward display of self-conscious artfulness and planning. Even as the content remains similar (seasonal change prompts emotion), it strikes the ear very differently than the knightly songs I explored in Chapter 3, where the conceit was often that the song arose spontaneously in reaction to the landscape, seemingly in real time.[73]

---

[70] RS 2101a. Although in *pedes cum cauda* form, this song does not align the shift to emotion or expression with the musical shift to the cauda, as did many of the songs I explored in Chapter 3.

[71] This song (MW 401) uses: leonine rhymes, paronym rhymes, homonym rhymes, rhymes of derivation, and echo rhymes. It shares its highly unusual meter and rhyme scheme (although not its melody) with only two other songs: "Touse de la ville" (RS 957) by Robert of Reims and "Mere Dieu" (RS 556) by Gautier de Coinci (who was also a cleric). Gilles also uses echo-rhymes in "Amours qui" (RS 257).

[72] Text edition follows Tischler, *Trouvère Lyrics*, VIII, no.1199. My translation. I am grateful to Eliza Zingesser for her assistance.

[73] Cf. Peraino, *Giving Voice to Love*, 76–77.

Example 4.1 "Biaus m'est prins tans" by Gilles le Vinier

In the second song in which Gilles uses the nature opening, "Biaus m'est prins tans,"[74] he is careful to make sure that his listeners do not assume that the speaker's experience in nature is what inspires thoughts of love or the song that they are hearing. Here, the description of seasonal change prompts the speaker to declare that he does not have a changeable heart, but rather, he always loves with his entire heart, meaning his sentiments are not dependent on the season. Gilles' song is in *pedes cum cauda* form, and he places the speaker's insistence on his unchanging heart in line 5 at the *cauda*, the moment of musical change (marked "B" in Example 4.1). The relationship between musical form and the content of the lyrics is thus in playful tension, poetic constancy set against musical change. Was Gilles aware of the way trouvères like Gace Brule and others I explored earlier often aligned the shift from observing nature in the *pedes* to feeling and sometimes singing in the *cauda*? Was Gilles actively writing against this formal device by insisting, at the moment of musical change, on his unwavering heart? This song also features an internal refrain of three syllables that always ends on the word "change" (*cangier*). In the sixth line of each stanza, this word-refrain

---

[74] RS 1280. A modern edition of the two melodies with which it is associated appears in Tischler, *Trouvère lyrics*, VIII, no.727.

interrupts the otherwise uniform decasyllabic lines. The song's unique poetic form is 10 ab'ab' b' 3A 10ab'. The surrounding lyric context of each stanza (and often, the word that precedes *cangier* within the stanza) causes the meaning of the word-refrain to shift throughout the song. The stanzaic melody and the word-refrain *cangier* continually repeat while the meaning of the refrain is perpetually changing as it reappears in each subsequent stanza's new lyrics. The melody and lyrics of the first stanza appear in Example 4.1.[75]

> I
>
> Biaus m'est prinstans au partir de fevrier,
> Ke primerole espanist el boskaige.
> Adont me vient fins talens d'envoisier,
> Plus k'en iver au felon tans sauvaige.
>
> 5   Non pas por cou ke j'aie cuer volaige
> Por *cangier*;
> Car tos jors aim et serf de cuer entier
> Et amerai tos jors ens mon eaige.

[At the end of February, spring is beautiful to me,/when the privet blooms in the woodland./Then comes to me the high desire to take pleasure,/more than in winter during the cruel, savage weather./Not because I have a fickle heart/—that *wavers*—/for always I love and serve with my entire heart/and I will love always for my whole life.][76]

The imagery of the nature opening continues in the second stanza, which is highly unusual in trouvère songs. It is here, in stanza II, that nature and personal feeling are brought into a poetic relationship, but Gilles does not use the formulation we have seen in which the sensory perception of nature inspires amorous feeling; instead, the speaker draws on an extended analogy, comparing the increase of feeling within his already full heart to the emergence of new spring growth on the laurel tree. Just as the evergreen laurel (already in leaf) flushes with still more delicate, new green growth during spring redoubling its leafy greenness, so love, revived in the speaker's heart, causes his suffering to grow. The shift from the speaker's description of the doubly green laurel to the way love redoubles his suffering occurs at the *cauda* (stanza 2, line 5). As Example 4.1 shows, the cauda's "B" melody thus

---

[75] Based on *T* 102v–103r.
[76] Translation my own. I thank Eliza Zingesser for her assistance.

coincides with line 5, where the song compares the natural image and the analogous experience in the speaker. Gilles' use of the term "iretage" (heritage) to describe the laurel's evergreen leaves surely betrays his work as a jurist, where that term, signifying a perpetual interest, was commonplace in wills and charters.[77] The elegance of his analogy might, too, be a reflection of his Latinate education, where analogies were a valued argumentative technique.

II

Tot ensement com il est del laurier,
Ki foillis est et vers a iretaige,
Plus finement commence a verdoier
Et rafreschir au tans ke rasouaige,
5   Si raverdist amors ens mon coraige
Sans *cangier*,
Fors tant k'adés se paine d'enforchier,
Et ke plus croist, plus doble mon malaige.

[Just as the laurel/that is in leaf and perpetually green/begins to green more delicately/and refresh itself in the calming weather,/thus revives love inside my heart/—without *changing*—/except that it always tries to grow/and the more it grows, the more it doubles my suffering.][78]

How might this song and the evocative way in which it aligns experiential musical structures with feeling and plant-life relate to Gilles le Vinier's own relationship to the natural world? As a clerk to the bishop of Arras, Gilles would have spent much of his time in the episcopal city. The Cathedral of Notre Dame and bishop's palace were adjacent to a leafy park, and the canons' houses were located inside it. Did Gilles enjoy lingering in the wooded, urban park next to the of the Cathedral of Notre Dame d'Arras? This park was quite large, home to a population of deer and rabbits and full of trees.[79] Did he there observe, and feel a connection to, the new spring growth on the laurel? The laurel, or Sweet

---

[77] Godefroy, *Dictionnaire*, IV, 463–64. Medieval exegetes associated evergreen leaves with the word of God, as represented by the leaf on the Tree of Life that does not wither. See Robertson, "Doctrine of Charity," 30.

[78] RS 1280. The text edition follows Gilles le Vinier, *Die lieder*, 40–41. I thank Eliza Zingesser for her assistance with my translation.

[79] This, we can surmise from the bishop's complaint in 1395 that the too-prolific rabbits and deer were the reason that the trees all needed to be replaced. See Duceppe-Lamarre, *Chasse et pâturage*, 85–86.

Bay Tree, had been naturalized in western Europe since Roman times and was rarely excluded from the plant lists of medieval horticultural treatises. It would have been present in Northern French woodlands.[80] Gilles, moreover, was a landowner. Surviving documents record his purchase and donation of significant tracts of land: he donated land in Wanquetin to the Church; he also donated two homes inherited from his parents to the abbey. Toward the end of his life, in 1248, he exchanged another plot of land for an annuity of wheat and oats.[81] It is interesting to witness the different relationship between landscape and identity that Gilles' songs project, compared not only to those of many of the knightly trouvères, but also to most of his fellow cleric-trouvères. While demonstrating careful observation of the growing patterns of plant-life and a positive disposition toward springtime, the speaker of "Biaus m'est prins tans" rejects the notion that his feelings are influenced by the changing seasons. Instead of drawing on the landscape as a source of inspiration or being directly moved to emotion by it, Gilles' speaker uses his observation of the laurel as a means for understanding and explaining the workings of his own heart; the natural world serves as an impetus for reflection and analogical thinking. Moreover, rather than projecting emotional attachment to expansive landscapes or dominion over them, the speaker's posture toward plant-life emphasizes small-scale detail and intimate, inward connection.

The Nature Opening and the Motet: Trees of Virtue and Trees of Vice

I have shown that in their songs, most of the cleric-trouvères did not connect the sensory and emotional appreciation of sweeping landscapes to identity. I now turn to a polyphonic musical repertory that many view as a site of clerical reception and commentary on vernacular song: the motet.[82] Most motets were created by layering different combinations of lyrics, melodies, and quotations of other songs over preexisting portions of liturgical polyphony or plainchant.[83] By combining diverse materials into a harmonious whole,

---

[80] See Harvey, *Medieval Gardens*, 30 and 168.

[81] See Berger, *Littérature et société*, 416.

[82] Others have explored the way in which motets comment on other genres of song. See, for example, Huot, *Allegorical Play*, 10 and Curran "Hockets Broken."

[83] The diversity of ways in which motets were composed is described in Everist, *French Motets* and Bradley, *Polyphony in Medieval*. Motets with vernacular tenors are discussed in Everist, "Motets, French Tenors." On motets transmitted without tenors, see Peraino, "Monophonic Motets."

motet composers could create amusing, parodic, or spiritually instructive juxtapositions.[84] The repertoire of hundreds of individual motets is preserved with near total anonymity in large motet collections;[85] however, when other sources occasionally attribute motets to an individual author, they normally credit a cleric, for example, Adam de la Halle, Petrus de Cruce, or Philip the Chancellor.[86] Scholars have long thought that in the case of the anonymous motets, the most likely composers and performers were clerics, particularly the minor clerics who were employed to sing the Parisian liturgical polyphony with which many motets are intimately connected.[87] Polyphonic motets are associated with the cities of the north such as Paris, Amiens, Cambrai, and Arras, areas where education levels were high.[88] Urban themes and scenery crop up in motet lyrics such as *On parole de batre*,[89] where the speaker of the triplum voice declares his preference for the pleasures of Paris over the toils of country life: "One speaks of threshing and winnowing,/Of digging and cultivating,/But these pleasures quite displease me,/For the only good life is to take one's ease/With good, clear wine and capon,/And to be

---

[84] The classic study of these juxtapositions is Huot, *Allegorical Play*.

[85] Everist suggests this tendency toward anonymity likely reflects the multiple authors whose hands left their mark on any given motet. See *French Motets*, 6.

[86] The first men credited with sacred polyphony were all *magistri* or had progressed to the rank of archbishop or bishop. See Wright, *Music and Ceremony*, 273. Five motets are included in the section of manuscript *W* among Adam de la Halle's complete works. Jacques de Liège credits Petrus de Cruce with two motets that are transmitted anonymously in *Mo*; see Huglo, "De Francon de Cologne." Medieval sources that attest to Philip the Chancellor's corpus of as many as eight motets. See Payne, *Philip the Chancellor*, xiii–xv. There is also a significant corpus of motets in which one of their voice parts is transmitted elsewhere as a trouvère song and attributed to an author. Saint-Cricq notes that clerics (Adam de la Halle, Moine de Saint-Denis, Richard de Fournival, Moniot d'Arras, Gautier de Coinci, and Guillaume le Vinier) dominate the attributions connected to this corpus. See Saint-Cricq, "Genre, Attribution, and Authorship," 187.

[87] See Page, *Owl and the Nightingale*, 144–47 and Wright, *Music and Ceremony*, 25. Although her recent study importantly revises older understandings of the mechanics of how motets were connected to liturgical polyphony (in many cases, reversing the order of influence), Bradley concurs with and indeed strengthens arguments made by Page and Wright that Parisian clerics were the motet's most likely composers. See *Polyphony in Medieval*, 250.

[88] On the cathedral of Notre Dame in Paris as a center for polyphonic performance and composition in the twelfth and thirteenth centuries, see Wright, *Music and Ceremony*. The major motet collections *Mo*, *Ba*, and *Cl* all seem to have been produced in Paris. The corpus of motets associated with areas other than Paris are discussed in Saint-Cricq, "Motets in Chansonniers." Among these other centers, urban areas still dominate. Amiens was also a center of polyphonic performance; Johnson uncovered references to two now lost manuscripts of organum connected to the cathedral. See Johnson, "Music at the Cathedral," 173 and 488. Motets tied to the city of Cambrai are discussed in Bradley, "Intertextuality, Song," chap. 7 in *Polyphony in Medieval*. The songbooks *M* and *T* both were produced in Arras and both transmit motets; the contents of *T* have particularly significant ties to Arras. A trove of motet lyrics appears in the Lorraine songbook *I*; on this manuscript, see especially Leach, "Adapting the Motet(s)?" and "A Courtly Compilation."

[89] For a study that positions songs and motets of this era within the rich sonic tapestry of medieval Paris, see Dillon, "Sound and the City," chap. 2 in *Sense of Sound*.

with good friends."[90] Some motets feature nuns and monks involved in amorous escapades.[91] Motets are full of quotations, allusions, and formal parallels
to other lyric genres; many bring such materials into contrast with an excerpt
of liturgical chant serving as their lowest voice.[92] Often, the commentary that
is implied through the juxtaposition of the nature opening with other topics
and genres is marked by parody, irony, and a self-conscious effacement of the
spontaneity that the nature opening communicated the songs of the knightly
trouvères. In their stance toward the nature opening, motets thus resemble
the songs of many of the cleric-trouvères explored earlier.

Vernacular motet composers seem to have drawn from the gamut of
themes, topics, and genres of the vernacular song traditions of their day, but
the love songs (and their nature openings) are not the best represented.[93]
Some motet parts refer to the nature opening directly as a poetic device,
invoking it in a writerly way as an opening gambit: the motet voice *Cest
quadruble*, for example, begins: "I did not compose this quadruplum for no
reason in a season during which even birds dare not sing."[94] The reference to

---

[90] Ll.1–6: "On parole de batre/et de foïr et de hanner;/mais ces deduis trop me desplaisent,/car
il n'est bone vie que d'estre a aise/de bon cler vin et de chapons/et d'estre aveuc bons compaignons"
(904). Edition and translation follow Stakel and Relihan, *Montpellier Codex*, 109. In place of a liturgical tenor, this motet voice is undergirded by an Old French market cry: "Frese nouvele, muere
France, muere, muere france!" See the discussion of this and other urban-themed motets in Dillon,
Sense of Sound, 86–90. A group of six motets include discussions of the pleasures of urban life
among a community of friends, two alluding to the status of the group as a confraternity. See Everist,
"Friends and Foals," 348–50.

[91] On motets involving monks and nuns, see especially Colton, "Articulation of Virginity" and
Clark, " 'S'en dirai chançonnette.' "

[92] The interpretation of motet lyrics within their polyphonic musical context has a long pedi-
gree stemming especially from foundational studies such as Everist, *French Motets* and the essays
in Pesce, *Hearing the Motet*. Much of the subsequent research is synthesized in the essays in Hartt,
Medieval Motets. Recent studies of the thirteenth-century vernacular motet have approached the
genre through questions of audibility and intelligibility (see Clark, " 'S'en dirai chançonnette' "), links
to devotional practices (Rothenberg, *Marian Symbolism*), sound studies (Dillon, *The Sense of Sound*),
connections to trouvère song (Saint-Cricq, "New Link"), and compositional process (Bradley,
Polyphony in Medieval), as well as intertextuality (Plumley, *Art of Grafted Song*).

[93] When the nature opening appears in motets, it often introduces a *pastourelle* vignette. On the diversity of poetic types in the motet repertoire and the relatively limited representation of the trouvère
love song, see the instructive remarks in Everist, *French Motets*, 154–58. There are motet voices that
feature abbreviated versions of the nature opening that reflect the alignment between sensation of
the landscape and feeling or song. See, for example, the motetus voice of *Sens penseir* (890)/*Quant
la saisons* (891)/*Qui bien aime*, the content of which is amplified by its triplum and vernacular tenor.
This motet is unique to the early fourteenth-century motet codex *Tu*. For a modern edition, see Auda,
Motets Wallons, II, 85–86. This motetus voice is also transmitted in *I, O, V,* and *U* as a vernacular song
(RS 505). On motet voices that are also transmitted as vernacular songs, see especially Saint-Cricq,
"Genre, Attribution, and Authorship."

[94] Ll.1–3: "Cest quadruble sans raison/n'ai pas fait en tel season/qu'oisel chanter n'ose" (798).
Translation modified slightly from Stakel and Relihan, *Montpellier Codex*, 8. A similarly self-
conscious reference the nature opening is found in *Le premier jour de mai* (521), ll.1–6: "At the beginning of May/I finished /this cheerful quadruplum/for at this time of year, lovers are/gallant and

the term for the motet voice part itself (the "quadruplum" is the top voice in a four-part motet) draws attention to the motet as a finished artistic product[95] and, specifically, a measured, polyphonic song that would have required careful planning. The motet composer situates the moment of composition squarely in the past, invoking the notion of being inspired by nature through a playful negation.[96] One of the more prominent of the known composers of the vernacular motet was Petrus de Cruce, a university-educated senior cleric who, by 1301 at the latest, was serving in the retinue of Bishop Guillaume de Maçon and lived at the episcopal palace near the cathedral of Amiens.[97] Petrus was a notable music theorist and the author of at least two vernacular motets with lyrics written in the style of trouvère love songs.[98] His two motets have long been viewed as stylistically distinctive, both featuring triplum voices in which the rhythmic unit of the breve is subdivided to such a degree that the top voice dramatically exceeds the motetus and tenor parts in its rhythmic activity and sheer number of notes. The resulting stratification has the effect of expanding the motet's time scale.[99] In Petrus' motet *S'Amours eüst* (600)/*Au renouveler* (601)/*Ecce[iam]* (M84), the motetus voice begins with an abbreviated reference to the nature opening: "At the rebirth of the joyous season,/I must begin a song."[100] He continues in a mode we have

joyful./But I found myself/distressed in love . . ." (Le premier jour de mai/Acordai/Cest quadruble renvoisié,/Car en cest tans sunt amant/Cointe et lié./Mes je me truis/D'amors desconseillié . . .), text and translation from Stakel and Relihan, *Montpellier Codex*, 9, and see the discussion in Dillon, *Sense of Sound*, 18–22. Compare also to *Au tans Pascor* (136), ll.1–10: "At Eastertide/most all those who sing because of the greenness and the flowers/lead a life of joy and gaiety./And I sigh and cry/when I feel the sorrow/which stays with me in cold weather/and in warm" (Au tans Pascor/Eminent joie et baudor/Tuit li pluisor/Qui chantant pour la verdor,/Por la flor./Et je, qui souspir et plor,/Quant sui a dolour,/Qui me dure/Par froidure/Et par chalour . . .), text and translation from Stakel and Relihan, *Montpellier Codex*, 68.

[95] Dillon draws attention to the way the use of "cest" (this) positions the motet part as no longer a product of the interior imagination but as a thing for others to behold. See Dillon, *Sense of Sound*, 22.

[96] I provide a more detailed reading of this motet in my *Refrain and the Rise*, 65–68.

[97] Johnson, "Music at the Cathedral of Amiens," 488.

[98] The motets are featured prominently as the first two in the seventh fascicle of *Mo*.

[99] Petrus is credited with a rhythmic innovation that modern scholars call "Petronian semiminims" in which the breve can be subdivided into four to seven semibreves. It is Jacobus who describes the practice and attributes it to Petrus in his *Speculum musicae*, citing this motet (where only subdivisions in four occur) as well as *Aucun ont trouvé* (106)/*Lonc tens* (107)/*Annuntiantes* (M9), in which Petrus subdivides the breve into groups of five, six, and seven semibreves. The citation appears in Jacobus Leodensis, *Speculum musicae*, VII, 36–37; the most recent reassessment of the dating of the *Speculum musicae* appears in Zayaruznaya, "Old, New." On Petronian style, see the lucid discussion in Desmond, *Music and the moderni*, 126–30; the musical language of the two motets directly attributed to Petrus as well as those written in a similar style (and possibly also by him) receives extensive and careful treatment in Maw, "Art of Diminution."

[100] Ll.1–2: "Au renouveler du joli tans/M'estuet commencier chançon" (601). Translation from Stakel and Relihan, *Montpellier Codex*, 81.

seen in the songs of other cleric-trouvères, by stressing that the cause of his impulse to begin his song is not seasonal change, but rather Amors.[101] This motetus voice is juxtaposed with the significantly more rhythmically active triplum melody, which utters a long-winded complaint about his torment by Amors and the fruitlessness of his suit. The lyrics are set syllabically to the heavily subdivided melody, resulting in a triplum that registers as a profusion of words.[102] Maw argues these subdivisions have the effect of imbuing Petronian tripla with an improvisatory immediacy as well as a sense of novelty;[103] the comparatively stodgy motetus *Au renouveler* is at a stylistic disadvantage in the competition for a listener's attention. Layering the motetus subject's song under the triplum's chatty reversal of its sentiment has the humorous effect of drowning it out. Petrus invokes the nature opening but undercuts its potential to prompt a spontaneous, emotional response to the natural world.[104]

Clerical commentary on natural imagery is fundamental to a complex of motets that includes a piece written by one of the most important composers of the thirteenth century: Philip the Chancellor, an influential theologian and chancellor of the University of Paris from 1218 until his death in 1236. The complex of motets shares the liturgical tenor *In odorem*, which is a chant that was sung at the Cathedral of Notre Dame in Paris in honor of the *semiduplex* feast of Saint Andrew on November 30th. The tenor, "In odorem" is an excerpt of the longer phrase "He [God] loved Andrew *in the odor of sweetness*" (Dilexit Andream *in odorem* suavitatis). Not only do the motets in this complex draw their pitches from the phrase "in odorem" within this chant as their tenor voice, but the melodies of their upper voices are nearly identical to those of a three-voice harmonization of *In odorem* that is transmitted in our oldest sources of Notre Dame polyphony—the clausula "In odorem," which was possibly written by the composer Perotin.[105] The full complex of works in question is summarized in Table 4.4.[106]

---

[101] Ll.3–6. See ibid.

[102] Tischler, *Montpellier Codex*, III, 61–62.

[103] See Maw, "Art of Diminution," 181.

[104] I have argued elsewhere that this is a frequently occurring posture toward the nature opening in vernacular motets. See the examples discussed in my "Songs of Nature," 145–52.

[105] The clausula "In odorem" appears in *F*, fasc.2, no.27 (fol.45r) and *W1*, fasc.8, no.22 (fol.91r/92r). On the attribution to Perotin, see Ludwig, *Repertorium*, I, 37.

[106] All pieces listed in the table share their melodies with the clausula. The motets with two voices use the clausula's tenor and duplum as their tenor and motetus parts.

Table 4.4 Motets Related to the 3-voice Clausula "In odorem"

Motet	Manuscripts	Notes on Transmission
Mens fidem seminat (495)	*Ma* fasc.6, no.14 (fol. 130v)	No tenor provided
	Bes, no.15	Text incipit extant (manuscript is lost)
Mens fidem seminat (495)/ *In odorem* (M45)	*F* fasc.9, no.1 (fol.399r)	First motet in fascicle 9; accompanied by decorated initial featuring (probably) Saint Andrew carrying a cross
	W2, fasc.8, no.11 (fol.150v)	Marginal annotation "Quant foilent" alludes to *Quant feuillent aubespine* (497)
Encontre le tens (496)/*Mens fidem seminat* (495)/*In odorem* (M45)	*Ba*, no.62 (fol.38r)	
	Cl, no.39 (fol.385v)	*Cl* records *Dieus fidem seminat* rather than *Mens fidem seminat*
Encontre le tens (496)/ *Quant feuillent aubespine* (497)/*In odorem* (M45)	*W2*, fasc.9, no.1 (fol.193r)	
	Mo, fasc.5, no.95 (fol.134v)	

Although the motet, *Mens fidem seminat* (495)/*In odorem* (M45), is transmitted anonymously in the music manuscripts where it appears, Payne has convincingly credited this work to Philip the Chancellor. His attribution is based not only on Philip's recognizable rhetorical style but also the motet's incorporation of extensive quotations from Philip's seminal theological *summa* on the nature of the good: the *Summa de bono*.[107] By composing new lyrics that could be sung to the middle of the clausula's three melodies (accompanied by its tenor voice), Philip turned this polyphonic chant setting into a two-voice motet.[108] This piece is found at the start of a collection of

---

[107] See Philip the Chancellor, *Motets and Prosulas*, 123.

[108] One cannot always assume that clausulae preceded the motets with which they share their music (on substitute clausulae that probably originated as motets, see especially Bradley, "Contrafacta and Transcribed," and *Polyphony in Medieval*, 108–9), however this is the likeliest scenario in this case. First, if the modern attribution of the clausula to Perotin is correct, Philip's re-texting of the clausula would be in line with the rest of his corpus—Philip wrote several lyrics to music composed by Perotin. On the role of Perotin in Philip's corpus and the close biographical connections between the two, see Wright, *Music and Ceremony*, 294–95; Payne, *"Aurelianis civitas"*; and Payne's comments

motets in *F*, a Parisian manuscript that transmits a large repertoire of poly-phonic settings of plainchant as well as the oldest known corpus of motets.[109] In *Mens fidem seminat*, Philip explores the virtues of faith, hope, and charity through horticultural analogies. Virtue, according to Philip, can be culti-vated just as a fruit is generated from a flower, which is produced by a bud, it-self generated from a seed (ll.6–9). Philip exhorts his readers and listeners to pursue virtue and thereby to become a tree that yields good fruit. The lyric's end alludes to a passage in the Gospel of Luke (6:43–44): "For there is no tree that bringeth forth evil fruit; nor an evil tree that bringeth forth good fruit. For every tree is known by its fruit. For men do not gather figs from thorns; nor from a bramble bush do they gather the grape."[110] Good trees, rooted in virtue, produce good fruit; bad trees, rooted in vice, produce bad fruit. Medieval theologians and poets alike used this natural image, often to very different ends.[111]

	Motetus:
	Mens fidem seminat.
	Fides spem germinat.
	Caritas exterminat
	Metum, et eliminat,
5	Mentem et illuminat.
	Germen fit de semine.
	Florem germen propinat.
	Fructum flos propaginat.
	Virtus fit hoc ordine.
10	Fides spei spes est ei,
	Radix et initium,

in Philip the Chancellor, *Motets and Prosulas*, xii–xiii). Second, the extensive use of hockets in the second half of this motet (which I discuss further below) is common in the three-voice clausula rep-ertoire while also less-typical of the early motet repertoire.

[109] The position of Philip's motet as the first in fascicle 9 of *F* is significant; not only is this a place of prominence, Bradley argues that the motets in this important manuscript (the first extant manu-script to transmit motets) may have been ordered according to their relative popularity. See Bradley, "Ordering in the Motet."

[110] Douay-Rheims Bible. https://biblehub.com/multi/luke. See also the similar passage in Matthew 7:16–20. The rich tradition of medieval allegorical and tropological readings of the Tree of Life and the Tree of Knowledge, many of which connect the two trees to the opposing concepts of *caritas* and *cupiditas*, receives extensive treatment in Robertson, "Doctrine of Charity."

[111] Among the trouvères, see especially Thibaut de Champagne, "Mauvès arbres ne puet florir" (RS 1410). For examples from the troubadour song corpus, see Thiolier-Mèjan, *Voici l'arbre d'amour*, 192–99.

Que sola maior omnium:
Extrema ligans medium,
Que vitium declinat,
15   Occium vitat, nos invitat
Cursus ad stadium,
Vite bravium.
Mentem ditat.
Fides spem maritat.
20   Miscet armonias;
Parit varias melodias.
Caritas est bonum
Mentem quod iustificat
Per gratiam,
25   Vere lucis donum
Quod tenebras purificat.
Hanc sitias.
Vanas scias
Linguas, prophetias,
30   Rerum copias.
Hanc tu capias;
Hanc tu sapias;
Vias devias
Per hanc fugias.
35   Arbor fias
Ut bonum parias
Fructum in odorem.

Tenor: In odorem [With an odor (of sweetness)]
[The mind sows faith./Faith sprouts hope./Charity expels fear,/turns it out of doors,/and enlightens the mind./A bud is formed from a seed./This bud produces a flower./The flower generates a fruit./This is how one cultivates virtue./The faith of hope is hope in a/root and origin,/which by itself/is greater than anything else:/the end securing the middle,/which shuns vice, eludes/idleness, and summons us/to the racecourse,/to the prize of life./It enriches the mind./Faith is coupled with hope./It blends the harmonies/and spawns sundry melodies./Charity is the good/that absolves the mind/through grace,/the gift of true light/that purges the shadows./Thirst for it./Come to recognize meaningless/speeches, false prophecies, and/the

lavishness of possessions./Cherish it,/savor it, and/through it/flee the crooked paths./Become a tree,/so that you may yield good/fruit with an odor (of sweetness).][112]

When joined with the tenor, *In odorem*, Philip's directive to cultivate faith, hope, and charity and to become a tree of virtue resonate with the chant's liturgical context and its discussion of Andrew's crucifixion; singers and listeners familiar with this chant likely connected Philip's reference to the tree with Andrew's martyrdom on the cross.[113]

Two additional motets represented in Table 4.4 use all three voices of the *In odorem* clausula, and both set the top voice to the text *Encontre le tens* (496):

Encontre le tens
De Pascour,
Que touz amanz
Maintent joie et baudour,
5   Puis n'i demeure
Que ne soie
Renvoisiez et plains de joie
Et d'amour.
Sans sejor
10 Veil faire un novel chant.
Ne pour quant
Ma joie est tournee en plour,
Si ne puis avoir l'amor
De cele qui mon cuer a
15 Et qui touz jors mes l'avra
Se li plaist; el[e] m'ocirra,
Tantost qu'on voudra.
Mon cuer a en sa baillie,
Face [en] quanque li plaira.
20 Sa grant biauté m'a si pris
Et sorpris
De s'amor sui si espris,

---

[112] Edition and translation follow that of Payne in Philip the Chancellor, *Motets and Prosulas*, 123.

[113] Medieval exegetes associated the Tree of Life with the cross and the redemption of Christ. See Robertson, "Doctrine of Charity," 25.

Bien vivrai en joie,
Se s'amor m'otroie;
25   Dieus doinst, qu'ele soit moie!
Si m'avroit trestout gari,
An Dieus, et resbaudi.
Ele a fresche la coulour,
Blanche comme flor
30   Est, c'e m'est avis;
Cheveus blons, front bien assis,
Les ieuz vairs rians,
Les sourcis haus et voutiz,
Bouche vermelle et plesant.
35   Dieus, ne me puis
Tenir, que s'amor
Ne demant!
Bele, que ferai,
Se vostre amor n'ai?
40   Las, autrement sui a la mort
Sans resort.
Se m'ociés,
Quant tot a vous m'acort,
Dieus, c'est a tort.

[In the season/of Easter,/when lovers all/revel in merriment and ardor, /I am no longer among them/because I am not/lighthearted and full of joy/and love./Without delay,/I want to compose a new song./But/my joy has turned to tears,/for I cannot have the love/of her who has my heart/and who always will,/if that please her; she will kill me as soon/as anyone asks her to./She has my heart in her power,/let her do with it as she pleases./Her great beauty has so captured me/and taken me,/I am so inflamed with love of her/that I will live in complete joy,/if she grants me her love;/may God grant that she be mine!/Then will she have completely cured me,/by God, and cheered me./ She has such fresh color,/as white as a flower,/it seems to me;/blond hair, a pleasingly shaped brow,/laughing, gray-blue eyes,/high arched eyebrows,/ pleasing, scarlet lips./God, I cannot/keep/from asking for her love./Fair one, what shall I do/if I have not your love?/Alas, otherwise death is my lot/

without recourse./You kill me/when I give myself entirely to you,/God, that is not right.][114]

The triplum voice begins with the nature opening and, in its approach, strongly resembles songs I explored earlier in which the speaker acknowledges that a kind of conventional alignment exists between springtime and joy for most people, but then claims he is not among them. He expresses a desire to write a new song, but his impulse is not generated through an encounter with a landscape. This lyric continues with the speaker's declaration of his love for this lady, a conventional description of her beautiful features, and his closing declaration that if she does not return his love, it will kill him. In the motet, *Encontre le tens* (496)/*Mens fidem seminat* (495)/*In odorem* (M45), this love lyric is encountered alongside Philip's *Mens fidem seminat*; the juxtaposition seems to offer a spiritual recuperation in which the unfulfilled, earthly desire for the lady expressed by the speaker of *Encontre le tens* (an example of cupidity) is redirected toward charity (love of God).[115] The nature opening of *Encontre le tens* is sounds against Philip's opening declaration: "The mind sows faith./Faith sprouts hope" (ll.1–2: Mens fidem seminat./Fides spem germinat.). Through this juxtaposition, the composer of the motet suggests that rather than hoping that springtime will initiate a state of cupidity (as the speaker of *Encontre le tens* wishes it would), one should follow Philip's instruction to cultivate faith in the mind in the same way that nature generates a sprout from a seed. Other juxtapositions similarly suggest that the proper reaction to nature is to imitate its generative processes in order to cultivate charity. This motet's ending combines Philip's advice that listeners become the tree that yields the good fruit of virtue (ll.35–37) with the lover's despondent reaction to his lady's indifference (ll.42–44). The juxtaposition directly contrasts the medieval values of charity and cupidity, which medieval exegetes connected to the two biblical trees: the Tree of Life (associated with charity) and the Tree of Knowledge of Good and Evil (associated with cupidity).[116] Undergirding the two texts is the tenor, *In odorem*. The sweet

---

[114] Lyrics and translation modified slightly from Stakel and Relihan, *Montpellier Codex*, 37.

[115] This reading of the motet connects it to other examples in which vernacular genres undergo spiritual recuperation. See Huot, "Earthly and Heavenly Revelry," chap. 2 in *Allegorical Play*, and Rothenberg, "The Assumption Story," chap. 2 in *Flower of Paradise*.

[116] Similar examples are discussed in Robertson, "Doctrine of Charity," 25–29.

odors of the springtime season might be seen as having been transformed into the odors of Andrew's martyrdom (divine fragrance was often associated with martyrdom) as well as the sweet odors of paradise.

As Table 4.4 shows, there is a third motet that shares its melodies with *In odorem* clausula: *Encontre le tens* (496)/*Quant feuillent aubespine* (497)/ *In odorem* (M45). This motet uses different lyrics to set the middle voice— *Quant feuillent aubespine*, rather than Philip's lyric *Mens fidem seminat*, accompanies the motetus melody. *Quant feuillent aubespine* is a *pastourelle*, a popular song type I explore at greater length in Chapter 5 in which a knight goes out riding in the countryside and encounters a shepherdess whom he attempts to seduce:

	Motetus:
	Qu[a]nt fuellent aubespin,
	Qu'oiseillon au matin
	Chantant cler en leur latin,
	Je, qui de penser n'ai fin
5	Et qui por adrecier tint
	Seur mon cheval a droiture
	Sentier lés un chemin,
	Trovai par desoz un pin
	Pastorale au cors fin,
10	Ou el[e] chantot
	[Et si notot]
	En son frestel menoit joie
	Ne quide, que nus hom l'oie.
	Je la vi simplete et coie,
15	Seule sans Robin.
	Vers li m'eslais,
	De moi li fis lais,
	A li m'otroi
	Du tout en m'amor li lais.
20	Esbahie
	Fu, si se deslie.
	Quant de li me vit pres,
	Si torn[e] a la fuie
	Et je apres.

25   Par la main l'ai prise;
        Ce que li dis,
        Mout petit prise,
        Ce m'est vis.
        S'amor qui m'atise
30   Beut, que je soi[e] a sa devise
        Ses amis.
        Au col li mis
        Mes bras et puis li dis:
        "Bele flour de lis,
35   Je sui vostre amis,
        A vous me rent pris."
        Tant fis et tant dis,
        Qu'audesus me mis,
        Ma volente fis
40   Tout a mon devis;
        Dous ris ot et cler vis.

[When the hawthorn bush is in leaf,/with the birds, in the morning,/singing in their language/I, who am endlessly rapt in thought,/and who set my course/on horseback keeping to a path alongside a road/found a true-hearted shepherdess/beneath a pine tree,/where she was singing/[and accompanying herself]/joyfully on her pipe,/she did not think that anyone heard her./I saw that she was simple and tranquil;/alone, without Robin./I approached her,/pulled her to me/and pledged/my love to her./Frightened/she was, and pulled away./When she saw me close to her/she turned and ran,/with me in pursuit./I took hold of her by the hand;/she perceived very little/of what I said,/it seemed to me,/that the love of her/which was exciting me/wanted me to be as she would/her sweetheart./Around her neck/I put my arms and said to her:/"Fair lily flower,/I am your sweetheart/and hand myself over as prisoner to you."/With enough talk and acts/I was able to put her under me/ and do my will/just as I desired;/she had a sweet laugh and a bright face.][117]

This motet presents a combination of lyric types in which the angst of unrequited love expressed in the triplum voice, *Encontre le tens*, is contrasted with

[117] Edition and translation modified slightly (with reference to the version of the texts in *W2*) from Stakel and Relihan, *Montpellier Codex*, 37–38.

the *pastourelle* lyric, *Quant feuillent aubespine*, which describes the speaker's sexual gratification.[118] Both vernacular voices start with the nature opening (which, as we saw earlier, is not efficacious for the speaker of *Encontre le tens*). In *Quant feuillent aubespine*, the nature opening prompts lust rather than elevated desire. In the context of this motet, where both upper voices are in the vernacular, readers or listeners may have connected the tenor incipit "In odorem" to the strong scent of the hawthorn to which the motetus text refers. As Table 4.4 shows, the motetus voice was transmitted very widely with Philip's lyric *Mens fidem seminat*. It is thus likely that many of those who listened to, read, or sang the motetus *Quant feuillent aubespine* within the context of this vernacular motet would have heard it with the lyrics of *Mens fidem seminat* already in mind. As Table 4.4 shows, the manuscript *W2* transmits both Philip's two-voice motet, *Mens fidem seminat* (495)/*In odorem* (M45), as well as *Encontre le tens* (496)/*Quant feuillent aubespine* (497)/*In odorem* (M45). *W2*, which was likely compiled in the 1240s, also includes the marginal cue "Quant foilent" next to its version of *Mens fidem seminat* (495)/ *In odorem* (M45), indicating an awareness of the concordance between the two works at the time of this manuscript's compilation and perhaps a desire to draw attention to it.[119]

Readers and performers may have encountered *Quant feuillent* with the lyrics of *Mens fidem seminat* jangling in their mind's ear, echoing behind the Old French *pastourelle* text in what Deeming has aptly termed "virtual polyphony."[120] Indeed, examining *Encontre le tens* (496)/*Quant feuillent aubespine* (497)/*In odorem* (M45) with knowledge of Philip's lyrics as an interpretive background quickly reveals striking parallels, particularly in the motet's second half, which appears in Example 4.2.[121] The example is based

---

[118] Huot discusses several examples in which the combination of texts produces juxtapositions between frustrated and gratified lust. See *Allegorical Play*, 41–47. Although she mentions this motet as an example, arguing that the two vernacular texts present a courtly lover participating in both poetic worlds (the love song and the *pastourelle*), her account does not address the tenor, the musical setting, or the broader family of works to which this motet belongs. See ibid., 46–47.

[119] A complete list of these motets in *W2* and the marginal cues appears in Bradley, "Musical Borrowing," 37.

[120] Deeming, "Music, Memory, and Mobility," 67–68. On the concept of the "mind's ear" in medieval thought as it relates to music, see Deeming, "Music and Contemplation," passim.

[121] The example produces the second half of the motet, starting with the repetition of the tenor. The motet tenor (like the clausula tenor) follows the chant's melisma on "In odo[rem]" while altering chant pitches fifty-five (up a step) and sixty-four (down a half-step). It also omits the final four pitches of the chant (on the syllable "rem"). The first tenor *cursus* uses the first sixty-six notes from the chant melisma (with the alterations mentioned); the second repeats this *cursus* nearly exactly, omitting the final pitch (the final cadence is thus on C rather than D).

Example 4.2 *Encontre le tens* (496)/*Quant feuillent aubespine* (497)/*In odorem* (M45), *Mo* 134v, mm.46–end, with lyrics of *Mens fidem seminat* by Philip the Chancellor

on the version of this motet in *Mo*, while also providing the lyrics of *Mens fidem seminat* under those of *Quant feuillent aubespine* for comparison.[122] The juxtaposition of the two vernacular lyrics in the second half, as well as their relationship to the sacred tenor and the memorative echo of Philip's Latin lyrics, combine to produce several potential commentaries on vernacular song that address the role of nature in both profane and divine love.

The second half of this motet is dominated by two lengthy hockets that engage all three of the voices. The hocket is a musical device in which a melody stops suddenly, interrupted by a rest, then restarts; this interruption can persist (sometimes at length) and in polyphonic settings, another voice can fill in the absent sound by interjecting notes into the void such that a composite melody is perceived, producing an effect akin to a modern bell choir. The length and dominance of the hockets in our motet are unusual compared to the genre as a whole.[123] Their presence here is likely the result of this motet's reliance on a clausula (where hockets are more common) for its melodies. Curran's exploration of medieval theoretical accounts of the hocket reveals that it was often understood as a device that entailed both breaking and integration,[124] whereby melodies were broken apart in one voice and fitted together with the aid of another.[125] The hockets jubilantly ring through our motet's three-voice texture. The first hocket (bracketed in Example 4.2) occurs during the triplum speaker's exclamation of his hope that his lady will return his love ("Then she will have completely cured me, by God! and cheered me").[126] The motet composer aligns the notes of the hocket, isolated between rests, with the speaker's own interjection within his exclamation: "by God!" ("an Dieus").[127] At this point in the motetus' *pastourelle* lyric, the speaker is describing his pursuit of the girl and her panicked reaction: "She saw me close to her, so she turned and ran and I followed."[128] Binding these two lyrics together through the hocket, this motet fuses the motetus speaker's

---

[122] The edition follows that of Tischler, *Montpellier Codex*, II, 98–101.

[123] Tischler identified this motet as one of only nine in the early motet corpus to include a hocket. See *Earliest Motets*, I, 93n40. Although Curran operates under the most inclusive definition of hocket of any recent accounts, these motet voices are among only twenty-eight within his corpus (which encompasses a total of 138 motet voices including hockets) that that he identifies as "extensive." See Curran, "Hockets Broken," 98–104.

[124] Interestingly, the "breaking" of the melodies is sometimes described in terms also used for felling trees and pruning. See Curran, "Hockets Broken," 45.

[125] Curran, "Hockets Broken," 39–56.

[126] Ll.27–28: "Si m'avroit trestout gueri,/En Dieus! et resbaudi."

[127] Other accounts note the coincidence of hockets with expressions of emotion. See Wolinski, "Hocketing," and Curran, "Hockets Broken."

[128] Ll.22–24: "Quant de li me vit pres,/Si torn[e] a la fuie et je apres."

active pursuit of sexual gratification with the unsatisfied desires expressed by the speaker of the triplum voice. By contrapuntally collapsing the previously independent melodies of the triplum and motetus voice into a single line, the motet composer suggests, too, that their two pursuits (elevated desire and carnal satisfaction) are interchangeable—two examples of cupidity. Moreover, those singers or listeners familiar with Philip's lyrics at this moment in the motetus part would hear, in their mind's ear, this this juxtaposition accompanied by Philips phrase: "It [Faith] is coupled with hope./ It blends the harmonies/and spawns sundry melodies."[129] In the process of fitting his lyrics to the *In odorem* clausula, Philip positioned these phrases within the hocket; his textual reference to the "blending of harmonies" is a clear reference to the impact of the hocket as a compositional device, where the two formerly distinct melodies are collapsed into a single, harmonious melody. In the full, three-voice version, the collapsed melody is punctuated by vertical sonorities (the harmonies?). When we consider the impact of the hocket in *Encontre le tens* (496)/*Quant feuillent aubespine* (497)/*In odorem* (M45), a listener who recalled Philip's lyrics would hear his lyrics "sundry melodies" at this moment, perhaps understanding them to refer to the two vernacular motet voices and their lyrics (evocative of the trouvère genres of love song and *pastourelle*) and their shared exploration of cupidity. Philip would undoubtedly have hoped that listeners aware of both versions would be inspired to spurn the sundry vernacular melodies.

The second hocket in this motet, which begins in m.67 (bracketed in Example 4.2), continues to engage the sonic palimpsest of Philip's Latin lyrics. Here, the two vernacular voices are both poised to declare their love: the speaker of the motetus voice puts his arm around the shepherdess' neck and prepares to profess his love (ll.32–33), while the speaker of the triplum adumbrates his lady's beautiful features and says he cannot keep from asking for her love (ll.35–37). Listeners familiar with Philip's lyrics would recall his words at this same musical juncture: "Thirst for it [charity]./ Come to recognize meaningless speeches" (ll.27–29). The professions of love by the subjects of the vernacular triplum and motetus would be understood as representations of these meaningless speeches. This final hocket positions the shared pursuit of cupidity in the vernacular triplum and motetus against Philip's exhortation to yearn instead for charity. The motet's close presents a final commentary on the relationships among the various lyrics. Here, the

---

[129] Ll.27–29: "Hanc sitias./Vanas scias/Linguas..."

triplum speaker laments that he will be killed if his lady does not give him
her love (ll.41–46) just as the speaker of the motetus voice "does his will"
(l.39: ma volonte fis) with the shepherdess (see Example 4.2, mm.77–end).[130]
This juxtaposition of sexual frustration with a sexual act lies at the crux of the
generic difference between trouvère love lyric and the *pastourelle*, as many
have noted.[131] But listening through the motetus lyrics, recalling the words
Philip positioned in this same melodic passage reveals a different, symbolic meaning: "And through it [Caritas]/Flee the crooked paths./Become a
tree,/So that you may yield good fruit/With an odor [of sweetness]."[132] In
the *pastourelle* lyric of motetus voice, recall that the knight was described as
riding along a path, and finding the shepherdess under a pine tree (ll.7–9).
We will see in Chapter 5 that paths are strongly connected to the genre of
the *pastourelle*, where the knight is very often described as riding on a path
from which he deviates to approach a shepherdess. Particularly in songs in
which a sex act occurs between the knight and shepherdess (including rape),
the knights often finds her sitting under a tree. For those aware of Philip's
lyric admonishing listeners to "flee the crooked paths" and become a tree of
virtue, the textual confluence at the motet's close would advise abandoning
the cupidity represented by vernacular song and pursuing charity.

There is no way to know for certain which of these motets was written
first. The presence of Philip's motet in *F* (the oldest source of Latin motets)
along with the clausula *In odorem* suggests its primacy. *Encontre le tens*
(496)/*Mens fidem seminat* (495)/*In odorem* (M45) appears in *Ba* and *Cl*,
motet manuscripts copied long after Philip's death (both likely date from
the turn of the fourteenth century), yet these manuscripts contain music
believed to have been composed much earlier. The motet *Encontre le tens*
(496)/*Quant feuillent aubespine* (497)/*In odorem* (M45) is transmitted in
W2, our oldest surviving manuscript of French motets, which was probably copied sometime in the 1340s, in the decade immediately following
Philip's death. Although no medieval evidence survives to demonstrate
the point, it is not impossible that Philip could have written these vernacular motets himself. Murray has argued that Philip wrote a *contrafactum*

---

[130] Unlike many *pastourelle* lyrics, there is no dialogue in the motetus; the speaker never records
the shepherdess' reaction to his declaration of love, nor does he record her consent to the sex act
described, which he claims to have accomplished "with enough deeds and words" (l.37: "Tant fis et
tant dis"). It should be noted that the phrase he uses to describe the sex act (ma volonte fis) is an expression often associated with rape in Old French song. See Gravdal, *Ravishing Maidens*, 2.

[131] See, for example, Huot, *Allegorical Play*, 42–47.

[132] Ll.33–36: "Vias devias/Per hanc fugias/Arbor fias/Ut bonum parias/Fructum in odorem."

of Bernart de Ventadorn's "Can vei la lauzeta" that inverted the meaning of the famous troubadour song; Philip rendered his lyrics to this piece in both Old French and Latin.[133] Even if it was not Philip who wrote the two vernacular motets, it certainly seems as though their composers were sympathetic to the point of view of *Mens fidem seminat* (495)/*In odorem* (M45), elaborating on its message and harnessing it as a critique of vernacular song genres. In *Encontre le tens* (496)/*Mens fidem seminat* (495)/*In odorem* (M45), the triplum voice and its love lyrics work with the lower voices to exhort listeners to pursue charity, amplifying the message of Philip's two-voice motet and juxtaposing his lesson with the vernacular lyric as a critique of its value system. The motet *Encontre le tens* (496)/*Quant feuillent aubespine* (497)/*In odorem* (M45) could engender different responses among audiences depending on their familiarity with the other version of its motetus voice (*Mens fidem seminat*). For those unfamiliar with Philips' hortatory lyrics, the piece may simply have been interpreted through the lens of parody, as one of many motets in which elevated desire and lust in the trouvère genres of the love song and *pastourelle* were contrasted, the *In odorem* tenor simply evoking the pleasant fragrances of springtime. The wide transmission of *Mens fidem seminat* (495)/*In odorem* (45) and the marginal annotation in *W2* drawing attention to its relationship to *Quant feuillent aubespine* suggest that knowledgeable listeners and readers likely apprehended the motet as a layered commentary that relied on Philip's lyrics as an absent presence. Such listeners likely heard the motet as a call to prize love of God over love of lady, trees of virtue over trees of vice.[134]

Together, this complex of pieces suggests commonalities in the approach clerics took to the nature opening in both songs and motets. Like the songs of the cleric-trouvères we saw earlier, some motet composers seem to approach the nature opening with distance and self-conscious manipulation. Their poetic response largely lacks the immediacy and emotional impact that

---

[133] Murray, "Clerical Reception of Bernart," 263–65. Additional *contrafacta* in Philip's corpus are discussed in Falck, "Zwei Lieder."

[134] Motets were likely cultivated by the minor clergy, perhaps specifically Parisian students. Philip's motet, with its admonition to seek *caritas*, is in keeping with other elements of his oeuvre in which he exhorts students to remember their clerical vows of chastity. Payne discusses a sermon Philip delivered in Orléans in 1229 (and a conductus Philip wrote in 1236 that resonates thematically with this sermon), in which Philip worked to convince the scholars to return to Paris during the Great Dispersal, a period in which the scholars fled Paris to avoid accountability for the role students played in inciting a violent riot in the city. Although Philip sided with the scholars in this episode, he also exhorted them to reform the conduct that contributed to the incident, focusing on their vows of chastity. See Payne, "*Aurelianis civitas*," 606–7.

characterized the songs of the knightly trouvères explored in Chapter 3.[135] The motet complex related to the *In odorem* clausula draws on quotation, the transformation of existing models, and a symbolic approach to nature imagery rooted in Scripture. The message of at least two of these motets (and perhaps all three) amounts of a rejection of the relationships between landscape, the emotion of (profane) love, and song production that the nature opening encapsulated in even stronger, theological terms. Yet arguably, the motets on *In odorem* can also be seen to suggest a deeply sympathetic response to plant-life. The scriptural verses upon which the closing lines of Philip's lyric, *Mens fidem seminat*, are based draw an analogy in which the heritability of plant characteristics is compared to the relationship between a person's character and their actions. Yet Philip does not merely draw an analogy in this motet (the person who cultivates virtue is like the biblical good tree that produces good fruit). He calls upon his listeners to *become* a tree. Like Gilles le Vinier, who saw in a greening laurel the emotion bursting from his already full heart, Philip (and the other anonymous motet composers who contributed to this complex of works) suggests a direct response to nature in which the desired result is not poetic production or profane love, but rather the cultivation of virtue.

Overall, there are broad similarities in the way cleric-trouvères approached the nature opening across the late twelfth through the early fourteenth centuries, and their posture toward it differed from the songs of the knightly classes. Most clerical trouvères rejected the nature opening entirely, omitting it from their songs. When knights began their songs with the nature opening, in contrast, they overwhelmingly wrote in the first-person and present tense, communicating a speaker's sensory emersion in a landscape; moreover, they often harnessed *pedes cum cauda* form to highlight the direct influence of the landscape on their emotions or their desire to sing. Those cleric-troouvères who did use the nature opening regularly wrote against it, whether directly deriding it, introducing oppositional conjunctions in place of the causal relationships favored by the knightly classes, or replacing the immediacy of the present tense favored by knightly trouvères with the subjunctive or conditional mood. Those who did embrace the nature opening,

---

[135] Indeed, with the exception of monophonic examples, the textual interplay of multi-voice motets is largely unsuited to the direct expression of individual sentiment, as Huot rightly explains: "Because of the multitude of singers, the performers are distinguished from both poet-composer and lover; we know that each of these characters cannot simultaneously be identified with the lyric 'I' and that the harmony of parts is due to the guiding, if invisible, hand of the author." *Song to Book*, 301.

such as Gilles le Vinier, did so in ways that were partial and which described small-scale observation of plant-life rather than grand, sweeping landscapes. The cleric-trouvères also differed from the knightly classes in their compositional approaches. By layering the nature opening under word refrains, echorhymes, or, in the motet repertoire, polytextuality, contrafaction, and symbolic intertexts, clerical composers often approached the nature opening with distance and compositional manipulation, all of which undermine its seeming immediacy in the knightly songs. This attitude may have reflected the urban surroundings of these composers, many of whom spent the majority of their careers in cities. It may also have been a posture toward nature that they adopted as part of a shared identity as cleric-trouvères. Their reaction may thus have stemmed from a belief that only God creates, and that human creativity can only strive in vain to imitate nature.[136]

---

[136] See Leach, "Nature's Forge," 73.

PART III

IN THE PASTURE AND THE GARDEN

5

Rural Landscapes and the *Pastourelle*

Boundaries, Spatial and Social

L'autrier mi chivachoie
Pencis com suis sovent
Leis un boix qui verdoie
Prés d'un preit lons de gent
Trovai pastoure qui gardoit sa proie.
Kant je la vix, ver li tornai ma voie . . .

The other day I was riding
Thoughtful as I often am
Alongside a wood that was greening;
Near a meadow far from people
I found a shepherdess guarding her flock.
When I saw her, I turned from my way toward her . . .

In medieval *pastourelle* songs, the narrator is nearly always at the edge of something, whether alongside wood, near a field, or between spaces bisected by his path.[1] He often tells us he is riding, beginning his song from the lofty position atop his horse. He normally finds a beautiful young shepherdess and dismounts, descending to her level. He must leave his path to bend his way toward her. She guards her "proie" (herd) but she is also the knight's "proie" (prey).[2] After the knight finds the shepherdess and they begin a dialogue, a shifting array of narrative outcomes unfold, from banter, to consensual sex, to rape. The *pastourelle* has been viewed as a kind of cultural release valve where the unconsummated desire knightly lovers expressed in their love songs was shifted to a context where it could potentially be gratified;[3] in the

---

[1] Paden, *Medieval Pastourelle*, I, 248.
[2] This pun is made explicit in "Hui main par un ajournant" (RS 292) in which the shepherdess tells the knight that since he wants to catch prey (proie) he should seek it in a higher place than she would be (st.8, ll.29–31). See Paden, *Medieval Pastourelle*, I, 284–85.
[3] See Zink, *La pastourelle*, 70–103.

Song, Landscape, and Identity in Medieval Northern France. Jennifer Saltzstein, Oxford University Press.
© Oxford University Press 2023. DOI: 10.1093/oso/9780197547779.003.0006

pastourelle, courtly love (with all its constraints) solicits its contrary.[4] Instead of prompting desire and elevated composition, as it did in the songs I explored in Chapter 3, the springtime opening becomes a source of open parody in the *pastourelle*, where the season inspires only lust.[5] *Pastourelle* characters transgress boundaries of status, personal space, propriety, and property. Social divisions find visual representation in a geography segmented by a distinct, patchwork pattern of land usage and bisected by roads. The spatial borders of the landscape are further echoed in structural features of the songs themselves, which readily traverse aesthetic confines of genre and form.[6] The *pastourelle* spills over the formal patterns that characterize other types of trouvère song.[7] The narrative encounter between a knight and a shepherdess can be featured in songs that are identical in their form to elevated love songs, but *pastourelle* narratives are equally at home in refrain songs, polyphonic motets, and genres associated with dance.[8] The speech of the two characters is often distinguished by the heightened musicality of the shepherdess' voice within their dialogue; she sometimes sings refrains found in other *pastourelle* songs.[9] Poetic and musical modelling draw *pastourelles* into dialogue with still more songs, coloring the listening experience for those in the know. Boundaries (spatial, aesthetic, and social) are constantly traversed.

The *pastourelle* is the first song genre I have explored that invokes, through its characters, the medieval peasantry. The images and voices of peasants that survive in my song corpus are literary, not authorial. Although it is theoretically possible that the voices of fictive medieval peasant characters could

---

[4] Zink, *La pastourelle*, 103.

[5] See Smith, *Medieval French Pastourelle*, 19–20. The springtime opening is even invoked as a pick-up line in "Hui main par un ajornant" (RS 292; st.3, ll.9–12). See Paden, *Medieval Pastourelle*, I, 282–83.

[6] See, for example, Callahan, "Hybrid Discourse."

[7] Modern scholars have created a wide array of generic terms for trouvère songs. The *pastourelle* was among a smaller group of those genres that was clearly recognized by medieval compilers. For example, the songbook *C* includes marginal annotations in a medieval hand labelling songs as "pastourelles" or "jeu-parti." The first layer of the songbook *I* is organized generically with separate sections for *grant chant, estampies, jeux-partis, pastourelles, ballettes*, and *sottes chansons*. However, songs in the poetic form of the *ballette* are sometimes placed in the *pastourelle* section if their theme features the encounter. See Atchison, *MS Douce 308*, 40–41 and Callahan, "Collecting Trouvère Lyric."

[8] Although the majority of *pastourelles* center on the encounter between a knight and shepherdess, there are others that feature related but distinct narratives, such as a knight who passively observes the shepherds interact with one another (often called the *bergerie* type). Subtypes within the *pastourelle* corpus are discussed in Paden, *Medieval Pastourelle*, x and Zink, *La pastourelle*, 28.

[9] Butterfield discusses the social through the lens of register (an approach influenced by Bec and Zumthor) and views the refrain as a crucial element of the mixing of poetic registers associated with differing social groups. See *Poetry and Music*, 125–32. On register in the context of the *pastourelle*, see Butterfield, *Poetry and Music*, 151–60.

have been appropriated directly from the mouths of the lower classes,[10] no surviving *pastourelles* are credited to medieval peasants. The authored songs in which peasants are represented were written by songwriters who were knights, clerics, urbanites, or professional performers—people who did not share the identities of the peasants they described. Although the "three orders" system (discussed in the Introduction) subordinated peasants to the clergy and knightly classes, the necessity of peasant labor was broadly recognized. Peasants were the dominant medieval social group, constituting around 90 percent of the population. Even as the knightly classes presented themselves as distinct from the other orders, poor knights would have been close to the land and close to their peasants.[11] The clergy often presented their own prayers, service, and preaching as a form of spiritual labor that they described using agricultural metaphors, particularly plowing and threshing.[12] Elites regarded peasants with deep-seated ambivalence, viewing them as members of an alien world while also realizing that their lifestyle conformed more closely than their own with God's intentions for humanity.[13] Medieval literature tended to represent peasants with a degree of contempt.[14] Songs preserved in writing, often in luxurious manuscripts (my object of study), surely do not provide a window into actual peasant lives, but rather into the ways other members of medieval society viewed the peasantry. These songs nonetheless suggest a great deal about how songwriters, patrons, and audiences may have defined their own identities against those of the peasants whose lives they depicted.

It might seem far-fetched at first glance for equestrian knights to encounter shepherdesses in the countryside, as they do in many *pastourelles*. And indeed, most accounts have argued that the terrain described in *pastourelle* songs is ahistorical, its location unfixed and floating, unattached to any specific point of reference.[15] Yet the fields, pastures, and woodland

[10] Bennett articulates her hope that songs, ballads, and proverbs written by clerks and students might have some origin in the oral cultures of the medieval countryside. Bennett, *A Medieval Life*, 52. This kind of optimistic speculation appears in much scholarship, as I will show in Chapter 6.

[11] Fossier, *Peasant Life*, 131.

[12] Freedman, *Medieval Peasant*, 33–34.

[13] See Freedman, *Medieval Peasant*, 12.

[14] According to Freedman, male peasants were commonly described in literature as cowardly and filthy whereas female peasants were depicted as potentially desirable and subject to sexual exploitation See Freedman, "Representations of Contempt" and "Peasant Bodies," chap. 6 and chap. 7 in *Medieval Peasant*.

[15] Smith, *Medieval French Pastourelle*, 20. Smith also characterizes the landscape as "a world somewhere between the court and raw nature." Ibid., 22. Butterfield places the genre in the context of the pastoral poetic mode, stating "the genre's highly conventional apparatus removes their encounter some distance from any genuine historical circumstance." Butterfield, *Poetry and Music*, 161.

settings in which *pastourelle* characters are placed were sites of interaction between medieval knights and peasants. Common rights to pasture animals would have applied to the meadowland, fields, and woodlands described in *pastourelle* songs, even if the land was owned by a lord.[16] In the middle ages, no single landowner held absolute or exclusive property rights to a plot of land.[17] Across most of Europe from the twelfth century onward, people distinguished between the right to the land (*dominum directum*) and the right to use the resources of a given area (*dominum utile*).[18] The nature of these rights and how they were exercised and enforced varied by region, but in most cases, lords were obliged by custom to allow neighboring villagers to use their land under certain circumstances.[19] On lordly arable, common rights pertained to fallow fields, where villagers were permitted to graze animals before the planting season (into early spring) and on the "stubble" of stems and stalks that remained after the harvest.[20] The use of the springtime opening in so many *pastourelle* songs thus places them temporally at the end of the common grazing season on such lordly landscapes.[21] Other *pastourelles*, as we shall see, are clearly situated in agricultural spaces between closely proximate medieval cities. These areas would have been part of the city's provisioning hinterland, areas that were, by the thirteenth century, densely settled with villages.[22]

If the prospect of the encounter between knight and peasant that lies at the heart of most *pastourelles* carries a certain historical plausibility, it seems wholly unlikely that actual interactions between knights and peasants prompted the mutual curiosity, attraction, and humor that characterizes their fictional representation in many *pastourelle* songs. Historical accounts show that such interactions involved persistent knightly victimization of peasants through theft, violence, and the destruction of property. The medieval tournament, which provided knights with essential military training, was, until the early fourteenth century, a group activity in which bands of knights competed over a wide swath of countryside. Warriors

---

[16] See the explanation in De Moor et al., "Comparing the Historical Commons," 15–31 at 15.

[17] See Van Bavel, *Manors and Markets*, 163.

[18] De Moor et al., "Comparing the Historical Commons," 24.

[19] De Moor, "Common Rights in Flanders," 117.

[20] In meadowlands around rivers, grazing was also permitted after the first mowing in August. De Moor, "Common Rights in Flanders," 117–18.

[21] One *pastourelle*, "Quant la sesons renouvele d'aoust" (RS 613), by Raoul de Beauvais, is specifically set in August at harvest time, as is "Au tans d'aoust que feuille de boschet" (RS 960).

[22] Jordan, *Great Famine*, 47 and Evergates, *Feudal Society*, 8.

fought for days over fields and even through village streets.[23] Although the goal of the thirteenth-century tournament (called the *mêlée*) was not to kill enemies but rather to win valuable prisoners to ransom while securing their horses and gear, in practice, there was little to no distinction in weaponry or tactics from actual warfare. The damage to peasant crops and homes was so significant that by convention, tournaments were not held during harvest time or during the period of early seedling growth in order to protect valuable crops on lordly lands.[24] When the knightly elite went to war, they fought in the countryside, where "looting, arson, capture of civilians for ransom, and rape continued to be inflicted almost casually upon civilian populations throughout the Middle Ages and beyond."[25] The booty knights stole on raids in the countryside enriched them, funding their courtly largesse.[26] Although some medieval critics descried the practice of destroying of towns, burning cities, laying waste to trees and crops, and killing livestock,[27] the targeting of noncombatants was generally viewed as licit when undertaken on lands owned by an enemy.[28] The commoners living there were viewed as supporters of the regime under attack, at a minimum through their taxes.[29] Hired soldiers, who lost their pay as soon as conflicts of the crown officially ended, would often continue to pillage their living from the peasantry during peacetime,[30] and peasants were vulnerable to the same violence and destruction during the private wars of the aristocracy.[31] Knights took great pains to distinguish themselves from agriculturalists, standing above those who toiled in the earth with their hands.[32] They seem to have viewed the peasantry as nearly a different

---

[23] Crouch, *Tournament*, 51 and Kaeuper, *Medieval Chivalry*, 213.

[24] Kaeuper, *Medieval Chivalry*, 220–21. The (still dangerous) individual contest did not replace the broadly destructive *mêlée* until the early fourteenth century.

[25] Kaeuper, *Medieval Chivalry*, 165 and Taylor, *Ideals of Knighthood*, 208–30.

[26] Kaeuper, *Medieval Chivalry*, 167.

[27] See the remarks of Ramon Llul quoted in Kaeuper, *Medieval Chivalry*, 181.

[28] Taylor, *Ideals of Knighthood*, 214–16.

[29] Kaeuper, *Medieval Chivalry*, 182 and Taylor, *Ideals of Knighthood*, 209 and 212–17.

[30] Taylor, *Ideals of Knighthood*, 218.

[31] Philippe de Beaumanoir argued that tradition supported the notion that every baron was the sovereign of his barony in the *Coutumes de Beauvaisis* of 1283; he argued for the right to private warfare and that crimes committed during such wars were permissible. See *Coutumes*, 612 and 610–18. Attempts by Louis IX to restrict private warfare contributed to the resistance to royal authority in the movement of 1314. See discussion in Taylor, *Ideals of Knighthood*, 123. The inherent conflict between knightly prowess and societal order is discussed in Kaeuper, *Chivalry and Violence*, esp. chap. 1, "The Problem of Public Order and the Knights."

[32] Kaeuper, *Medieval Chivalry*, 72, Kaeuper, *Chivalry and Violence*, 189, and Van Bavel, *Manors and Markets*, 170.

species—the living antithesis of courtly life.[33] Class solidarity within aristocratic culture helped to normalize brutality toward social inferiors.[34] For most medieval peasants, the sight of a mounted knight approaching would surely have inspired terror.

The relationships between identity and place that I have traced in earlier chapters are perhaps nowhere as closely intertwined as in the *pastourelle*. We will see that *pastourelle* dialogues between knights and rural herders play out in landscapes marked by elements of both realism and symbolism. The way composers place their characters on a well-mapped terrain could reflect accurate customs of land usage or the symbolic projection of social boundaries. This chapter will pay special attention to the way these songs highlight ties between geography, identity, and, in some cases, violence, questioning how sung representations of the rural landscape relate to the lived environment at the time of their composition. I begin with a survey of the terrain described in a large corpus of *pastourelle* songs to establish the conventional contours of the genre's landscape. I then contrast this broad corpus songs with a smaller subset of *pastourelles* that depict rape. I show that the outcome in these songs is often signaled from the outset through the shepherdess' location on the land, demonstrating how knightly and peasant identities could be symbolically mapped onto the *pastourelle* terrain. The final section turns to reception history, considering how *pastourelles* could be implicated in identity formation in the context of Arras, a Northern French urban area where the genre was widely cultivated. Considering the *pastourelle* within this context highlights the ways in which urban composers, patrons, and audiences who did not inhabit the rank or geography of the *pastourelle* characters may nonetheless have harnessed the *pastourelle* to conceptualize their identities in relation to the literary figures of the knight and peasant.

Space, Place, and Identity in *Pastourelle* Narratives

The physical landscape of the *pastourelle* has been viewed as one of its defining characteristics. Scholars often describe the *pastourelle* landscape as existing in between the brute nature of the forest and the civility of court; the

---

[33] Kaeuper, *Medieval Chivalry*, 194. This fact provides an explanation for the common knightly ploy of calling the shepherdess noble in appearance, a trope evident in Marcabru's early Occitan *pastorela*, "L'autrier jost'una sebissa."

[34] Taylor, *Ideals of Knighthood*, 227.

remoteness from the court creating, according to many, the conditions for the genre's more violent examples.[35] In light of the more detailed image of the Northern French land that I provided in Chapter 1, I wish to interrogate with greater specificity the physical terrain of the *pastourelle* and relationships between landscape, identity, and violence depicted in these songs. I will explore the topography in *pastourelles* that depict rape in the following section. Here, I survey a corpus of seventy-five *pastourelle* songs that do not depict rape. My aim in examining this substantial corpus of examples is to establish conventional characteristics of the genre's physical landscapes and their relationship to the *pastourelle* characters to serve as a basis for comparison in the next section.[36]

Collectively, *pastourelle* songs chart a particular rural topography, invoking the orchards, grain fields, and grazing areas that, as I showed in Chapter 1, often surrounded medieval estates, villages, and cities. Occasionally, through references to the more rarified topography of gardens and the forest, we seem to catch glimpses of the domain (*demesne*) of an aristocratic estate, and in rare cases, even the lordly forest. The knight's location sometimes goes unspecified, but often he is in the middle of a journey between two cities. Sometimes he even triangulates his location, specifying, as in "D'Ares a Flandres alloie," that he is riding from Arras to Flanders, and finds the shepherdess outside Lille.[37] He is nearly always riding on a road or

---

[35] Smith, *Medieval French Pastourelle*, 18–22, at 21.

[36] This section is based on the edition Paden, *Medieval Pastourelle*, and is focused on seventy-five *pastourelles* that do not depict rape. There is no one complete edition of *pastourelle* lyrics and no edition collects their melodies. The number of extant *pastourelle* songs can vary significantly depending on the editor's generic criteria. Establishing a definitive generic corpus lies outside the scope of this chapter. The first published edition of *pastourelles* appeared in 1870 (Bartsch, *Altfranzösische Romanzen und Pastourellen*). Bartsch classified one hundred eighty-two authored and anonymous Old French songs as *pastourelles* and included these alongside examples from a variety of other song genres that he termed "romances." In the most comprehensive study of the genre to date, Zink argued for the elimination of fifteen of songs Bartsch had categorized as *pastourelles* and the addition of five songs Bartsch did not include. See Zink, *La pastourelle*, 32–33. Rivière published a new edition in 1974 that was limited to the anonymous *pastourelles*, He rejected, on generic grounds, twenty-seven of the anonymous songs Bartsch had originally classified as *pastourelles* and added *pastourelles* found in the motet manuscript *Mo* (which Bartsch did not consult). See Rivière, *Pastourelles*, 8–13. Paden's *Medieval Pastourelle* includes a significant corpus of both authored and anonymous *pastourelle* songs (including twenty songs not found in Bartsch), placing these alongside antecedents and imitations from other linguistic traditions. Published editions by Bartsch, Rivière, and Paden each overlap partially and none is comprehensive.

[37] "D'Ares a Flandres aloie" (RS 1683; Arras, Flanders, and Lille). Other songs that mention specific cities or regions include: "De Saint Quentin a Cambrai" (RS 61), "En Hachicourt l'autre jour chivachoie" (RS 1701; Achicourt), "Je me levai ier matin de Langres" (RS 1369; Bar to Langres), "L'autrier defors Picarni" (RS 1050; Picardy), "L'autrier tout seus chevauchoie" (RS 1362; Paris); "L'autrier quant je chevauchoie" by Andrieu (RS 1699; Arras and Douai), among others.

path.[38] His location on a boundary finds expression in the adverbs of place that saturate these songs, telling us that he is along, beside, outside, or between things. Orchards and gardens, which are among the most intensively cultivated of medieval outdoor spaces, are less common as descriptors of the knight's location.[39] When the knight's position on the landscape is specified, he tends to be riding along a field or meadow[40] or near a wooded area.[41] In several songs, the knight borders a *breuil*, a term that can mean a coppice, thicket, or small wood, but which was also used to describe walled game parks.[42] We saw in Chapters 2 and 3 that male aristocratic identity was intimately connected with woodlands; thus his location, while plausibly realistic, was also deeply symbolic. If the knight typically rides on a path near a wood, the most common place for the shepherdess to appear is in a nearby field, meadow, or prairie,[43] grazing her sheep. In some songs, the shepherdess is literally standing in the knight's path.[44] She often appears shading herself under a tree.[45] Overall, the songs project a high degree of knowledge of plant-life, specifying individual tree species and specific modes of plant growth. The girl is sometimes found in the *buisson* (brushland)[46] or a field of heather;[47] these densely vegetated areas grew up after forest clearances.[48] She may be found in a woodland or grove. She is less often found in an intensively cultivated space like a garden or orchard.[49] When the songs culminate in consensual sex or the agreement to engage in it, leafy bowers provide the

---

[38] See, for example, "De Més a friscor l'autre jour" (RS 1991), "Pencis l'altrier alloie mon chemin" (RS 1360), and "Quant li dous estés" by Simon d'Authie (RS 1381).

[39] The knight wanders along an orchard in "Pensis, chief enclin" by Ernoul li Vielle (RS 1365) and enters an orchard in the motet voice "Quant repaire la verdor" (438); in "L'autrier chevauchoie" (RS 1693) he is riding near a garden.

[40] He rides in a prairie in "Onques jor de ma vie" (RS 1226); in the motet voice "Hui matin a l'ajornee" (217) and the song "Je me chevauchoie" (RS 1706), he is riding through a small meadow.

[41] See, for example, "Dalés Loncpré ou boskel" by Jehan Erart (RS 570), "L'autrier quant chevauchoie" by Jehan Bodel (RS 1702), and "Pres d'un boix et lons de gent" (RS 680).

[42] "Les le breuil" by Jehan Erart (RS 993) and "Chevauchoie les un breuil" (RS 994).

[43] See, for example, "A l'entrant de mai" (RS 85), "L'autrier chevauchoie seus" by the Comte de la Marche (RS 2046), and "Or voi iver defenir" (RS 1394).

[44] See "Dalés Loncpré ou boskel" by Jehan Erart (RS 570) and "L'autre jour je chevauchoie" (RS 974).

[45] See, for example, "Je me chevauchoie" (RS 1706; behind the branches of a little elm) and "L'autrier chevauchai mon chemin" by Jehan Erart (RS 1361; under a pine), among others.

[46] See, for example, "Pastourelle vi seant" (RS 605) and "Pencis l'autrier aloie mon chemin" (RS 1360).

[47] See "Au par issir de la campagne" (RS 47) and "L'autrier quant chevauchoie" (RS 1703).

[48] Van Bavel, *Manors and Markets*, 23.

[49] See, for example, "L'autrier tout seus chevauchoie" by Richard de Semilli (RS 1362) and the voices of the motet, *Pour escouter* (779)/*L'autre jour* (780)/*Seculorum amen*. In "L'autre jour par un matin" (RS 1373), the garden setting puns on the girl's name (*Lijart*).

desired privacy.[50] Overall, the songs convey a rural landscape consisting of a patchwork of areas devoted different land usages (fields, pastures, brushland, and woodland) that border each other in close proximity, their boundaries seemingly delineated by a road or path.

The characters of the *pastourelle* are situated in a landscape that realistically reflects some aspects of rural land management and the ways in which nobles and peasants would have dwelled in these spaces. The focus on fields, pastures, coppices, and brushland conjures up the provisioning hinterland of a major city—land that was agricultural and excluded the orchards and gardens that required more regular tending and were thus situated nearer to dwellings. Arable tended to be located close to villages, whereas grazing and pasturing in heaths and "wastelands" (uncultivated spaces) would be situated farther from the town. It is thus reasonable that a shepherdess grazing sheep might be in a remote location.[51] In the songs, the shepherdess is usually in a field, a place where a person of her rank would have had grazing rights under certain circumstances and at certain times of year. Although no laborers other than the shepherdess (sometimes her rustic friends) are present, when sex occurs, the privacy of a leafy cover is sought, suggesting the potential for onlookers to intrude.

In important ways, however, *pastourelle* landscapes did not reflect the land management schemes that predominated during the thirteenth century, when the majority of the songs were written. Medieval farming underwent a process that has been called "cerealization" in which agriculture shifted toward grain as the primary crop. Cerealization was driven by population growth, and it stimulated further growth; it led to the conversion of as much land as possible to arable. The clearing of forests accelerated.[52] Few wooded areas remained as "common waste" (uncultivated woodland); most of those that did were private property. Because of the high monetary value of wood,[53] lords carefully monitored woodland common rights, often severely limiting the use of their woodlands by local people[54] and employing professional foresters to manage them.[55] With introduction of the heavy

---

[50] The search for such a leafy, private place is discussed directly in "Par dessous l'ombre" by Jehan de Braine (RS 1830), where the knight suggests he and the shepherdess construct a leafy hut.

[51] Van Bavel, *Manors and Markets*, 129.

[52] In many regions, woodlands were cleared completely. See, for example, Van Bavel, *Manors and Markets*, 24.

[53] Wood often provided significant seigneurial income. Commercial wood sales produced seven to eight percent of all royal and ducal revenue at the turn of the thirteenth century in Normandy and the royal domain; this commercialization was relatively new. See Keyser, "Woodland Management," 377.

[54] De Moor, "Common Rights in Flanders," 119.

[55] Keyser, "Woodland Management," 380.

plow, the clay soils located near wetlands that had formerly been too difficult to cultivate could be plowed more easily and converted to fields. These
areas had once provided excellent grazing and their conversion to arable
diminished what had been common pastureland. Indeed, despite housing
global textile industries, Flanders and Artois saw local wool production decline between the eleventh and thirteenth centuries.[56] Arable, moreover, was
consolidated to increase productivity.[57] As early as the twelfth century in
much of Northern France and the Low Countries, the patchwork of crops
grown on individual peasant fields that had surrounded villages was being
converted to single, large, open fields managed through collective, compul-
sory systems of crop rotation. The soil of the entire village would be split into
three large open fields devoted to one crop each year, alternating between a
spring grain, a winter grain, and a fallow field. The lord's *demesne* was often
managed in separate, smaller, open fields but it could also be situated among
the peasants' plots. The introduction of oats within this system facilitated the
shift to horses (who favored oats) as the primary draught animal. This open
field system not only allowed for the most efficient use of the land, the consol-
idation of fallow land created a large, communal grazing area where animals
fed on the "stubble" left behind after the harvest. This communal stubble was
necessary since so much pastureland had been plowed and planted. Because
the work of plowing, harvesting, and pasturing was coordinated, the open
field system eliminated the need for the roads and hedges that once been required to keep livestock and equipment from damaging neighboring crops.[58]

The descriptions of the landscape we find in many *pastourelle* songs, in
which a patchwork of fields, woodland, and brushland is bordered by roads
and paths, was thus not contemporary at the time the songs were written.[59]
Such songs describe a pattern of land use that lay in the recent past,[60] evoking

---

[56] Textile producers in the region imported wool, often from England. See Van Bavel, *Manors and Markets*, 133 and 155. Flemish cities even joined the Hanse of London for procuring wool. See Van Bavel, *Manors and Markets*, 113.

[57] The history of open field systems is discussed in Hoffman, "Origin of the Common Fields."

[58] See Van Bavel, *Manors and Markets*, 135–38. This system was not used everywhere (no-tably, Flanders stopped using it during the second half of the thirteenth century), but it was in use in Hainault, Artois, and most of Northern France. See Van Bavel, *Manors and Markets*, 138–39. There were also large open fields near Paris and throughout Champagne. See Renes, "Open Field Landscapes," 141–42.

[59] Occasionally, the descriptions are realistic and contemporary, including references to a fallow field (*lairis* or *gaschiere*) in "D'Ares a Flandres alloie" (RS 1683) and Jehan Bodel's "L'autrier quant chevauchoie" (RS 1702). In Guillaume le Vinier's *bergerie* "Je me chevauchai pensis" (RS 1587), the narrator is riding beside a fallow field.

[60] The poetic landscape is thus not (as Butterfield argues in *Poetry and Music*, 162) representative of the idealized past of the pastoral mode.

the nucleated villages that dominated the countryside during the previous century.[61] If it is often not, strictly speaking, realistic, how might this landscape symbolically configure relationships between identity and place? The next section considers this question in the context of *pastourelles* that depict rape or attempted rape.

Boundaries Transgressed: Topographies of Rape in the *Pastourelle*

The *pastourelle* presents a spectrum of narrative possibilities that would have been known to its audiences, a spectrum that included rape.[62] It was illegal for knights to rape women, but both historical and literary sources implicate knights of all ranks in rapes; chronicles even record cases of knights raping nuns.[63] Instances of rape (including the rape of noble women) pervade medieval romance, many of them carried out by elite knightly characters.[64] Rape was a feature of medieval literature and of life.[65] In an influential essay published in 1985, Kathryn Gravdal drew critical attention to the rapes depicted in the *pastourelle* genre, demonstrating that these songs constituted a large portion of the corpus as a whole.[66] I omitted this subset of *pastourelle* songs from the corpus discussed in the previous section; it is to these songs and their landscapes that I now wish to turn. We will see that the topography of *pastourelles* in which rape is depicted, and the placement of the characters

[61] These arrangements were still in use in some regions, particularly those in which manorial lords were most powerful. See Van Bavel, *Manors and Markets*, 140.

[62] For a lucid overview of *pastourelle* narrative conventions and scholarly approaches to *pastourelle* lyrics, see Smith, *Medieval French Pastourelle*, chap. 1, "The Medieval French Pastourelle."

[63] Kaeuper, *Medieval Chivalry*, 204. Further examples of rapes committed by knights are discussed in Rieger, "Motif du viol," 243–44.

[64] Kaeuper notes that in the Post-Vulgate *Quest for the Holy Grail*, King Arthur rapes a virgin he finds while hunting. *Medieval Chivalry*, 325n12.

[65] Kaeuper, *Medieval Chivalry*, 325.

[66] Gravdal identified twenty-five Old French *pastourelle* songs and motets in which the male subject rapes or attempts to rape the shepherdess. Gravdal, "Camouflaging Rape," 362n4. She explores this corpus more fully in the context of medieval law in Gravdal, *Ravishing Maidens*. In a response to this article, Paden argued that a slightly smaller number (twenty) of Old French songs depicted rape (by his rendering, this represents 18 percent of the 109 songs in which the issue was germane) and that four others depicted attempted rape or had "overtones of rape." See Paden, "Rape in the Pastourelle," 333. With two exceptions, my analysis here takes Gravdal's larger corpus into account. I have added Jehan Bodel's "L'autrier me chevauchoie lés" (RS 1702), which describes a rape but was not included her sample; I eliminated "Je chevauchai l'autrier la matinee" (RS 527; Bartsch III, no.12), which I do not believe represents rape. For a thorough review of literature that has addressed the issue of rape in the *pastourelle*, see Smith, *Medieval French Pastourelle*, 31–38.

Table 5.1 Distribution of Anonymous *Pastourelles* Describing Rape or Attempted Rape

	K	N	P	X	C	I	U	(Me)	S	Ba	Cl	Mo	W2	C (troub.)	G (troub.)
RS 72					X										
RS 75				X	X										
RS 392				X											
RS 534	X	X		X											X*
RS 583									X						
RS 599	X	X	X	X											
RS 1257	X						X*								
RS 1364				X	X*								X		
RS 1695		X						(X)							
RS 1698a	X														
RS 1707					X										
RS 1984	X	X	X	X											
M 227												X			
M 497												X	X		
M 528d											X				
M 716										X		X			
M 717										X		X			

on the landscape in these songs, differs importantly from those examples in which the knight does not resort to violence.

I do not wish to position these "rape *pastourelles*" as a distinct subgenre. Examining the placement of rape *pastourelles* across their surviving manuscripts shows that they were aesthetically diverse and not characterized by a robust transmission history. Few were widely transmitted in the middle ages, as Tables 5.1 and 5.2 show.[67] Their reach was fairly extensive, however; we find them not only in songbooks associated with Artois, Metz, and Paris, but also translated into Occitan and preserved in two troubadour

---

[67] Only one of these songs, "L'autrier par la matinee" (RS 529) by Thibaut, Roi de Navarre, was widely transmitted, appearing in seven extant manuscript contexts and across different songbook families. The survival of the others is sparse: nineteen of the songs are transmitted in only one or two manuscripts; nine of the songs are unique, transmitted in one manuscript alone; and six survive in a single manuscript family. In Table 5.1, entries marked with a * indicate that the copy of the song in that manuscript lacks the description of the rape.

Table 5.2 Distribution of Authored *Pastourelles* Describing Rape or Attempted Rape

Author	#	M	Mt	T	K	N		P	X	V	C	I	B	W2
Ernoul li Vielle	RS 19	X												X (as the duplum of a three-voice motet)
	RS 973	X												
Huitace de Fontaines	RS 1700							X						
Jakes d'Amiens	RS 1681										X			
Jake de Cambrai	RS 1855										X	X		
Jehan Bodel	RS 1702	X		X										
Perrin d'Angecourt	RS 573				X	X		X	X					
Thibaut IV, Roi Navarre	RS 529		X	X	X	X (in a missing part of the manuscript)		X	X				X	

songbooks.[68] One of these songs is transmitted in *S*, where it appears as the first of eight lyrics copied between an Old French translation of a Latin treatise on falconry and a copy of Brunetto Latini's *Li livres dou tresor*.[69]

The *pastourelles* depicting rape present us with a diverse array of forms, from the traditional AAB form (*pedes cum cauda*) we witnessed in many of the trouvère love songs featured in Chapter 3,[70] to songs with refrain

---

[68] An Occitan version of the lyrics of the first twenty-three lines of "Quant voi nee" (RS 534) are entered into a flyleaf of the troubadour songbook *G* (produced in Lombardy), on fol.143r (edited in Rivière, *Pastourelles*, II, 26–27; diplomatic edition in Carapezza, *Il canzoniere occitano*, 589). "Chevauchai mon chef enclin" (RS 1364) is rendered in Occitan in troubadour songbook *C* (which was produced in Southern France) as "Ge me chivaujoy" (attributed to Gautier de Mursin). The Occitan version retains several Old French words such as "l'erbete," "forestier," and "bergiere." The differences between the surviving lyrics are discussed in Rivière, *Pastourelles*, II, 17–18. The broader corpus of Old French songs transmitted in Occitan songbooks is addressed in Rosenberg, "French Songs in Occitan." The Occitanization of French songs is discussed in Zingesser, *Stolen Song*, chap.5, "Rustic Troubadours."

[69] "Quant pré reverdoient" (RS 583). See fols.87v–88v.

[70] "L'autrier par la matinee" (RS 529) and "L'autrier quant je chevauchoie" (RS 1698a).

structures,[71] to motet voices,[72] a *lai*,[73] and a song possibly based on a Latin conductus.[74] Nine of the songs survive without musical notation and across those that have melodies, no two musical/poetic structures are alike. Only one nobleman is represented: Thibaut IV, king of Navarre. The other songs are anonymous or are attributed to authors about whom we know little to nothing (such as Ernoul li Vielle, Huitace de Fontaines, and Jacques de Cambrai). Perrin d'Angicourt is included in the section of songbook *a* devoted to professional musicians from the north, and he is pictured with an organ.[75] As I mentioned in Chapter 2, what little evidence we have regarding the biographies of Jacques d'Amiens suggests he may have been a cleric. The lack of biographical documentation of these few authors prevents us from developing a detailed view of when and where these songs and motets may have been composed, yet a few observations are possible. Around a third of the surviving songs were possibly written by clerics, if, to the song by Jacques d'Amiens, we add the rape *pastourelles* that survive as voices in polyphonic motets (which, as we saw in Chapter 4, may have been written by clerics).[76] Most of the named authors were associated with urban areas.[77] The songs appear in sources copied during the second quarter of the thirteenth century,[78] as well as in manuscripts that were produced during the fourteenth

[71] "Au tens novel" (RS 573), "Hier main" (RS 1700), and "L'autre jour me chevachoie" (RS 1707) are songs with changing refrains (*chanson avec des refrains*).

[72] This includes both voices of the motet, *Hé Marotele* (M716)/*En la praierie* (M717)/*Aptatur* (which appears on *Mo* 112v and 198v, and *Ba*, 18v, and which I discuss at length in Saltzstein, "Rape and Repentance.") as well the motet voices "Quant fuellent aubespine" (M 497; *W2* 194r and *Mo* 135r) and "L'autrier chevauchoie" (M 227; *Mo* 148r).

[73] "L'autrier chevauchoie pensant" (RS 1695).

[74] "Quant voi nee" (RS 534) shares its music with the Latin conductus *Ortum floris*. There is no scholarly consensus regarding compositional priority between the two songs. See the discussion in Marshall, "Old French Lyric," 121–25. This song survives in *C*, *K*, and *N*. The version of the lyrics in *C* includes the lines "Une grant loee/Et demie a duree/La joie de moi et de li/Ainz qu'ele fust finee" (st.3, ll.17–20) after the sex act occurs, suggesting that it was consensual (this is the version presented in Paden, *Medieval Pastourelle*, I, 278–83). The version of the lyrics found in *K* and *N* does not include these lines, which is why I include it in this discussion. Studies of *contrafacta* involving conductus include Tischler, *Conductus and Contrafacta* and Everist, *Discovering Medieval Song*, 255.

[75] Perrin's songs suggest that he was connected with Charles I, King of Naples. It is possible that Perrin was the "Pierre d'Angicourt" who served as rector of the chapel of Castel Vairano outside Naples, a familiar of the king, however, we cannot be certain that the two men were the same. Noted in Harper, "Pierre d'Angicourt and Angevin Construction," 154n18. On Perrin's possible connections to Charles I, see Maillard, *Roi-trouvère*, 29 and Dyggve, *Onomastique des trouvères*, 195–96.

[76] On the relationship between rape and clerical masculinity see Skoda, *Medieval Violence*, 146–49.

[77] Jacques d'Amiens (Amiens), Jehan Bodel (Arras), Huitace de Fontaines (Arras), Richart de Semilli (Paris), and Perrin d'Angecourt (Arras).

[78] "Por conforter mon corage" (RS 19) is transmitted as a song in *M* but also as a motet voice in *W2*, one of the earliest motet manuscripts, the copying of which may have occurred during the 1240s. Although "En mi forest" (RS 1257) appears in *U*, the earliest portions were likely compiled during the 1220s, the stanza in which the rape is described does not appear this manuscript.

century, a period when fewer *pastourelle* songs are extant.[79] The exact percentage of rape *pastourelles* relative to the genre as a whole has been disputed, but it is in the teens by most estimations.[80] Their relatively sparse transmission, less than robust authorial attribution, and heterogeneous musical and poetic features should discourage the view that rape *pastourelles* represent a separate subgenre of the Old French *pastourelle*. Rather, rape was a narrative outcome that appeared in songs spanning many forms and genres that were transmitted throughout the genre's long history. These songs existed as part of a spectrum of possibilities that gave the *pastourelle* its narrative shape.

What relationships do these songs construct between landscape, identity, and sexual violence? Like other *pastourelles*, the descriptions of place in songs that describe rape and attempted rape tend to highlight boundaries of various types, particularly between the woods, the fields, and paths or roads. Like other *pastourelles*, songs depicting rape are saturated with adverbs of place, representing the characters along or between things.[81] Unlike the *pastourelles* I discussed in the previous section, the songs that represent rape specify the knight's location less frequently, simply stating that he was out riding or omitting his position altogether, suggesting a reluctance to place him in an identifiable location.[82] Those that do place the knight spatially most often associate him with the woods, a location closely tied, as I have shown, to knightly identity.[83] In one anonymous song, the speaker claims to be in his own forest, a location that marks him as a high-ranking magnate.[84] Forest (*foresta*) was a legal term used to describe the large, wooded areas prized for hunting, woods that were generally naturally occurring rather than planted, and occupied hundreds to tens of thousands of hectares. Forests lay at the

---

[79] See, for example, *I*, which is believed to have been produced in the early fourteenth century. Even if the repertoire may itself have been older, the manuscript dating would reveal continuing interest in these *pastourelles* at the time of compilation. On the musical sections of this manuscript see Leach, "Adapting the Motet(s)?" and "A Courtly Companion."

[80] I view this percentage as significant regardless of whether we adopt the larger or smaller estimate.

[81] The knight's location is along a wooded area in "Ier matin ge m'en aloie lonc" by Jacques d'Amiens (RS 1681), and "L'autrier quant chevauchoie" by Jehan Bodel (1702); along brushland in "Hier matinet delez un vert boisson" by Jacques de Cambrai (RS 1855) and "L'autre jour moi chivachai" (RS 72); along a meadow in "Quant pré reverdoient" (RS 583). In in "L'autrier par la matinee" by Thibaut IV, King of Navarre (RS 529), the knight is between a wood and an orchard when he finds the shepherdess.

[82] Only one song triangulates the knight's position, in this case, between Arras and Douai, outside of Gavrelle. See "Entre Arras et Douai" (RS 75).

[83] See "Pour conforter mon corage" by Ernoul de Gastinais (RS 19), "Hier main" by Huitace de Fontaines (RS 1700), "En mi forest" (RS 1257), and "Ier matin je m'en aloie" by Jacques d'Amiens (RS 1681).

[84] "En mi forest" (RS 1257).

very top of the hierarchy of medieval arboreal zones;[85] the counts of Hainaut
and Artois, for example, held dozens.[86]

The physical location of the shepherdess differs significantly between rape
pastourelles and the broader corpus of *pastourelles* I surveyed in the previous
section. Although some songs place her in a pasture or a meadow (the most
common place she is found across the in the corpus I surveyed in the previous
section),[87] rape *pastourelles* more often place the shepherdess in a wooded
setting.[88] Their descriptions of these landscapes are specific and detailed,
invoking a broad range of fairly technical terms to differentiate between
glades, groves, planted woodlands, and deep forest. Several of these songs
place the girl under a bush or tree,[89] a position that insinuates privacy. In
"Chevachai mon chief enclin," for example, the knight finds the shepherdess
shading herself under a hawthorn.[90] She is immediately defensive after he
greets her, threatening him with her club and dog. After he announces his intention to take her virginity, he warns that her cries will not be heard "for we
are in the deep forest."[91] Realizing she is trapped, she threatens to cry out so
loudly that "There's not a shepherd in the wood/or a forester in this forest"[92]
who will not know what the knight has done. This terminology strongly
suggests they are located deep within a lordly forest. In "L'autrier par la matinee" by Thibaut IV, the knight finds the shepherdess sitting under a bush,
then puts her onto his saddle and rides toward a wood.[93] The focus on woodland settings as the shepherdess' location in rape *pastourelles* is conspicuous.

The location of the rape is rarely omitted from these songs. Very often,
the narrator tells us that rape happens on the grass, sometimes after the

---

[85] The terminology of lordly forest ecosystems is explained in Duceppe-Lamarre, *Chasse et pâturage*, 142–48. On forests as medieval status symbols, see Rackham, "Medieval Countryside," 22 and Creighton, *Designs Upon the Land*, 153.

[86] Duceppe-Lamarre, *Chasse et pâturage*, 39.

[87] See "Entre Arras et Douai" (RS 75), "Por conforter mon corage" (RS 19), and in the two upper voices of the motet, *Hé Marotele* (M716)/*En la praierie* (M717)/*Aptatur*, which I have argued else-where represent the same scene (see my "Rape and Repentance," 590). Although a lacuna prevents us from knowing her position in "Trespensant d'une amourete" by Ernoul li Vielle (RS 973), the knight dismounts near her in a field, suggesting this is her location.

[88] "Au tens novel" by Perrin d'Angicourt (RS 573), "Hier matinet" by Jacques de Cambrai (RS 1855), "Chevachai mon chief enclin" (RS 1364), "L'autrier par la matinee" (RS 529), "L'autrier chevauchoie pensant" (RS 1695), "Hier main" (RS 1700), "Quant fuellent aubespine" (M 497). In "En mi forest" (RS 1257), the shepherdess is in an orchard within a lordly forest.

[89] See "En mi forest" (RS 1257), "Chevachai mon chief enclin" (RS 1364), "Quant pré reverdoient" (RS 583), "L'autrier chevauchoie pensant" (RS 1695), and "Quant fuellent aubespin" (M 497).

[90] "Chevauchai mon chief enclin" (RS 1364). For a modern edition, see Paden, *Medieval Pastourelle*, I, 224–27.

[91] St.4, l.42: "car nos sons en perfont gaut."

[92] "n'ait pastor en cest boscaige/Ne fourestrier en cest gaul" (st.4, ll.45–46).

[93] See st.5, ll.58–60. Thibaut IV, *Lyrics of Thibaut*, 150–53.

knight throws the shepherdess down.[94] The cultivated spaces that are marked most clearly by human intervention such as gardens and orchards make rare appearances.[95] Some songs specify a field or meadow.[96] The rape also happens under a tree in several cases, in the privacy of a leafy canopy or shadow.[97] In "En mi forest," the knight finds and rapes the shepherdess under a grafted tree (an *enté*), its presence in the forest serving as a reminder that medieval woodlands were not wild.[98] With the rare exceptions, woodlands tended to be planted and actively managed by landowners as a productive pasture.[99] Fruit trees (which were often grafted) were common in such woodlands.[100] Grafting was associated with marriages between characters of different social ranks in medieval literature,[101] and the verb *enter* (to graft) was used in conjunction with nonnoble men who married noblewomen.[102] These songs clearly use the grafted tree to symbolize sexual contact between characters of different social ranks. Marder underscores the transformative nature of grafting, where a scion or graft (the shoot of a young tree) is inserted into an incision made in a root stock of a different species of tree. If the graft succeeds, the plasticity and receptivity of vegetal life allow the root stock to take on the characteristics of the graft, either producing the graft's flowers and fruit alongside its own or by changing and acquiring the

---

[94] See: "Quant fuelle chiet" (RS 392), "Au tens nouvel que cil oisel" by Perrin d'Angicourt (RS 573), "Quant voi nee" (RS 534), "Quant voi la flor nouvele paroir" (RS 599), "Chevachai mon chief enclin" (RS 1364), "L'autrier chevauchoie pensant" (RS 1695), "L'autrier quant je chevauchoie" (RS 1698a), and "Hier matinet" by Jacques de Cambrai (RS 1855). See also the motet voice, "Hé Marotele" (M 716). Although the forest floor in dense, modern woodlands tends to lack grass, the pasturing of cows and pigs in medieval woods suppressed saplings and fertilized the soil, creating a forest structure in which trees were spaced more widely apart and the canopy was laced with grassy clearings. See Duceppe-Lamarre, *Chasse et pâturage*, 70.

[95] In "L'autrier par la matinee" by Thibaut IV (RS 1695), the characters are between a wood and an orchard. In "L'autrier chevauchoie pensant" (RS 529), the shepherdess sits in a grove of hazel trees that in an orchard that lies within a garden.

[96] See "Hier matinet delez" by Jacques de Cambrai (RS 1855) and "Quant voi nee" (RS 534).

[97] "Quant pré reverdoient" (RS 583), "En mi forest" (RS 1257), and "Hier main" (RS 1700).

[98] "En mi forest" (RS 1257). I thus disagree with Smith's characterization of the setting of the medieval *pastourelle* as a liminal space between the tamed aristocratic garden and the "savage" forest (representative of "brute nature"). See Smith, *Medieval French Pastourelle*, 18–19.

[99] On planting in medieval woodlands, see Duceppe-Lamarre, *Chasse et pâturage*, 145–46 and Harvey, *Medieval Gardens*, 15–17. On woodland management, see Keyser, "Woodland Management."

[100] Duceppe-Lamarre, *Chasse et pâturage*, 69.

[101] Butterfield, "Enté," 72. Grafting was also symbolic of aesthetic hybridization in medieval music. Johannes de Grocheio associated grafting with practices of quotation. See ibid., 67–68, and the discussion in Plumley, *Art of Grafted Song*, 21–22. Compilers adopted this usage in conjunction with the *motet enté*, a subgenre of motet that includes refrains. See Butterfield, "Enté," Everist, *French Motets*, 82–89, and Peraino, "Monophonic Motets."

[102] See "Enter" in Godefroy, *Lexique de l'ancien français*, 212. In the *pastourelle* "L'autrier quant je chevauchoie" (RS 1699), a knight finds a lady in a garden shading herself under an *enté*; she is a noblewoman unhappily married to a peasant.

characteristics of the graft. This transformation only occurs when the sap of the graft flows into the trunk—as Marder explains, successful grafting is a difficult feat: "membranes, tissues, liquids, and surfaces must be exposed to one another in all their nudity for a graft to work, to exercise its transformative influence."[103] The mechanics of grafting, with its forced insertion of the graft into the root stock and required transfer of fluids, are an obvious metaphor for the rape that occurs in the two *pastourelles*.

The placement of the shepherdess in the woods rather than a meadow or field is significant. We have already seen that woods are symbolic of knightly identity. But the preponderance of woodland settings in the rape *pastourelles* is also telling because sheep (the animal the shepherdess normally guards) were rarely pastured in medieval woodlands.[104] Although common grazing rights potentially pertained even to lordly woodlands, cows and pigs were normally the only livestock that were permitted to graze there. Sheep and goats inflicted enormous damage on woodlands,[105] and the value of wood was so high that landowners typically forbade pasturage of such animals there, even in cases in which common rights permitted the grazing of cows and pigs.[106] Moreover, because woodland became rarer after the great clearances of the tenth and eleventh centuries, lords severely limited its use; most woodlands in Flanders, for example, were private property.[107]

The prevailing view holds that knightly violence occurs in *pastourelles* because the knight is located outdoors, away from the civilizing influence of the court and thereby loosed from courtly constraints.[108] My analysis suggests a different aspect of the way these songs represent relationships between identity and place. In those *pastourelles* in which the shepherdess is raped, the composer most often locates her in a spatial context that was deeply symbolic of male aristocratic identity and within which a shepherdess' presence would have been unlikely or even proscribed, since custom often forbade the grazing of sheep in woodlands. The songs thus seem to insinuate, through the shepherdess' location, the knight's (far greater) transgression to come. The spatial articulation of these characters reflects knowledge of social dynamics

---

[103] See Marder, *Grafts: Writing on Plants*, 15–17, quotation at 17.

[104] See Duceppe-Lamarre, *Chasse et pâturage*, 60–62.

[105] Duceppe-Lamarre, *Chasse et pâturage*, 71.

[106] Illegal pasturing was punished most harshly near coppices, underscoring its economic implications. See Duceppe-Lamarre, *Chasse et pâturage*, 68.

[107] De Moor, "Common Rights in Flanders," 119.

[108] See Smith, *Medieval French Pastourelle*, 18–21, Zink, *Pastourelle*, 95–96, and Butterfield, *Poetry and Music*, 162.

of these rural spaces. Their composers created an imagined landscape that was coded through realistic markers of status and identity, articulating a geography contoured by symbolic social boundaries as well as the potential for their violent transgression.[109] The outcome for the shepherdess in these songs may have been predictable for listeners familiar with the terrain.

Urban Composers and Rural Life: *Pastourelle* Landscapes of Arras

We have just seen that medieval composers could use landscape symbolically to delineate the status of the *pastourelle's* two primary characters, the knight and shepherdess, superimposing physical spaces and social boundaries. Although *pastourelle* songs tend to present a binary social structure in which only two strata (knights and peasants) are present, excluding the increasing number of people who inhabited medieval cities,[110] urban composers and audiences seem to have cultivated the genre with enthusiasm during the thirteenth century. Some of the oldest surviving *pastourelles* are attributed to Jehan Bodel of Arras, and many other composers associated with urban centers wrote *pastourelles*, including, among others Moniot de Paris, Guillaume le Vinier, Jacques d'Amiens, Jacques de Cambrai, Jean de Renti, Jean de Neuville, Richart de Semilli, and Jehan Erart.[111] Some of these composers transported their *pastourelles* to urban settings,[112] but for the most part, urban composers set their *pastourelles* in the countryside. The gap between the landscapes and identities featured in these *pastourelles* and the identities of their composers and audiences is significant, setting these songs apart from many I explored in chapters 3 and 4 in which the landscapes and identities depicted in songs were closely aligned

---

[109] For a discussion of relationships between identity, geography, and violence in relation to American woodlands, see Finney, *Black Faces, White Spaces*.

[110] Smith argues that the genre represents a fantasy of the simpler social structure of the recent past, reflecting elite social anxiety regarding the emergence of an urban, moneyed middle class. See Smith, *Medieval French Pastourelle*, 66–69.

[111] Noted in Zink, *La pastourelle*, 54.

[112] See, for example, Moniot de Paris' "Je chevauchoie l'autrier" (RS 1255), a *pastourelle* set on the Seine in which the shepherdess is replaced by a woman unhappily married to a villein whose husband lives on the Grand Point (st.3, ll.22–24). Dyggve, *Moniot d'Arras et Moniot de Paris*, 197–200. See also Richard de Semilli, "L'autrier tout seus chevauchoie" (RS 1362), and "L'autrier chevauchoie delez Paris" (RS 1583), a song in which the shepherdess also mentions Saint Denis (st.1, l.5). Richard de Semilli, *Lyrics of Richard*, 29.

with those occupied by their authors.[113] In medieval society, the lives of ordinary people in urban areas differed from their rural counterparts. This
was due not only to factors such as urban population density, cosmopoli-
tanism, and the wider range of occupations available—urban dwellers often
enjoyed rights and freedoms unknown in the countryside. The rise of guilds
and confraternities contributed to a growing sense of civic identity.[114] Most
cities were surrounded by a wall, a porous barrier that physically separated
their interior from what was outside. How might a song genre focused on
the interaction between knights and peasants in agricultural spaces speak to
composers, audiences, and patrons in urban contexts? How might they have
defined their own urban identities against characters occupying agricultural
spaces? I consider these questions through the *pastourelles* (and *pastourelle-*
infused works) of three songwriters from the bustling, cosmopolitan urban
center of Arras: Jehan Bodel, Adam de la Halle, and Jehan Erart.

The five *pastourelles* attributed to the playwright, composer, and cleric
Jehan Bodel (d. 1210) were among the earliest attributed songs in the Old
French genre (their transmission appears in Table 5.3).[115]

Jehan's songs exhibit a broad range of poetic and musical forms, as well
as narrative scenarios and outcomes, ranging from *pastourelles* in which the
narrator observes the shepherds without participating (a narrative type that
scholars call the *bergerie* or "objective" *pastourelle*), to *pastourelles* featuring
rape or attempted rapes, to a *pastourelle* that alludes to political events.[116]
Table 5.4 summarizes stylistic features of his songs, which, like his narratives,
exhibit variety.

Jehan was an urban cleric and his play, the *Jeu de Saint Nicholas*, prominently features taverns, currency, and other emblems of the city. Yet he writes

---

[113] The surviving corpus of authored *pastourelles* divides fairly evenly between authors of high and
low social rank (Zink, *La pastourelle*, 54). *Pastourelles* written by knightly trouvères could potentially align the identities of the author and narrator. Smith rightly notes the potential for humorous
exploitation of this alignment, as in, for example, in "L'autrier par la matinee" (RS 529) by Thibaut
IV, in which the knightly narrator departs after hearing the shouts of the shepherdess' lover from
the woods. The notion that a king and military commander such as Thibaut would quit the scene
rather than confront a (likely unarmed) shepherd surely lent a comic tone to this song, particularly
if performed by the author himself. See Smith, *Medieval French Pastourelle*, 65. Zink argued that
the knight was humiliated often enough that it would be impossible to view the *pastourelle* genre
as merely an aristocratic vehicle for mocking peasants, as critics had once claimed. He viewed
antifeminism as the perspective that most unified these songs. See Zink, *La pastourelle*, 57–65.

[114] Symes articulates this relationship in the context of Arras. See *A Common Stage*.

[115] Jehan claimed that he worked as a clerk to the elected officials (*echevins*) who governed the
Town of Arras. See the discussion of Jehan's life in Symes, *A Common Stage*, 38–42. The table of
contents of *M* shows that compilers planned to include the full corpus of five *pastourelles* attributed to
Jehan, although only two appear in the songbook. All five of Jehan's *pastourelles* appear in *T*; three of
them are copied in succession (fols.85r–86r).

[116] See the editions of Bodel's lyrics in Brasseur, "Les *pastourelles*." The melodies can be consulted
in Tischler, *Trouvère Lyrics with Melodies*.

Table 5.3 Transmission of Jehan Bodel's Song Corpus

RS Number	Index of *M*: Songs attributed to Jehan Bodiaus (Er)	*M*	*T*	*U*	*C*
141	Entre le bois		78r		
367	Les un pin verdoiant	98v*–99r	85v–86r		
571	Lautre ior les un boschel		85r		
578	Contre le dous tans	99r	109r–109v (attributed to Aubuins)		
1702	Hui main me chemin' (attributed a second time to Guiot de Dijon)		85r–85v	74v–75r Ruled for musical notation (none entered)	139v–140r Ruled for musical notation (none entered)

Table 5.4 Style Features of Jehan Bodel's Songs

RS #	141	367	571	578	1702
pedes cum cauda	no	no	no	no	yes
Tonal center/ Secondary Tonal center	D	G/D	C/D	D/G	D/C
Refrains	no	vdB 1408	no	vdB 1883	no
Large leaps	5th	no	4th	no	no
Internal motivic repetition	yes	no	yes	yes	yes
Range	9th	9th	7th	8ve	9th
Meter	heterometric	isometric (Hélinand Strophes) + refrain	heterometric	heterometric	isometric
Narrative type	*bergerie*	"classic"	*bergerie*	"classic"	"classic"

pastourelles that are remarkably evocative of rural life. They contrast with many examples I explored previously in their realism and the degree to which they accurately portray land use practices that were contemporary at the time of writing. Jehan refers to specific species of trees and modes of arboreal growth.[117] His description of springtime in "Contre le dous tans" includes an evocative image of newly sprouted grass that is "pointing" from the ground.[118] Jehan's understanding of grazing customs is evident in "L'autre jor les un boschel," which features a shepherdess whose lover has abandoned her in anger after she allowed her lamb to run away into the woods.[119] In "Entre le bos," where Robin chides Marion to redirect her sheep out of the oat field back to the grass, Jehan demonstrates his knowledge of current farming practices.[120] As we saw earlier, oats were being cultivated as a result of newer schemes of crop rotation. This song is a *bergerie* in which, between the woods and the plains and far from the village, the narrator finds Marion guarding her animals.

I	Entre le bos et le plaine
	Trovai de ville lontaigne
	Tose de grant beauté plaine
	Ses bestes gardant.
5	Cler chantoit come seraine,
	Et Robins a vois autaine
	Li respond ens flahutant;
	Et je por oïr lor samblant
	Descendi, si entendi
10	Ke cele li dist tant:
	"Robin, bien fust avenant
	K'eüssïens chapel d'un grant,
	De la flor permeraine."
II	A cest mot Robins l'achaine
15	Ki por s'amor ert em paine.
	"Marïon," fait il, "amaine
	Tes bestes avant
	Ke ne passent ens l'avaine;

---

[117] In "L'autrier me chevauchoie" (RS 1702), the knight rides along a grove of fir trees (*sapinoie*); in "Les un pin" (RS 367), he finds the shepherdess under a pine tree.

[118] "Qu'erbe point novele" (RS 578) l.2. References to the lyrics refer to Brasseur, "Les *pastourelles*."

[119] RS 571.

[120] RS 141, st.2, ll.16–19.

Met le ens l'erbe foraine.

20 Ton chapel ferai avant

Mais mout me feroies dolant

Se le cri de ton ami

Avoie por noiant,

Car Perrins se va vantant

25 Ke de çou dont me vois penant

K'il en keudra la graine."

[I: Between the woods and the plain,/I encountered a young girl of striking beauty/from a remote village/keeping her animals./She sang with a clear voice like a siren/And Robin, in sonorous voice/responded to her with a refrain on his flute./As for me, to find out what they were doing,/I dismounted to hear/what she was saying to him:/"Robin, it would be very nice/if we could each have a crown of equal size/made of new flowers." II: With these words, Robin,/who was making great efforts to be loved/called out "Marion, lead/your animals forward/so that they do not pass through the oats;/graze them in the grass outside the field./I will make your crown beforehand,/but you will give me a great deal of pain/if you ignore/your lover's call,/for Perrin boasts /that all in spite of my efforts,/it is he who will reap the grain."][121]

Bodel's song "Entre le bos" appears in Example 5.1.[122] Although not in *pedes cum cauda* form, describing this song as through-composed does little

Example 5.1 Jehan Bodel, "Entre le bos"

---

[121] This text Brasseur's edition: Bodel, "Les *pastourelles*," 264–65.

[122] Example 5.1 follows *T* 78r, which preserves this song's only surviving melody.

justice to the subtle motivic repetition that permeates it (and most of Bodel's melodies, as Table 5.4 shows).

Three distinctive motives (labelled X, Y, and Z in Example 5.1) reoccur throughout the first eight lines. The rising open fifth of the X motive lends an annunciatory quality to the narration in lines 1, 4, and 5.[123] The sonic character of the stanza undergoes a shift in line 9, when the knight descends to hear Marion speak. Bodel introduces a new rhyme sound that appears in this line alone ("di").[124] The narrator then tells us that he hears Marion ask Robin to make them both wreaths of new flowers (ll.11–13). Marion's words, which the narrator quotes to us, are sung to an inversion of the annunciatory open fifth figure (marked with a * in Example 5.1), which is inverted as a descending open fifth in her request in line 11.[125] The second of the song's two stanzas record Robin's affirmative response to Marion's request as well as his apprehension that a competitor for her affections, Perrin, has boasted that he will reap the "grain" of Robin's efforts to please her.[126] Bodel's poetic placement of Robin's apprehension at the end of the second stanza ensures that it is sung to the same melodic segment as Marion's request, a symmetrical compositional technique that underscores the complementary nature of the rustic couple's relationship.

Although the knight in "Entre le bos" is a benign observer, in other songs, Jehan portrays knights as a violent presence in the countryside. In two of the three songs in which the knightly character interacts with the shepherdess, he attempts rape.[127] In "Contre le douz tans novel," the knight finds the shepherdess not in a field or wood, but on the mount of Cassel, a location near to where the army of the French King Philip Augustus found itself trapped in August of 1199 during a conflict with the counts of Flanders and Hainaut; the shepherdess bemoans the devastation both armies have wrought on the countryside.[128] Bodel's recurring emphasis on knightly violence would likely

---

[123] As Table 5.4 shows, such large leaps are relatively unusual in Bodel's songs.

[124] Here, I follow Brasseur's segmentation of the song. Raynaud/Spanke splits line 9 into two separate lines (3 + 4 syllables), whereas Brasseur views the rhyme within line 9 as internal. Cf. Bodel, "Les pastourelles," 262 and Spanke, G. Raynaud's Bibliographie, 54.

[125] This gesture also echoes the cadence of l.6, which describes Robin's sonorous voice ("a vois autaine").

[126] St.2, ll.24–26.

[127] "Les un pin" (RS 367) and "L'autrier me chevauchoie" (RS 1702), where the knight rapes the shepherdess after violently killing a wolf that has taken one of her lambs. Jehan tells us that the knight attacks the wolf with a blow of such violence (Un cop de tel randon, st.2, l.28) that the wolf dies.

[128] RS 578. M attributes this song to Bodel in both the table of contents and on 99r, where the song is copied. It should be noted however that this same song is listed a second time in table of contents of M where it is attributed to Guiot de Dijon, and that T attributes the song to "Aubuin," likely Aubouin de Sézanne (109r).

have spoken directly to his contemporaries of turn of the century Arras, weary of their position in the middle of a power struggle between Count Philip II of Flanders and the king of France, Philip II.[129]

If the *pastourelle* genre often pits knights against shepherds, Jehan's songs transparently side with the latter. His shepherds and shepherdesses are wily and clever, boldly bargaining with the knight[130] and engaging in schemes in which the knight is ridiculed or made to feel foolish. In "Les un pin" the knight is drawn to observe the shepherdess and her lover share affection under a pine tree.[131] After Robin goes into the woods, the knight approaches her, asking her for a kiss. After she agrees to give him three kisses to appease his desire, he "miscounts," taking six instead, prompting her playful admonition that he keep their original bargain. His desire doubled, he throws her under him as she cries out three times; hearing her cry, Robin and three friends run out of the woods, prompting the knight to leave, since force was on their side. Bodel harnesses the musical structure to help assure listeners that the shepherdess is not in real danger, because she took measures to protect herself (and these prove successful). Bodel wrote this song in Hélinand stanza, a sophisticated poetic form he would also use in his *Congés*, which features twelve-line stanzas, each divided into two hexasyllabic halves; the rhyme scheme of the stanza's second half inverts that of the first. To the end of all five stanzas in this song, Bodel also attached a refrain, extending each to fourteen lines.[132] As shown in Example 5.2, Bodel designed the musical setting to highlight the textual structure.[133]

The musical form, ABC ABC DEF $D^1E^1F^1$ GG^1 (marked above the staff in Example 5.2) allots a melodic unit to each rhyme. The melody also emphasizes the hexasyllabic halves by repeating the first three melodic units in lines 4–6 and repeating the three melodic segments set to lines 7–9 in lines 10–12. The melody is thus fashioned to draw further attention to the

---

[129] See the summary in Symes, *A Common Stage*, 53–56. "Contre le douz tans novel" may have been understood allegorically through the lens of this conflict, as Bruckner has argued: the shepherdess represents, through her position of inferiority vis the knight, the commune of Arras; she enters into a struggle with a superior power and has at least a chance to prevail. Bruckner, "Jehan Bodel's Political Pastourelle," 128.

[130] Unsuccessfully and at significant cost in "L'autrier me chevauchoie" (RS 1702), where the shepherdess is raped after attempting to trick the knight.

[131] RS 367, st.1.

[132] See the notes on versification and meter in Brasseur, "Les *pastourelles*, 280–81.

[133] Example 5.2 is based on *T* 85v–86r, which transmits the full melody and text. The version in *M* that begins on 99v lacks the song's opening (a segment of the folio was removed at some point in the manuscript's history). The portion of the first stanza that survives on 99r (beginning on the last word of st.1, l.9) preserves the same basic pitch strand with few (very minor) differences.

Example 5.2 Jehan Bodel, "Les un pin"

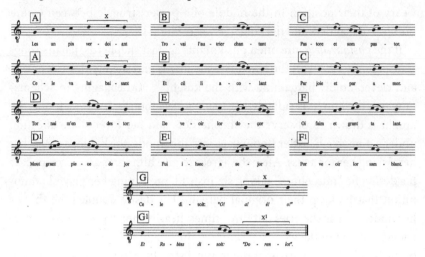

Hélinand stanza.[134] This ensures that the rhyme sounds are sung to the same or very similar melodic segments throughout. Tonally, Bodel's melody is carefully planned around its cadential pitch (g), which is reinforced at the end of the stanza (as the cadential pitch of F') and in the starting pitches of the A melody and both halves of the refrain. The refrain's two halves (G and G[1]) are sung reciprocally by the shepherdess and Robin, their meaning and phrasing shifting subtly throughout the song. In the first stanza, after they embrace, the shepherdess sings the nonsense vocables "O a e o!"; to this, Robin replies "Dorenlot!" Bodel's melody highlights their diegetic song as an emblem of their suitability and reciprocity as a couple. The brief melody is antiphonal, its cue ("Cele disoit" or "she said/sang" and "Et Robins disoit" or "And Robin said/sang") set to the same pitches (see Example 5.2).[135] The upper neighbor figure that sets the final three syllables of the shepherdess' song (d-e-d) is transposed down a fifth and inverted in Robin's "Dorenlot" (g-f-g), mirroring her song in his own vocal range. These motives are bracketed and marked x and x[1] in Example 5.2; the motive derives from the cadence of the A melody, also bracketed and marked x). As the song progresses, it becomes clear that even as the knight attempts to press his advantage, Robin is always in earshot. In stanza 2, after the knight sits beside the shepherdess

---

[134] Globally, we can think of the form as aa bb' CC', which, as Rosenberg, Switten, and le Vot note, approximates the ballade. See Rosenberg et al., *Songs of the Troubadours and Trouvères*, 265.

[135] Robin's cue ("Et Rob-ins di-soit") is one syllable longer than Marion's ("Cele disoit").

and requests her love, the girl speaks not a word, and Bodel's refrain subtly shifts to provide her response: "Instead, she said: "'O! a! é! o!'/and Robin, in the woods, 'Dorenlot.'"[136] The refrain functions as a signal between the shepherdess and her lover; his response assures her that he is always in earshot, ready to protect her. The need for his proximity arises in the final stanza, after the knight he throws her under him as she cries out three times. Robin and three of his friends respond immediately, rushing out from the woods while the knight runs off. The final refrain, "No longer was there any talk of 'O! a! é! o!'/Robin no longer said 'Dorenlot,'"[137] shows that the refrain, which is no longer necessary, was the couple's signal. In this song, we find the *pastourelle* couple in command of the space they inhabit and of their contact with the knight and his violent tendencies. As a whole, Jehan Bodel's *pastourelle* corpus demonstrates knowledge of rural land management. His melodic settings suggest his sympathy for and perhaps even his identification with his peasant characters, and his tone invites audiences to identify with them.[138]

Although no monophonic *pastourelle* songs are attributed to him, Adam dramatized the encounter at the heart of the *pastourelle* in one of the earliest surviving vernacular plays, his *Jeu de Robin et Marion*. This play suggests Adam's deep familiarity with the relationships between landscape and identity articulated in the *pastourelle* song tradition. The *pastourelles* of *arrageois* trouvères such as Jehan Bodel, Jehan Erart, and Guillaume le Vinier, among others, may have provided him with important models for this play, which expands the cast of characters beyond the shepherdess and knight to a group of their rustic friends.[139] Adam's urban home (which he depicted in his other play, the *Jeu de la feuillée*) was a far cry from the rural landscapes

---

[136] St.2, ll.13–14. Ançois disoit: "O! a! é! o!"/Et Robins el bois: "Dorenlot!"

[137] St.5, ll.13–14. Puis n'i ot dit: "O! a! é! o!"/Robins ne dit puis: "Dorenlot."

[138] Although Bodel's *fabliaux* include the foolish peasant characters that are a typical locus of humor within the genre, his sympathy toward them is also suggested in "The peasant of Bailleul." See Dubin, *The Fabliaux*, 496–503. Jehan's portrayal of peasant life also resonates with the songs of the cleric-trouvère Guillaume le Vinier, whose three *pastourelles* eschew the seduction narrative. In two, Guillaume's narrators describe scenes of seasonal peasant dances: "Le premier jour de Mai" (RS 87) and "Quant ces moissons song cuillies" (RS 1350). In the third, "Je me chevauchai pensis" (RS 1587), a narrator observes a shepherdess using a hemp leaf to learn whom she will marry. The expression Guillaume uses to describe her process of divination (l.65: "Quant fis ma chenneviere") was also used to refer to plowing and other agricultural activities. See remarks of Ménard in Guillaume le Vinier, *Guillaume le Vinier*, 236.

[139] See remarks in Brusegan, "Symbolisme champêtre," 119. Ungureanu credited the poets of Arras with introducing variations on the narrative of encounter, including the extended cast of characters associated with the *bergerie*, and argued that these songs were a generic precedent for Adam's dramatization. See *Bourgeoisie naissant*, 165–69. Blanchard also argued that the dramatized *pastourelle's* origins lay in the *bergerie*. See Blanchard, *La pastorale en France*, 17–45.

described in *pastourelle* songs, and Adam probably wrote the *Jeu de Robin et Marion* in a location even farther afield from its rural, Northern French setting: the Angevin court in Naples, where, from around 1284 and most likely until his death around 1288, Adam served Robert II, count of Artois.[140] The play was brought back home to Arras where it was clearly well loved after Adam's death.

How might the *Jeu de Robin et Marion* have resonated with audiences in the urban context of Arras?[141] Adam's engagement with the *pastourelle* subject matter shared the positive attitudes toward the shepherds and shepherdess that we saw in Jehan Bodel's songs. As Brownlee argues, by transforming the *pastourelle*, with its linear narrative told from the perspective of the knight, into a drama in which the knight is just one of a large cast of characters, Adam de la Halle allows Marion, Robin, and their peasant friends to speak (and sing) in their own voices, dramatically elevating their status while simultaneously demoting the knight from his former position as the genre's controlling narrator.[142] Through the songs the characters sing throughout the play (many of which are intertextual refrains used in related songs that survive) Adam often introduces musical subtexts that bring the narrative possibilities of the genre into relief through clever references for knowing audiences.[143] The play opens by eschewing the framework through which the knight controlled the narrative of the songs. Instead, Adam opens with Marion singing a *rondet*, "Robin m'aime" (ll.1–8),[144] allowing the character of Marion to sing for herself from the start and to express her contentment with her shepherd lover. The refrain she sings is a reference that connects Adam's play to two other *pastourelle* songs that together articulate the genre's spectrum of narrative possibilities: in one, the shepherdess sings the refrain just

---

[140] On this dating, see Symes, "The 'School of Arras,'" 29. Adam may have composed his *Jeu de Robin et Marion* against the backdrop of widespread unrest that spread throughout the kingdom after 1282, when an Angevin soldier incited a peasant rebellion in Palermo after he sexually assaulted an Italian woman. Although numerous accounts consider how Adam's story of shepherdess forcefully pursued by a knight might have resonated in performance in this charged context (notably Butterfield, *Poetry and Music*, 163–68, but see the summary of this literature in Smith, *Medieval French Pastourelle*, 108–9), Symes argues that it is difficult to develop a political reading of this play that would be in accord with an Angevin agenda. See Symes, *A Common Stage*, 263–66.

[141] Symes brilliantly explores the ways in which the play speaks to the identity of its likely patron, Count Robert II of Arras, expressing his taste for theatricality. See Symes, *A Common Stage*, chap. 5, "Lives in the Theater."

[142] See Brownlee's still unsurpassed reading, "Transformations of the Couple," 419–21. The range of interpretations that have been proposed in the vast literature on this play is summarized in Smith, *Medieval French Pastourelle*, chap. 2, "Adam de la Halle's *Jeu de Robin et Marion*: Lyric Fantasy Meets Theater."

[143] Butterfield, *Poetry and Music*, 151–60 and Saltzstein, "Refrains in the *Jeu*."

[144] Line numbers refer to Adam de la Halle, *Oeuvres complètes*.

before being raped, and in the other, she sings the refrain while refusing the knight.[145] The play's knight, Aubert, must wait until Marion finishes singing to make his entrance.[146] He does so not with an emotive springtime opening, but rather, he merely sings that he is returning from a tournament. Although he makes no reference to the setting in the text,[147] Adam's play thus begins with Marion's sung reminder of the undercurrent of rape in the *pastourelle* genre upon which it is based, as well as Aubert's reference to the knightly violence and destruction of the countryside that occurred during tournaments.

Adam's familiarity with the physical landscapes represented in the *pastourelle* song corpus is evident in his play, which charts a familiar rural terrain. The encounter between Marion and the knight, Aubert, is amplified into three distinct scenes. In his first request, Aubert asks Marion, "Now tell me, sweet shepherdess,/would you like to come with me,/and play on this beautiful horse/along this copse in the valley?"[148] As I showed earlier, a "little wood" (*bosket*) or copse was the sort of place where sex (whether consensual or not) would be likely to occur.[149] After Marion refuses him, Aubert rides away, finally singing a conventional opening for a *pastourelle* song: "This morning I went riding along the edge of a wood; I found a kind shepherdess; a king never saw one more beautiful...."[150] He rides off singing this *pastourelle*, which takes its cue from many others in which the knight is situated along the edge of a wooded area. When the knight encounters Marion a second time, she rebuffs him quickly, asking him to keep to his path;[151] when he asks her to help him find his bird, Marion tells him "Go along this little hedge/ I think that you will find it there."[152] Hedges, which we did not encounter at all in the *pastourelle* corpus, were used as barriers around parks to prevent game from escaping. By suggesting that he follow "this little hedge" (cest

---

[145] See "Au tens nouvel que cil oisel" (RS 573) by Perrin d'Angicourt, where the shepherdess sings the refrain "Robin m'aime" at the end of the stanza preceding the rape, and "A l'entrant de mai" (RS 85), in which a shepherdess sings the refrain as part of her lengthy refusal of the knight. Discussed in Butterfield, *Poetry and Music*, 152–56. For additional surviving contexts for this refrain, see Ibos-Augé, *REFRAIN*. http://refrain.ac.uk/view/abstract_item/1633.html.

[146] On this inverted structure, see Brownlee, "Transformations of the Couple," 423.

[147] None of the three manuscripts in which the *Jeu de Robin et Marion* survives (*W, Aix*, and fr.1569) include stage directions.

[148] Ll.68–71: "Or me dites douche bergiere/Vauriés vous venir avoec moi/Jeuer seur che bel palefroi/Selonc che bosket en che val."

[149] Brusegan argued that Adam intended the terms "bosket" and "val" as sexual innuendoes. See her "Le *Jeu de Robin et Marion*," 121.

[150] Ll. 97–102: "Hui main jou chevauchoie les l'oriere d'un bois/Trouvai gentil bergiere/Tant bele ne vit roys...."

[151] L.286: Pour dieu sire ales vo chemin.

[152] Ll.292–93: Alés selonc cest haiete/Je cuit que vous l'i trouverés.

haiete), she not only asks him to leave but also uses a reference to the built environment to reinforce the symbolic, social boundaries between them. In her final encounter with Aubert, the knight carries Marion off on his horse after her refusal. Having lost Marion, Robin and his friend Gautier hatch a plan to get her back; they scheme to hide themselves behind the bushes.[153] Their plan is comically cowardly and ineffectual (Marion will later berate Robin for this cowardice); however, within the generic realm of the *pastourelle*, the bushes would be the sort of place where a rape might occur. Robin's plan thus reflects a long tradition of spatial coding in the *pastourelle* landscape that we observed in the songs explored earlier, where wooded locations are associated with sexual activity and sometimes rape. Relationships between landscape, identity, and violence that lay on the landscape's surface in earlier *pastourelle* songs continue to exert influence in Adam's late thirteenth-century dramatization.

The popularity of *pastourelles* in medieval urban settings may seem straightforwardly escapist, composers and audiences vicariously experiencing identities that lay in contrast with their own. Yet the sympathetic ways in which both Jehan Bodel and Adam de la Halle portrayed the peasantry and the realism of Jehan's depiction of land use practices should remind us that the ties between cities like Arras and their surrounding countryside were close. The economies of cities and their provisioning hinterlands were fluid and marked by constant crossover.[154] Although medieval urbanites held a strong sense of collective identity, they were also dependent on the surrounding villages for virtually all of their food. Medieval agricultural surpluses were, by modern standards, small; and transportation was difficult and costly. Fossier estimated that feeding the population of Arras at its height (around 30,000–35,000 people) required around three thousand square kilometers of productive arable land,[155] a rural expanse that would have encompassed as many as one hundred sixty-five individual villages.[156] Cities often had rights to force producers from the surrounding countryside or those shipping grain on bordering rivers to sell their grain there.[157] As Fossier explained, although medieval Arras is remembered primarily for its

---

[153] Ll. 368–72: "Now, let's see what will become of them/please; and let's "bush" ourselves/all three of us behind these bushes/because I want to help Marion/if you'll help me with the rescue." (Or esgardons leur destinee,/Par amours; si nous embuissons/Tout troi derriere cel buissons,/Car je voeil Marion sekeure/Se vous le m'aidés a reskeure).

[154] Van Bavel, *Manors and Markets*, 122.

[155] Fossier, "Arras et ses campagnes," 18.

[156] Fossier, "Arras et ses campagnes," 22.

[157] Van Bavel, *Manors and Markets*, 109.

cultural achievements, "these cultural traits could not develop without the rural substrate that supplied it with grain, wool, and people."[158]

Indeed, many medieval town-dwellers were recent transplants; toponyms suggest that the urban inhabitants of Arras had largely relocated from the nearby countryside.[159] As Kowaleski explains, "Towns were distinct from the countryside, but they were of the countryside too . . . many townspeople were in origin peasants, and given the essential role of migration in sustaining urban life in the Middle Ages, we might not be too far off in thinking that the quintessential townsperson was not someone born, bred, and dead within town walls, but instead a risk-taking migrant."[160] This scenario likely pertained in the decades around 1200, when Jehan Bodel was writing such convincing descriptions of rural land use. But even in the mid- and late thirteenth century, when *arrageois* trouvères like Guillaume le Vinier, Jehan Erart, and Adam de la Halle and their audiences lived, many city-dwellers would have descended relatively recently from farmers.[161] It is thus unsurprising that some urban *pastourelle* composers portrayed rural characters sympathetically or were astute in their understanding of the rural land use practices that may have lain, if not in their own memories or in their recent family history, in the memories of many in their audiences. Because of the high demand for servants, medieval urban populations skewed female; urban women had often left behind strenuous manual labor in favor of higher wages, lighter work, and more varied diets.[162] How might such women have reacted to the works I have discussed, should they have heard them?[163] The figure of the shepherdess may well have reminded them of difficult lives they had escaped. The fictional elevation of the shepherdess figure in works by

---

[158] "ces traits de culture n'auraient pu se developper sans le substrat rural qui l'alimente en grains, en laine et en hommes." Fossier, "Arras et ses campagnes," 25.

[159] Fossier, "Arras et ses campagnes," 22.

[160] Kowaleski, "Medieval People," 600.

[161] This helps to explain the popularity of the anonymous play, the *Courtois d'Arras*, in which a farmer moves to the city and is quickly parted from his money, returning home to his father's farm, a story Symes argues spoke to the anxieties of recent urban transplants. See Symes, *A Common Stage*, 71–80.

[162] Kowaleski, "Medieval People," 581. The skeletons of medieval peasant women of this era show lives marked by heavy lifting and squatting and suggest they performed just as much heavy labor as men did. See ibid., 494–95.

[163] The makeup of the audiences for Adam's plays is a matter of speculation. The *Jeu de Robin et Marion* may have been performed publicly in Arras (Symes argues that Adam's other play, the *Jeu de la feuillée*, was performed publicly, outdoors in Arras, perhaps on a yearly basis. See *A Common Stage*, 231) and the worn state of the manuscripts preserving it suggest repeated use. Given that many women lived and worked as musicians and performers in Arras (see Dolce, " 'Soit hom.' ") it seems possible that they were also included in audiences of the play.

Jehan Bodel and Adam de la Halle may have been welcomed by this audience in particular.

The most prolific composer of thirteenth-century *pastourelles*, Jehan Erart of Arras, suggests a different facet of *pastourelle* reception and urban identities. Although we know almost nothing about Jehan from historical sources,[164] in Chapter 2, I showed that the songbook *a* situates him within a section of trouvères that were professional entertainers.[165] Jehan's *pastourelles* are often narrated by knights whose requests are fulfilled easily and without violence. In several songs, the shepherdess complains that her lover is staying away too long,[166] Robin's distance serving as a rationale for her acquiescence to the knight's advances. Such songs may speak to the influence of Jehan's patrons, some of whom seem to have been wealthy, high-interest moneylenders from the urban patriciate of Arras. In honor of one of these patrons, a certain "Gerard" (possibly Gherart Aniel),[167] Jehan wrote the highly unusual song, "Nus chanters" (RS 485). Jehan honors the death of his protector, singing, "Death, you have ravished my wheat and my vetch, and my garden,"[168] directly correlating artistic patronage with agricultural production.[169] Jehan then mentions having "placed his hopes" in Robert Crespin, suggesting he aspired to the patronage of a member of the richest moneylending family in Arras.[170] Finally, in his envoi, Jehan sends his song to "Pierron Wyon" and "Wagon," members of the Wion family of moneylenders based in Arras.[171]

"Nus chanters" is fascinating in its combination of agricultural metaphors, direct appeals to noted usurers, and noble pretensions. Sponsoring songs such as Jehan's *pastourelles* may have been in keeping with the affectations of

---

[164] Indeed, we do not even know if the songs attached to this name were written by one person or two. There were two men named Jehan Erart are inscribed in the register of the Carité de Notre Dame des Ardents d'Arras in 1258 and 1259. The compositional output attributed to this name could be by either of these men or both.

[165] See Table 2.2c.

[166] See "Les le brueill" (RS 993) and especially "Dales Longpre" (RS 570), where the shepherdess' refrain encapsulates this sentiment. A modern edition and translation are available in Paden, *Medieval Pastourelle*, 175–79.

[167] Dyggve, *Onomastique des trouvères*, 151. Rosenberg argues that this is the only surviving lament that is directed at a patron. See Rosenberg, "Lyric Death Laments," 45–54. An edition can be found in Rosenberg, Tischler, and Grossel, *Chansons de Trouvères*, 726–29.

[168] St.5, ll. 29–30: "Mors, tolu m'as et men blé et me veche/Et mes cortieus;/Tos les mes as ravis."

[169] Vetch is a nitrogen-fixing, flowering legume used as a cover crop to replace nutrients in spent soil.

[170] St. 5, l.35: "Robers Crespins, ou j'ai mon espoir mis."

[171] Pierres Wion was mentioned as a judge in several *jeux-partis*. He was *échevin* before 1260 and again in 1263. See Dyggve, *Onomastique des trouvères*, 203. Pierre's brother, "Wagon" (sometimes Vaugon Guion or "Vuaghes Wions") is mentioned in the *envoi* of "Pour la meillour qu'onques formast" (RS 2108) by Jehan le Cuvelier and served as *échevin* in 1265. See Dyggve, *Onomastique des trouvères*, 247–48.

the urban patriciate in Arras, including the wealthy moneylending families. Symes has illuminated the socially fluid and theatrical character of medieval Arras, arguing that social upstarts were eager to confuse distinctions between old families and new wealth.[172] Members of the patrician elite in Arras tended to marry each other or members of the local nobility. They often owned significant portions of urban land as well as land in the surrounding countryside: the Wions held land near the city, the Crespins owned land to the east and southeast, and the Loucharts (another family of prominent moneylenders in Arras) held property in the surrounding countryside near Bapaume. The urban rich kept manors on their lands and would have needed to spend time on their estates, supervising the harvests and the employees who worked the land for them.[173] Might these financiers have sponsored *pastourelles* by trouvères like Jehan Erart in part to assume the mantle of the aristocracy and project this identity to audiences in Arras? Might they have imagined themselves in the position of the *pastourelle* knight, particularly the knights who were so easily gratified in Jehan's songs? Might such role-play have reminded them of how far their families had climbed from the rank occupied by the shepherds and shepherdesses the knight encounters? Patronizing and hearing *pastourelle* songs may have reminded this specific audience of changes in their relationships to the land, underscoring their relatively new status as landowners, giving voice to their noble aspirations, and defining their identities against the figure of the peasant.

The medieval *pastourelle* tied identity to landscape in ways that could be oriented to either the past, the future, or both at once. Through an anachronistic landscape with its roots in the recent past, some songs aligned not only the identities but also the actions of knight and peasant characters with specific rural spaces. These songs spatialized identity, conceptualizing social difference symbolically through physical boundaries. Viewed within the context of their urban reception history, other *pastourelle* songs underscored the potential for those whose social status had changed to imagine a familial past or a desired future through poetic representations of rural space.

---

[172] Symes, *A Common Stage*, 154. The medieval bourgeoise classes were anxious to join the knightly classes; they were quick to adopt coats of arms, hold tournaments, and intermarry with knightly families. See Kaeuper, *Chivalry and Violence*, 194.

[173] See Fossier, "Arras et ses campagnes," 23. See also Van Bavel, *Manors and Markets*, 108–9.

6

The Song-Space of the Medieval Garden

Performance and Privacy in the *Rondet*

The majority of land, both around medieval cities and villages as well as on estates, was devoted to agricultural production and careful resource management. Yet by the thirteenth century, relatively large portions of medieval estates began to be reserved for ornamental spaces—areas designed not exclusively for agricultural productivity and valued for their ability to provide sensory pleasures.[1] These garden spaces were strongly associated with aristocratic women, both in their use as well as their design and management. Space was gendered in the middle ages, with women more often occupying rooms, houses, and quarters in the cities and villages, while men tended to occupy streets, highways, fields, cities.[2] The garden, however, was an outdoor space with strong ties to women. The late fourteenth-century aristocratic household manual *Le menagier de Paris* stated directly that garden management was the role of the lady of the house.[3] Eleanor of Castile (queen of Edward I) personally oversaw her own royal gardens, employing Aragonese gardeners and an Italian vintner, and importing apple cuttings from France.[4] Because crowding was a feature of even elite medieval households, the promise of time spent alone (or in the clandestine company of a lover) amid the healing presence of plant-life[5] could rank among the greatest of all possible luxuries. Making wreaths and garlands out of flowers was a common pastime of

---

[1] Garden spaces could still be managed productively, and medieval people would not have distinguished between beauty and use with regard to plant-life. See Dowling, "Landscape of Luxuries." Records of gardens among the lower classes are generally scarce since the produce was not often sold, however tithes offer glimmers of the mixture of herbs, beans, fruit, and flowers grown in the kitchen gardens of the peasantry. See Delmaire, "Note sur le dime," 232–34.

[2] See Hanawalt and Kobialka, "Introduction," ix–xviii, at x.

[3] Creighton, *Designs upon the Land*, 176.

[4] Creighton, *Designs upon the Land*, 175.

[5] The medicinal benefits of plants were believed to extend to the very act of viewing them. See Rawcliffe, "Delectable Sightes," 11.

Song, Landscape, and Identity in Medieval Northern France. Jennifer Saltzstein, Oxford University Press.
© Oxford University Press 2023. DOI: 10.1093/oso/9780197547779.003.0007

aristocratic women, who did this while seated on the turf, fashioning flowers into various arrangements for their own adornment and for the liturgy.[6] Flowers were scattered on the floor and in beds in aristocratic households.[7] The baths aristocratic women took were infused with flowers and medicinal spices, setting these ladies apart from others with their perfume. The gardens attached to castles directly supplied the flowers for these rituals.[8]

This chapter will focus on a song genre that was often set in gardens and other non-agricultural outdoor spaces—the medieval *rondet*. I will argue that a subset of the songs in this genre seems to offer glimpses of the ornamental portions of medieval estates and focuses on the experience of women in such areas. For musicologists and medieval literary scholars, the *rondet* will initially seem an unlikely genre through which to investigate such connections since it has long scholarly associations with orally transmitted dance songs once thought to emanate from medieval peasants. These associations have obscured the topography the songs describe, which often evokes physical spaces that seem elite and ornamental. These songs focus on the kinds of experiences such landscapes allowed for women by introducing concepts of privacy, overhearing, and voyeurism, concepts that some songs enact through their musical forms. They also seem to offer a glimpse of how some medieval women may have experienced the dynamics of place, space, and privacy as they enjoyed time spent in the outdoors.

The Medieval *Rondet*: Aspects of Genre, Register, and Transmission

Main se leva bele Aeliz;
Dormez, jalous, ge vos en pri!
Biau se para, miex se vesti
Desoz le raim.
Mignotement la voi venir
Cele que j'aim.
(Jean Renart, *Roman de la Rose*, vv.310–15)[9]

---

[6] Stannard, "Uses of Plants," 89.

[7] Rawcliffe, "Delectable Sightes," 10.

[8] Woolgar, *The Senses*, 138–43.

[9] Boogaard, *Rondeaux et Refrains*, no.2. In this chapter, all *rondets* and their refrains will be referred to through their number in Boogaard's edition, which will henceforth be abbreviated as "vdB."

[Fair Alice got up in the morning;/*sleep well, I pray you jealous one!*/Adorned and so prettily dressed/under the branches./*I see her come dancing along, the one I love best.*][10]

Scenes like this one abound in the thirteenth-century *rondet* corpus—a lovely girl rises and beautifies herself then dances outdoors under a leafy canopy or amid the blossoms of a garden. Many songs in the *rondet* genre include references to dancing, particularly a dance known as the *carole*. *Rondet* lyrics feature both men and women exuberantly expressing their love and eagerly anticipating reunions with lovers. Their brief narratives unite gardens, the joy of movement, and reciprocal desire. There is often a tantalizing suggestion of privacy, as seen here in Alice's position under the branches. Some of these songs suggest privacy hoped for but already at risk (here, because of a jealous husband). The *rondet* offers intriguing glimpses of the pleasure garden (a relatively novel ornamental outdoor space) and the experiences it offered.

The *rondet* was a monophonic refrain song genre that featured a brief narrative strophe interlaced with a refrain. The form varies considerably, but many *rondets* are in either six lines or eight lines, as in this example:

J'ai mon cuer del tout abandouné
A vous, ma douce amie.
C'est la jus c'on dis ens mi le pré
J'ai mon cuer del tout abandoné
Gieus et baus i avoit assamblé
Quant rose est espanie.
J'ai mon cuer del tout abandouné
A vous, ma douce amie.[11]

[*I have wholly surrendered my heart*/to you, my dear lover./Over there, they say, in the meadow/*I have wholly surrendered my heart*/games and dances were going on/when the rose was in bloom./*I have wholly surrendered my heart*/to you, my dear lover.][12]

The rhyme scheme *a b a b a b* and feminine rhyme sound used here is fairly typical. In *rondet* form, the refrain closes the song, appearing at the end

---

[10] Translation follows Jean Renart, *The Romance of the Rose*, 22.
[11] vdB 159.
[12] This *rondet* appears with the tenor *Letabitur* as a rondeau-motet in *T*. Translation modified from Saint-Cricq, Doss-Quinby, and Rosenberg, *Chansonnier de Noailles*, lviii.

(and, if, as in this case, the song has eight lines, also at the beginning). The refrain's first line can also recur in the middle of the narrative strophe (its position varies). The *rondet's* structure is "rounded" just as its name suggests. The earliest known examples of this genre survive in a narrative romance written sometime in the first quarter of the thirteenth century, Jean Renart's *Roman de la Rose.*[13] Jean Renart integrates the lyrics of sixteen *rondets* as well as lyrics from a variety of other trouvère song types and refrains within this narrative. A total of 198 songs in something like this *rondet* form survive from the thirteenth and early fourteenth centuries; the genre was thus robust and long-lived. I will focus here on a subset of thirty-three *rondets* often referred to as the "Bele Aaliz" and "C'est la jus" songs.[14] The former type, which account for nine of the thirty-three *rondets*, feature a young girl named Alice who adorns herself and heads into a garden to dance. The "C'est la jus" songs often describe dancers assembled beneath a shade tree. These thirty-three songs are formally varied. Seven are in the eight-line form illustrated above. An additional fourteen are in a six-line format similar to the *rondet* above but lacking the initial refrain. There are a significant number of *rondets* among this subset of the repertory (twelve in all) that are not in either the refrain forms just described. Four *rondets*, for example, end with a refrain but do not use a refrain in the song's opening or internally within the strophe. Their sources are diverse. Nearly half are quoted within the narrative of a romance.[15] Two are included in a section of eight *rondets* attributed to the trouvère Guillaume d'Amiens in the songbook *a*, seven others appear in *Mo* and *T*, and two are transmitted in *k*, a manuscript that provides space for music notation that was never entered. Music survives for the minority of the thirty-three *rondets*; only eight *rondets* are transmitted with notation.[16]

There is some indication that medieval observers recognized the *rondet* as a genre, although the evidence is ambiguous. In the only thirteenth-century theoretical text that seems to describe the features of the surviving *rondets*,

[13] This date range is based on the title of the romance's dedicatee. See Baldwin, "A Political Reading," 51 and 64–65. The most recent assessment of the dating of this romance (which is thought to have been written between 1202 and 1218), appears in Martina, "Pour la datation."

[14] Everist discusses these song types in the context of the motet repertoire. See Everist, "The Rondeau Motet."

[15] In addition to Jean Renart's *Roman de la Rose*, three other *rondets* are quoted within other romances: the *Lai d'Aristote*, the *Sone de Nansay*, and *Meliacin*.

[16] In twelve of the thirty-three *rondets*, neither the *rondet* nor its refrain survives with music in any source. There are thirteen *rondets* in which the refrain survives with musical notation in a different source; whether or not that melody would have been associated with the refrain of the *rondet* is unknown.

Johannes de Grocheio emphasizes the repetition at the song's beginning and end.[17] It is not certain, however, that the Latin terms Grocheio used such as *rotunda, rotundella,* and *rondellus* were equivalent to the Old French term *rondel,*[18] which is the term some songbooks attach to pieces of this type.[19] Modern scholars often refer to "rondels" as "rondets de carole."[20] The inclusion of the word "carole" in the generic designation for medieval *rondets* attests to a general assumption that the surviving *rondets* record music that accompanied the popular medieval dance known as the *carole.* This dance was performed in urban and rural environments by all members of medieval society, young and old, from aristocrats, to clerics, to farmers and servants. References to the *carole* abound in sermons and confessors manuals, where the dance frequently served as an exemplum of the sins of lust and pride. Three of these sermons quote lyrics the preachers claim to be *carole* songs.[21] The dance appears with some regularity in narrative romances, where it is variously performed by all social groups and by both sexes.[22] The moralists and poets agree that the dancers adorned themselves with floral garlands. Scandalized priests and confessors claim that *caroles* sometimes occurred in urban cemeteries and took place on saints' days, and that the women beautified themselves with cosmetics and donned wigs made from the hair of the dead.[23] No treatises on choreography survive from the medieval

---

[17] Grocheio, "On secular music," 69.

[18] Falck argues that Grocheo was likely describing a group of sixty songs in fascicle 11 of *F,* some of which end with a cue that directs the singers back to the song's beginning. Ibid., 42–43. Caldwell shows that Latin refrain songs from this era are preserved in ways that provide significantly more information about their performance, often using descriptive cues. See Caldwell, "Cueing Refrains."

[19] See, for example, the manuscript that transmits the complete works of Adam de la Halle (*W*), in which Adam's polyphonic *rondets* open with the rubric "li rondel Adan" on fol.32v. See also the songbook *a* which announces the start of the eight rondets by Guillaume d'Amiens with the rubric "Rondel Willaume damiens li Paigniers" on fol.117r. Further, the last section of songbook *I,* which groups songs by genre, contains a corpus of motet and *rondet* lyrics. Each of the other sections of song lyrics in this book is grouped by genre and contains a heading identifying the genre by name. Although two spaces were left between the "sottes chansons" and the combined motet and *rondet* section that follows, no rubric was entered. See comments in Atchison, *Oxford Bodleian MS Douce 308,* 539n747 and the helpful introduction in Doss-Quinby, Rosenberg, and Aubrey, *The Old French Ballette.*

[20] In the case of the later thirteenth-century examples by composers such as Adam de la Halle and Guillaume d'Amiens, scholars often use the term *rondeaux* to distinguish these later, more formally regular examples from the early, irregular *rondets.*

[21] These sermons not only quote *rondets* but also comment on them, in some cases, glossing their lyrics with reference to the *Song of Songs.* See the editions and discussion in Hunt, "La chanson au sermon"; see also Stevens, *Words and Music,* 177. The three lyrics quoted in medieval sermons are vdB 42–44.

[22] Guillaume de Lorris' *Roman de la Rose* features an iconic representation of the dance; descriptions also survive in *Le tournoi de Chauvency, Li restor du Paon,* and many other romances. A survey of references to the *carole* appears in Mullally, "Choreography," chap. 5 in *The Carole.*

[23] Page, *Owl and the Nightingale,* 115.

period, and the descriptions of the dance in the romances and sermons are quite vague, referring to the dancers holding hands, clapping, and stamping their feet.[24] Some medieval references describe a round dance in which the dancers clasp hands and step to the left, joining the right foot to the left.[25]

Was the *rondet* actually sung during *caroles*, as the modern generic designation *rondet de carole* would suggest? The evidence is not especially strong. Four *rondets* are sung by characters early in the narrative of Jean Renart's *Roman de la Rose* during a scene in which young men and ladies dance hand in hand in a green meadow;[26] another is sung during a May festival.[27] These scenes likely influenced perceived connections between the genre and dancing. Yet the term *carole* is not, by and large, connected to the music or lyrics of the *rondet* in medieval sources (Jean Renart does not use the term in these scenes). Turn-of-the-century romance philologists were keenly interested in the *rondet* because they hoped these songs represented a written trace of otherwise lost medieval folk songs that medieval peasants had sung to accompany popular May dances.[28] Although several of the medieval romances that describe *caroles* insert lyrics and even notated melodies following their descriptions, many of these insertions are refrains not *rondets*, and the narratives usually cue these songs with the more general term *chancon* or *chansonette*, rather than *rondet*, *rondet de carole*, or *rondel*.[29] In her reassessment of the relationship between the *carole*, the *rondet*, and the refrain, Butterfield reminds us that the romances upon which the early

[24] Ibid. For a review of literature on various theories regarding the choreography, see Mullally, "Theories," chap. 4 in *The Carole*.

[25] See Mullally, *The Carole*, 49. It should be noted, however, that all but one of the references to leftward motion occur in moralizing texts in which the symbolism of the left may have motivated the descriptions. Ibid., 47. Other references to the *carole* suggest processional movement. See discussion in Page, *Owl and the Nightingale*, 114–15. A broad overview of medieval music and dance appears in Stevens, "The Dance Song," chap. 5 in *Words and Music*. Chaganti productively traces the ambiguities and lacunae in our evidence of the *carole*, which, she argues, call for speculative reenactment. See *Strange Footing*, 190–98.

[26] These are "C'est tot la gieus, enmi les prez" (vdB 5), "C'est la jus desoz l'olive" (vdB 6), "Main se levoit Aaliz," (vdB 7), and Main se leva la bien fete Aeliz" (vdB 8), in Renart, *Roman de la rose*, 25–26.

[27] "Tout la gieus, sor rive mer" (vdB 14), in Renart, *Roman de la rose*, 75. Renart's *Rose* is the main evidentiary basis for connecting the *rondet* and *carole* in Page, *Voices and Instruments*, 78–84.

[28] See Jeanroy, *Origines de la poésie lyrique*, 106–13 and Bédier "Les fêtes de mai." Although these theories are essentially unprovable, in my previous work on the Old French refrain, I have argued that the surviving musical evidence does not support them. See the longer discussion in my *Refrain and the Rise*, 8–16.

[29] Mullally, *The Carole*, 64 and 79. In romances such as Jean Renart's *Roman de la Rose* and Jacquemart Giéllée's *Renart le Nouvel*, refrains, not *rondets*, are cued by the term "rondet a carole." Haines, *Medieval Song*, 72–75, and Peraino, "Et pui conmencha," 4. In the *Roman de la violette*, a refrain is called a "cançonnete a karole." See Butterfield, *Poetry and Music*, 57. There are also instances in which romances interpolate *rondets* into narrative contexts that lack references to dancing entirely. See Mullally, *The Carole*, 87.

philologists relied so heavily for evidence were highly mediated sources of information about the social practices they described.[30] Instead, Butterfield believes that the interpolation of *rondets* and refrains in Jean Renart's *Roman de la Rose* is a rhetorical device designed to convey "spontaneous, unstructured, oral performance"; she views the caroling scene at the opening of this romance as a carefully controlled representation of orality, not a historical record of an oral performance practice.[31] Butterfield's astute analysis gives us license to imagine that the *rondet* may not have accompanied the *carole*; we can thus begin to reimagine this genre and its contexts.

Re-placing the *Rondet*: "Bele Aeliz" and "C'est la jus" on the Landscape of the Estate

Associations between the *rondet* genre and the lower classes (influenced by early assertions of the genre's "popular" origin)[32] endured in many subsequent studies. Bec, for example, assigned the *rondet* to a category he termed *popularisant*, in contrast with the *aristocratisant* trouvère love songs (the *grand chant*).[33] Zumthor adopted the more flexible notion of high and low registers, associating the *rondets* to the low register.[34] Yet placing the *rondet* and other genres at the low end of a class-based hierarchy is no longer justifiable after Aubrey's meticulously argued critique of such approaches.[35] She has convincingly shown that the stylistic features that scholars had used to characterize songs such as the *rondet* as somehow "low" or "popular" are also found in the trouvère love songs these same scholars viewed as representing a literate, aristocratic "high style." Her careful research cautions against creating equivalences between musical style and social hierarchies. Even among those scholars who postulated a "high/aristocratic" and "low/ popular" system of registers governing the trouvère song corpus, few later

---

[30] Butterfield, *Poetry and Music*, 50–53.

[31] Butterfield, *Poetry and Music*, 53. Butterfield argues that the *caroles* featured in the *Roman de la violette* and *Le tournoi de Chauvency* are similarly stylized rather than naïvely realist. See Ibid., 54–59.

[32] The early philologists believed *rondets* were oral and popular in their origin, and that they only found favor with the aristocratic classes later in their development. See Bedier, "Les fêtes de mai," 160–61 and Jeanroy, *Origines*, xix–xxiii.

[33] For a schematic of the two registers and their characteristics, see Bec, *La lyrique française*, 34. His discussion of the *rondet* appears on ibid., 223–28.

[34] See especially Zumthor, *Toward a Medieval Poetics*, 195–204.

[35] See Aubrey, "Reconsidering 'High Style." For a systematic review of secondary literature in which modern scholars place medieval song genres into high/low categories, see ibid., 76–81.

accounts mapped those categories straightforwardly onto medieval social classes. Indeed, most scholars agreed that the *rondet*, even when it described the activities of clearly lower-status characters, could have been performed and enjoyed in aristocratic venues.[36] Whatever oral or popular venues in which their melodies or lyrics might have originated, what survives was filtered through the culture of the aristocrats who funded its preservation and the clerics who composed and copied so much of it.[37]

I would argue that interest in the supposed popular origins of the *rondet* has obscured the landscapes in which they are set, which (in contrast to the *pastourelle* songs I explored in Chapter 5) are notably non-agricultural. Some of characters featured in the "C'est la jus" and "Bele Aaliz" *rondets* strike us as rustic, a factor that surely encouraged scholars to view the songs as emanating from the lower classes—the shepherd and shepherdess characters Robin and Marion make several appearances. Even when they describe rustic characters, however, the geographical location that forms the setting of these songs strongly suggests that of a medieval rural estate. In the "C'est la jus" songs, the dancers are typically assembled in an orchard or meadow. In one *rondet*, this meadow is specifically called the "roi pree," or "king's meadow,"[38] a term that designated meadowland owned by a king or prince, but over which the lower classes living nearby would have held common rights to pasture their animals, collect firewood, or otherwise be present on the land.[39] In many parts of Europe, virtually all of the land was owned by a lord, yet the "right to the soil" did not guarantee the exclusive right to use the land. Common rights entitled villagers to use resources in certain areas under certain circumstances.[40] Because open lands such as rough pastures, heaths, and even some wooded lands on seignorial estates were subject to these common rights, they were an elite location in which one could sometimes expect the lower classes to be present.[41] The presence of lower-class characters thus

---

[36] Ibid., 91.

[37] Something like this belief prompts Stevens to adopt the hybrid term "courtly-popular" to describe the "low register" songs. See *Words and Music*, 162 and 175. Butterfield also relies upon this term, which she deems "usefully compromising." See Butterfield, *Poetry and Music*, 6–7.

[38] vdB 164.

[39] On the nature of common rights in Europe, see the essays in De Moor, Shaw-Taylor, and Warde, *Management of Common Land.*

[40] The regulation of common lands differed (often significantly) by region. See De Moor, Shaw-Taylor, and Warde, "Comparing the Historical Commons," 23–25.

[41] Harvey, *Medieval Gardens*, 115. The grounds of aristocratic estates were also maintained by large staffs of paid gardeners, ensuring that laborers of low rank would be on hand much of the time.

need not prevent us from imagining that the narratives of these songs could have been set on an aristocratic estate.

The topography the songs describe is much more closely aligned with estates than the areas in or around Northern French cities, towns, and villages. The "Bele Aaliz" songs are clearly set on an estate landscape—the narrative often culminates with Alice entering a beautiful garden. There could hardly be a more emphatic marker of aristocratic status than a pleasure garden, and the association between women and such landscapes was strong. The landscapes featured in other *rondets* also evoke estate grounds. The meadowlands they frequently mention were not sown crops but natural growth associated with the floodplains of small rivers.[42] Meadowland was typically not plentiful in urban environments, where open lands were largely devoted to wheat crops and vineyards. The public meadows created at the turn of the fourteenth century in Italian cities such as Florence, Padua, and Sienna, were a novelty. Further, as I discussed in Chapter 5, villages in Northern France were often surrounded by open fields, large plots in which the individual holdings of peasants were consolidated for greater efficiency. Some of the "C'est la jus" songs describe a dance that takes place under a tree that offers shade and even the suggestion of privacy under its boughs. This description is evocative of a tree with a tall trunk and long, spreading branches that provide a canopy. A tree fitting this description would have been a less-common sight in many areas of medieval Northern France due to the woodland clearances discussed in Chapter 1. By the thirteenth century, even in regions such as Champagne, which had once been heavily wooded, dramatic increases in villages and towns (as well as industries such as smelting and tile-making) required intensive use of the forest.[43] The wooded areas in the environs of Paris had been largely cleared by the late twelfth century.[44] Coppiced woodlots were far more common than tall trees, and coppices grow differently than other trees. In a coppice, the central trunk of the tree is removed so that poles of small wood can grow up around the base. Rather than producing branches that bend down from a trunk, a coppice produces branches stand upright from the ground. The height of trees in medieval wood lots was often tightly regulated and kept relatively short so that the coppices would receive optimum sunlight.[45] An estate was the likeliest place one might find a tall tree

---

[42] Hoffmann, *An Environmental History*, 175.

[43] See Keyser, "Woodland Management," 365.

[44] Keyser, "Woodland Management," 353–54.

[45] Some regulations explicitly stipulated, for example, that the canopy could be no more than 25 feet high. See Keyser, "Woodland Management," 380.

with low-hanging branches.[46] Moreover, the alder trees that receive mention in several songs grew best in wet meadowland, an ecosystem that was associated with estates.[47] Having relocated the landscape songs these songs describe to the grounds of an estate, it is now possible to contemplate how they might speak to the kinds of experiences that were possible for women on such terrain.

Ornamental Landscapes: Experiencing Space, Place, and Movement through the *Rondet*

The "Bele Aeliz" and "C'est la jus" *rondets* encode an experience of space and place. They often describe characters dancing or advancing from one location to another. The emphasis on movement in their lyrics accords well with descriptions of the design of medieval pleasure gardens and their architectural underpinnings. An important agricultural text that survives from the early fourteenth century and includes a wealth of information about the design of medieval gardens: Piero de' Crescenzi's *Liber ruralium commodorum*, written between 1304 and 1309.

Piero was a Bolognese lawyer from a landowning family.[48] Skepticism regarding the realism of his reflections is justifiable since Piero copied much of his treatise directly from Albertus Magnus' thirteenth-century *De vegetalibus*[49] (and Albertus copied much of his own work from classical sources).[50] Yet the chapters of Piero's *Liber ruralium commodorum* dedicated to ornamental gardens are seemingly original; no classical or medieval source for them has been found.[51] The landscape Piero describes is remarkably similar to the elements of his own estate (which are described in his

---

[46] Estates also included coppices as well as pollarded trees. Pollarding involves cutting a tree trunk high enough above the ground that deer cannot eat the suckers before they can form poles of wood. Although a pollard has higher branches, the branches also stand vertically rather than reaching outward or bending downward. See the description in Rackham, "Pre-existing Trees," 5.

[47] Duceppe-Lamarre, *Chasse et pâturage*, 70.

[48] Bauman, "Tradition and Transformation," 112.

[49] Piero's sources are discussed in Epstein, *Medieval Discovery of Nature*, 29–35. Whereas Piero duplicated large portions of Albertus Magnus' treatise (including parts of his discussion of pleasure gardens; cf. the relevant excerpt of Albertus translated in Harvey, *Medieval Gardens*, 6), he added many original observations. Calkins, "Piero de' Crescenzi," 159.

[50] Although he relies heavily on classical sources, some of Albertus' material was clearly drawn from his own observation as well as occasional conversations with the peasantry (*rustici*). See Epstein, *Medieval Discovery of Nature*, 19–25. Further, Albertus often contradicts his sources, seemingly based on personal observation. See Bauman, "Tradition and Transformation," 113.

[51] Bauman, "Tradition and Transformation," 120.

will),[52] suggesting that they reflect his direct experience and observation of his own land. His extensive discussion of grafting "has all the enthusiasm of a practical gardener who has much hands-on experience."[53] Piero describes the ideal garden for those of moderate means and for kings and princes, separating the gardens appropriate to these ranks into different chapters. The garden for those of moderate means is essentially an orchard, featuring trees spaced into even rows and separated by a strip of meadowland that was to be mowed twice per year.[54] He recommends that this orderly space be surrounded by a thorny rose hedge. For kings and princes, Piero describes a landscape that strongly suggests elements of the medieval deer park, a heavily managed space that was both designed for pleasure and to provide a suitable habitat for the animals aristocrats enjoyed hunting and eating. It should be large (over twelve acres) and should be created in a site with a spring flowing through it. It should be surrounded by walls and include habitats for many different types of animals: a planted grove to provide cover for deer, a stocked fishpond, and a bird house for many kinds of songbirds. Piero advises that it should also have places where the king and queen can meet with barons or lords (weather permitting), including rows of trees that provide walks and bowers and even a living room created by the training of fruit trees and vines into walls and a roof.

Piero advocated a specific garden design meant to foster sensory engagement with plants. The garden was revealed step by step, as the viewer walked through it.[55] His perspective steeped in humoral medicine, Piero extolled the benefits that the garden would provide to those who lingered within it:

Along the edge of the garden should be planted fragrant herbs of all kinds, such as rue, sage, basil, marjoram, mint, and the like, and also flowers of every type, such as violet, lily, rose, water iris, and the like. Between these plants and the level turf raise and form [another] turf in the fashion of a seat, flowering and pleasant. Plant trees or train vines on the turf against the heat of the sun. . . . There should be no trees in the middle of the turf, but this level place should rather enjoy free and pure air, since that air is

---

[52] Bauman, "Tradition and Transformation, 112.
[53] Epstein, *Medieval Discovery of Nature*, 32.
[54] If meadowland is not mowed periodically or grazed, it quickly reverts to woodland.
[55] Howes, "Literary Landscapes," 205.

healthier, and also since spiders' webs stretched from one branch to another would block the way and contaminate the faces of those passing through.[56]

As Piero describes his design, which is calculated to maximize human engagement with plant-life, he seems constantly aware of how a garden's visitors will move through the space, whether enjoying the dappled shade of vines, stopping to rest on a turf seat, or passing between trees.

The "Bele Aaliz" and "C'est la jus" songs are similarly preoccupied with space, place, and movement. In this example, the space is constantly delimited within the brief lyric:

La jus, desoz la raime
Einsi doit aler qui aime
Clere i sourt la fontaine
Y a!
Einsi doit aler qui bele amie a.[57]

[Over there, under the branches/*that's the way those who love should go*/a clear fountain springs up/there!/*That's the way the one who has a fair lover should go.*][58]

The first line that binds songs of this lyric type together, "Over there," opens the song by casting the listener's mind's eye across a landscape to a point not immediately perceived. The narrator describes a location that is "over there" "under" the leafy canopy, adding in vv.3–4 that a fountain springs up there. The poetry of the *rondet* is saturated by verbs denoting movement through space[59] as well as prepositions and demonstrative pronouns. As brief as these songs are, their narrators are nonetheless painstakingly specific about the geographical positioning of the features and characters they describe, as though they are trying to help listeners locate a spot in their field of view and observe it

---

[56] In circuitu vero eius herbae aromaticae omnium generum platentur, ut sunt ruta, salvia, basilicon, maiorana, menta et similes, et similiter omnis generis flores, sicut viola, lilium, rosa, gladiolus et similia. Inter quas herbas et caespitem planum sit caespis elevatior et quasi per modum sedilium aptatus, florens et amoenus. In caespite etiam contra vim solis plantandae sunt arbores aut vites decendae. . . . In medio autem caespitis nihil sit arborum, sed potius ipsa planities libero gaudeat aëre et sincero, quia ille aër salubrior est, et etiam aranearum telae extensae de ramo arboris ad ramum impedirent et inficerent vultus transeuntium. . . ." Crescenzi, *Liber ruralium*, 100–101.

[57] vdB 1.

[58] My translation.

[59] These dynamics are at work in nearly all of the "C'est la jus" songs. Noted by Zumthor, *Toward a Medieval Poetics*, 202.

alongside them. The narrator's vantage point is far enough away to assume the listener will need multiple locators to spot it, but close enough to observe the activities of the dancers and to overhear their songs. In the "Bele Aaliz" *rondets*, the lyrics often highlight the maiden's movements, as she rises, dresses, and walks out, presumably from an interior space, into the garden or grounds.

> Aaliz main se leva.
> *Bon jor ait qui mon cuer a!*
> Biau se vesti et para
> Desoz l'aunoi.
> *Bon jor ait qui mon cuer a!*
> *N'est pas o moi!*[60]

[Alice arose in the morning./*Greetings to her who has my heart!*/Beautifully she dressed and went out/under the alder tree./*Greetings to her with all my heart!*/*It's not with me.*][61]

The lyric charts movement forward, seemingly from an interior space toward the castle grounds, as we encounter Alice rising, dressing, and walking out to the alder tree.[62] Unlike the knightly love songs I explored in Chapter 3, *rondets* are narrative—an unnamed observer communicates their brief scenes to us in the past tense. Who is the observer in these songs, and who is being observed? The following section explores how these songs reflect gendered differences in the kinds of experiences available to medieval men and women on the lands the songs describe.

The Promise of Privacy: Watching, Being Watched, and Overhearing in the *Rondet*

In their form, *rondets* have often been viewed as hybrid, drawing in elements of other genres and connecting to other works through their refrains, which are sometimes intertextual (meaning they are quoted in additional poetic and musical contexts).[63] They have also been seen as a muddle of diverse

---

[60] vdB 9.

[61] My translation.

[62] The narrative motion of rising, dressing, and going outside also appears in vdB 2, 7, and 42.

[63] An account of the portion of *rondet* refrains that appear intertextually in other medieval songs, motets, narratives, and other sources appears in my *Refrain and the Rise*, 13–16.

thematic elements and registers that do not exactly cohere.[64] The refrains that both frame and insert themselves within the strophes of *rondets* are often described as disjunctive, interrupting and disrupting the brief narratives of the strophes, and it is not difficult to find examples to support this view.[65] These kinds of discontinuities suggested to many that the strophe and refrain of the *rondet* genre were voiced by different performing forces, a chorus who sang the repeated refrains and a soloist who took the strophe, or the reverse.[66]

Yet across the thirty-three *rondets* of the "Bele Aaliz" and "C'est la jus" lyric type, the voice of the refrains is not always disruptive. In many cases, the voice of the refrain and the voice of the strophe appear continuous, not disjunctive, as in this example from Jean Renart's *Roman de la Rose*:

C'est la jus, desoz l'olive,
Robins enamine s'amie.
La fontaine i sort serie
Desouz l'olivete.
E non Deu! Robins enamine bele Marïete.[67]

[It's over there, under the olive tree,/*Robin is taking his lover.*/The fountain flows tranquilly/under the little olive grove./*In the name of God! Robin is taking beautiful little Marie.*]

In this song, it would be unproblematic to assume that the refrain and the strophe share the same impersonal narrative voice; there is nothing particularly disjunctive about their relationship.[68]

In many of the *rondets* considered disjunctive in earlier accounts, the narrative strophe contrasts with a refrain that features an exuberant expression of love in a first-person voice. This dynamic has often been viewed from a socio-anthropological perspective as evidence of the choral performance of

---

[64] Zumthor stated, "We often perceive this register as not really being expressively cohesive but rather as a jumble of debris." Zumthor, *Toward a Medieval poetics*, 202.

[65] See especially vdB 7.

[66] Jeanroy, *Origines*, 106–13. Although she does not adopt Jeanroy's theory wholesale, Butterfield's account continues to argue that the refrains, with their first-person expression of love, interrupt the narrative strophe of the *rondet*. Butterfield reverses the elements of Jeanroy's theory, arguing that it was the refrain that was an element of individualistic expression and was more often assigned to the soloist in medieval romances, whereas the strophe was repetitive and thus communal, designed for choral performance. See Butterfield, *Poetry and Music*, 46–49.

[67] vdB 6.

[68] See also vdB 1.

refrains within the carol dance or a literary representation of such a performance scenario.

C'est la jus en la praele
Or ai bone amor novele!
Dras i gaoit Perronele.
Bien doi joie avoir:
Or ai bon' amor novele
a mon voloir.[69]

[It's over there in the meadow/*Now I have a new love!*/Peronele was washing
her clothes in the brook./*Now have a new love/to my liking!*][70]

A different view of the relationship between the strophe and the refrain is
also possible. In this *rondet* and others, the refrains could represent passages
of direct speech voiced by a character the narrator is describing—that is,
that this narrator is quoting the songs he hears Perronele singing, and the
refrain, "Or a bone amor novele," is a synecdoche for the full song Perronele
sings as she washes her clothes in the brook.[71] This relationship is implied—
none of these short songs include cues such as "she said" or "she sang" to
introduce the refrains. However, many other narrative song genres within
the trouvère corpus use refrains in exactly this way, often without cueing
them.[72] This relationship is evident in "C'est la jus c'on dit es prés," where the
refrain seems to be in the voice of a character named in the strophe:

C'est la jus c'on dit es prés
Jeu et bal i sont cries
Emmelos i veut aler
A sa mere en acquiert grés
Par Dieu, fille, vous n'irés;
Trop y a des bachelers au bal.[73]

---

[69] vdB 10.
[70] My translation.
[71] See also vdB 5, vdB 11, and vdB 93. Peraino was the first to argue that some refrains function
through the device of synecdoche. See Peraino, "*Et pui conmencha*," 2–4.
[72] Cf. Burns, "Sewing Like a Girl," 99–126.
[73] vdb 44.

[It's over there, in the fields, they say/games and dances are called there/ Emmelot wants to go there/she asks her mother for permission./*By God, girl, you will not go;/there are too many young knights at the dance.*][74]

This example, which was quoted in a medieval sermon, features a single refrain at the song's close. The refrain is not preceded by text such as "her mother replied," but it clearly represents the mother's response to Emmelot's request.[75]

Of the total corpus of thirty-three *rondets* in the "C'est la jus" and "Bele Aaliz" type, it is common for the refrains to be narratively continuous with the strophe or, as in the song just quoted, to plausibly exist as an un-cued reported song within the narrative (the truly disjunctive refrains are in the minority). Hearing these *rondets* as narrative songs interlaced with un-cued quotations adds texture to their descriptions of the outdoors and draws attention to the ways in which some of these songs explore dynamics of privacy, looking on, and overhearing. Many of the "C'est la jus" and "Bele Aaliz" songs feature narrators who observe (mainly) female characters from a distance and report their actions. *Rondets* often emphasize the role of viewers, as in this example, in which the narrator describes having caught sight of the dancers:

C'est la gieus, en mi les prez
J'ai amors a ma volente.
Dames i ont baus levez.
Gari m'ont mi oel.
J'ai amors a ma volenté;
Teles com ge voel.[76]

[Down there in the meadow/*I have the love of my heart's desire.*/The ladies had begun the dance/when my eyes saw one./*I have the love of my heart's desire;/all I require.*][77]

---

[74] My translation.

[75] It is something like this dynamic that motivates Bédier's elaborate argument that the *rondets* were strung together into longer, theatrical performances. See his "Fêtes de mai," 165.

[76] vdB 16.

[77] Translation is modified from that of Terry and Durling from Jean Renart, *Romance of the Rose*, 92.

In another *rondet*, the speaker of the refrain repeats a reference to having seen his lover coming, virtually sputtering with references to seeing her:

C'est la jus, desoz l'olive.
La, la voi venir, m'amie.
La fontaine i sort serie,
El jaglolai soz l'anunoi.
La voi, la voi, la voi,
La bele la blonde; a li m'otroi.[78]

[It's over there, under the olive./*Her, I see her coming, my lover.*/The fountain flows clearly there/and burbles under the alder tree./*Her, I see her coming, see her, see her,/the beautiful blonde; I've granted myself to her.*][79]

This element of voyeurism is in keeping with what is known about medieval garden settings and castles more broadly. Castle architecture prioritized surveillance as a central function, with the greatest opportunities for observation afforded to the lord. As I mentioned in Chapter 1, the mottes on which castles were built increased the field of view.[80] Even in early defensive castles, the most expansive views were made accessible to the lord alone; accounts of Charlemagne's private *solarium* at Aachen describe an elevated room where he could privately observe the comings and goings of his visitors.[81] Viewing was also intrinsic to the experience of being in the garden, a factor that both Albertus Magnus and Piero de' Crescenzi noted. Albertus emphasized from the outset that gardens were "mainly designed for the delight of two senses, viz, sight and smell."[82] Garden design focused on sight not only through the visual attraction of flowers and greenery but also through the careful curation of views and sight-lines through the space. Piero advised his readers to build their palaces to the south of the garden expressly so that in the palace shadow, they could enjoy viewing the garden even in the hot season—unhindered by the heat of the sun.[83] When records show the addition of new windows to the various castles renovated under the direction of Eleanor of Provence (wed to Henry III in 1236), they specify which part of the garden the window should

---

[78] vdB 17.
[79] My translation.
[80] Creighton, *Early European Castles*, 90.
[81] Creighton, *Early European Castles*, 120–21.
[82] Harvey, *Medieval Gardens*, 6.
[83] Crescenzi, *Liber ruralarium*, 102.

overlook, and excavations of these castles show that the windows had built-in seats to aid in viewing the gardens.[84] Castles also often included garden spaces designed specifically for women; these gardens were buried deep into the architecture of the castle, hidden from the male gaze, visible and accessible only from women's chambers.[85] Queen Eleanor's privy garden was located under her chamber and was hidden from view by a large timber fence.[86]

Even in the more communal gardens and meadows on aristocratic estates, the outdoors attracted, in part, because of the promise of privacy, whether along the paths between the fruit trees of a walled orchard or under the branches of a shady tree. Yet it is a kind of privacy that can seem insecure in the *rondet*, a dynamic evident in this example by the trouvère Guillaume d'Amiens, which combines the "C'est la jus" lyric type with elements of the *pastourelle* song genre:

Prendés i garde, s'on me regarde;
S'on me regarde, dites le moi.
C'est tout la jus en cel boschiage.
Prendés i garde, s'on me regarde
La pastourelle u gardoit vaches.
Plaisant brunete a vous m'otroi.
Prendés i garde, s'on me regarde;
S'on me regarde, dites le moi.[87]

[*Please be watchful, if someone is looking at me;/if someone is looking at me, tell me.* It's over there in that little woodland./*Please be watchful, if someone is looking at me./*The shepherdess guards cows there./Pretty brunette, I grant myself to you./*Please be watchful, if someone is looking at me;/ if someone is looking at me, tell me.*]

Here, the strophe places a shepherdess "over there in that little woodland," elaborating that she guards her cows there.[88] We learn in verse 6 that the strophe is a first-person narration, and that the narrator hopes to pledge himself to the shepherdess he is describing. Again, there are no cues here, but it

---

[84] Creighton, *Designs upon the Land*, 178.
[85] Gilchrist, "The Contested Garden" and Richardson, "Gender and Space."
[86] Creighton, *Designs upon the Land*, 178. On the class-based hierarchical design of castle gardens, see ibid., 65.
[87] "Prendés i garde" (vdB 93), *a* 119v.
[88] As I mention in Chapter 5, peasants often held common rights to graze cows in lordly woodlands; the song thus presents a realistic scenario.

Example 6.1 "Prendes y garde" by Guillaume d'Amiens, *a* 119v

seems plausible that the refrain represents a song the shepherdess is singing. In the *pastourelle* song genre (in which a shepherdess is the central character), the knight often finds the shepherdess because he hears her singing song. And in this *rondet*, the character who voices the refrain is rather obsessively (and rightly) worried that someone is watching her.

In the stylistic context of the corpus of ten notated songs attributed to Guillaume in the songbook *a*, the melody of "Prendes i garde" is highly unusual. Its range is restricted to just a fifth. Although five of Guillaume's nine *rondets* feature the relatively narrow melodic range of a sixth to an octave,[89] the remaining four *rondets* and his other two songs have rather sweeping ranges of an octave to a ninth.[90] The song is also permeated by a declamatory, repeated pitch (a) which occupies an extraordinary amount of the melodic space of "Prendes i garde," as shown in Example 6.1. Guillaume sets the first four of these syllables to this repeated a. In the second verse, which has nine syllables, Guillaume sets the first four to the same repeated a. Overall, Guillaume's melodies tend toward both graceful, stepwise arc shapes[91] that contrast with passages featuring adventurous leaps[92] and triadic ascents, as

[89] His *rondets* "Jamais ne serai saous" (vdB 85), "Ses trés dous regars" (vdB 87), "De ma dame vient" (vdB 90), "C'est la fins" (vdB 92), and "Prendés i garde" (vdB 93) span either an octave or a sixth.

[90] See "Amours me maint u cuer" (vdB 84), "Dame, pour men lonc sejour" (vdB 86), "Je canterai" (vdB 88), and "Hareu, conment mi mainterrai" (vdB 89), as well as "Puis que chanters" (RS 2) and "Amours me fait" (RS 1004).

[91] He uses these in his "B" melodies in particular. See "Amours me maint u cuer" (vdB 84), "Jamais ne serai saous" (vdB 85), "Hareu, conment mi mainterrai" (vdB 89), and "De ma dame vient" (vdB 90).

[92] "Amours me maint u cuer" (vdB 84), "Dame, pour men lonc sejour" (vdB 86), "Je canterai" (vdB 88), and "De ma dame vient" (vdB 90) all feature leaps of a fourth or greater. In "C'est la fins" (vdB

well as descents through the melodic interval of a fifth.[93] The melodic repetition in "Prendes i garde" is thus unique within Guillaume's corpus, as is the focus on the melody's apex, given his preference for arc-shapes.

It is possible that Guillaume composed this unusual melody to amplify elements of the song's lyrics that emphasize viewing and being seen. First, the repeated pitches communicate a sense of urgency, particularly since they occur at the melody's apex. The melody seems to mimic the sound of the girl's voice as she calls out to someone in the distance. Moreover, the relationship between the brief narrative and the *rondet*'s melodic form extend themes of voyeurism. As in all surviving notated *rondets*, the lyrics of the strophe in Guillaume's song are set to the same melody as its refrain. From a narrative perspective, one senses the speaker of the strophe eavesdropping on the singer of the refrain. Within the fiction of this brief song, he seems to actually overhear her—and as listeners first hear his narration in line 3, sung to the melody of the refrain's first and second lines, they can imagine that his character has heard the song of the shepherdess and re-texted it, improvising his narrative verses to the pitches of her melody.

The melody and lyrics of Guillaume's refrain from this *rondet*, "Prenes i garde, s'on me regarde/s'on me regarde dites le moi,"[94] also appear within an anonymous motet: *S'on me regarde* (908)/*Prennés i garde* (909)/*Hé, mi enfant*. The motet is transmitted uniquely in a section of *Mo* believed to date from the early fourteenth century.[95] Very little is known about Guillaume d'Amiens, although his author portrait in *a*, which depicts him as a painter, has engendered much speculation. His residence in Amiens seems to be confirmed by the census of 1301–1302, which lists him as the owner of a house in the city. His death date is not known,[96] nor can we make many inferences about his status or patrons based on the existing evidence, although *a* includes his works in the section largely devoted to urban, professional performers. Whereas existing knowledge of relevant chronologies prevents

---

92), a leap of a fifth appears within its intertextual refrain. Although several of the melodies with which this refrain appears in its other surviving contexts are recognizably similar to that used in Guillaume's *rondet*, none of the refrain's melodic concordances use such a large leap.

[93] This characteristic feature of Guillaume's melodic style is evident in "Amours me maint u cuer" (vdB 84), "Hareu, conment mi mainterrai" (vdB 89), "De ma dame vient" (vdB 90), and "C'est la fins" (vdB 92).

[94] The refrain is vdB 1531.

[95] The piece appears in fascicle 8, fols. 375v–376v. For the most recent summary of arguments regarding the dating of *Mo* fascicle 8, see Bradley and Desmond, "Introduction."

[96] Johnson, "Music at the Cathedral of Amiens," 467.

Example 6.2 "Prendes i garde" melody in (a) Guillaume d'Amiens' *rondet* and
the (b) triplum, (c) motetus, and (d) tenor voices of the motet, S'on me regarde
(908)/*Prennés i garde* (909)/*Hé, mi enfant*

us from knowing for certain whether the motet quoted the refrain directly
from Guillaume's *rondet*, it would be reasonable to make such an assumption
in this case.[97] But more tellingly, as Everist has demonstrated, the motet is
largely generated from the refrain material, which, through compositional
techniques such as voice exchange, permeates the motet setting. Moreover,
the newly composed French tenor is written in the shape of an irregular
six-line *rondet*, a structure that the upper voices amplify through their own
counterpoint.[98]

In this brief motet, the refrain melody serves as material for much of the
composition, permeating the setting of both all parts. The refrain does not
actually appear in full, verbatim in any voice. Example 6.2 compares the refrain melody in Guillaume's *rondet* with the opening phrases of the motet. To
facilitate comparison, the pitches of the refrain "Prendes i garde" are num-
bered; these numbers are written above the pitches in the motet in which
they are used. The motetus part begins with the lyrics and melody of the
refrain's first two phrases ("Prenes i garde/s'on me regarde"), then continues
in v.3 with newly composed lyrics and music ("trop sui gaillarde . . .").

In the opening phrase, the motetus intones the lyrics and melody of the
refrain's first two poetic lines in a near exact quotation.[99] At verse 3 (m.3), the

[97] The sources of the two works give us no help in establishing a compositional chronology.
Curran's meticulous consideration of the scribal hand of fascicle 8 of *Mo* has lent further weight to a
possible dating in the 1290s, roughly contemporary with *a*. See Curran, "A Palaeographical Analysis."
[98] Everist argues that this piece is a member of a small subset of the late thirteenth-century motet
repertoire that is stylistically more similar to the polyphonic songs of the fourteenth century than
other motets. He offers an extensive analysis of the melodic patterning and reuse of refrain material
from Guillaume's *rondet*. See Everist, "Motets, French Tenors," 390–98.
[99] The motetus melody is transposed from a to e' and missing pitch 9; it inserts a new pitch (e') on
the downbeat of measure 2.

motetus includes a new phrase of melody and text ("I am too cheeky": *trop sui gaillarde*), before returning, in verse 4 (m.4), to a near exact quotation of the refrain's fourth verse and its final four pitches.[100] The triplum voice begins, in m.1–2, with a near exact quotation of the refrain from pitches 6 through 21 (these pitches correspond to the second half of line 1 through line 3).[101] The motetus part is set at the same pitch as the refrain and begins with a near identical quotation of pitches 1 through 10.[102]

After measure 4, as the motet lyrics continue with a new narrative, the phrases of the refrain's melody constantly echo through the texture through the technique of voice exchange. The refrain's melody permeates the setting of two different but closely related narratives in the new lyrics that follow the quotation of the refrain in the motet's opening. The lyrics of the two parts share much of their lexical content, but it is kaleidoscopically reorganized in such a way that, despite its fragmentation, nonetheless results in a virtually identical narrative in both texts.[103] The triplum and motetus lyrics each describe a young girl who both delights in catching the eye of her lover and fears the eye of her jealous husband, whom she believes is also watching her.[104] In the lyrics, which appear below, the refrain text is underlined and the textual phrases shared between the voices are in bold:

Triplum:
<u>**S'on me regarde,**</u>
<u>**S'on me regarde,**</u>
<u>Dites le moi;</u>
Trop sui gaillarde,
Bien l'aperchoi.
Ne puis laissier
Que mon regard ne s'esparde,
Car tes m'esgarde

---

[100] This segment is transposed and, like m.2, inserts e' before quoting pitches 18 through 21 of the refrain.

[101] The triplum is also transposed from a to e.' It omits pitch 9 and, like the motetus, inserts e' prior to pitch 6 as well as between pitches 18 and 19.

[102] The tenor omits pitch 5 (instead, it repeats pitch 4 two additional times in m.2), inserts a and g between pitches 6 and 7, and adds e between pitches 9 and 10.

[103] For a chart that illustrates the phrases shared between the two texts and the pattern of their reorganization, see Everist, "Motets, French Tenors," 397.

[104] Motets in which the voices are unified in their poetic register or narrative perspective form a category that Grau has termed, following Bakhtin, "homoglossic." See the helpful discussion in Grau, "Hearing Voices," 79–86.

Dont mout me tarde
Qu'il m'ait o soi,
Qu'il a, en foi,
De m'amour plain otroi.
Mais tel ci voi
Qui est, je croi—
Feu d'enfer l'arde!—
Jalous de moi.
Mais pour li d'amer ne recroi,
Car par ma foi,
Pour nient m'esgarde;
Bien pert sa garde:
J'arai rechoi.

[If someone is watching me,/if someone is watching me,/tell me;/I am too cheeky,/I see it clearly,/I cannot keep my gaze/from wandering,/for someone is looking at me/whom I am eager to be with,/for in truth he has/full right to my love./But I see someone else here/who, is I think—/May he burn in hell!—/jealous of me./But in spite of him I will not renounce love,/for to tell the truth/he guards me in vain;/His surveillance is for naught:/I will find a hiding place.]

Motetus:
<u>Prénes i garde</u>
<u>S'on me regarde;</u>
Trop sui gaillarde.
<u>Dites le moi.</u>
Pour Dieu, vous proi,
Car tes m'esgarde
Dont mout me tarde
Qu'il m'ait o soi,
Bien l'aperchoi.
Et tel chi voi
Qui est, je croi—
Feu d'enfer l'arde!—
Jalous de moi.
Mais pour li
D'amer ne recroi.

Pour nient m'esgarde;
Bien pert sa garde:
J'arai rechoi
Et de mon ami le dosnoi.
Faire le doi:
Ne serai plus couarde.

[Please take note/if someone is watching me;/I am too cheeky—/do tell me./In God's name, I beg you,/For someone is looking at me/whom I am eager/to be with,/I see him clearly./And I see someone else here/who is, I think—/May he burn in hell!—/jealous of me./But in spite of him I will not renounce love./He guards me in vain;/his surveillance is for naught:/I will find a hiding place/and have pleasure with my lover I must do so,/and be a coward no longer.]

Tenor:
Hé, mi enfant!
[Ho, my child!][105]

In these new texts, seemingly spun off from the lyrics of the refrain they share with the *rondet* by Guillaume d'Amiens, the motet composer significantly amplifies the dynamics of viewing, being seen, listening, and overhearing suggested in the original *rondet*.[106] Guillaume's *rondet*, which featured a shepherdess guarding cows in a little woodland, offered a hint of the *pastorelle* lyric type without fleshing out a full *pastourelle* narrative. The *pastourelle* lyric context does not inform the motet, *S'on me regarde* (908)/ *Prennés i garde* (909)/*Hé, mi enfant*, although a listener familiar with both pieces would likely associate the girl in this motet with the shepherdess of the *rondet*. The motet does not mention an outdoor setting; rather, its lyric type is often described as the *mal mariée*, which features an unhappily married young woman who complains about her jealous husband and schemes to meet with her lover. We saw that the original *rondet* highlighted the gaze of the girl's lover; the motet composer adds the suggestion of a second male

---

[105] Text and translation modified slightly from Doss-Quinby, Grimbert, Pfeffer, and Aubrey, *Women Trouvères*, 231–37.

[106] The voyeurism of the motet's upper voices is discussed in Peraino, *Giving Voice to Love*, 202–3. Viewing and spectatorship connect this work to the idea of the dance, where dancers can function as both performers and spectators, watching themselves participate. See Chaganti, *Strange Footing*, 58 and 214.

observer (her jealous husband). Further, the newly composed tenor's brief incipit "Ho, my child!" (Hé, mi enfant!) could easily be understood as a salutation to the girl voiced from the subject-position of one of these two male onlookers. Whether the tenor voice represents her lover (whose gaze she desires) or her husband (whose gaze she spurns) is for listeners to determine.

The dynamic of overhearing I explored in Guillaume's *rondet* is also operative in the motet, where the tenor's melody opens with a slightly altered version of the motive from the refrain's opening verse, with its distinctive repeated pitches, as Example 6.2 shows.[107] Just as in the *rondet*, we might imagine the subject of the tenor heard this melody from the girl's song, retexting it with his salutation. Musically speaking, the tenor's melody governs the shape of the composition—the upper voices are coordinated with its irregular *rondet* structure.[108] The notion of attempted control through surveillance that is discussed in the narrative scenario is thus insinuated by the counterpoint itself. The brief piece focuses intently on and even amplifies elements of the refrain that deal with viewing, listening, and overhearing. Its suggestion of surveillance is a reminder that the privacy medieval people sought in the outdoors (particularly if they were women) was often more aspirational than real.[109] It also foregrounds interesting tensions between the desire for privacy and the pleasures of being on display, highlighting the female subject's conflicting feelings about being watched (depending on who is looking).[110]

Garden settings offered new experiential possibilities; its dynamics were enacted through the musical structure of motets and *rondets* whose lyrics used the "C'est la jus" and "Bele Aelis" lyric types. These songs tended to associate ornamental outdoor settings with women, and with both the pleasures and anxieties surrounding being seen and being overheard. These songs include textually feminine voices but (with the exception of "Prendes i garde" by Guillaume d'Amiens) are anonymous. Although the makers of medieval manuscripts largely neglected to record the names of their authors (as

---

[107] The motive begins each of the major sections of the motet, thus marking out its altered *rondet* form.

[108] See discussion in Everist, "Motets, French Tenors," 396.

[109] For other songs in which characters are overlooked or overheard in garden settings, see, for example, "Deduxans suis et joliette, s'amerai" (RS 59a), "En un vergier" (RS 594), "Quant voi la flor nouvele" (RS 599), and "Je me levai ier main" (RS 1371).

[110] Compare to Anna Grau's discussion of the autopanegyric mode used in feminine-voiced motet lyrics. Grau, "Gendered Voices," 205–6.

I discussed in the Introduction), it is possible that these songs could have been written by persons of any gender or status.[111] Whether they reflect the desires, impulses, and experiences of historical medieval women is unknown, but elite women were certainly an important audience for them when they were quoted in romances like Jean Renart's *Rose*. Elite women could also have patronized the anonymous composers who wrote many of these songs. Did women recognize themselves in these descriptions? Or did these songs reflect the ways men (for example, songwriters like Guillaume d'Amiens or male patrons) viewed women? Whereas the answers to these questions are a matter of conjecture, the connections the *rondets* in this chapter draw between gardens and women are an apt reflection of certain aspects of elite feminine identity, and their focus on viewing and overhearing reflects emerging notions of privacy.

---

[111] On female authorship and the concept of textual femininity and the motet corpus, see especially Grau, "Gendered Voices," 203–5.

Conclusions

Nature, Culture, and Change in
the Middle Ages and Beyond

During the long thirteenth century, the songs of the trouvères defined the identities of knight, lady, cleric, and peasant through specific modes of being in the outdoors. For trouvères who were knights (explored in Chapter 3), the nature opening expressed an ideal of sensory emersion in (and emotional connection to) the land, a key component of knightly self-image and aspiration. The landscapes described in these songs resembled a medieval aristocratic estate, thus the songs expressed an identity in which land, love, and singing intertwined in the figure of the knightly songwriter. In Chapter 4, I demonstrated that the cleric-trouvères tended to define their identities against the nature opening. These songwriters eschewed the device entirely or manipulated it in ways that cleverly drained it of its immediacy. Rather than linking emotion and song production to immersion in sweeping landscapes, those cleric-trouvères who did use nature imagery in their songs expressed intimate, small-scale engagement with plants and their growing patterns or put forth symbolic, biblical interpretations of plant-life. Songs set in agrarian landscapes allowed songwriters, patrons, and audiences to contrast their own identities through comparison to the figure of the medieval peasant, as I showed in Chapter 5. In the *pastourelle*, the figure of the shepherdess was defined through the articulation of boundaries that were spatial and symbolically social. The shepherdess' physical placement in spaces associated with knightly identity potentially prefigured his use of violence against her. In other songs, agrarian landscapes seemed to reflect geographies that songwriters and their audiences had recently vacated, as in the case of Jehan Bodel and his urban audiences. For Jehan Erart's newly wealthy bourgeois patrons in Arras, the landscape of the countryside may have engaged their elite aspirations and flattered their (relatively new) status as landowners. Songs that placed women in the estate's ornamental spaces, explored in Chapter 6, emphasized the important role elite women played in designing

Song, Landscape, and Identity in Medieval Northern France. Jennifer Saltzstein, Oxford University Press.
© Oxford University Press 2023. DOI: 10.1093/oso/9780197547779.003.0008

and inhabiting gardens while associating them with both the pleasures of movement and display as well as anxieties regarding privacy.

The broad corpus of songs and songwriters explored in this book show that the relationships between landscape and identity they describe could be realistic, aspirational, or anachronistic. The songs of Gace Brulé were seemingly autobiographical, plausibly based on direct observation of the land, and may have expressed personal sentiment. In similar songs by the Vidame de Chartres and Raoul de Soissons however, the landscapes described aligned imperfectly with the biographies of their songwriters, reflecting relationships between landscape and identity prized by the peer group to which they belonged but that were not fully realized in their own lives. In other cases, such as the *pastourelles* of Jehan Bodel, the landscape described was realistic but not current, reflecting the land-use patterns of earlier generations.

These songs, and the relationships they project between landscape and identity, continued to be received, recorded, and presumably loved by patrons and audiences well into the fourteenth century. This continuity is surprising given the historical changes it conceals. The decades around 1300 were marked by destabilizing weather conditions that accompanied the gradual winding down of the Medieval Climate Anomaly (described in Chapter 1). I am not aware, however, of any trouvère songs in which a speaker laments the catastrophic rains that led to the Great European Famine of 1314–22, or of any songs that convey a sense that the seasons, the weather, or nature in general had betrayed people. Fourteenth-century French poetic works that discuss these miserable conditions are relatively uncommon. The anonymous lyrics of the songbook *Penn* (an important later source of *pastourelles*) are striking and atypical in their pessimism and frank discussion of politics and natural disasters:[1] aging peasant farmers relay their memories of the aftermath of the Black Death;[2] shepherds lament livelihoods that have been ruined;[3] and peasant characters, in thinly veiled language, descry the damage wrought by knights on the peasantry during the Hundred Years' War.[4] Guillaume Machaut wrote his narrative *dit* the *Jugement dou Roi de Navarre* sometime after 1349; this poem opens with a well-known description of the Black Death that self-consciously inverts the springtime

---

[1] The *Penn* lyrics are edited in Kibler and Wimsatt, "Development of the Pastourelle."
[2] Kibler and Wimsatt, "Development of the Pastourelle," no. VI, ll.61–65.
[3] Kibler and Wimsatt, "Development of the Pastourelle," no. IV.
[4] Kibler and Wimsatt, "Development of the Pastourelle," nos. VI and VII, discussed on 32–35.

opening, instead invoking autumn as the context for the outbreak. Machaut includes the traditional elements of the springtime opening but situates them in the past tense, the opening rhyme pair contrasting the homonyms "esté" (summer) and "esté" (had been); autumn, and the conditions with which it is symbolically aligned, are aligned with the narrator's melancholy.[5] After the Plague has subsided the narrator leaves his self-imposed quarantine to go hunting, noting that the mild weather soothes his body and that he enjoys hearing the birds singing melodious songs.[6] In response to the spring-like conditions, he completely forgets his prior melancholy.[7] The realism of this introduction is so unusual that many commentators criticized it as being un-related and irrelevant to the *dit* that followed.

Overall, the songs of the trouvères explored in previous chapters demon-strate the long cultural continuity of relationships between landscape and identity, even amid significant changes in land use and built environments. A number of the songbooks discussed in this book are believed to have been produced after 1300,[8] yet they take no notice of calamities of the century, continuing to highlight songs featuring the nature opening and the harmo-nious, emotional, and artistically generative relationships it articulates be-tween the singer and the landscape. The songs of the later knightly-trouvères and some of the songbooks produced around the turn of the fourteenth cen-tury suggest the relevance of nostalgia, which, as Boym influentially argued, often seeks to project an idealized version of the past into the future.[9] I con-clude by considering relationships between nature, culture, and change in two works, one medieval and one modern. First, I examine continuities between the approach to the nature opening in Guillaume de Machaut's *Remede de Fortune*[10] (a mid-fourteenth-century narrative into which songs are interpolated) and the nature openings of the thirteenth-century

---

[5] Ll.1–2. Guillaume de Machaut, *Jugement dou Roy de Navarre*.

[6] Ll.526–529.

[7] L.543. Butterfield notes the historicity of this opening in which Machaut overlays a pastoral landscape with the real social dynamics of the Black Death, a time when the movement from court and city to country associated with the classical pastoral realistically reflected a common medieval strategy used to evade infection. Butterfield, "Politics of Plague," 17–20.

[8] This is likely true, for example, of the songbooks B, I, L (B and L are thought to have once been joined in the same book), Q, R, Z, and a. See the descriptions in Aubrey, "Sources, MS: Secular Monophony." Oxford Music Online, https://www-oxfordmusiconline-com. Plumley underscores the long "shelf life" of trouvère song in the fourteenth century. See Plumley, *Art of Grafted Song*, 415.

[9] As Boym stated, "One is nostalgic not for the past the way it was, but for the past the way it could have been. It is this past perfect that one strives to realize in the future." See Boym, *Future of Nostalgia*, 351

[10] The dating of the *Remede* is uncertain. It may have been composed prior to 1349, when Machaut served king John of Luxembourg and, after the king's death in 1346, his daughter Bonne

cleric-trouvères. The continuities in Machaut's approach suggest the durability of relationships between landscape and identity forged by the cleric-trouvères, even amid changing social and climatic conditions. I close with a text that bears witness to an even longer legacy of medieval configurations of land and identity—Aldo Leopold's iconic *A Sand County Almanac* (1949)—exploring how Leopold's humorous resituating of medieval lordship speaks to modern efforts to understand relationships between nature and culture in periods of climatic change.

Continuities Amid Change in Machaut's *Remede de Fortune*

Machaut's biography combines the courtly and clerkly worlds, as discussed in Chapter 2.[11] There are suggestions that in addition to the broad array of classical, biblical, and philosophical texts that constituted his literary frame of reference, Machaut may also have been familiar with elements of the songs I explored in Chapters 3 and 4, including those of Thibaut IV and Adam de la Halle, as well as the version of the *Roman de Fauvel* found in fr.146.[12] Like Adam, Machaut never invokes the springtime opening in the way the knightly trouvères explored in Chapter 3 do.[13] However, the

of Luxembourg. See the summary of proposed dates in Earp, *Guillaume de Machaut*, 213–14 and Leach, *Guillaume de Machaut*, 227. Accounts that claim Bonne was among Machaut's patrons are summarized in Earp, *Guillaume de Machaut*, 25–26. The *Remede* was certainly compete by 1357, when Machaut refers to it in his datable work, the *Confort d'Ami*. See Earp, *Guillaume de Machaut*, 213. All texts of the *Remede* follow Machaut, *The Boethian Poems*, which is based upon Paris, BNF fr.1584. Translations follow this edition with some slight modifications.

[11] See the discussion in Leach, *Guillaume de Machaut*, 124.

[12] On Machaut's possible knowledge of songs by Adam de la Halle, see the summary of literature in my "Musical and Poetic Legacies," 359–60; on allusions to trouvère songs in Machaut's motets and his *Lay de plour*, see especially Boogaart, "Encompassing Past and Present" and Plumley, *Art of Grafted Song*, 282–91. Machaut's probable knowledge of the version of the *Roman de Fauvel* found in fr.146 and his quotations and allusions to "Pour recouvrer alegiance" in his *Lay mortel* were first proposed by Schrade, "Guillaume de Machaut and the Roman de Fauvel." But see the discussion in Dillon, *Medieval Music-Making*, 278–81.

[13] In Machaut's *rondeau* "Rose liz" (R10), in which his lady surpasses the sensory delights of the springtime season and possesses all the goodness of Nature, the lady supplants the nature opening. Moreover, Rothenberg argues that this song is directed at the Virgin Mary, as was Machaut's *Lay de Nostre Dame* (L15/10), in which Machaut self-consciously inverts the springtime opening, invoking only the season ("Contre ce doulz mois de may") as the setting for the composition of his *lay*, which he writes in honor of Mary. See the discussion of these works in Rothenberg, *Flower of Paradise*, 89–91. In other cases, for example, Machaut's *ballade* "De toutes flours" (B31), natural imagery is used abstractly in ways that idealize or sublimate the lady. See the discussion in Kelly, *Medieval Imagination*, 148–49. Numbering reflects that used in Earp, *Guillaume de Machaut*.

device figures importantly in several of his narrative poems.[14] The nature opening also serves an important function in Machaut's *Remede de Fortune*, a work that amplifies and extends the relationships between landscape and identity explored in earlier chapters in the context of trouvère song. The *Remede* features a narrator-protagonist who is a clerkly author figure that readers would likely have identified as Machaut himself. After the narrator-protagonist fails to admit to his lady that he loves her, he flees to the Park of Hesdin. In this garden setting, the protagonist meets Hope, an allegorical character who will both embody and supplant the springtime opening. In language that explicitly recalls the songs explored in Chapter 3, Hope inspires the protagonist to compose a new love song in a new musical language. Machaut's invocation of the springtime opening in this extended narrative sequence demonstrates the long reach of its associations between nature and poetic inspiration while also aligning Machaut with the poetic stance of the cleric-trouvères I explored in Chapter 4.

Machaut sets the majority of the narrative of the *Remede* in the outdoors in parks and gardens, ornamental landscapes adjacent to a manor house. The springtime opening occurs during the longest and arguably most important narrative sequence of the *Remede*, which occurs in the Garden Park of Hesdin, a real, 2,200 hectare deer park and pleasure garden created by Robert II of Artois in 1292 that Machaut likely saw with his own eyes in the 1330s.[15] As Farmer has shown, the Garden Park of Hesdin was an outdoor space shaped so profoundly by human artifice that little of it lacked human intervention.[16] As a hunting park, Hesdin was a habitat for the species required for the hunt and the aristocratic table, especially rabbits, carp, herons, fallow deer, and horses.[17] Countess Mahaut of Artois managed the park carefully to maximize the production of exotic meats and other luxury products that enhanced the status of her household.[18] There was nothing wild or natural about many of the park's animal species, which were imported; and

---

[14] In addition to the *Jugement dou Roy de Navarre*, mentioned above, Machaut's *Dit dou vergier*, written sometime in the 1330s, begins with a springtime opening that reflects the influence of the *Roman de la Rose* by Guillaume de Lorris. The clerk and narrator of Machaut's *Jugement du roy de Behaingne* (written before 1346) also begins his story with the springtime opening, and this opening is re-narrated at two subsequent points in the plot. See the discussion in Brownlee, *Poetic Identity*, 161–62. On the dating of this and Machaut's other *dits*, see Earp, *Guillaume de Machaut*, 189–94.

[15] Van Buren "Reality and Literary Romance," 123 and *Le Jugement du roy de Behaigne*, 36.

[16] Farmer, "Aristocratic Power," 644–80.

[17] Farmer, "Aristocratic Power," 655–76.

[18] Dowling, "Landscape of Luxuries," 369.

extraordinary investments in human labor and capital were required for their maintenance.[19] The park was famous for housing not only exotic animals but also mechanical marvels such as elaborate fountains and automata.[20]

Among all outdoor spaces, gardens are those in which nature is most deliberately and intensively shaped by culture. The Garden Park of Hesdin was an extreme human attempt to exert control over nature, clearly functioning as a demonstration of aristocratic power.[21] Yet Robert II and his descendants went to great lengths to make the artificial elements look and feel natural: the park's famous mechanical monkeys were cloaked in real fur to make them look more lifelike, and the meadows, fields, woodland, and marshes were designed to look naturalistic.[22] The Park of Hesdin was a space where visitors were meant to experience nature and culture in dialogue, and to see culture as the dominant force. These extraordinary human interventions in the natural world continued during the Great Transition, when unpredictable weather disrupted agricultural cultivation of all kinds.[23] Countess Mahaut even continued to expand the park against royal decrees during the years of the Great European Famine when food production was failing to meet regional needs.[24]

The Garden Park of Hesdin is an apt setting for the central narrative sequence of Machaut's *Remede*, which is an extended exploration of relationships between nature and culture. In ways that recall relationships between gardens and privacy that I explored in Chapter 6, Machaut repeatedly reminds readers that it is the narrator's desire for privacy that leads him to Hesdin. The story opens with the narrator-protagonist's failure to admit to his lady that he has written a *lay* in her honor (which would be tantamount to revealing his feelings for her), and he flees in tears and attempts "to reach some hidden place . . . Because I didn't want to meet anyone."[25] He spots the beautiful Park of Hesdin, a park he cannot enter because it is enclosed (surrounded by high walls) and the road leading to it is not open to everyone.[26] Finding a trail leading to a gate, "in a remote spot far from people,"[27]

---

[19] Farmer, "Aristocratic Landscape," 648.
[20] Machaut's protagonist describes these marvels in ll.813–17.
[21] Farmer, "Aristocratic Landscape," 674.
[22] See Farmer, "Aristocratic Landscape," 676 and Truitt, *Medieval Robots*, 127.
[23] Campbell, "Nature and Society," chap. 1 in *Great Transition*.
[24] Farmer, "Aristocratic Landscape," 648.
[25] Ll.775 and 779.
[26] Ll. 790–793.
[27] "En un destour et loing de gent" l.797.

he sees no one inside, which makes him happier: "because I wanted to be all alone, if I could."[28] The nature opening and the connections the trouvères drew between experience in a landscape and feeling or poetic production (explored in Chapters 3 and 4) is crucial to the narrative sequence involving the park. In Machaut's hands, the springtime topos is implicated in multiple narrative temporalities and layered under several different literary allusions. In the *Remede*, Machaut presents his readers with a real, historical, outdoor locale he likely experienced directly, but he mediates his account of it so heavily that it quickly turns to metafiction. Machaut foregrounds the human representation of nature through cultural artifice, a strategy that echoes the aims of Hesdin's designers.

The artifice of the *Remede* lies close to the surface of the work and Machaut draws heavily on several literary models. The multilayered, first-person narrative voice of the *Remede*, in which a clerkly poet-author figure narrates a story he experienced in his youth, directly inspired by the portion of the *Roman de la rose* written by Guillaume de Lorris.[29] The narrative structure is modelled on Boethius' *Consolation of Philosophy*. Machaut transforms Boethius' prosimetrum work by replacing the figure of Lady Philosophy with a lady named Hope. Unlike Lady Philosophy, Hope consoles the lover not by teaching him to overcome suffering through virtue, but rather, by providing him with the sufficiency (*souffissance*) to endure suffering and continue both to love and to compose.[30] Her "remedy" thus keeps the narrator-protagonist in a state of amorous suffering bearable enough that he can continue to generate song.[31] The *Remede*, as many have noted, is a didactic text that functions both as an Ovidian *ars amatoria* as well an *ars poetica*.[32] After an early failure to admit his authorship of a *lay* and thus reveal his love for his lady (a failure that is both amorous and poetic), the narrator-protagonist will learn, through the teachings of Hope, to be a more successful lover and composer.[33]

[28] Ll.803–804.

[29] Extensive narrative parallels between the two texts are identified in Huot, *Song to Book*, 258–59. On Machaut's transformation of the narrative voice of the *Rose*, see Brownlee, *Poetic Identity*, 20–21. Approaches to Machaut's narrative voice are summarized in Swift, "The Poetic I," 15–32.

[30] Machaut's use of Boethius as a model for the *Remede* is discussed in many accounts including, among others, Huot, "Machaut and the Consolation of Poetry," 169–95; Armstrong and Kay, *Knowing Poetry*, 91–94; Kay, "Touching Singularity," 21–38; and Kelly, *Machaut and the Medieval*, 23–27.

[31] Armstrong and Kay, *Knowing Poetry*, 94.

[32] The didactic function of the lyrics is discussed by Hoepffner in Guillaume de Machaut, *Oeuvres de Guillaume de Machaut*, 2, xxxiv–liv; Calin, *A Poet at the Fountain*, 70; and Brownlee, *Poetic Identity*, 37–39; and Leach *Guillaume de Machaut*, 11, among others.

[33] I use the term "narrator-protagonist" following Brownlee. See "Machaut's *Remede de Fortune*," 2.

In the Park of Hesdin, the narrator-protagonist composes a *complainte* in which he bewails his powerlessness in the face of Fortune.[34] Hope appears miraculously and demonstrates, for the lover, a new way of loving and singing. Her central lesson takes the form of a pair of songs, the second of which is polyphonic and is written in a new musical style that musicologists call the *ars nova*.[35] Hope's teachings take the form a debate with the narrator-protagonist in which she refutes the argument of his *complainte* point by point. Upon finishing her first song, the *chanson roïal* "Joie, plaisence," Hope asks if she has debated (*debatu*) the case well and asks whether there were themes or arguments (*tenson*) that pleased or displeased him (ll.2040–2042); she finishes her speech by saying "I won't debate this further."[36] Machaut's word choice evokes the academic mode of scholastic disputation that was a primary method of instruction in medieval universities.[37] After engaging in this clerkly dispute with the narrator-protagonist, Hope gives him her ring and explains her relationship to lovers. She says that just as the sun's rays and the advent of summer illuminate the world and adorn the formerly barren winter landscape with the warmth and greenness of springtime, so her radiance shines over all lovers who are in love, bringing them the joy and pleasure of love.[38] She uses a specifically horticultural metaphor of the grafted scion to explain that she is the true mother of all lovers, ensuring that the shoot grafted onto their heart from love sprouts flowers, leaves, new fruit, and seed.[39] In this lengthy passage, which occurs near the midpoint of the *dit* and culminates in Hope revealing her identity and naming herself, Hope both embodies and supplants the key aspects of the springtime opening. She describes her influence on lovers as similar to the power springtime exerts when it transforms winter landscapes and inspires love. In what follows, she, not the landscape or the songs of birds, will inspire and instruct the narrator-protagonist to love in a new way and to compose a new kind of song.

The narrator-protagonist proves an eager student; while the he listens in a mnemonic trance, Hope sings the first polyphonic song in the narrative,

[34] The role of Fortune in the *Remede* has received extensive treatment. See Brownlee, "Machaut's *Remede de Fortune*," 5, and especially Leach, *Guillaume de Machaut*, chap. 5.

[35] The most recent treatments of the emergence of *ars nova* practices are Desmond, *Music and the Moderni*, and Zayaruznaya, "Old, New."

[36] A toy ne m'en quier plus debatre. L.2090.

[37] On the influence of scholastic disputation on medieval music, see Novikoff, *Medieval Culture of Disputation*, 147–55. On Machaut's Latin and vernacular models for his debate poetry, see Cayley, "Machaut and Debate Poetry," 103–18.

[38] Ll. 2196–2240.

[39] Ll. 2244–2246.

the *baladelle* "En amer,"[40] a song written in a style fundamentally different from the songs earlier interpolated into the *Remede*, and in a form with few musical precedents.[41] Hope's *baladelle* is saturated with minims, the smallest rhythmic value that could be written at that time.[42] He learns Hope's song completely, memorizing its music and its lyrics before she is done singing it.[43] Recording Hope's song in his memory is an immersive, sensory experience that requires "That all the faculties/of the five senses God had given to me/ were so directed toward this end."[44] It is not until the narrator-protagonist leaves Hesdin that Machaut includes a hyperbolic invocation of the spring-time opening, focused on the birdsong that often inspired trouvères to re-member their beloved or to sing: "Now the birds in more than/thirty thousand places were/singing away, as if competing with/one another, their throats opened wide,/and they made the whole garden/resound with their song. . . ."[45] The narrator-protagonist states that the birds had been singing from the outset, but that prior to Hope's teaching, he had been unable to perceive the sound of their songs: "My senses had been so dulled/I'd taken no notice/of the birds or their clamor."[46] Now, properly instructed in a new method of loving and singing, and buoyed by the sweet music of the birds, the narrator-protagonist claims he is in the proper state of mind to express him-self.[47] The memory of Hope and the expectation of seeing his lady prompt him to compose, on the spot, his own *balade*, "Dame de qui." In this song, he demonstrates his mastery of Hope's teachings. The musical setting includes long hockets and uses substantial passages of syncopation, features associ-ated with *ars nova* musical style.[48] As several scholars have argued, the pres-ence of these stylistic features functions at a narrative level to demonstrate

---

[40] It is perhaps Hope's status as a mnemonic vision in this sequence that allows her to sing a poly-phonic song by herself. See Enders, "Music, Delivery, and the Rhetoric of Memory," 554.

[41] See the discussion in Everist, "Machaut's Musical Heritage," 157.

[42] See Leach, *Guillaume de Machaut*, 152–54.

[43] Ll. 2904–2918.

[44] Ll. 2913–2915: "Que toute l'inclination/Des.v. sens que Diex m'a donné/Y estoient si ordonné."

[45] Ll. 2981–2986: "Et plus de.xxx. mille liex/Tout aussi com par estrivées/Chantoient, les gueules baées,/Si qu'il faisoient restentir/Tout le vergier. . . .

[46] Ll. 2989–2991: "Mes scens estoit si pervertis/Qu'encor ne m'estoie avertis/Des oisillons, ne de leur noise."

[47] L. 3004.

[48] Although hockets and syncopation are present in thirteenth-century polyphony, the more ex-tensive use of these features was facilitated by fourteenth-century rhythmic innovations. A pithy summary of *ars nova* musical style appears in Everist, "Machaut's Musical Heritage," 143. The focus on the new style in the narrative of the *Remede* has been clarified by the recent shifting forward of the practices associated with the *ars nova*. See Desmond, *Music and the* Moderni, 238 and Zayaruznaya, "Old, New," 104.

the protagonist's internalization and absorption of the musical style of Hope's *baladelle* and thus her teachings on both love and composition.[49]

What role does the springtime opening play in the protagonist's new compositional style? The suddenness with which his perception of the birdsong is followed by first the memory of Hope and the lady, and then the composition of "Dame de qui," strongly evokes the springtime openings of the knightly trouvères.[50] Yet the spectacle of the protagonist purportedly performing polyphonic music alone directly undercuts the immediacy and realism that the springtime opening conveyed in its classic form. Moreover, as Brownlee has shown, the model of direct inspiration from nature that Machaut seems to evoke in this passage is itself a self-conscious (and inverted) literary allusion to Guillaume de Lorris' *Rose*.[51] In the *Rose*, the narrator-protagonist enters a garden after hearing birdsong; in the *Remede*, the protagonist hears the birdsong upon departing from the garden. Brownlee further notes that Hope's appearance in the narrative as a super-human interlocutor is a visibly literary gesture that would have immediately brought Machaut's Boethian model to the surface. The presence of such recognizable literary allusions in this narrative sequence would have focused a medieval reader's attention on Machaut, the clerkly author-poète who orchestrates the experiences of fictional characters within his narrative.[52] These models would prevent readers (even those who might attempt to suspend disbelief and accept Machaut's act of pseudo-autobiography) from perceiving the narrator-protagonist's experience as unmediated or spontaneous.

Machaut's mediated treatment of the springtime opening with regard to the protagonist of the *Remede* thus resonates strongly with the approach we saw in Chapter 4 in the songs of most of the clerical trouvères.[53] Machaut invokes birdsong and the protagonist composes "Dame de qui" immediately after hearing it. Yet he is only able to hear the birds after absorbing the teachings of Hope and internalizing the *ars nova* features of her new *baladelle*. Hope

---

[49] The argument that the musical works in the *Remede*'s narrative (and their notational style) demonstrate the narrator-protagonist's compositional progression from the style of the troubadours and trouvères to *ars nova* musical practices was made first and with great clarity by Switten, "Le *Remede de Fortune* au carrefour," 101–18.

[50] Machaut's knowledge of trouvère song is discussed in Boogaart, "Quotations and Their Function."

[51] Brownlee, "Machaut's *Remede de Fortune*," 11.

[52] Brownlee, "Machaut's *Remede de Fortune*," 7–8 and 11.

[53] This continuity between Machaut's authorial self-presentation and the way the nature opening is used in the songs of the cleric-trouvères I explore in Chapter 4 is in keeping with many studies that explore how Machaut's works project a clerkly authorial identity. See, for example, Brownlee, *Poetic Identity*, Cerquiglini, *'En engin si soutil'*; Leach, *Guillaume de Machaut*, and others.

must activate the birdsong, stimulating the protagonist's capacity to perceive it. Hope presents herself as a substitute springtime who possesses its qualities and is equally effective in inspiring lovers to love; the protagonist learns through Hope's clerkly argumentation and through study of her two musical exempla. His memorization of her *baladelle* is described using explicitly scribal metaphors: "Just as I've written it down,/[it] was inscribed on my heart/through true and certain understanding/one hundred times better and more properly/than any clerk might copy it/by hand on parchment or a wax tablet."[54] Machaut presents musical composition as an art dependent on clerkly modes of teaching and learning, not as inspired spontaneously by sensory experiences in the natural world. Indeed, it is the studious memorization of Hope's song that the protagonist describes as a sensory experience.[55] The Garden Park of Hesdin, a spectacularly artificial natural environment, is thus an apt setting for Machaut's apotheosis of writerly craft and musical and literary artifice. His transformation of the springtime opening in the *Remede* and other works demonstrates clear continuities with the songs explored earlier in Chapter 4, reflecting a century of engagement with this trope among cleric-trouvères. Whereas his own experience as a court cleric likely enabled similar or even greater contact with estate landscapes as that of the knightly trouvères explored in Chapter 3, his treatment of the nature opening reflects longstanding relationships between song, landscape, and identity among clerical vernacular composers. Amid changes (cultural and environmental), Machaut's *Remede* and its treatment of the nature opening thus demonstrates continuities with the past. The resilience of these relationships in the face of significant historical change suggests that once entangled with identity, songs have a way of projecting attitudes toward nature into the future.

Culture, Identity, Climate, and Change, Medieval and Modern

Given the climate-related challenges human societies currently face, I suspect that few readers will have approached this book without some degree of curiosity about relationships between nature and culture during the last major era of climatic change, and about how those relationships might illuminate

---

[54] Ll.2942–2946: "Estoit en mon cuer en escript/Par vray certein entendement/Mieux .c. fois et plus proprement/Que clers ne le porroit escrire/de main en parchemin n'en cire."
[55] L.2914.

present conditions on earth.[56] Some may even wonder what (if any) lessons modern people might draw from the example of medieval Northern France. To broach such questions risks profound anachronism. Yet it is always worth remembering that scholarship does not occur within a vacuum, and indeed, as Haines astutely observes, "More often than not, the Middle Ages were studied with one eye firmly fixed on the present."[57] Since the sixteenth century (or arguably, the late thirteenth century), consciously or not, those who have sought to understand trouvère song examined it through perspectives that were strongly related not only to their own interests and priorities, but also to their value systems. Early antiquarians (wealthy collectors who shared much with the original patrons of medieval songbooks) focused on royal and aristocratic trouvères. Post-revolutionary scholars elevated urban, educated, composers like Adam de la Halle.[58] Even the foundational work of seemingly dispassionate philologists like Bedier was conducted in contexts in which nationalism played a key role.[59]

Greater awareness of one's motivations might temper the potential for anachronism. And further, the examples explored in this book plainly defy simplistic parallels between past and present. The Medieval Climate Anomaly and tumultuous transition to the Little Ice Age were importantly dissimilar to the current state of climatic change. The modern climate crisis is man-made, caused by human beings in industrial societies burning fossil fuels. It has been exacerbated by slow acceptance of accountability among those most responsible and slow progress in replacing fossil fuels with other sources of energy. Medieval climate change, by contrast, was caused primarily by changes in natural processes (such as sunspot activity, volcanic eruptions, and ocean circulation patterns) that were divorced from human action.[60] And although medieval people bore no responsibility for these changes, they were quick to blame themselves, assuming the changes to their climate and resulting disasters were a punishment for their sins.[61]

[56] Cronon, "Uses of Environmental History."

[57] Haines, Eight Centuries, 50.

[58] Haines, "The Changing Song," chap. 2 in Eight Centuries, and Alden, "Excavating Chansonniers."

[59] See Nycrog, "Warrior Scholar," and Corbellari, "Joseph Bedier."

[60] The first example of a large-scale shift in climate caused by human activities may be the so-called Orbis Spike, a drop in CO_2 observed in glacial ice cores dated to 1610 that was significant enough to delay the next period of glaciation. The Orbis Spike has been attributed to reforestation that followed the mass mortality of native peoples caused primarily by the European contact that began in 1492. Although some have posited the Orbis Spike as the start of the "Anthropocene" (see Lewis and Maslin, "Defining the Anthropocene"), the nuclear age has gained acceptance as its starting point.

[61] In Machaut's Jugement dou Roy de Navarre, for example, after seeing humans descend into corruption, greed, and strife, Nature cooks up storms as punishment, and in the narrative, it is these

It is also important to remember that previous attempts to extrapolate lessons from history about current environmental crises have misinterpreted the medieval European example. In his widely influential article, "The Historical Roots of Our Ecologic Crisis," first published in *Science* in 1967, White argued that the ecological crises of the early fourteenth century had their roots in medieval readings of the Book of Genesis, where God granted humans dominion over the earth.[62] Others argued that the Great European Famine was caused by medieval farmers who, in an attempt to feed a fast-growing population, had exhausted their soil by planting too much grain while fallowing and manuring too little.[63] Historians later showed that these critiques of resource management (and the blame they placed on medieval people) were wrong, demonstrating that medieval people regulated their resources specifically to prevent depletion.[64] Moreover, where twentieth-century theories stressed the centrality of human actions (primarily over-population and its effects on farming practices), more recent studies suggest that changing climate often played an outsized role.[65] Although their sweeping claims were not borne out by more detailed histories of medieval agricultural management, these theories nonetheless resonated with activists in the modern environmental movement who saw in the medieval example a potent warning against environmental overexploitation.[66] More recently, the medieval example has been harnessed in arguments against the established fact that contemporary climate change has anthropogenic causes. Commentators have pointed to the Medieval Climate Anomaly and Little Ice Age in order to suggest that current changes in climate are natural, not caused by humans, and therefore need not prompt a human response.[67]

The relationships between nature and culture that I have charted in Northern France during the long thirteenth century are thus distinct from

punitive storms that give rise to the haze of filth and vapors that causes people to become ill with the buboes associated with the Black Death. See Machaut, *Debate Poems*, ll.257–70. https://d.lib.roches ter.edu/teams/text/palmer-machaut-thedebateseries-navarre.

[62] See the discussion in Hoffman, *An Environmental History*, 87–91.

[63] This neo-Malthusian hypothesis was put forth by Michael Postan in the mid-twentieth century; In 1980, Charles Bowlus similarly argued that the crises of the fourteenth century were the result of human overexploitation of natural resources. Explanation and later criticism of Postan's view can be found in Jordan, *Great European Famine*, 26–35 and Hoffman, *An Environmental History*, 161–67; on Bowlus' argument, see Hoffman, *An Environmental History*, 330–46.

[64] See especially Dowling and Keyser, "Introduction," 1–3, and the essays in Dowling and Keyser, eds., *Conservation's Roots*.

[65] Campbell, *Great Transition*, 205.

[66] See Hoffman, *An Environmental History*, 343–44.

[67] See Will, "Climate Change's Instructive Past."

current conditions and it would be unwise view the era as a direct ana-
logue to our current one. Nonetheless there are interesting parallels. The
cultural formation of identities through connections to urban or rural
landscapes connects the medieval French context to the modern era. The
intertwining of landscape and identity in trouvère song shows us how long-
lived such associations could be, even when the material circumstances
of those who embraced particular identities were in imperfect alignment with those identities. Into the fourteenth century, an era when royal
and aristocratic courts were growing more urban and artistic production
more professionalized,[68] aristocratic songbook patrons and compilers continued to copy songs by Gace Brulé and others in which identity was articulated through emotional and artistically generative ties to expansive, estate
landscapes. During a period in which he lived and worked on aristocratic
estates, Guillaume de Machaut's authorial posture toward the nature opening
in the *Remede* recalls generations of mostly urban, clerical composers. Songs
whose lyrics claim they were prompted directly by sensory engagement with
flourishing plant-life and the ideal environmental conditions of the Medieval
Climate Anomaly continued to be composed, copied, and presumably sung
and read, during the disastrous transition to the Little Ice Age. The example
of medieval song is a reminder that identities can be relatively impervious to
social and environmental change.

For medieval people, damaging impacts of climate change that they experienced were not prevented by their prayers, nor could they have been
reversed through different land management regimes. In contrast, much of
the modern environmental crisis has been caused by cultural choices, and
many of its remedies will thus extend beyond the reach of science.[69] Those
who hope to mitigate current impacts of climate change and prevent even
worse scenarios in the future argue that human behaviors and lifestyles in
resource-intensive societies must change. This might seem, at first blush,
much easier to accomplish than the technological feats through which
modern scientists are creating novel methods of energy generation. Yet I have
shown that cultural images can be remarkably durable, projecting values into
the future—the songs and songbooks explored in this book helped to propel
attitudes and behaviors long after their authors and compilers were dead.

---

[68] See Vale, *The Princely Court.*
[69] See the remarks in Allen and Dawe, "Ecomusicologies," 11.

Indeed, an example of precisely this point survives in an unlikely place, namely Aldo Leopold's *A Sand County Almanac*, a book that has exerted profound influence on modern views of ecology and conservation. Leopold famously criticized what he described as the "Abrahamic concept of land" (alluding to biblical dominion over the earth), which he argued led to its commodification and abuse. He advocated instead that humans view the land as a community to which they belonged.[70] Yet the celebration of this kind of belonging in his chapter "July" bears playful echoes of medieval lordship. Leopold writes that at dawn (when the county clerk is asleep), his dominion extends well beyond his 120 acres: "At daybreak I am the sole owner of all the acres I can walk over. . . . expanses unknown to deed or map are known to every dawn, and solitude, supposed no longer to exist in my county, extends on every hand as far as the dew can reach."[71] Leopold writes that before daybreak, his "emblems of sovereignty" are his coffee pot and notebook and that "like other great landowners," he has tenants, such as sparrows who "announce their fiefdom" through their "clear tenor chant" and the robin who claims his elm branch through insistent "caroling."[72] When this avian chorus runs out of breath and he can feel the sun, Leopold writes that the shrinking of this landscape to the "mean dimensions known to county clerks" is announced by the clank of cowbells and the roar of his neighbor's tractor.[73] Leopold playfully installs himself as lord and sovereign of the biotic community to which he belongs.[74]

Attempting to live up to the vision of ecological relationships that Leopold cherished in his less playful moments would involve significant changes to the ways many humans view themselves and their place on the land. The enduring relationships between landscape and identity explored in this book suggest that enacting such changes will be no small undertaking.

[70] Leopold, *Sand County Almanac*, viii.
[71] Ibid., 41.
[72] Ibid., 42.
[73] Ibid., 44.
[74] Beusterien and Callicott, "Politics through the Animal," 61–62.

Acknowledgments

This book originated as a study of medieval cleric-trouvères, which was generously supported by a summer stipend from the National Endowment for the Humanities in 2014. It was through my engagement with the University of Oklahoma's Arts and Humanities Forum in 2015, where I first explored the relevance of nature and the environment to my song corpus, that the book began to take its current form. I am grateful for the discussions, feedback, and bibliographic suggestions offered by my cohort of fellows: Robert Bailey, Laurel Smith, Peter Soppelsa, Todd Stewart, Zev Trachtenberg, and our director, Janet Ward. I am especially grateful to the National Endowment for the Humanities for a year-length fellowship that provided me with necessary research leave to develop these connections further in 2016–17. Conducting the final editing during a Summer Residency at the National Humanities Center was a unique privilege. I am grateful to the OU Arts and Humanities Forum for helping to fund the residency and to librarians Brooke Andrade, Sarah Harris, and Joe Milillo for placing the contents of a very long bibliography at my fingertips. I gratefully acknowledge that Skye van Duuren set my musical examples. Financial support for his work and for high-resolution images from the Bibliothèque nationale de France was provided by the Office of the Vice President for Research and Partnerships and the Office of the Provost of the University of Oklahoma. My article "Songs of Nature in Medieval Northern France: Landscape, Identity, and Environment" (published in the *Journal of the American Musicological Society* in 2019) was an important impetus for this book. As I significantly re-thought that material in the intervening years and expanded my study into new repertoire, I continued to mull over the copious and invaluable comments and suggestions provided by the seven anonymous peer reviewers. I gratefully acknowledge their diligence.

I presented various parts of this book (in person or virtually) to audiences at the Annual Meeting of the American Musicological Society (held in Rochester, NY, in 2017 and Boston, MA, in 2019), the Southwest Chapter of the AMS (2022), the International Congress of Medieval Studies at Kalamazoo (2022), "Nostalgia, Music, and Music Studies" held at UCLA

(2022), and at colloquia and distinguished lecture series held at the UCLA, the University of North Texas, Case Western Reserve University, Northwestern University, the Eastman School of Music, New York University, and the Yale Lectures in Medieval Studies. I am also grateful for feedback I received locally from the University of Oklahoma's Arts and Humanities Forum and the School of Music's Norton Lecture Series, as well as the Red Earth Group of the Oklahoma Sierra Club. Those in attendance at these events offered comments and questions that shaped my thinking as did conversations with Suzannah Clark, Mike Lee, Juan Meneses, Brooke McCorkle Okazaki, Matt Schullman, and Jane Wickersham. Marisa Galvez, Sarah Kay, Roberta Magnusson, Carol Symes, and Eliza Zingesser offered valuable leads, answered questions, and provided bibliographic suggestions. Eliza Zingesser assisted me with several of the translations in this book (these are noted within the text); any errors that remain are my own. Early feedback from Judith Peraino and John Haines was crucial, allowing me to strengthen aspects of my argument and methodological framework. Rick Keyser offered key bibliographic suggestions, detailed responses to many queries, and helpful comments on early drafts. Long and pleasurable conversations with Mary Caldwell, Brian Chance, Rachel May Golden, Lori Kruckenberg, and David J. Rothenberg helped me clarify and refine my thinking. Aaron S. Allen provided sustained engagement with this project over the course of several years through correspondence, conversations, and by reading drafts. His influence is felt across these pages. Sarah Hines offered needed historical perspective, encouragement, and levity at key moments. Joyce Coleman was an intellectually generous interlocutor at all stages of this project and provided valuable feedback on several chapters. I am indebted to Mary Caldwell, Brian Chance, and the anonymous reviewer at Oxford University Press for reading the full manuscript. Their comments, questions, and suggestions improved the final version considerably.

Drafting my manuscript during a global pandemic was a challenge I could never have anticipated. Completing and submitting it in December of 2021 would have been impossible without a sabbatical provided by the University of Oklahoma and a semester-length writing grant provided by the University of Oklahoma Arts and Humanities Forum. Under such unprecedented and unforeseen circumstances, this generous leave from my teaching duties would have remained insufficient without childcare and writing retreats facilitated by Chloe, Mom and Dad, and especially Brian. I dedicate this book to Brian and Remi with all my love.

APPENDIX

"Au renouveau" by Gace Brulé

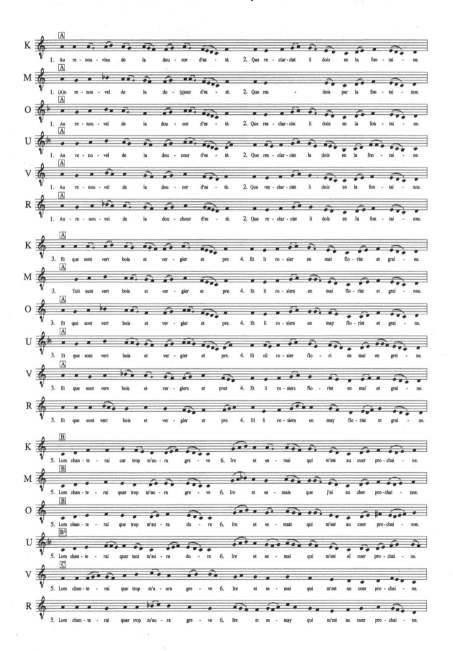

K 7. Et fins a - mis a tort a - chai - son 8. Est mult souvent de le - gier es - fre - e.

M 7. Et fins a - mis a tort a - choi - son - ez. 8. Est mont sou - vent de le - gier es - frez.

O 7. Car fins à - mis a tort a - choi - son - ez. 8. Est mont sou - vent de le - gier ef - fra - ez.

U 7. Don fins a - manz est tost o - qui - son - nez 8. Et molt so - vent de le - gier ef - fria - ez.

V 7. Et fins a - mis a tort a - choi - sons 8. Est mont sou - vent de le - gier ef - fre - ez.

R 7. Et fins a - mis a tort a - choi - son - ne 8. Est mult sou - vent de le - gier ef - fr - se.

Manuscript and Print Sources

Manuscripts Transmitting Trouvère Song

A ("Chansonnier d'Arras") Arras, Médiathèque municipal, 657
https://bvmm.irht.cnrs.fr/mirador/index.php?manifest=https://bvmm.irht.cnrs.fr/iiif/24762/manifest

B Bern, Burgerbibliothek, codex 231
https://e-codices.ch/de/list/one/bbb/0231

C Bern, Burgerbibliothek, codex 389
http://www.e-codices.unifr.ch/en/list/one/bbb/0389

F London, British Library, Egerton 274
http://www.bl.uk/manuscripts/FullDisplay.aspx?ref=Egerton_MS_274

G London, Lambeth Palace Library 1681

I Oxford, Bodleian Library, Douce 308
https://digital.bodleian.ox.ac.uk/objects/dd9d1160-196b-48a3-9427-78c209689c1f/surfaces/637930c2-4d46-4616-8980-6c16717d5268/

K Paris, Bibliothèque de l'Arsenal 5198
https://gallica.bnf.fr/ark:/12148/btv1b550063912/f27.image

L Paris, Bibliothèque nationale de France, fonds français 765
https://gallica.bnf.fr/ark:/12148/btv1b8454670d/f105.item

M ("Chansonnier du Roi") Paris, Bibliothèque nationale de France, fonds français 844
https://gallica.bnf.fr/ark:/12148/btv1b84192440/f21.image

M^t (*Libellus* of Songs by Thibaut IV, Roi de Navarre) Paris, Bibliothèque nationale de France, fonds français 844

Me Chansonnier de Mesmes (lost)

N Paris, BNF, fr. 845
https://gallica.bnf.fr/ark:/12148/btv1b6000955r/f11.image

O ("Chansonnier Cangé") Paris, Bibliothèque nationale de France, fonds français 846
https://gallica.bnf.fr/ark:/12148/btv1b6000950p/f27.image

P Paris, Bibliothèque nationale de France, fonds français 847
https://gallica.bnf.fr/ark:/12148/btv1b8454673n/f15.image

R Paris, Bibliothèque nationale de France, fonds français 1591
https://gallica.bnf.fr/ark:/12148/btv1b8454668b

S   Paris, Bibliothèque nationale de France, fonds français 12581
     https://gallica.bnf.fr/ark:/12148/btv1b53000323h/f767.image

T   ("Chansonnier de Noailles") Paris, Bibliothèque nationale de France, fonds
     français 12615
     https://gallica.bnf.fr/ark:/12148/btv1b60007945/f13.image

U   ("Chansonnier Saint Germain") Paris, Bibliothèque nationale de France, fonds
     français 20050
     https://gallica.bnf.fr/ark:/12148/btv1b60009580/f9.image

V   Paris, Bibliothèque nationale de France, fonds français 24406
     https://gallica.bnf.fr/ark:/12148/btv1b84386028/f15.image

W   Paris, Bibliothèque nationale de France, fonds français 25566
     https://gallica.bnf.fr/ark:/12148/btv1b6001348v

X   ("Chansonnier Clairambault") Paris, Bibliothèque nationale de France, fonds
     français 1050
     https://gallica.bnf.fr/ark:/12148/btv1b530003205/f23.image

Y   Fragment from St. Lô

a   ("Chansonnier du Vatican") Vatican City, Biblioteca Apostolica Vaticana, reg.
     lat. 1490
     https://digi.vatlib.it/view/MSS_Reg.lat.1490

b   Vatican City, Biblioteca Apostolica Vaticana, reg. lat. 1522
     https://digi.vatlib.it/view/MSS_Reg.lat.1522

k   Paris, Bibliothèque nationale de France, fonds français 12786
     https://gallica.bnf.fr/ark:/12148/btv1b60003511

Manuscripts Transmitting Troubadour Song

C   Paris, Bibliothèque nationale de France, fonds français 856
     https://gallica.bnf.fr/ark:/12148/btv1b8419246t/f1.item

D   I-MOe R 4, 4 Modena, Biblioteca estense universitaria, alfa.r.4.4
     http://bibliotecaestense.beniculturali.it/info/img/mss/i-mo-beu-alfa.r.4.4.html

G   Milan, Biblioteca Ambrosiana R 71 sup.
     http://213.21.172.25/0b02da8280051bf4

Manuscripts Transmitting Motets

Ba   Bamberg, Staatsbibliothek, lit. 115

Bes   Besançon, Bibliothèque municipal I, 716

Cl   Paris, Bibliothèque nationale de France, nouvelles acquisitions françaises 13521

F   Florence, Biblioteca Medicea Laurenziana, Pluteus 29.1

Ma   Madrid, Biblioteca Nacional, 20486

Mo   Montpellier, Bibliothèque Inter-Universitaire, Section Médicine, H196

W2   Wolfenbüttel, Herzog August Bibliothek, 1099

Primary Texts in Print and Online

Adam de la Halle. *Oeuvres Complètes*. Edited by Pierre Yves Badel. Paris: Librairie Général Française, 1995.

Adam de la Halle. *Le jeu de Robin et Marion*. Edited and translated by Jean Dufournet. Paris: Flammarion, 1989.

Atchison, Mary. *The* Chansonnier *of Oxford Bodleian MS Douce 308: Essays and Complete Edition of Texts*. Aldershot and Burlington, VT: Ashgate, 2005.

Auda, Antoine, ed. *Les* Motets Wallons *du manuscrit de Turin, Vari 42*. Brussels: Author, 1953.

Bartsch, Karl. *Altfranzösische Romanzen und Pastourellen*. Leipzig: Vogel, 1870.

Beaumanoir, Philippe de. *The* Coutumes de Beauvaisis *of Philippe de Beaumanoir*. Edited by F. R. P. Akehurst. Philadelphia: University of Pennsylvania Press, 2015.

Berger, Roger, ed. *La nécrologe de la Confrérie des jongleurs et des bourgeois d'Arras (1194–1361)*. Arras: Commission départementale des monuments historiques du Pas-de-Calais, 1963 and 1970.

Carapezza, Francesco. *Il canzoniere occitano G*. Naples: Liguori Editore, 2004.

Charles d'Anjou. *Roi-trouvère du XIIIè siècle: Charles d'Anjou*. Edited by Jean Maillard. N.P.: American Institute of Musicology, 1967.

Châtelain de Coucy. *Chansons attribuées au Chastelain de Couci (fin du XIIe–debut du XIIIe siècle)*. Edited by Alain Lerond. Paris: Presses Universitaires, 1964.

Conon de Béthune. *Les chansons de Conon de Béthune*. Edited by Axel Wallensköld. Paris: Honoré Champion, 1921.

Crescenzi, Piero de'. *Liber ruralium commodorum (Book on Rural Arts)*. Translated by Johanna Bauman. *Studies in the History of Gardens and Designed Landscapes* 22, no.2 (2002): 99–141. htps://doi.org/10.1080/14601176.2002.10435257.

Doss-Quinby, Eglal, Joan Tasker Grimbert, Wendy Pfeffer, and Elizabeth Aubrey, eds. *Songs of the Women Trouvères*. New Haven: Yale University Press, 2001.

Doss-Quinby, Eglal, and Samuel N. Rosenberg, eds., and Elizabeth Aubrey, mus. ed. *The Old French Ballette: Oxford, Bodleian Library, Douce 308*. Geneva: Droz, 2006.

Dubin, Nathaniel E. *The Fabliaux: A New Verse Translation*. Introduction by R. Howard Bloch. New York: Liveright Publishing Corporation, 2013.

Everist, Mark, and Anne Ibos-Augé. *REFRAIN*, accessed January 17, 2021. http://refrain.ac.uk/information.html.

Gace Brulé. *The Lyrics and Melodies of Gace Brulé*. Edited and translated by Samuel N. Rosenberg and Samuel Danon, music edited by Hendrik van der Werf. New York: Garland, 1985.

Geoffrey of Villehardouin. "The Conquest of Constantinople." Translated by Caroline Smith. In *Chronicles of the Crusades*. London: Penguin Classics, 2008.

Giles le Vinier. "Die Lieder des altfranzösischen Lyrikers Gille le Vinier." Edited by Albert Metcke. Dissertation, University of Halle, 1906.

Guillaume de Machaut. *Guillaume de Machaut, the Complete Poetry and Music*, Vol. 2: *The Boethian Poems*, edited and translated by R. Barton Palmer, music edited by Uri Smilansky. Kalamazoo, MI: Medieval Institute Publications, 2019.

Guillaume de Machaut. *Le jugement du roy de Behaigne and Remede de Fortune*. Edited by James I. Wimsatt and William W. Kibler. Athens: The University of Georgia Press, 1989.

Guillaume de Machaut. *Le jugement dou Roy de Navarre*. In *Guillaume de Machaut: The Complete Poetry and Music*, Vol. 1: *The Debate Series*, edited by R. Barton Palmer and Yolanda Plumley. Kalamazoo, MI: Medieval Institute Publications, 2016. https://d.lib. rochester.edu/teams/text/palmer-machaut-thedebateseries-navarre.

Guillaume le Vinier. *Les poésies de Guillaume le Vinier*. Edited by Philippe Ménard. Geneva: Droz, 1970.

Hoepffner, Ernest, ed. *Œuvres de Guillaume de Machaut*. 3 vols. Paris: Société des Anciens Textes Français, 1908–21.

Jakemes. *Le roman du Châtleain de Couci et de la Dame de Fayel par Jakemes*. Edited by John E. Matzke and Maurice Delbouille. Paris: Société des anciens textes français, 1936.

Jean de Joinville. "The Life of Saint Louis." Translated by Caroline Smith. In *Chronicles of the Crusades*. London: Penguin Classics, 2008.

Jean Renart. *The Romance of the Rose or Guillaume de Dole by Jean Renart*. Edited by Patricia Terry and Nancy Vine Durling. Philadelphia: University of Pennsylvania Press, 1993.

Jeanroy, Alfred. *Le chansonnier d'Arras: reproduction et phototypie*. Paris: SATF, 1925.

Jehan Bodel. "Les *pastourelles* de Jehan Bodel." Edited by Annette Brasseur. In *Arras au moyen âge*, edited by Marie-Madeline Castellani and Jean-Pierre Martin, 257–302. Arras: Artois Presses Université, 1994.

Jehan Bodel. *L'oeuvre de Jehan Bodel*. Edited by Charles Foulon. Paris: P.U.F., 1958.

Jehan Erart. *The Songs of Jehan Erart, 13th-Century Trouvère*. Edited by Terence Newcombe. Corpus Mensurabilis Musicae 67. American Institute of Musicology: NP, 1975.

Jehan Erart. *Les poesies du trouvère Jehan Erart*. Edited by Terence Newcombe. Geneva: Droz, 1972.

Johannes de Grocheio. *Ars musice*. Edited and translated by Constant J. Mews, John N. Crossley, Catherine Jeffreys, Leigh McKinnon, and Carol J. Williams. Kalamazoo, MI: Medieval Institute Publications, 2011.

Kibler, William W., and James I. Wimsatt. "The Development of the Pastourelle in the Fourteenth Century: An Edition of Fifteen Poems with an Analysis." *Medieval Studies* 45 (1983): 22–78.

Le Roux de Lincy, Antoine. *Les quatre livres des rois, traduits en français du xiiie siècle*. Paris: Imprimerie royale, 1891.

Moniot d'Arras and Moniot de Paris. *Moniot d'Arras et Moniot de Paris: trouvères du XIIIe siècle*. Edited by Holger Niels Petersen Dyggve. Helsinki: Société de littérature finnoise, 1938.

Paden, William D. *The Medieval Pastourelle*. 2 vols. New York: Garland, 1987.

Paterson, Linda M. *Troubadours, Trouvères, and the Crusades*, accessed January 17, 2021. https://warwick.ac.uk/fac/arts/modernlanguages/research/french/crusades/.

Philip the Chancellor. *Motets and Prosulas*. Edited by Thomas B. Payne. A-R Editions: Middleton, WI, 2011.

Raoul de Soissons. *Die Lieder Raouls von Soissons.* Edited by Emil Winkler. Halle: Max Niemeyer Verlag, 1914.

Richard de Fournival. *Beasts of Love: Richard de Fournival's "Bestiaire d'amour" and a Woman's Response.* Edited by Jeanette Beer. Toronto: University of Toronto Press, 2003.

Richard de Semilli. *Lyrics of Richard de Semilli.* Edited by Susan M. Johnson. Binghamton, NY: Medieval & Renaissance Texts & Studies, 1992.

Rivière, Jean Claude. *Pastourelles.* Geneva: Droz, 1974.

Rosenberg, Samuel N. and Hans Tischler. *The Monophonic Songs in the Roman de Fauvel.* Lincoln: University of Nebraska Press, 1991.

Rosenberg, Samuel N., Hans Tischler, and Marie-Geneviève Grossel, eds. *Chansons des trouvères: Chanter m'estuet.* Paris: Librairie Général Français, 1995.

Rosenberg, Samuel N., Margaret Switten, and Gérard le Vot, eds. *Songs of the Troubadours and Trouvères: An Anthology of Poems and Melodies.* New York: Garland, 1998.

Saint-Cricq, Gaël, Eglal Doss-Quinby, and Samuel Rosenberg, eds. *Motets from the Chansonnier de Noailles.* Middleton, WI: A-R Editions, 2017.

Thibaut de Blaison. *Les poésies de Thibaut de Blaison.* Edited by Terence H. Newcombe. Geneva: Droz, 1978.

Thibaut IV, de Champagne. *The Lyrics of Thibaut de Champagne.* Edited and translated by Kathleen J. Brahney. New York: Garland, 1989.

Thibaut IV, de Champagne. *Les chansons: Textes et melodies.* Edited by Christopher Callahan, Marie-Geneviève Grossel, and Daniel E. O'Sullivan. Paris: Champion, 2018.

Tischler, Hans, ed. *The Earliest Motets (to c.1270): A Complete Comparative Edition.* New Haven: Yale University Press, 1982.

Tischler, Hans, ed. *Trouvère Lyrics with Melodies: Complete Comparative Edition.* Corpus mensurabilis musicae 107. 15 vols. Neuhausen: Hänsler-Verlag's American Institute of Musicology, 1997.

Tischler, Hans, ed., and Susan Stakel and Joel Relihan, trans. *The Montpellier Codex.* 4 vols. Recent Researches in the Music of the Middle Ages and Early Renaissance 2–7. Madison, WI: A-R Editions, 1978–85.

Traill, David A., ed. and trans. *Carmina Burana.* 2 vols. Cambridge, MA: Harvard University Press, 2018.

van den Boogaard, Nico H. J. *Rondeaux et Refrains du XIIe siècle au début du XIVe.* Paris: Klincksieck, 1969.

van der Werf, Hendrik. *The Chansons of the Troubadours and Trouvères: A Study of the Melodies and Their Relation to the Poems.* Utrecht: A. Oosthoek's Uitgeversmaatschappij, 1972.

van der Werf, Hendrik. *Trouvères-Melodien.* 2 vols. Basel: Bärenreiter Kassel, 1979.

Bibliography

Aberth, John. *An Environmental History of the Middle Ages: The Crucible of Nature.* New York: Routledge, 2013.

Alden, Jane. "Excavating Chansonniers: Musical Archaeology and the Search for Popular Song." *Journal of Musicology* 25, no.1 (2008): 46–87. https://doi-org.ezproxy.lib.ou.edu/10.1525/jm.2008.25.1.46.

Allen, Aaron S., and Kevin Dawe. "Ecomusicologies." In *Current Directions in Ecomusicology: Music, Culture, Nature,* edited by Aaron S. Allen and Kevin Dawe, 1–15. New York: Routledge, 2015.

Allen, Peter L. *The Art of Love: Amatory Fiction from Ovid to the* Romance of the Rose. Philadelphia: University of Pennsylvania Press, 1992.

Armstrong, Adrian, and Sarah Kay. *Knowing Poetry: Verse in Medieval France from the* Rose *to the* Rhétoriqueurs. Ithaca, NY: Cornell University Press, 2011.

Aubrey, Elizabeth. "Genre as a Determinant of Melody in the Songs of the Troubadours and the Trouvères." In *Medieval Lyric: Genres in Historical Context,* edited by William D. Paden, 273–96. Urbana: University of Illinois Press, 2000.

Aubrey, Elizabeth. *The Music of the Troubadours.* Bloomington: Indiana University Press, 1996.

Aubrey, Elizabeth. "Reconsidering 'High Style' and 'Low Style' in Medieval Song." *Journal of Music Theory* 52, no.1 (2008): 75–122.

Aubrey, Elizabeth. "Sources, MS III, 3 and 4: Secular Monophony, Occitan and French." In *Oxford Music Online.* Oxford University Press, 2001–. Article published 2001. https://www-oxfordmusiconline-com.

Baldwin, John W. *Aristocratic Life in Medieval France: The Romances of Jean Renart and Gerbert de Montreuil, 1190–1230.* Baltimore: Johns Hopkins University Press, 2002.

Baldwin, John W. *The Government of Philip Augustus: Foundations of French Royal Power in the Middle Ages.* Berkeley: University of California Press, 1986.

Baldwin, John W. *Knights, Lords, and Ladies: In Search of Aristocrats in the Paris Region, 1180–1220.* Philadelphia: University of Pennsylvania Press, 2019.

Baldwin, John W. "Le tournoi de Chauvency." In *Lettres, musique et société en Lorraine médiévale: autour du* Tournoi de Chauvency *(Ms. Oxford Bodleian Douce 308),* edited by Mireille Chazan and Nancy Freeman Regalado, 7–24. Geneva: Librairie Droz, 2021.

Baldwin, John W. *Masters, Princes, and Merchants: The Social Views of Peter the Chanter and His Circle.* 2 vols. Princeton: Princeton University Press, 1970.

Baldwin, John W. "'Once there was an emperor . . . .': A Political Reading of Jean Renart." In *Jean Renart and the Art of Romance: Essays on* Guillaume de Dole, edited by Nancy Vine Durling, 45–82. Gainesville: University Press of Florida, 1997.

Baldwin, John W. *Paris, 1200.* Stanford: Stanford University Press, 2010.

Baltzer, Rebecca. "Thirteenth-Century Illuminated Miniatures and the Date of the Florence Manuscript." *Journal of the American Musicological Society* 25, no.1 (1972): 1–18.

Barbieri, Luca. "Thibaut le chansonnier, Thibaut le posthume: sur la réception de la lyrique française dans la tradition manuscrite." *Critica del testo* 18, no.3 (2015): 199–233.

Barrow, Julia. *The Clergy in the Medieval World: Secular Clerics, Their Families and Careers in North-Western Europe, c.800–c.1200.* Cambridge: Cambridge University Press, 2015.

Baudin, Arnaud. *Emblématique et pouvoir en Champagne: les sceaux des comtes de Champagne et de leur entourage (fin XIe–début XIVe siècle).* Langres: Éditions Dominique Guéniot, 2012.

Baudin, Arnaud. "Enquête sur le premier sceau de Thibaud IV le Chansonnier (1214–1232)." In *Actes des tables rondes de la Société française d'héraldique et de sigillographie,* edited by Jean-Luc Chassel, 31–37. Paris: Société française d'héraldique et de sigillographie, 2007.

Bauman, Johanna. "Tradition and Transformation: The Pleasure Garden in Piero de' Crescenzi's *Liber ruralium commodorum*." *Studies in the History of Gardens and Designed Landscapes* 22, no.2 (2002): 117–21. https://doi.org/10.1080/14601176.2002.10435257.

Bec, Pierre. *La lyrique Française au moyen age (XIIe–XIIIe siècles): Contribution à une typologie des genres poétiques médiévaux.* 2 vols. Paris: Picard, 1977.

Beck, Corinne, and Fabrice Guizard. "La forêt ressources." In *La forêt au moyen âge*, edited by Sylvie Bépoix and Hervé Richard, 107–21. Paris: Les Belles Lettres, 2019.

Bédier, Joseph. "Les fêtes de mai et les commencemens de la poésie lyrique au moyen age." *Revue des Deux Mondes* 135, no.1 (1896): 146–72.

Bedos-Rezak, Brigitte Miriam. *When Ego Was Imago: Signs of Identity in the Middle Ages.* Leiden: Brill, 2010.

Bennett, Judith M. *A Medieval Life: Cecilia Penifader and the World of English Peasants Before the Plague.* 2nd ed. Philadelphia: University of Pennsylvania Press, 2020.

Bent, Margaret, and Andrew Wathey. "Introduction." In *Fauvel Studies: Allegory, Chronicle, Music, and Image in Paris Bibliothèque Nationale de France, MS français 146,* edited by Margaret Bent and Andrew Wathey, 1–24. Oxford: Clarendon Press, 1998.

Benton, John. "The Court of Champagne as a Literary Center." *Speculum* 36, no.4 (1961): 551–91.

Berberich, Christine, Neil Campbell, and Robert Hudson. "Introduction." In *Land & Identity: Theory, Memory, and Practice,* edited by Christine Berberich, Neil Campbell, and Robert Hudson, 17–37. Amsterdam and New York: Rodopi, 2012.

Berger, Roger. *Littérature et société arrageoises au XIIIe siècle: les chansons et dits artésiens.* Arras: Mémoires de la Commission Départementale des Monuments Historiques du Pas-de-Calais, Archives départementales, 1981.

Bernard, Vincent, et al. "À l'Ouest, des ressources forestières diversifiées." In *La forêt au moyen âge,* edited by Sylvie Bépoix and Hervé Richard, 243–58. Paris: Les Belles Lettres, 2019.

Birrell, Jean. "Common Rights in the Medieval Forest: Disputes and Conflicts in the Thirteenth Century." *Past and Present* 117, no.1 (1987): 22–49.

Blanchard, Joël. *La pastorale en France aux XIVe et XVe siècles: recherches sur les structures de l'imaginaire medieval.* Paris: Champion, 1983.

Boogaard, Nico H. J. van den. *Rondeaux et refrains du XIIe siècle au début du XIVe.* Paris: Klincksieck, 1969.

Boogaart, Jacques. "Encompassing Past and Present: Quotations and Their Function in Machaut's Motets." *Early Music History* 20 (2001): 1–86.

Bowers, Roger. "Guillaume de Machaut and His Canonry of Reims, 1338–1377." *Early Music History* 23 (2004): 1–48.

Boynton, Susan. "Women's Performance of the Lyric Before 1500." In *Medieval Woman's Song: Cross-Culutral Perspectives*, edited by Anne L. Klinck and Ann Marie Rasumssen, 47–65. Philadelphia: University of Pennsylvania Press, 2001.

Bradley, Catherine A. "Contrafacta and Transcribed Motets: Vernacular Influences on Latin Motets and Clausulae in the Florence Manuscript." *Early Music History* 32 (2013): 1–70.

Bradley, Catherine A. "The Earliest Motets: Musical Borrowing and Re-use." PhD diss., Cambridge University, 2011.

Bradley, Catherine A. "Ordering in the Motet Fascicles of the Florence Manuscript." *Plainsong and Medieval Music* 22, no.1 (2013): 37–64.

Bradley, Catherine A. *Polyphony in Medieval Paris: The Art of Composing with Plainchant.* Cambridge: Cambridge University Press, 2018.

Bradley, Catherine A., and Karen Desmond, "Introduction." In *The Montpellier Codex: The Final Fascicle. Contents, Contexts, Chronologies*, edited by Catherine A. Bradley and Karen Desmond, 1–10. Woodbridge: Boydell & Brewer, 2018.

Brownlee, Kevin. "Authorial Self-Representation and Literary Models in the *Roman de Fauvel.*" In *Fauvel Studies: Allegory, Chronicle, Music, and Image in Paris Bibliothèque Nationale de France, MS français 146*, edited by Margaret Bent and Andrew Wathey, 73–104. Oxford: Clarendon Press, 1998.

Brownlee, Kevin. "Machaut's *Remede de Fortune*: The Lyric Anthology as Narrative Progression." In *The Ladder of High Designs: Structure and Interpretation of the French Lyric Sequence*, edited by Doranne Fenoaltea and David Lee Rubin, 1–25. Charlottesville: University Press of Virginia, 1991.

Brownlee, Kevin. *Poetic Identity in Guillaume de Machaut.* Madison, WI: University of Wisconsin Press, 1984.

Brownlee, Kevin. "Transformations of the Couple: Genre and Language in the *Jeu de Robin et Marion.*" *French Forum* 14, no.1 (1989): 419–33.

Bruckner, Matilda Tomaryn. "What Short Tale Does Jehan Bodel's Political *Pastourelle* Tell." *Romania* 120, nos.477/478 (2002): 118–31.

Burgwinkle, William. "The Chansonniers as Books." In *The Troubadours: An Introduction*, edited by Simon Gaunt and Sarah Kay, 246–62. Cambridge, UK: Cambridge University Press, 1999.

Burns, E. Jane. "Sewing Like a Girl: Working Women in the *chansons de toile.*" In *Medieval Woman's Song: Cross Cultural Approaches*, edited by Anne L. Klinck and Anne Marie Rasmussen, 99–126. Philadelphia: University of Pennsylvania Press, 2002.

Burns, E. Jane, Sarah Kay, Roberta Kreuger, and Helen Solterer. "Feminism and the Discipline of Old French Studies: 'Une Bele Disjointure.'" In *Medievalism and the Modernist Temper*, edited by R. Howard Bloch and Stephen G. Nichols, 225–66. Baltimore: Johns Hopkins University Press, 1996.

Busby, Keith. *Codex and Context: Reading Old French Verse Narrative in Manuscript.* 2 vols. Amsterdam and New York: Rodopi, 2002.

Butterfield, Ardis. "Enté: A Survey and Reassessment of the Term in Thirteenth-and Fourteenth-Century Music and Poetry." *Early Music History* 22 (2003): 67–101.

Butterfield, Ardis. "Pastoral and the Politics of Plague in Machaut and Chaucer." *Studies in the Age of Chaucer* 16 (1994): 3–27.

Butterfield, Ardis. *Poetry and Music in Medieval France: From Jean Renart to Guillaume de Machaut.* Cambridge: Cambridge University Press, 2002.

Bynum, Caroline Walker. "Did the Twelfth Century Discover the Individual?" *The Journal of Ecclesiastical History* 31 (1980): 1–17.

Caldwell, Mary Channen. "Cueing Refrains in the Medieval Conductus." *Journal of the Royal Musical Association* 143, no.2 (2018): 273–324.

Caldwell, Mary Channen. *Devotional Refrains in Medieval Latin Song.* Cambridge: Cambridge University Press, 2022.

Calin, William. *A Poet at the Fountain: Essays on the Narrative Verse of Guillaume de Machaut.* Lexington: University of Kentucky Press, 1974.

Calkins, Robert G. "Piero de' Crescenzi and the Medieval Garden." In *Medieval Gardens*, edited by Elisabeth Blair MacDougall, 157–73. Washington, D.C.: Dumbarton Oaks, 1986.

Callahan, Christopher. "Collecting Trouvère Lyric at the Peripheries: The Lessons of MSS Paris, BnF fr. 20050 and Bern, Burgerbibliothek 389." *Textual Cultures* 8, no.2 (2013): 15–30.

Callahan, Christopher. "Hybrid Discourse and Performance in the Old French Pastourelle." *French Forum* 27, no.1 (2002): 1–22.

Callahan, Christopher. "Strategies of Appropriation in Jacques de Cambrai's Devotional Contrafacts." In *A Medieval Songbook: Trouvère MS C*, edited by Elizabeth Eva Leach, Joseph W. Mason, and Matthew P. Thompson, 158–73. Woodbridge: The Boydell Press, 2022.

Campbell, Bruce M. S. *The Great Transition: Climate, Disease and Society in the Late-Medieval World.* Cambridge: Cambridge University Press, 2016.

Cayley, Emma. "Machaut and Debate Poetry." In *A Companion to Guillaume de Machaut*, edited by Deborah McGrady and Jennifer Bain, 103–18. Leiden: Brill, 2012.

Cerquiglini, Bernard. *Éloge de la variante: histoire critique de la philologie.* Paris: Seuil, 1989.

Cerquiglini-Toulet, Jacqueline. *'En engin si soutil': Guillaume de Machaut et l'écriture au XIVe siècle.* Paris: Champion, 1985.

Chaganti, Seeta. *Strange Footing: Poetic Form and Dance in the Late Middle Ages.* Chicago: University of Chicago Press, 2018.

Chapelot, Jean, and Robert Fossier. *The Village and House in the Middle Ages.* Translated by Henry Cleere. Berkeley and Los Angeles: University of California Press, 1985.

Clark, Suzannah. "'S'en dirai chançonete': Hearing Text and Music in a Medieval Motet." *Plainsong and Medieval Music* 16, no.1 (2007): 31–59.

Clark, Suzannah. "When Words Converge and Meanings Diverge: Counterexamples to Polytextuality in the Thirteenth-Century Motet." In *A Critical Companion to Medieval Motets*, edited by Jared C. Hartt, 205–24. Woodbridge: The Boydell Press, 2018.

Cohen, Jeffrey J. *Medieval Identity Machines.* Minneapolis, MN: University of Minnesota Press, 2003.

Coldwell, Maria V. "*Jougleresses* and *Trobairitz*: Secular Musicians in Medieval France." In *Women Making Music: The Western Art Tradition, 1150–1950*, edited by Jane Bowers and Judith Tick, 39–61. Urbana and Chicago: University of Illinois Press, 1986.

Colton, Lisa. "The Articulation of Virginity in the Medieval *Chansonne de nonne*." *Journal of the Royal Musical Association* 133, no.2 (2008): 159–88.

Colvin, Howard M. "Royal Gardens in Medieval England." In *Medieval Gardens*, edited by Elisabeth Blair Macdougall, 7–22. Washington, D.C.: Dumbarton Oaks Research Library and Collection, 1986.

Corbellari, Alain. "Joseph Bédier, Philologist and Writer." In *Medievalism and the Modernist Temper*, edited by R. Howard Bloch and Stephen G. Nichols, 269–85. Baltimore: University of Maryland Press, 1996.

Crane, Susan. *The Performance of the Self: Ritual, Clothing, and Identity During the Hundred Years War.* Philadelphia: University of Pennsylvania Press, 2002.

Creighton, Oliver. *Designs Upon the Land: Elite Landscapes of the Middle Ages.* Woodbridge: Boydell, 2009.

Creighton, Oliver. *Early European Castles: Aristocracy and Authority, AD 800–1200.* London: Bristol Classical Press, 2012.

Cronon, William. "The Trouble with Wilderness; Or, Getting Back to the Wrong Nature." In *Uncommon Ground: Rethinking the Human Place in Nature*, edited by William Cronon, 69–90. New York: W.W. Norton, 1996.

Cronon, William. "The Uses of Environmental History." *Environmental History Review* 17, no.3 (1993): 1–22.

Crouch, David. *The Chivalric Turn: Conduct and Hegemony in Europe before 1300.* Oxford: Oxford University Press, 2019.

Crouch, David. *Tournament.* New York: Bloomsbury, 2005.

Cummings, John. "*Veneurs s'en vont en Paradis*: Medieval Hunting and the 'Natural' Landscape." In *Inventing Medieval Landscapes: Senses of Place in Western Europe*, edited by John Howe and Michael Wolfe, 33–56. Gainesville: University Press of Florida, 2002.

Curran, Sean. "Hockets Broken and Integrated." *Early Music History* 39 (2017): 31–104.

Curran, Sean. "A Palaeographical Analysis of the Verbal Text in Montpellier 8: Problems, Implications, Opportunities." In *The Montpellier Codex, The Final Fascicle: Contents, Contexts, Chronologies*, edited by Catherine A. Bradley and Karen Desmond, 32–65. Woodbridge: Boydell & Brewer, 2018.

Curtius, Ernst Robert. *European Literature and the Latin Middle Ages.* Translated by Willard R. Trask. New York: Harper & Row, 1963.

Deeming, Helen. "Music and Contemplation in the Twelfth-Century *Dulcis Jesu memoria*." *Journal of the Royal Musical Association* 139, no.1 (2014): 1–39.

Deeming, Helen. "Music, Memory, and Mobility: Citation and Contrafactum in Thirteenth-Century Sequence Repertories." In *Citation, Intertextuality, and Memory in the Middle Ages and Renaissance*, Vol. 2: *Cross-Disciplinary Perspectives on Medieval Culture*, edited by Giuliano di Bacco and Yolanda Plumley, 67–81. Exeter: Exeter University Press, 2013.

Deeming, Helen, and Elizabeth Eva Leach, eds. *Manuscripts and Medieval Song: Inscription, Performance, Context.* Cambridge: Cambridge University Press, 2015.

Delmaire, Bernard. "Note sur la dime des jardins, 'mes' et courtils dans la France du nord au moyen âge." In *Campagnes médiévales: l'homme et son espace, études offertes à Robert Fossier*, edited by Elizabeth Mornet, 231–46. Paris: Publications de la Sorbonne, 1955.

Delumeau, Jean. *History of Paradise: The Garden of Eden in Myth and Tradition.* Translated by Matthew J. O'Connell. Urbana and Chicago: University of Illinois Press, 2000.

De Moor, Martina, Leigh Shaw-Taylor, and Paul Warde. "Common Land and Common Rights in Flanders." In *The Management of Common Land in North West Europe, c. 1500–1850*, edited by Martina De Moor, Leigh Shaw-Taylor, and Paul Warde, 113–41. Turnhout: Brepols, 2002.

De Moor, Martina, Leigh Shaw-Taylor, and Paul Warde. "Comparing the Historical Commons of North West Europe: An Introduction." In *The Management of Common Land in North West Europe, c. 1500–1850*, edited by Martina De Moor, Leigh Shaw-Taylor, and Paul Warde, 15–31. Turnhout: Brepols, 2002.

De Moor, Martina, Leigh Shaw-Taylor, and Paul Warde, eds. *The Management of Common Land in North West Europe, c. 1500–1850.* Turnhout: Brepols, 2002.

Dembowski, Peter F. "Vocabulary of Old French Courtly Lyrics: Difficulties and Hidden Difficulties." *Critical Inquiry* 2, no.4 (1976): 763–79.

Desmond, Karen. *Music and the Moderni, 1300–1350: The ars nova in Theory and Practice.* Cambridge: Cambridge University Press, 2018.

Dillon, Emma. "The Art of Interpolation and the *Roman de Fauvel*." *Journal of Musicology* 19, no.2 (2002): 223–63.

Dillon, Emma. *Medieval Music-Making and the Roman de Fauvel*. Cambridge: Cambridge University Press, 2002.

Dillon, Emma. *The Sense of Sound: Musical Meaning in France, 1260–1330*. Oxford and New York: Oxford University Press, 2012.

Dillon, Emma. "Unwriting Medieval Song." *New Literary History* 46, no.4 (2015): 595–622.

Dolce, Brianne. "'Soit hom u feme': New Evidence for Women Musicians and the Search for the 'Women Trouvères.'" *Revue de musicologie* 106, no.2 (2020): 301–28.

Doss-Quinby, Eglal, Joan Tasker Grimbert, Wendy Pfeffer, and Elizabeth Aubrey, eds. *Songs of the Women Trouvères*. Yale: Yale University Press, 2001.

Dowling, Abigail P. "Landscape of Luxuries: Mahaut d'Artois's (1302–1329) Management and use of the Park at Hesdin." In *Rural Space in the Middle Ages and Early Modern Age: The Spatial Turn in Premodern Studies*, edited by Albrecht Classen, 367–88. Berlin: De Gruyter, 2012.

Dowling, Abigail P., and Richard Keyser. *Conservation's Roots: Managing for Sustainability in Preindustrial Europe, 1100–1800*. New York: Berghahn Books, 2020.

Dragonetti, Roger. *La technique poétique des trouvères dans la chanson courtoise: contribution à l'étude de la rhétorique médiévale*. Bruges: De Tempel, 1960.

Dronke, Peter. *The Medieval Lyric*. 3rd ed. Cambridge: D. S. Brewer, 1996.

Duby, Georges. *The Chivalrous Society*. Translated by Cynthia Postan. Berkeley: University of California Press, 1977.

Duby, Georges. *Rural Economy and Country Life in the Medieval West*. Translated by Cynthia Postan. London: Edward Arnold, 1968.

Duceppe-Lamarre, Fraçois. *Chasse et pâturage dans les forêts du nord de la France: pour une archéologie du paysage sylvestre (XIe–XVIe siècles)*. Paris: L'Harmattan, 2006.

Dyer, Christopher. "Woodlands and Wood-Pasture in Western England." In *The English Rural Landscape*, edited by Joan Thirsk, 97–121. Oxford: Oxford University Press, 2000.

Dyggve, Holger Petersen. "Chansons françaises du XIIIe siècle (Colart le Boutellier, Gaidifer, Wasteblé, etc.)." *Neuphilologische Mitteilungen* 30, no.4 (1929): 177–214.

Dyggve, Holger Petersen. *Gace Brulé: Trouvère Champenois*. Helsinki: Société Neophilologique, 1951.

Dyggve, Holger Petersen. *Onomastique des trouvères*. Helsinki: Société de littérature finnoise, 1934.

Dyggve, Holger Petersen. "Personnages historiques figurant dans la poésie lyrique française des XIIe et XIIIe siècles, xxii: le Vidame de Chartres." *Neuphilologische Mitteilungen*, 45 (1944): 161–85.

Earp, Lawrence. *Guillaume de Machaut: A Guide to Research*. New York: Garland, 1995.

Enders, Jody. "Music, Delivery, and the Rhetoric of Memory in Guillaume de Machaut's *Remède de Fortune*." *Proceedings of the Modern Language Association* 107, no.3 (1992): 450–64.

Épaud, Frédéric. "Les forêts et le bois d'oeuvre dans le bassin parisien." In *La forêt au moyen âge*, edited by Sylvie Bépoix and Hervé Richard, 142–53. Paris: Les Belles Lettres, 2019.

Epstein, Marcia Jenneth, ed. and trans. *'Prions en chantant': Devotional Songs of the Trouvères*. Toronto: University of Toronto Press, 1997.

Epstein, Steven A. *The Medieval Discovery of Nature*. Cambridge: Cambridge University Press, 2012.

Evergates, Theodore. *The Aristocracy in the County of Champagne, 1100–1300*. Philadelphia: University of Pennsylvania Press, 2007.

Evergates, Theodore. "Aristocratic Women in the County of Champagne." In *Aristocratic Women in Medieval France*, edited by Theodore Evergates, 74–110. Philadelphia: University of Pennsylvania Press, 2010.

Evergates, Theodore. *Feudal Society in the Bailliage of Troyes under the Counts of Champagne, 1152–1284*. Baltimore: Johns Hopkins University Press, 1975.

Evergates, Theodore. *Marie of France: Countess of Champagne, 1145–1198*. Philadelphia: University of Pennsylvania Press, 2019.

Everist, Mark. *Discovering Medieval Song: Latin Poetry and Music in the* Conductus. Cambridge: Cambridge University Press, 2018.

Everist, Mark. *French Motets in the Thirteenth Century: Music, Poetry and Genre*. Cambridge: Cambridge University Press, 2004.

Everist, Mark. "Friends and Foals: The Polyphonic Music of Adam de la Halle." In *Musical Culture in the World of Adam de la Halle*, edited by Jennifer Saltzstein, 311–51. Leiden: Brill, 2019.

Everist, Mark. "Machaut's Musical Heritage." In *A Companion to Guillaume de Machaut*, edited by Deborah McGrady and Jennifer Bain, 143–58. Leiden: Brill, 2012.

Everist, Mark. "Motets, French Tenors, and the Polyphonic Chanson ca. 1300." *Journal of Musicology* 24, no.3 (2007): 365–406.

Everist, Mark. "The Rondeau Motet: Paris and Artois in the Thirteenth Century." *Music & Letters* 69, no.1 (1988): 1–22.

Falck, Robert. "Zwei Lieder Philipps des Kanzlers und ihre Vorbilder. Neue Aspekte musikalischer Entlehnung in der mittelalterlichen Monodie." *Archiv für Musikwissenschaft* 24 (1967): 81–98.

Falck, Robert. "*Rondellus*, Canon, and Related Types before 1300." *Journal of the American Musicological Society* 25, no.1 (1971): 38–57.

Fallows, David. "Lai." In *Oxford Music Online*. Oxford University Press, 2001–. Article Published 2001. https://www-oxfordmusiconline-com.

Farmer, Sharon. "Aristocratic Power and the 'Natural' Landscape: The Garden Park at Hesdin, ca. 1291–1302." *Speculum* 88, no.3 (2013): 644–80.

Ferruolo, Stephen. *The Origins of the University: The Schools of Paris and Their Critics, 1100–1215*. Stanford: Stanford University Press, 1985.

Finney, Carolyn. *Black Faces, White Spaces: Reimagining the Relationship of African Americans to the Great Outdoors*. Chapel Hill: University of North Carolina Press, 2014.

Freedman, Paul. *Images of the Medieval Peasant*. Stanford: Stanford University Press, 1999.

Fossier, Robert. "Arras et ses campagnes au moyen âge." In *Arras au moyen âge: Histoire et littérature*, edited by Marie-Madeleine Castellani and Jean-Pierre Martin, 15–26. Artois: Presses Université, 1994.

Gallé, Hélène and Danielle Quéruel. "La forête dans la littérature médiévale." In *La forêtau moyen âge*, edited by Sylvie Bépoix and Hervé Richard, 25–84. Paris: Les Belles Lettres, 2019.

Galvez, Marisa. `Songbook: How Lyrics Became Poetry in Medieval Europe*. Chicago: University of Chicago Press, 2012.

Galvez, Marisa. *The Subject of Crusade: Lyric, Romance, and Materials, 1150 to 1500*. Chicago: University of Chicago Press, 2020.

Gatti, Luca. "Author Ascriptions and Genre Labels in C." In *A Medieval Songbook: Trouvère Manuscript C*," edited by Elizabeth Eva Leach, Joseph W. Mason, and Matthew P. Thompson, 75–81. Woodbridge: The Boydell Press, 2022.

Gatti, Luca. *Repertorio delle attribuzioni discordanti nella lirica trovierica*. Rome: Sapienza Università Editrice, 2019.

Gennrich, Friedrich. *Bibliographie der ältesten französischen und lateinischen Motetten.* Summa musicae medii aevi 2. Darmstadt, 1957.

Gennrich, Friedrich. *Grundriss einer formenlehre des mittelalterlichen Liedes (als Grundlage einer musikalischen Formenlehre des Liedes).* Halle: Max Niemeyer, 1932.

Gennrich, Friedrich. "Simon d'Authie: ein pikardischer Sänger des XIII. Jahrhunderts." *Zeitschrift für romanische Philologie* 67 (1951): 49–104.

Gifford, Terry. "Pastoral, Anti-pastoral, Post-pastoral." In *The Cambridge Companion to Literature and the Environment*, edited by Louise Westling, 17–30. Cambridge, UK: Cambridge University Press, 2014.

Gilchrist, Roberta. "The Contested Garden: Gender, Space and metaphor in the English Castle Garden." In *Gender and Archaeology: Contesting the Past*, edited by Roberta Gilchrist, 109–145. London: Routledge, 1999.

Glacken, Clarence. *Traces on the Rhodian Shore: Nature and Culture in Western Thought from Ancient Times through the Eighteenth Century.* Berkeley: University of California Press, 1976.

Godefroy, Frédéric. *Dictionnaire de l'ancienne langue française et de tous ses dialectes du IXe au XVe siècle.* 10 vols. Paris: F. Vieweg, 1881–1902.

Le Goff, Jacques. "Note sur société tripartite, idéologie monarchique et renouveau économique dans la crétienté du IXe au XIIe siècle." In *Pour un autre Moyen Age: temps, travail, et culture en Occident: 18 essais*, 80–90. Paris: Gallimard, 1977.

Golden, Rachel May. *Mapping Medieval Identities in Occitanian Crusade Song.* Oxford: Oxford University Press, 2020.

Grant, Edward. *God and Reason in the Middle Ages.* Cambridge: Cambridge University Press, 2001.

Grau, Anna Kathryn. "Hearing Voices: Heteroglossia, Homoglossia, and the Old French Motet." *Musica Disciplina* 58 (2013): 73–100.

Grau, Anna Kathryn. "*Jonete et jolie*: Polyphony and Gendered Voices in the Old French Motet." In *Gender and Voice in Medieval French Literature and Song*, edited by Rachel May Golden and Katherine Kong, 203–29. Gainesville: University Press of Florida, 2021.

Gravdal, Kathryn. "Camouflaging Rape: The Rhetoric of Sexual Violence in the Medieval *Pastourelle*." *Romanic Review* 76, no.4 (1985): 361–97.

Gravdal, Kathryn. *Ravishing Maidens: Writing Rape in Medieval French Literature and Law.* Philadelphia: University of Pennsylvania Press, 1991.

Griffiths, Quentin. "Royal Counselors and Trouvères in the Houses of Nesle and Soissons." *Medieval Prosopography* 18, no.1 (1997): 123–37.

Grossel, Marie-Geneviève. "Thibaut de Champagne et Gace Brulé: Variations sur un même ideal." In *Thibaut de Champagne: Prince et poète au XIIIe siècle*, edited by Yvonne Bellanger and Daniel Quéruel, 107–118. Lyon: La Manufacture, 1987.

Guesnon, Adolphe. "Nouvelles recherches biographiques sur les trouvères artésiens." *Le Moyen Âge* 15 (1902): 137–73.

Guesnon, Adolphe. "Recherches biographiques sur les trouvères artésiens." *Bulletin historique et philologique du comité des travaux historiques et scientifiques* (1894): 420–36.

Guiette, Robert. *D'une poésie formelle en France au moyen age.* Paris: Nizet, 1972.

Guillemain, Bernard. "Chiffres et statistiques pour l'histoire ecclésiastique du Moyen Âge." *Le Moyen Âge* 59 (1953): 341–65.

Haines, John. "Aristocratic Patronage and The Cosmopolitan Vernacular Songbook: The *Chansonnier du Roi (M-trouv.)* and the French Mediterranean." In *Musical Culture in the World of Adam de la Halle*, edited by Jennifer Saltzstein, 95–120. Leiden: Brill, 2019.

Haines, John. *Eight Centuries of Troubadours and Trouvères: The Changing Identity of Medieval Music*. Cambridge: Cambridge University Press, 2004.

Haines, John. "Erasures in Thirteenth Century Music." In *Music and Medieval Manuscripts: Paleography and Performance*, edited by John Haines and Randall Rosenfeld, 60–88. Burlington VT: Ashgate Publishing, 2004.

Haines, John. *Medieval Song in Romance Languages*. Cambridge: Cambridge University Press, 2010.

Haines, John. "The Songbook for William of Villehardouin, Prince of the Morea (Paris, Bibliothèque nationale de France, fonds français 844): A Crucial Case in the History of Vernacular Song Collections." In *Viewing the Morea: Land and People in the Late Medieval Peloponnese*, edited by Sharon E. J. Gerstel, 57–109. Washington, D.C.: Dumbarton Oaks Research Library and Collection, 2013.

Haines, John. "Vers une distinction *leu/clus* dans l'art music-poétique des troubadours." *Neophilologus* 81 (1997): 341–47.

Hanawalt, Barbara A., and Michal Kobialka. "Introduction." In *Medieval Practices of Space*, edited by Barbara A. Hanawalt and Kobialka, ix–xviii. Minneapolis: University of Minnesota Press, 2000.

Harper, Alexander. "Pierre d'Angicourt and Angevin Construction." *Journal of the Society of Architectural Historians* 75, no.2 (2016): 140–57.

Harvey, John. *Medieval Gardens*. Beaverton, OR: Timber Press, 1981.

Hasenohr, Geneviève. "Les systèmes de repérage textuel." In *Mise en page et mise en texte du livre manuscript*, edited by H. Jean-Martin and J. Vezin, 273–88. Paris: Editions du Cercle de la Librairie-Promodis, 1990.

Hexter, Ralph J. *Ovid and Medieval Schooling: Studies in Medieval School Commentaries on Ovid's 'Ars amatoria,' 'Epistulae Ex Ponto,' and 'Epistulae Heroidum.'* Munich: Arbeo Gesellschaft, 1986.

Hoffmann, Richard C. *An Environmental History of Medieval Europe*. Cambridge: Cambridge University Press, 2014.

Hoffmann, Richard C. "Medieval Origins of the Common Fields." In *European Peasants and their Markets*, edited by William N. Parker and Eric L. Jones, 23–71. Princeton: Princeton University Press, 1975.

Howes, Laura L. "Narrative Time and Literary Landscapes in Middle English Poetry." In *Inventing Medieval Landscapes: Senses of Place in Western Europe*, edited by John Howe and Michael Wolfe, 192–207. Gainesville: University Press of Florida, 2002.

Huglo, Michel. "De Francon de Cologne à Jacques de Liège." *Revue belge de Musicologie* 34/35 (1980/1981): 44–60.

Huglo, Michel. "Le contexte folklorique et musical du charivari dans le *Roman de Fauvel*." In *Fauvel Studies: Allegory, Chronicle, Music, and Image in Paris Bibliothèque Nationale de France, MS français 146*, edited by Margaret Bent and Andrew Wathey, 277–84. Oxford: Clarendon Press, 1998.

Hult, David. *Self-Fulfilling Prophecies: Readership and Authority in the First* Roman de la Rose. Cambridge: Cambridge University Press, 1986.

Hunt, Tony. "De la chanson au sermon: 'Bele aalis' et 'Sur la rive de la mer'." *Romania* 104, no.4 (1983): 433–56.

Hunt, Tony. *Miraculous Rhymes: The Writing of Gautier de Coinci*. Cambridge, UK: D.S. Brewer, 2007.

Huot, Sylvia. *Allegorical Play in the Old French Motet: The Sacred and the Profane in Thirteenth-Century Polyphony*. Stanford: Stanford University Press, 2007.

Huot, Sylvia. *From Song to Book: The Poetics of Writing in Old French Lyric and Lyrical Narrative Poetry*. Ithaca, NY: Cornell University Press, 1987.

Huot, Sylvia. "Guillaume de Machaut and the Consolation of Poetry." *Modern Philology* 100, no.2 (2002): 169–95.

Jacob, Uri. "'Chevalier mult estes guariz' and the 'Pre-chansonnier' Vernacular Lyric." *Plainsong and Medieval Music* 30, no.2 (2022): 119–40.

Jaeger, C. Stephen. "Courtliness and Social Change." In *Cultures of Power: Lordship, Status, and Process in Twelfth-Century Europe*, edited by Thomas N. Bisson, 287–309. Philadelphia: University of Pennsylvania Press, 1995.

Jeanroy, Alfred. *Les origines de la poésie lyrique en France au moyen age*. 4th ed. Paris: Honoré Champion, 1925.

Johnson, Glenn Pierr. "Aspects of Late Medieval Music at the Cathedral of Amiens." PhD diss., Yale University, 1991. 2 vols.

Johnson, Matthew. *Behind the Castle Gate: From the Middle Ages to the Renaissance*. London: Routledge, 2002.

Jordan, William Chester. *The Great Famine: Northern Europe in the Early Fourteenth Century*. Princeton: Princeton University Press, 1996.

Jordan, William Chester. "The Representation of the Crusades in the Songs Attributed to Thibaud, Count Palatine of Champagne." *Journal of Medieval History* 25, no.1 (1999): 27–34.

Kaeuper, Richard W. *Chivalry and Violence in Medieval Europe*. Oxford: Oxford University Press, 1999.

Kaeuper, Richard W. *Medieval Chivalry*. Cambridge, UK: Cambridge University Press, 2016.

Karp, Theodore. "Thibaut de Blaison." In *Oxford Music Online*. Oxford University Press, 2001–. Article published in 2001. https://www.oxfordmusiconline.com.

Kay, Sarah. *Parrots and Nightingales: Troubadour Quotations and the Development of European Poetry*. Philadelphia: University of Pennsylvania Press, 2013.

Kay, Sarah. *The Place of Thought: The Complexity of One in Late Medieval French Didactic Poetry*. Philadelphia: University of Pennsylvania Press, 2007.

Kay, Sarah. *Subjectivity in Troubadour Poetry*. Cambridge, UK: Cambridge University Press, 1990.

Kay, Sarah. "Touching Singularity: Consolation, Philosophy, and Poetry in the French *Dit*." In *The Erotics of Consolation: Desire and Distance in the Late Middle Ages*, edited by Catherine E. Léglu and Stephen J. Milner, 21–38. Basingstoke, UK: Palgrave Macmillan, 2008.

Keen, Maurice. "Chivalry and the Aristocracy." In *The New Cambridge Medieval History*, edited by Michael Jones, 6:209–21. Cambridge: Cambridge University Press, 2000.

Kelly, Douglas. *Machaut and the Medieval Apprenticeship Tradition: Truth, Fiction, and Poetic Craft*. Cambridge: D.S. Brewer, 2014.

Kelly, Douglas. *Medieval Imagination: Rhetoric and the Poetry of Courtly Love*. Madison: University of Wisconsin Press, 1978.

Kelly, Douglas. "The Medieval *Moi Multiple*: Names, Surnames, and Personifications." In *Shaping Identity in Medieval French Literature: The Other Within*, edited by Adrian P. Tudor and Kristin L. Burr, 15–29. Gainesville: University Press of Florida, 2019.

Keyser, Richard. "The Transformation of Traditional Woodland Management: Commercial Sylviculture in Medieval Champagne." *French Historical Studies* 32, no.3 (2009): 353–84.

Koerner, Joseph Leo. *Caspar David Friedrich and the Subject of Landscape*. 2nd ed. London: Reaktion Books, 2009.

Kowaleski, Maryanne. "Medieval People in Town and Country: New Perspectives from Demography and Bioarchaeology." *Speculum* 89, no.3 (2014): 573–600.

Krause, Kathy M., and Alison Stones, eds. *Gautier de Coinci: Miracles, Music, and Manuscripts*. Turnhout, Belgium: Brepols, 2006.

Lalou, Élisabeth. "La chancellerie royale à la fin du règne de Philippe IV le Bel." In *Fauvel Studies: Allegory, Chronicle, Music, and Image in Paris, Bibliothèque Nationale de France, MS français 146*, edited by Margaret Bent and Andrew Wathey, 307–20. Oxford: Clarendon Press, 1998.

Leach, Elizabeth Eva. "A Courtly Compilation: The Douce Chansonnier." In *Manuscripts and Medieval Song: Inscription, Performance, Context*, edited by Helen Deeming and Elizabeth Eva Leach, 221–46. Cambridge: Cambridge University Press, 2015.

Leach, Elizabeth Eva. "Adapting the Motet(s)? The Case of *Hé bergier* in Oxford MS Douce 308." *Plainsong & Medieval Music* 28, 2 (2019): 133–47.

Leach, Elizabeth Eva. "Do Trouvère Melodies Mean Anything?" *Music Analysis* 38, nos.1–2 (2019): 3–46.

Leach, Elizabeth Eva. *Guillaume de Machaut: Secretary, Poet, Musician*. Ithaca, NY: Cornell University Press, 2011.

Leach, Elizabeth Eva. "Nature's Forge and Mechanical Production: Writing, Reading, and Performing Song." In *Rhetoric Beyond Words: Delight and Persuasion in the Arts of the Middle Ages*, edited by Mary Carruthers, 72–95. Cambridge: Cambridge University Press, 2010.

Leach, Elizabeth Eva. "The Provenance, Date, and Patron of Oxford, Bodleian Library, MS Douce 308." *Speculum* 97, no.2 (2022): 283–321.

Leach, Elizabeth Eva. *Sung Birds: Music, Nature, and Poetry in the Later Middle Ages*. Ithaca, NY: Cornell University Press, 2007.

Leach, Elizabeth Eva, and Jonathan Morton. "Intertextual and Intersonic Resonances in Richard de Fournival's *Bestiaire d'amour*: Combining Perspectives from Literary Studies and Musicology." *Romania* 135 (2017): 131–51.

Lecco, Margherita. "Lo 'charivari' del 'Roman de Fauvel' e la tradizione della 'Mesnie Hellequin." *Mediaevistik* 13 (2000): 55–85.

Lecco, Margherita. "Per un'interpretazione del III 'lai del *Roman de Fauvel*' nel ms. Paris BNF, fr.146, 'Pour recouvrere alegiance." *Romania* 128 (2010): 193–212.

Leclerq, Jean. *Love of Learning and the Desire for God: A Study of Monastic Culture*. Translated by Catharine Misrahi. New York: Fordham University Press, 1962.

Lévêque-Fougre, Mélanie. "The Lorraine Repertory of *C*." In *A Medieval Songbook: Trouvère MS C*, edited by Elizabeth Eva Leach, Joseph W. Mason, and Matthew P. Thompson, 20–43. Woodbridge: The Boydell Press, 2022.

Le Gentil, Pierre. "A propos du 'Guillaume de Dole." In *Mélanges de linguistique romane et de philologie médiévale offerts à M. Maurice Delbouille*, edited by Madeline Tyssens, II: 381–97. Gembloux: Duculot, 1964.

Leopold, Aldo. *A Sand County Almanac and Sketches Here and There*. Oxford: Oxford University Press, 1949.

Livingstone, Amy. "Nobility of Blois-Chartres: Family and Inheritance, 980–1140." PhD diss., Michigan State University, 1992.

Livingstone, Amy. *Out of Love for My Kin: Aristocratic Family Life in the Lands of the Loire, 1000–1200*. Ithaca, NY: Cornell University Press, 2010.

Lower, Michael. *The Barons' Crusade: A Call to Arms and Its Consequences.* Philadelphia: University of Pennsylvania Press, 2005.

Lower, Michael. "The Burning at Mont-Aimé: Thibaut of Champagne's Preparations for the Barons' Crusade of 1239." *Journal of Medieval History* 29, no.2 (2003): 95–108.

Ludwig, Friedrich. *Repertorium organorum recentioris et motetorum vetustissimi stili. Band 1: Catalogue raisonné der Quellen.* Reprint, New York: Institute for Medieval Music, 1910.

Lug, Robert. "Katharer und Waldenser in Metz: Zur Herkunft der ältesten Sammlung von Trobador-Liedern (1231)." In *Okzitanistik, Altokzitanistik und Provenzalistik: Geschichte und Aufrag einer europäischen Philologie,* edited by Angelica Rieger, 249–74. Frankfurt and Berlin: Peter Lang, 2000.

Lug, Robert. "Politique et littérature à Metz autour de la guere des amis (1231–1234): le témoignage du chansonnier de Saint-Germain-des-Prés." In *Lettres, musique, et société en Lorraine médiévale: autour du 'Tournoi de Chauvency' (Ms. Oxford Bodleian Douce 308),* edited by Mireille Chazan and Nancy Freeman Regalado, 451–86. Geneva: Droz, 2012.

Maillard, Jean. *Roi-trouvère du XIIIème siècle: Charles d'Anjou.* N.P.: American Institute of Musicology, 1967.

Mann, Jill. *Chaucer and Medieval Estates Satire: The Literature of Social Classes and the General Prolog to the Canterbury Tales.* Cambridge: Cambridge University Press, 1973, repr. 2009.

Marder, Michael. *Grafts: Writings on Plants.* Minneapolis: University of Minnesota Press, 2016.

Marder, Michael. *Plant-Thinking: A Philosophy of Vegetal Life.* New York: Columbia University Press, 2013.

Marshall, J.H. "Textual Transmission and Complex Musico-Metrical Form in the Old French Lyric." In *Studies in honor of T. B. W. Reid,* edited by Ian Short, 119–84. London: Anglo-Norman Text Society, 1984.

Martina, Piero Andrea. "Pour la datation basse du Roman de la Rose ou de Guillaume de Dole." *Romania* 138, no.1–2 (2020): 203–8.

Maschke, Eva M. "*Porta salutis ave*: Manuscript Culture, Material Culture, and Music." *Musica Disciplina* 58 (2013): 167–229.

Mason, Joseph W. "Debatable Chivalry: A *Jeu-parti* by the Duke of Brittany and Its Context." *Medium Aevum* 87, no.2 (2018): 255–76.

Mason, Joseph W. "Structure and Process in the Old French *Jeu-parti*." *Music Analysis* 38 (2019): 47–79.

Maw, David. "'Je le temoin en mon chant': The Art of Diminution in the Petronian Triplum." In *The Montpellier Codex: The Final Fascicle. Contexts, Contents, Chronologies,* edited by Catherine A. Bradley and Karen Desmond, 161–83. Woodbridge: D.S. Brewer, 2018.

McAlpine, Fiona. "Establishing a Trouvère Musical Style: The Songs of the Vidame de Chartres." In *Liber Amicorum John Steele: A Musical Tribute,* edited by Warren Drake, 1–36. Stuyvesant, NY: Pendragon Press, 1997.

McGrady, Deborah, and Jennifer Bain, eds. *A Companion to Guillaume de Machaut.* Leiden: Brill, 2012.

Merriman, Peter, George Revill, Tim Cresswell, Hayden Lorimer, David Matless, Gillian Rose, and John Wylie. "Landscape, Mobility, Practice." *Social & Cultural Geography* 9, no.2 (2008): 191–212.

Mitchell, W. J. T. "Imperial Landscape." In *Landscape and Power,* edited by W. J. T. Mitchell, 5–34. Chicago: University of Chicago Press, 1994, reprinted 2000.

Mölk, Ulrich, and Friedrich Wolfzettel, *Répertoire métrique de la poésie lyrique française des origins à 1350*. Munich: Fink Verlag, 1972.

Morgan, Lucy. "Early Modern Edens: The Landscape and Language of Paradise." *Studies in the History of Gardens & Designed Landscapes* 27, no.2 (2012): 142–48.

Mullally, Robert. *The Carole: A Study of a Medieval Dance*. Aldershot: Ashgate, 2011.

Murray, David. "Clerical Reception of Bernart de Ventadorn's 'Can vei la lauzeta mover' (PC 70, 34)." *Medium Aevum* 85, no.2 (2016): 259–77.

Novikoff, Alex J. *The Medieval Culture of Disputation: Pedagogy, Practice, and Performance*. Philadelphia: University of Pennsylvania Press, 2013.

Nykrog, Per. "A Warrior Scholar at the Collège de France: Joseph Bédier." In *Medievalism and the Modernist Temper*, edited by R. Howard Block and Stephen G. Nichols, 286–307. Baltimore: Johns Hopkins University Press, 1996.

Oksanen, Eljas. *Flanders and the Anglo-Norman World, 1066–1216*. Cambridge, UK: Cambridge University Press, 2012.

O'Neill, Mary. *Courtly Love Songs of Medieval France: Transmission and Style in the Trouvère Repertoire*. Oxford: Oxford University Press, 2006.

O'Sullivan, Daniel E. *Marian Devotion in Thirteenth-Century French Lyric*. Toronto: University of Toronto Press, 2005.

O'Sullivan, Daniel E. "The Northern *Jeu-parti*." In *Musical Culture in the World of Adam de la Halle*, edited by Jennifer Saltzstein, 153–88. Leiden: Brill, 2019.

Paden, William D. "Christine de Pizan as a Reader of the Medieval Pastourelle." In *Conjunctures: Medieval Studies in Honor of Douglas Kelly*, edited by Keith Busby and Norris J. Lacy, 387–405. Leiden: Brill/Rodopi 1994.

Paden, William D. "Rape in the Pastourelle." *Romanic Review* 80 (1989): 331–49.

Page, Christopher. *Discarding Images: Reflections on Music and Culture in Medieval France*. Oxford: Clarendon Press, 1993.

Page, Christopher. "Listening to the Trouvères." *Early Music* 25, no.4 (1997): 638–59.

Page, Christopher. *The Owl and the Nightingale: Musical Life and Ideas, 1100–1300*. Berkeley: University of California Press, 1989.

Page, Christopher. "Tradition and Innovation in BN fr. 146: The Background to the Ballades." In *Fauvel Studies: Allegory, Chronicle, Music, and Image in Paris Bibliothèque Nationale de France, MS français 146*, edited by Margaret Bent and Andrew Wathey, 353–94. Oxford: Clarendon Press, 1998.

Page, Christopher. *Voices and Instruments in the Middle Ages: Instrumental Practice and Songs in France 1100–1300*. Berkeley and Los Angeles: University of California Press, 1987.

Palmer, R. Barton, and Uri Smilansky, eds. *Guillaume de Machaut, the Complete Poetry and Music*, Vol. 2: *The Boethian Poems*. Kalamazoo, MI: Medieval Institute Publications, 2019.

Paris, Paulin. "Chansonniers des trouvères." In *Histoire littéraire de la France*, edited by Paulin Paris, vol. 23, 512–831. Paris: Firmin Didot, 1856.

Parisse, Michel. "Le tounoi en France, des origines à la fin du XIIIe siècle." In *Das ritterliche Turnier im Mittelalter: Beiträge zu einer vergleichenden Formen- und Verhaltensgeschichte des Rittertums*, edited by Josef Fleckenstein, 175–211. Göttingen: Vandenhoeck & Ruprecht, 1985.

Parker, Ian. "A propos de la tradition manuscrite des chansons de trouvères." *Revue de Musicologie* 64, no.2 (1978): 181–202.

Parker, Ian. "Notes on the Chansonnier Saint-Germain-Des-Prés." *Music & Letters* 60, no.3 (1979): 261–80.

Paterson, Linda M. *Troubadours, Trouvères, and the Crusades*, accessed January 17, 2021. https://warwick.ac.uk/fac/arts/modernlanguages/research/french/crusades/

Payne, Thomas B. "*Aurelianis civitas*: Student Unrest in Medieval France and a Conductus by Philip the Chancellor." *Speculum* 75, no.3 (2000): 589–614.

---. *Philip the Chancellor: Motets and Prosulas*. A-R Editions: Middleton, WI, 2011.

Pearsall, Derek and Elizabeth Salter. *Landscapes and Seasons of the Medieval World*. London: Elek, 1973.

Peraino, Judith A. "*Et pui conmencha a canter*: Refrains, Motets, and Melody in the Thirteenth-Century Narrative, *Renart le Nouvel*." *Plainsong and Medieval Music* 6, no.1 (1997): 1–16.

Peraino, Judith A. *Giving Voice to Love: Song and Self-Expression from the Troubadours to Guillaume de Machaut*. Oxford: Oxford University Press, 2011.

Peraino, Judith A. "Monophonic Motets: Sampling and Grafting in the Middle Ages." *The Musical Quarterly* 85, no.4 (2001): 644–80.

Pesce, Dolores, ed. *Hearing the Motet: Essays on the Motet of the Middle Ages and Renaissance*. New York: Oxford University Press, 1997.

Peters, Gretchen. *The Musical Sounds of Medieval French Cities: Players, Patrons, and Politics*. Cambridge: Cambridge University Press, 2012.

Pfeffer, Wendy. *The Change of Philomel: The Nightingale in Medieval Literature*. New York, Bern, and Frankfurt am Main: Peter Lang, 1985.

Philips, Jenna. "Singers without Borders: A Performer's *Rotulus* and the Transmission of *Jeux Partis*." *Journal of Medieval History* 45 (2019): 55–79.

Plumley, Yolanda. *The Art of Grafted Song: Citation and Allusion in the Age of Machaut*. Oxford: Oxford University Press, 2013.

Pluskowski, Aleks. "Predators in Robes: Materialising and Mystifying Hunting, Predation and Seclusion in the Northern European Medieval Landscape." In *Centre, Region, Periphery: Proceedings of the International Conference of Medieval and Later Archaeology, Basel, Switzerland*, edited by G. Helmig, B. Scholkmann, and M. Untermann, Vol. 2, 243–47. Basel: Archäologische Bodenforschung Basel-Stadt, 2002.

Poe, Elizabeth. *Compilatio: Lyric Texts and Prose Commentaries in Troubadour Manuscript H (Vat. Lat. 3207)*. Lexington, KY: French Forum, 2000.

Prinet, Max. "L'Illustration héraldique du Chansonnier du roi." In *Mélanges de linguistique et de littérature offerts à M. Alfred Jeanroy par ses élèves et ses amis*, 521–37. Paris: Éditions E. Droz, 1928.

Quinlan, Meghan. "When Courtly Song Invades History: Lyricizing Blanche de Castille." In *Gender and Voice in Medieval French Literature and Song*, edited by Rachel May Golden and Katherine Kong, 93–120. Gainesville: University Press of Florida, 2021.

Rackham, Oliver. "The Medieval Countryside of England: Botany and Archaeology." In *Inventing Medieval Landscapes: Senses of Place in Western Europe*, edited by John Howe and Michael Wolfe, 13–32. Gainesville: University Press of Florida, 2002.

Rackham, Oliver. "Pre-Existing Trees and Woods in Country House Parks." *Landscapes* 5, no.2 (2004): 1–17.

Ragnard, Isabelle. "The Songs of Adam de la Halle." In *Musical Culture in the World of Adam de la Halle*, edited by Jennifer Saltzstein, 189–230. Leiden: Brill, 2019.

Räkel, Hans-Herbert S. *Die musikalische Erscheinungsform der Trouvèrepoesie*. Bern: Paul Haupt, 1977.

Rawcliffe, Carol. "'Delectable Sightes and Fragrant Smelles': Gardens and Health in Late Medieval and Early Modern England." *Garden History* 36, no.1 (2008): 3–21.

Regalado, Nancy. "Masques réels dans le monde de l'imaginaire: le rite et l'écrit dans le charivari du Roman de Fauvel, ms. B.N. fr. 146." In *Masques et déguisements dans la littérature médiévale*, edited by Marie-Louise Ollier, 111–26. Montréal: Presses de l'Université de Montréal, 1988.

Renes, Hans. "Open Field Landscapes and Research in the Netherlands and Europe." In *Peasants and their Fields: The Rationale of Open-Field Agriculture*, edited by Christopher Dyer, Erik Thoen, and Tom Williamson, 121–61. Turnhout: Brepols, 2017.

Ridder-Symoens, Hilde. "Mobility." In *A History of the University in Europe*, Vol. 1: *Universities in the Middle Ages*, edited by Hilde Ridder-Symoens, 280–304. Cambridge: Cambridge University Press, 1992.

Richardson, Amanda. "Gender and Space in English Royal Palaces c.1160–1547: A Study in Access Analysis and Imagery." *Medieval Archaeology* 47, no.1 (2013): 131–65.

Richardson, Amanda. "'Riding like Alexander, Hunting like Diana': Gendered Aspects of the Medieval Hunt and its Landscape Settings in England and France." *Gender & History* 24, no.2 (2012): 253–70.

Rieger, Dietmar. "Le motif du viol dans la littérature de la France médiévale entre norme courtoise et réalité courtois." *Cahiers de Civilisation Médiévale* 31 (1988): 241–67.

Robertson, D. W. "The Doctrine of Charity in Mediaeval Literary Gardens: A Topical Approach Through Symbolism and Allegory." *Speculum* 26, no.1 (1951): 24–49.

Robertson, Kellie. *When Nature Speaks: Medieval Literature and Aristotelian Philosophy*. Philadelphia: University of Pennsylvania Press, 2017.

Rosenberg, Samuel N. "Colin Muset and the Question of Attribution." *Textual Cultures* 1, no.1 (2006): 29–45.

Rosenberg, Samuel N. "French Songs in Occitan Chansonniers: An Introductory Report." *Tenso* 13, no.2 (1998): 18–32.

Rosenberg, Samuel N. "The Old French Lyric Death Laments." In *Le gai savoir: essays in memory of Manfred Sandmann*, edited by Mechtild Cranston, 45–54. Madrid: Studia Humanitatis, 1983.

Rosenwein, Barbara. *Generations of Feeling: A History of the Emotions, 600–1700*. Cambridge, UK: Cambridge University Press, 2016.

Rothenberg, David J. *The Flower of Paradise: Marian Devotion and Secular Song in Medieval and Renaissance Music*. Oxford: Oxford University Press, 2011.

Ruffo, Kathleen Wilson. "Courting Convention, Compiling Context: Chansonnier Iconography and Beyond in Machaut's MS C." In *Poetry, Art, and Music in Guillaume de Machaut's Earliest Manuscript (BnF fr. 1586)*, edited by Lawrence Earp and Jared C. Hartt, 157–94. Turnhout: Brepols, 2021.

Ruffo, Kathleen Wilson. "The Illustration of Notated Compendia of Courtly Poetry in Late Thirteenth-Century Northern France." PhD diss., University of Toronto, 2000.

Saint-Cricq, Gaël. "Genre, Attribution, and Authorship in the Thirteenth Century:Robert de Reims vs 'Robert de Rains'." *Early Music History* 38 (2019): 141–213.

Saint-Cricq, Gaël. "Motets in Chansonniers and the Other Culture of the French Thirteenth-Century Motet." In *A Critical Companion to Medieval Motets*, edited by Jared Hartt, 225–42. Rochester: Boydell & Brewer, 2018.

Saltzstein, Jennifer. "Adam de la Halle's Fourteenth-century Musical and Poetic Legacies." In *Musical Culture in the World of Adam de la Halle*, edited by Jennifer Saltzstein, 352–64. Leiden: Brill, 2019.

Saltzstein, Jennifer. "Cleric-Trouvères and the *Jeux-partis* of Medieval Arras." *Viator* 43, no.2 (2012): 147–63.

Saltzstein, Jennifer. *Musical Culture in the World of Adam de la Halle*. Leiden: Brill, 2019.

Saltzstein, Jennifer. "Rape and Repentance in Two Medieval Motets." *Journal of the American Musicological Society* 70, no.3 (2017): 583–616.

Saltzstein, Jennifer. *The Refrain and the Rise of the Vernacular in Medieval French Music and Poetry*. Cambridge: D.S. Brewer, 2013.

Saltzstein, Jennifer. "Songs of Nature in Medieval Northern France: Landscape, Identity, and Environment." *Journal of the American Musicological Society* 72, no.1 (2019): 115–80.

Scheludko, Dimitri. "Zur geschidite des Natureinganges bei den Trobadors." *Zeitschrift für französische Sprache und Literatur* 60, no.5/6 (1937): 257–334.

Schrade, Leo. "Guillaume de Machaut and the *Roman de Fauvel*." *Miscelánea en homenaje a Monseñor Anglés*, Vol. 2, 843–850. Barcelona: Consejo superior de investigaciones cientificas, 1958–61.

Schwan, Eduard. *Die altfranzösischen Liederhandschriften: ihr Verhältniss, ihre Entstehung, und ihre Bestimmung, eine litterarhistorische untersuchung*. Berlin: Weidmann, 1886.

Schwinges, Rainer Christoph. "Student Education, Student Life." In *A History of the University in Europe*, Vol. 2: *Universities in the Middle Ages*, edited by Hilde de Ridder-Symoens, 195–243. Cambridge: Cambridge University Press, 1992.

Short, Brian. "Forests and Wood-Pasture in Lowland England." In *The English Rural Landscape*, edited by Joan Thirsk, 122–49. Oxford: Oxford University Press, 2000.

Skoda, Hannah. *Medieval Violence: Physical Brutality in Northern France 1270–1330*. Oxford: Oxford University Press, 2013.

Smalley, Beryl. *The Study of the Bible in the Middle Ages*. Oxford: Blackwell, 1952.

Smith, Geri L. *The Medieval French Pastourelle Tradition: Poetic Motivations and Generic Transformations*. Gainesville: University Press of Florida, 2009.

Spanke, Hans. "Die Gedichte Jehan's de Renti und Oede's de la Couroierie." *Zeitschrift für französische Sprache und Literatur* 32 (1908): 157–218.

Spanke, Hans. *G. Raynauds Bibliographie des altfranzösischen Liedes*. Leiden: Brill, 1980.

Spanke, Hans. "Sequenz und lai." *Studi medievali* 11 (1938): 37–68.

Spiegel, Gabrielle. "History, Historicism, and the Social Logic of the Text in the Middle Ages." *Speculum* 65, no.1 (1990): 59–86.

Spiegel, Gabrielle. *Romancing the Past: The Rise of Vernacular Prose Historiography in Thirteenth-Century France*. Berkeley and Los Angeles: University of California Press, 1995.

Stannard, Jerry. "Alimentary and Medicinal Uses of Plants." In *Medieval Gardens*, edited by Elisabeth Blair MacDougall, 69–92. Washington, D.C.: Dumbarton Oaks Research Library and Collection, 1986.

Stevens, John. *Words and Music in the Middle Ages: Song, Narrative, Dance and Drama, 1150–1350*. Cambridge: Cambridge University Press, 1986.

Stones, Alison. *Manuscripts Illuminated in France: Gothic Manuscripts, 1260–1320*. 4 vols. London and Turnhout: Harvey Miller and Brepols, 2013-2014.

Stones, Alison. "Notes on the Artistic Context of Some Gautier de Coinci Manuscripts." In *Gautier de Coinci: Miracles, Music, and Manuscripts*, edited by Kathy M. Krause and Alison Stones, 65–98. Turnhout: Brepols, 2006.

Swift, Helen J. "The Poetic I." In *A Companion to Guillaume de Machaut*, edited by Deborah McGrady and Jennifer Bain, 15–32. Leiden: Brill, 2012.

Switten, Margaret Louise. *The "Cansos" of Raimon de Miraval: A Study of Poems and Melodies*. Cambridge, MA: Medieval Academy of America, 1985.

Switten, Margaret Louise. "Guillaume de Machaut: Le *Remede de Fortune* au carrefour d'un art nouveau." *Cahiers de L'Association Internationale des Études Françaises* 41 (1989): 101–18.

Symes, Carol. *A Common Stage: Theater and Public Life in Medieval Arras*. Ithaca, NY: Cornell University Press, 2007.

Symes, Carol. "Doing Things Beside Domesday Book." *Speculum* 93, no.4 (2018): 1048–1101.

Symes, Carol. "The 'School of Arras' and the Career of Adam." In *Musical Culture in the World of Adam de la Halle*, edited by Jennifer Saltzstein, 21–50. Leiden: Brill, 2019.

Taylor, Craig. *Chivalry and the Ideals of Knighthood in France During the Hundred Years War*. Cambridge: Cambridge University Press, 2013.

Taylor, Patrick, ed. *The Oxford Companion to the Garden*. Oxford: Oxford University Press, 2006.

Thiolier-Méjean, Suzanne. *Voici l'arbre d'amour: nature et culture dans la poésie médiévale d'Oc*. Paris: L'Harmattan, 2018.

Thirsk, Joan. *The Agrarian History of England and Wales*, Vol. 4: *1500–1640*. Cambridge: Cambridge University Press, 1967.

Tilley, Christopher. *A Phenomenology of Landscape: Places, Paths and Monuments*. Oxford, Berg: 1994.

Tischler, Hans. *Conductus and Contrafacta*. Ottawa: Institute of Medieval Music, 2001.

Trabut-Cussac, Jean-Paul. "Itinéraire d'Édouard Ier en France, 1286–1289." *Bulletin of the Institute of Historical Research* 25, no.72 (1952): 160–203.

Truitt, Elly Rachel. *Medieval Robots: Mechansim, Magic, Nature, and Art*. Philadelphia: University of Pennsylvania Press, 2015.

Tyssens, Madeline ed. *"Intavulare." Tables de chansonniers romans. Chansonniers français 1, a (B.A.V., Reg. Lat. 1490), b (B.A.V, Reg. Lat. 1522), A (Arras, Bibliothèque Municipale 657)*. Studi e testi 388. Cité du Vatican: Biblioteca Apostolica Vaticana, 1998.

Uitti, Karl D. "From *Clerc* to *Poète*: The Relevance of the *Romance of the Rose* to Machaut's World." In *Machaut's World: Science and Art in the Fourteenth Century*, edited by Madeline Pelner Cosman and Bruce Chandler, 209–16. New York: New York Academy of Sciences, 1978.

Ungureanu, Marie. *La bourgeoisie naissante: société et littérature bourgeoises d'Arras aux XIIe et XIIIe siècles*. Arras: Mémoires de la Commission départementale des monuments historiques du Pas-de-Calais, 1955.

Vale, Malcolm. *The Princely Court: Medieval Courts and Culture in North-West Europe, 1270–1380*. Oxford: Oxford University Press, 2001.

Van Bavel, Bas. *Manors and Markets: Economy and Society in the Low Countries, 500–1600*. Oxford: Oxford University Press, 2010.

Van Bavel, Bas. "The Emergence and Growth of Short-term Leasing in the Netherlands and Other Parts of Northwestern Europe (Eleventh–Seventeenth Centuries): A Chronology and a Tentative Investigation into its Causes." In *The Development of Leasehold in Northwestern Europe, c.1200–1600*, edited by Bas Van Bavel and Philipp Schofield, 179–213. Turnhout: Brepols, 2009.

Van Buren, Anne Hagopian. "Reality and Literary Romance in the Park of Hesdin." In *Medieval Gardens*, edited by Elisabeth B. Macdougall, 115–34. Washington, D.C.: Dumbarton Oaks Research Library and Collection, 1986.

Van Dam, Petra J. E. M. "New Habitats for the Rabbit in Northern Europe." In *Inventing Medieval Landscapes: Senses of Place in Western Europe*, edited by John Howe and Michael Wolfe, 57–69. Gainesville: University Press of Florida, 2002.

Van der Werf, Hendrik. *The Chansons of the Troubadours and Trouvères: A Study of the Melodies and Their Relation to the Poems*. Utrecht: A. Oosthoek's Uitgeversmaatschappij, 1972.

Verger, Jacques. *Men of Learning in Europe at the End of the Middle Ages*. Notre Dame, IN: Notre Dame University Press, 2000.

Wallensköld, Axel, ed. *Les chansons de Conon de Béthune*. Paris: Honoré Champion, 1921.

Watkins, Holly. *Musical Vitalities: Ventures in a Biotic Aesthetics of Music*. Chicago, IL: University of Chicago Press, 2018.

Weeda, Claire. "The Fixed and the Fluent: Geographical Determinism, Ethnicity, and Religion c. 1100–1300." In *The Routledge Handbook of Identity and the Environment in the Classical and Medieval Worlds*, edited by Rebecca Futo Kennedy and Molly Jones-Lewis, 93–113. New York: Routledge, 2015.

Wei, Ian P. *Intellectual Culture in Medieval Paris: Theologians and the University, c.1100–1330*. Cambridge: Cambridge University Press, 2012.

Whalen, Logan and Rupert T. Pickens. "Gardens and Anti-Gardens in Marie de France's 'Lais.'" *Romance Philology* 66, no.1 (2012): 185–210.

Wickham, Chris. *Medieval Europe*. New Haven: Yale University Press, 2016.

Wilhelm, James. *The Cruelest Month: Spring, Nature, and Love in Classical and Medieval Lyrics*. Yale: Yale University Press, 1965.

Wilkin, Alexis and John Naylor. "Introduction: Dynamic Interactions, Developing a Unified Approach to Urban-Rural Interaction." In *Town and Country in Medieval Northwestern Europe: Dynamic Interactions*, edited by Alexis Wilkin, John Naylor, Derek Keene, and Arnoud-Jan Bijsterveld, 1–34. Turnhout: Brepols, 2015.

Will, George. "Climate Change's Instructive Past." *Washington Post*, January 7, 2015.

Wimsatt, James I., and William W. Kibler, eds. *Le jugement du roy de Behaigne and Remede de Fortune*. Athens: The University of Georgia Press, 1989.

Winiwarter, Verena. "The Art of Making the Earth Fruitful: Medieval and Early Modern Improvements of Soil Fertility." In *Ecologies and Economies in Medieval and Early Modern Europe: Studies in Environmental History for Richard C. Hoffman*, edited by Scott C. Bruce, 93–114. Leiden: Brill, 2010.

Wolfzettel, Friedrich. "Au carrefour des discours lyriques: le trouvère Richard de Fournival." *Romania* 115 (1997): 50–68.

Wolinski, Mary. "Hocketing and the Imperfect Modes in Relation to Poetic Expression in the Thirteenth Century." *Musica Disciplina* 58 (2013): 393–411.

Woolgar, C. M. *The Senses in Late Medieval England*. New Haven: Yale University Press, 2006.

Wright, Craig. *Music and Ceremony at Notre Dame of Paris, 500–1500*. Cambridge: Cambridge University Press, 1989.

Wright, Nicholas. *Knights and Peasants: The Hundred Years War in the French Countryside*. Woodbridge: Boydell and Brewer, 1998.

Zadora-Rio, Elisabeth. "Parcs à gibier et garennes à lapins: contribution à une étude archéologique des territoires de chasse dans le paysage médiéval." *Hommes et terres du Nord* 2–3 (1986): 133–39.

Zayaruznaya, Anna. "Old, New, and Newer Still in Book 7 of the *Speculum musice*." *Journal of the American Musicological Society* 73, no.1 (2020): 95–148.

Zink, Michel. *The Invention of Literary Subjectivity*. Translated by David Sices. Baltimore: Johns Hopkins University Press, 1999.

Zink, Michel. *La pastourelle: poésie et folklore au moyen âge*. Paris: Bordas, 1972.

Zink, Michel. "The Place of the Senses." In *Rethinking the Medieval Senses: Heritage, Fascinations, Frames*, edited by Stephen G. Nichols, Andreas Kablitz, and Alison Calhoun, 93–101. Baltimore: Johns Hopkins University Press, 2008.

Zingesser, Eliza. *Stolen Song: How the Troubadours Became French*. Ithaca, NY: Cornell University Press, 2020.

Zumthor, Paul. "De la circularité du chant." *Poétique* 2 (1970): 129–40.

Zumthor, Paul. *Toward a Medieval Poetics*. Translated by Philip Bennett. Minneapolis: University of Minneapolis Press, 1992.

Song Index

For the benefit of digital users, indexed terms that span two pages (e.g., 52–53) may, on occasion, appear on only one of those pages.

Tables and figures are indicated by *t* and *f* following the page number

General Index

For the benefit of digital users, indexed terms that span two pages (e.g., 52–53) may, on occasion, appear on only one of those pages.

Tables and figures are indicated by *t* and *f* following the page number